WOMEN AND CANADIAN
PUBLIC POLICY

WOMEN AND CANADIAN PUBLIC POLICY

JANINE BRODIE

This book is based on a seminar series
sponsored by The Robarts Centre for Canadian Studies
in the winter of 1993.

HARCOURT
BRACE
CANADA

Harcourt Brace & Company, Canada

Toronto   Montreal   Fort Worth   New York   Orlando
Philadelphia   San Diego   London   Sydney   Tokyo

Requests for permission to make copies of any part of the work should be mailed to: Permissions, College Division, Harcourt Brace & Company, Canada, 55 Horner Avenue, Toronto, Ontario M8Z 4X6.

Every reasonable effort has been made to acquire permission for copyright material used in this text, and to acknowledge all such indebtedness accurately. Any errors and omissions called to the publisher's attention will be corrected in future printings.

Canadian Cataloguing in Publication Data

Main entry under title:

Women and Canadian public policy

Includes bibliographical references and index.
ISBN 0–7747–3459–0

1. Women – Government Policy – Canada.   2. Women –
Canada – Social conditions.   3. Women's rights –
Canada.   I. Brodie, M. Janine, 1952– .

HQ1236.5.C2W6 1996   305.4'0971   C94–932759–X

Publisher: Heather McWhinney
Editor and Marketing Manager: Daniel J. Brooks
Projects Manager: Liz Radojkovic
Projects Co-ordinator: Megan Mueller
Director of Publishing Services: Jean Davies
Editorial Manager: Marcel Chiera
Supervising Editor: Semareh Al-Hillal
Production Editor: Sheila Barry
Production Manager: Sue-Ann Becker
Production Co-ordinator: Carol Tong
Copy Editor: Beverley Beetham Endersby
Cover and Interior Design: Dave Peters, revised by Opus House
Typesetting and Assembly: Sharon Moroney
Printing and Binding: Hignell Printing Limited

♾ This book was printed in Canada on acid-free paper.

1 2 3 4 5   00 99 98 97 96

PREFACE

C anada, like all Western democracies, is currently experiencing a significant shift in the form of the state and its governing practices. Daily, our newspapers are filled with dire warnings about how, among other things,

▶ Canada must adjust in order to trade competitively in the new international market;

▶ federal and provincial governments must cut back their activities and their spending in order to become more efficient and reduce constraints on private-sector investment;

▶ social programs must be reduced and transformed to help those displaced by the new economic realities to enter the work force and become self-sufficient.

All of these messages mark a distinct departure from the governing assumptions of the postwar period. Following the Second World War, all Western liberal democracies, including Canada, designed their own particular versions of what is commonly called "the Keynesian welfare state." Although the versions differed somewhat, this particular state form was universally founded on similar assumptions and governing instruments. The postwar years brought new shared understandings about state intervention in the economy, expansion of the social-welfare system and government commitment to full employment, and changes to the very meaning of citizenship itself. The postwar Keynesian state asserted the primacy of the public good over the "invisible hand" of the market and generated expectations that the state was responsible for meeting the basic social needs of its citizens. Moreover, an assumption was commonly made that it was the responsibility of the state to cushion national economies against disruptive international conditions.

It is now widely recognized that the pillars of the Keynesian welfare state have not survived the combined forces of prolonged economic crisis, the so-called globalization of production, and neo-liberal governing practices. The broad consensus that formed the foundation of the postwar welfare state has given way to a very different set of assumptions about the role of governments and the rights of citizens. It is now widely believed that the only means left to correct the mounting problems of slow economic growth, rising government debts, and widespread unemployment is restructuring. In Canada, restructuring entails

maximizing exports, reducing social spending, curtailing state economic regulation and enabling the private sector to reorganize the national
economy as part of a continental trading bloc.

These new tenets of governing are rapidly transforming Canadian
politics and public-policy priorities. Yet, little attention has thus far
been paid to the impact these policy changes have had and will have
on the everyday lives of Canadian women. The essays in this book are
a first step in attempting to address this issue. This volume took shape
in the winter of 1994, when a number of my colleagues at York
University and I met at weekly seminars to contemplate the consequences that restructuring would have for Canadian women. This seminar series was organized during my tenure as the Robarts Chair in
Canadian Studies and was sponsored by the Robarts Centre of
Canadian Studies at York. It combined the expertise of feminist academics from a wide spectrum of disciplines, including political science,
law, social work, sociology, and women's studies. This cross-fertilization of ideas proved very rewarding during the seminar series, and we
hope that it has also enriched this volume.

From the outset, the participants in the series emphasized that
restructuring is affecting every facet of women's lives and that any
exploration of Canadian women and public policy should not be limited
to only those areas traditionally viewed as "women's issues." We begin,
therefore, from the perspective that all public-policy issues are, in
effect, "women's issues." Although policy-makers may believe that their
initiatives in a particular policy field are gender-neutral, the essays in
this volume argue that this is rarely the case: because the organization
of Canadian society remains profoundly gendered, men and women
usually have quite separate experiences of policy changes.

Since restructuring involves significant changes in social, economic,
and political life, many kinds of issues could have been examined in
this volume. In a sense, the essays here only "scratch the surface" of
the countless and often contradictory effects that the current round of
restructuring is having and will have on Canadian women. However, we
believe that the issues examined here provide a strong foundation for
further research in the areas of restructuring, public policy, and gender.

ORGANIZATION OF THE TEXT

Structurally, this volume has four components. In the introduction,
I discuss how traditional approaches to women and the state fail
to address the current shift in state form and the attendant fundamental changes in the ground rules. The introduction provides students
with an understanding of what is at stake in this current round of
restructuring and how it entails nothing less than a historic shift in

social organization and governing practices. Parts I–III of the text explore the gendered impacts of restructuring within the realms of the economy, the welfare state, and the regulation of private life.

Many of the essays discuss the process of restructuring as it has been manifest in provincial politics in Ontario. The constitutional division of powers and responsibilities among jurisdictions in Canada means that many of the changes that affect national politics must be enacted at the provincial level. Nevertheless, there is a surprising convergence among provinces' responses to this current period of fundamental change. The fiscal crisis of the state and the demands of continental integration are making very similar demands on and realizing very similar responses from the provincial governments, regardless of partisan stripe. The Ontario case, then, invites us to examine the convergence of provincial responses to restructuring, and to explore when and why some provinces have been more flexible in relation to the emerging new order than have others.

Part I examines how the current restructuring of the economy is affecting women in the workplace and in the home. In Chapter 1, Isabella Bakker discusses how changes in macro-economic policies and thinking, while generally perceived as being gender-neutral, actually make women's lives invisible and, at the same time, place new burdens on women and society's other marginalized actors. In Chapter 2, Judy Fudge continues this line of inquiry by demonstrating how changes in macro-economic policies are inscribed in labour-market policy and labour relations, disadvantaging women and erecting new barriers to political action. In Chapter 3, Patricia McDermott examines how relatively new policy initiatives, such as those governing pay and employment equity, fail to achieve their stated goals and how their objectives are being compromised by the new order. In Chapter 4, Barbara Cameron uses the case of new reproductive technologies to demonstrate how international trading agreements, such as the North American Free Trade Agreement (NAFTA), set very severe constraints on government. It is largely prohibited from regulating the economy to protect women from potential harms or to provide public services designed to promote women's equality.

Part II of the text focusses on how the erosion of the welfare state and changes in thinking about social welfare and citizenship are affecting the everyday lives of Canadian women in very different ways. In Chapter 5, Pat Armstrong describes the negative effect that the erosion of the health-care system is having on women working in that system and women who are served by it. Cutbacks in health-care spending and new management models are effectively shifting such caregiving to the home, thus making it part of the unpaid labour of women. In Chapter 6, Patricia Evans shows how new welfare thinking is explicitly targeting single mothers as "the problem" in the welfare system. Public policies are progressively redefining these disproportionately poor Canadians as employable and responsible for the maintenance of their children, even though the state has failed to provide necessary supports such as a national day-care system. In Chapter 7, Christina Gabriel examines post-war citizenship from the rather different angle of how multicultural policy has failed to incorporate the perspectives and address the needs of women of colour. These women are often at the margins of the state bureaucracy, which tends to see either race or gender, and not the intersection of the two, in the everyday lives of women of colour.

Since this volume takes the position that restructuring involves nothing less than a profound change in cultural forms, Part III provides an intensive examination of the current reregulation of many aspects of our private lives. In Chapter 8, Thelma McCormack examines the assumptions informing the Royal Commission on the New Reproductive Technologies. She concludes that its findings were based on biased assumptions about the primacy of the nuclear family and biological parenthood and, if implemented, would effectively limit the reproductive choices of women. The next two essays, by Brenda Cossman and Shelley A.M. Gavigan, take on the issue of the family more directly, especially as it applies to lesbians and women of colour, respectively. These essays discuss, in different ways, the privilege that the state accords to the heterosexual nuclear-family unit and how the designation "family" is problematic for lesbians and often denied to women of colour and poor women.

The final two essays in this volume speak more directly to policy areas frequently designated as "women's issues." In Chapter 11, Lise Gotell argues that the recent intensification of state interest in the criminalization of pornography is directly linked to the changing political economy. Finally, in Chapter 12, Andrea Levan similarly demonstrates how recent federal-government initiatives in the area of violence against women strengthen the policing arm of the state rather than addressing the material needs of women who are abused by men.

FEATURES OF THE TEXT

Each chapter in this volume has been organized to be used as a teaching unit in the subject area under investigation. The essays have been written and revised to be accessible to an undergraduate audience in a variety of disciplines. Each chapter provides a clear introduction to the policy area and an extensive discussion of the impact that past and present policy initiatives are having on the lives of Canadian women. A number of additional features are included in the text to facilitate learning and class discussion. A glossary of key terms used throughout the text is provided. As well, each chapter contains extensive references and suggested readings for students who wish to pursue further the topics and policy areas disussed. Finally, each chapter includes "Questions to Consider" designed to focus and facilitate class discussion and to help students prepare for essays and examinations.

ACKNOWLEDGEMENTS

Many people are responsible for the success of the 1994 Robarts Chair's seminar series and for the innovative quality of the essays in this volume. First and foremost, I would like to express my gratitude to the contributors, who readily agreed to participate in the seminar series and respond to rounds of editing with good humour and enthusiasm. This collection is a reflection of the strength of York University's community of feminist scholars and their ongoing commitment to work together to create multidisciplinary programs and publications. In this regard, I would especially like to thank the Osgoode Centre for Feminist Legal Studies; Dean Marilyn Pilkington, of Osgoode Hall; Kenneth McRoberts, former director of the Robarts Centre for Canadian Studies; Daniel Drache, the current director of the Robarts Centre for Canadian Studies; David Shugarman, Master of McLaughlin College; and York president Susan Mann for their support of this project and of collaborative feminist research at York. I am also indebted to the Social Sciences and Humanities Research Council (SSHRC) for its support of my ongoing research on women and restructuring.

The transformation of a series of discussions into a teaching volume is not accomplished without the assistance of considerable outside expertise and guidance. The contributors to this volume owe a special debt to Megan Mueller and Daniel Brooks of Harcourt Brace & Company for their enthusiastic support of this project, and to James Murray, who helped with many details, including the index. The contributors also benefited greatly from the detailed review of the manuscript undertaken by Dr. Sandra Burt of the University of Waterloo. A very special thank you, however, is due to Krystyna Tarkowski at the Robarts Centre, who made sure that this project was a success from beginning to end. Thanks, Krys, for everything! Finally and always, I am grateful to my dear friends and loved ones—especially, Isa Bakker, Susan O'Rourke, Lise Gotell, and Brodie Nutbrown—for enriching my life.

Janine Brodie
November 1994
Toronto

A Note from the Publisher

Thank you for selecting *Women and Canadian Public Policy* by Janine Brodie. The author and publisher have devoted considerable time to the careful development of this book. We appreciate your recognition of this effort and accomplishment.

We want to hear what you think about *Women and Canadian Public Policy*. Please take a few minutes to fill in the stamped reader reply card at the back of the book. Your comments and suggestions will be valuable to us as we prepare new editions and other books.

BRIEF CONTENTS

CONTENTS

PART II RESTRUCTURING THE STATE

Canadian Women, Changing State Forms, and Public Policy

Janine Brodie

When I was driving through the Maritime provinces in summer 1994, I was struck by a series of images that I thought rather nicely illustrated the central theme that informs the essays in this volume. The chapters in this book demonstrate, from very different perspectives, that Canada is currently experiencing a dramatic shift in state form. This shift involves changing the rules, expectations, and opportunities that Canadian women have lived with for most of the postwar period. Canada, as our politicians seem fond of telling us and as our newspapers remind us daily, is currently undergoing the painful exercise of restructuring. Among other things, this process has brought about continental economic integration and the collapse of the branch-plant manufacturing sector, a seemingly uncontrollable public debt, the erosion of the public sector and the welfare state, and the impetus to redesign the social safety net. Yet, while terms such as "restructuring," "globalization," and "competitiveness" have become a part of our everyday language, how this discourse informs Canadian public policy and the everyday lives of Canadian women is given little attention.

During my trip to the Maritime provinces, I was immediately struck, upon entering New Brunswick, by how much road construction was going on and, especially, by the number of women on the road crews. Of course, these women were not operating the heavy machinery; instead, they had the mind-numbing task of turning a sign—slow/stop, slow/stop, slow/stop—for hours on end. Nevertheless, my first impression was that this represented a marked improvement. It was not so long ago that only male college students got these relatively well-paying summer jobs, and female students were relegated to summer waitressing for minimum wage, a job that always offered few employment protections and often involved sexual harassment. As I approached the second construction site, however, I realized that my first impression had been dead wrong. These women were not college students; they were older and responsibility, stress, and poverty showed in their faces. As one construction site passed into another, the scene was repeated again and again. In fact, during my stay in the province, I don't think I saw one man signalling traffic to slow or stop.

I do not know whether this recurring spectacle was coincidental, nor did I ask. But my mind immediately turned to what I had been reading about New Brunswick—the province that federal Human Resource Development Minister Lloyd Axworthy calls an "incubator of reform." He coined the phrase in praising the province for its initiatives in social-welfare reform, which, he said, "rather than using (**social assistance**) in a passive way for people to get some limited income security, ... gives them a launching pad into the job market" (*Globe and Mail*, November 17, 1993, p. A1). These initiatives, NB WORKS and the Self-Sufficiency Project, attempt to nudge single parents (read: women) from the welfare rolls onto the job market. More recently, the federal and Manitoba governments have launched a $26.2-million program to help that province's 4000 single parents who are currently on welfare find work (*Globe and Mail*, September 10, 1993, p. A4). (Patricia Evans's essay in this volume traces Ontario's adoption of a similar policy.) In each case, **single mothers** are being targeted as "a problem" within the existing welfare system. Legislation and practice are rapidly transforming mothers previously seen as unemployable into burdens on the state—potential members of the labour force who are responsible for their own maintenance and that of their children.

The issue is not that the state should resist welfare-policy reforms that provide single mothers on welfare, or any other disadvantaged group, with good jobs, some dignity, and a means to financial security and independence. Rather, the issue is whether, in a period of so-called jobless recovery, such initiatives can reasonably be expected to succeed. New Brunswick's premier, Frank McKenna, suggests that the likelihood of jobs becoming available should not be a concern: "if you have the training, the jobs will take care of themselves" (*Globe and Mail*, January 15, 1993). However, critics of the new thinking about "active" social policy are less convinced (McFarland, 1993). My point is simply that the policy universe, the economy, and politics are undergoing a period of flux in which questions regarding the appropriate role for the state in the economy and the rights of citizenship are being recast, renegotiated, and reregulated.

French philosopher Michel Foucault once suggested that social scientists begin their analysis with a basic assumption—namely, not "that everything is evil but rather that everything is dangerous" (quoted in Fink-Eitel, 1992, p. 10). Foucault was not advocating a philosophy of extreme paranoia. Instead, he was pointing out that the way we think about social problems is profoundly political. Power and knowledge are intimately related; within each historical period, they construct systems of domination and oppression, exclusion and silence, and perceptions of self and other. The current period of restructuring in Canada, which is based on new ideas about the economy and the state, is no different. As the essays in this volume attempt to show, the process of restructuring is changing the issues and challenges Canadian women face in their ongoing struggle for equality. Our project in this book is not to lament the passing of the old order, although evidence suggests that the shift away from it has left Canadian women disproportionately disadvantaged. Instead, our goal is to point to how the rapidly changing political and policy universe is creating new dangers that Canadian women must recognize and challenge. Our point here is that it is contingent upon feminists to examine closely the policy shifts that affect women's everyday lives in order to identify the various webs of subordination and domination on which the emerging order rests.

CANADA AND THE NEW GLOBAL ORDER

Uncertain Politics

The 1993 federal election made clear what had been increasingly apparent since the implementation of the Canada–U.S. Free Trade Agreement (CUFTA) in 1989. Canadian voters roundly rejected, and, indeed, struck a death blow to, the federal Conservative party for betraying their trust, eroding their social-security system, and forcing their family members into the growing ranks of the unemployed—all in the name of "efficiency" and "competitiveness." But the election made clear that this collective rage was not triggered by the loss of the postwar **Keynesian welfare state**, which the Conservatives had been working to dismantle with determination and assuredness since they came to power in 1984. Even though public-opinion polls show that most Canadians continue to support their social programs, the only party promising anything like a return to the "good old" Keynesian days—the federal New Democratic Party—was dismissed during the campaign as the "New Preservation Party" and was abandoned at the polls by all but its most loyal supporters.

Perhaps not since the 1935 federal election, which also was held during a prolonged period of economic turmoil and restructuring, had voters been offered such fundamental choices at the polls. In 1993, each of the federal parties had a different interpretation of Canada's economic and political crisis and a different prescription for change. For most of the postwar period, Canada's three major parties had shared a vision of the appropriate relationship among the state, the economy, and the home. This vision, sometimes called the "Keynesian" or "postwar" consensus, rested on three fundamental planks:

▶ the development of a comprehensive social-welfare system,

▶ the use of **macro-economic** levers to control inflation or stimulate growth and protect the national economy from international disturbances, and

▶ adherence to a more liberalized international trading regime. (Brodie, 1990, p. 149)

The three major parties had been committed to these principles, arguing only about how much welfare or how much government intervention in the economy was appropriate. Indeed, until the mid-1980s, political commentators often referred to the federal Liberal and Conservative parties as "Tweedledum and Tweedledee" or "The Boys from Bay Street," and to the New Democratic Party as simply "Liberals in a hurry"! However, since the mid-1970s, prolonged economic crisis and the rise of neoliberal rhetoric and governing practices have dramatically changed the political landscape and the way that policy-makers assess both the causes of and the "cures" for Canada's ongoing social problems. The federal party system now houses new challengers with profoundly different prescriptions for Canadian development, nationhood, and citizenship, although the system is increasingly silent about the gender order. In other words, the postwar pattern of politics has been pushed aside, throwing into stark relief the uncertain and contested political space women now occupy (Brodie and Jenson, 1995).

The New Neoliberal Consensus

Canada, like all Western democracies, is currently experiencing a significant shift in state form and governing practices. It is now widely acknowledged that the foundations of the Keynesian welfare state (KWS) have been undermined by the combined forces of prolonged recession, the so-called globalization of production, and neoliberal governing practices. The broad consensus that grounded the KWS and structured the pattern of federal politics for almost a half-century has gradually, but certainly, given way to a very different set of assumptions about the role of government and the rights of citizens. These new assumptions lead to new forms of domination, at the same time reshaping the familiar ones rooted in gender, race, and class.

The new governing orthodoxy—"the neoliberal consensus"—holds that changing international realities put roughly the same demands on all governments; namely, that they

▶ maximize exports,

▶ reduce social spending,

▶ curtail state economic regulation, and

▶ enable market forces to restructure national economies as parts of transnational or regional trading blocs (Friedman, 1991, p. 35).

On the basis of these principles, Canadian governments are increasingly rejecting their former roles as promoters of domestic welfare and protectors of the national economy against unstable international forces. In the process, they have largely abandoned as futile the post-war goals of full employment and an inclusive social safety net. As Lloyd Axworthy announced, in *Improving Social Security in Canada: A Discussion Paper,*

> today's social security system doesn't deliver enough of what Canadians need, and spends too much money in the wrong places.... This generation must use its ingenuity to rebuild our social programs for a new era, just as an earlier generation after the Second World War forged solutions to meet the social needs of the post-war period.... the key to dealing with social insecurity can be summed up in a single phrase: helping people get and keep jobs. This means many things, from action to improve the business climate for entrepreneurs, to getting the government's finances in order. (Canada, 1994, pp. 9–10)

Governments are effectively acting as the midwives of globalization, transforming the state apparatus, development strategies, and regulations to respond to the "perceived exigencies" of a global economy (Cox, 1991, p. 337). In particular, assumptions and governing practices are being refashioned to achieve the illusive and abstract states of "flexibility" and "competitiveness."

This neoliberal world view was first championed by the Reagan administration in the United States, and by Margaret Thatcher's Conservatives in Great Britain in the early 1980s. It was put at the top of the Canadian political agenda by the long-awaited report of the Macdonald Commission (Royal Commission on the Economic Union and Development Prospects for Canada), released in 1985. The commission successfully advanced the position that free trade with the United States and a neoliberal economic agenda were the *only* viable economic-development strategies left to Canada. With respect to free trade, in particular, Canadians were told to close their eyes and take "a leap of faith" because the globalization train had already left the station. If Canadians did not "jump aboard," they would most surely be left behind and would forfeit their living standards. Consequently, in its report, the commission advised all Canadian governments, federal and provincial, to

▶ adopt a market-driven development strategy,

▶ facilitate adjustment by reducing regulations on industry, and

▶ create new opportunities for private-sector growth (Brodie, 1990, pp. 218–223).

The Macdonald Commission had been appointed in 1982 by the federal Liberal party, which, at the time, seemed incapable of reversing the worst economic downturn Canada had had since the 1930s. Postwar macro-economic policies appeared unable to cope with stagflation—an increase in both inflation and joblessness. However, the newly elected Conservative government, under the leadership of Brian Mulroney, was quick to embrace the commission's prescriptions for economic renewal. In fact, the outgoing Trudeau government could not have given the Conservative party a better gift. It quickly launched into free-trade talks with the United States, although only two years earlier all but one of the Conservative leadership candidates (John Crosbie), including Brian Mulroney, had roundly rejected the idea as a threat to Canadian jobs and sovereignty. The Conservative party also began, tentatively at first, to carve away at the welfare state.

An uncompromising neoliberal world view came to dominate the Mulroney government's front benches after its re-election in 1988 and the implementation of the Canada–U.S. Free Trade Agreement in 1989. Throughout the late 1980s, the Mulroney government had used mounting federal deficits as a rationale for cutting back the welfare state. By the early 1990s, however, the Conservatives' attack was directly linked to making Canada more "competitive"—primarily by forfeiting economic terrain to the private sector (Abele, 1992, p. 1). In its 1992 Budget Speech, for example, the Conservative government announced that its primary legislative priority was to promote greater "reliance on the private sector and market forces." Ranked immediately below this were the related goals of deficit reduction, inflation control, free trade, and the development of a new consensus about the role of government. For the federal Conservatives, a restructured economy required a restructured government that would provide only those public services that were "affordable" and did not interfere with Canadian "competitiveness" (*Toronto Star*, November 8, 1992). Indeed, so committed was the ruling party to this new world view that it attempted to make it constitutional in the early stages of the ill-fated **Charlottetown Accord** negotiations (Brodie, 1992).

More of the Same

Historians may very well judge the Mulroney regime to be one of the most radical and overtly ideological in Canadian history. It ultimately collided with the Canadian voters in 1993, when they gave a landslide victory to the federal Liberal party. The Liberals promised little else than to be more compassionate managers of the economic transition. Since the election, moreover, the new government has charted the same neoliberal course and has used similar governing instruments, primarily the budget, to erode Canada's social safety net. The Liberal government, for example, ratified the North American Free Trade Agreement (NAFTA) in January 1994, even though it had failed to secure the side agreements it had identified during the election campaign as prerequisites for Canada's signing NAFTA. The Liberals also gave deficit reduction priority over employment and infrastructure development and have continued to attack the social-welfare system and system of federal–provincial cost-sharing that had been built up piecemeal during the postwar years.

The new minister of finance, Paul Martin, Jr., wore workboots instead of Bay Street brogues when he delivered his first budget on February 22, 1994. Although this choice of footwear was meant to convey to the public that the Liberal party was about jobs, it did not signal that the new federal government was preparing to repair Canada's fraying social safety net. Instead, Martin told Parliament that, "for years, governments have been promising more than they can deliver, and delivering more than they can afford. That has to end. We are ending it" (*Toronto Star*, February 23, 1994, p. A1). In the process, the federal government has begun a total redesign of the social-welfare system, a strategy begun within the federal bureaucracy during the Mulroney regime. In other words, the postwar KWS, is no more.

In sum, then, the past decade has seen discredited most of the familiar assumptions that grounded governing practices in the postwar years. Daily, we receive a barrage of messages about the imperatives of trade, the deficit, a "jobless" recovery, the survival of our health-care system, the necessity for redesigning our social programs ... the list goes on. These policy changes, represent more than a series of ad hoc responses to a weak national economy and the changing global order. Instead, these changes represent a paradigm shift in governing practices—a historic remodelling of state form that, in turn, enacts changes, some intended and some not, in cultural forms, political identities, and the very terrain of the political. Restructuring, in other words, "conveys the notion of a 'brake,' if not a break, in secular trends, and a shift toward a *significantly different order and configuration of social, economic and political life*. It thus evokes a sequential combination of falling apart and building up again, deconstruction and attempted reconstitution" (Soja, 1989, p. 159; emphasis added).

WOMEN, RESTRUCTURING, AND THE STATE

Women and Restructuring

Feminists have not stood passively by as the new order emerged. Women's organizations in English Canada have been in the forefront of the broad-based political coalition, sometimes called the "popular sector," that has opposed neoliberal premises and governing practices ever since they were transplanted to Canadian soil in the early 1980s (Cameron, 1989). Feminists also have been among the few to emphasize, as Isabella Bakker's essay in this volume points out, that restructuring is not a gender-neutral macro-economic process but, instead, has been enacted precisely on the field of gender (see also Bakker, 1994).

In fact, a growing body of gender-sensitive research, including the essays in this volume, provides compelling evidence to show that the gendered impacts of restructuring are pronounced and multiple. Feminist academics and women's organizations have linked restructuring to the intensification and feminization of poverty, especially among single mothers and elderly women. They also point out that women, whether as clients or as state workers, have been disproportionately affected by ever-growing cuts to social-welfare spending and by the reduction of the public sector. Finally, the women's movement and statistical data consistently demonstrate that the gendered impacts of restructuring are unevenly distributed among women; restructuring has exacted the heaviest toll among young women, immigrant women, women of colour, and working-class women, especially in the manufacturing sector (Leger and Rebick, 1993; Gavigan, this volume). As Judy Rebick, former president of the National Action Committee on the Status of Women (NAC), summarizes, "all the 'vanguard destructive forces' of the right are hitting women first—teleworking, part-time work—all of that hits women first" (Rebick, 1994, p. 58).

Key front-line women's organizations recognized, from the beginning, that the neoliberals' vision of a minimalist state and an unfettered global capitalism threatened the very foundations of second-wave feminism's equity agenda. Throughout the 1960s and 1970s, the dominant current of the English-Canadian women's movement had consistently linked the achievement of gender equality with federal state activism, whether through the elaboration of the social safety net, regulation, or law reform (Brodie, 1995; McCormack, Gotell, and Levan, this volume). Key feminist policy demands, such as universal and affordable child care, income security, the protection of women from male violence, **affirmative action**, and **pay equity**, call for more, not less, governmental intervention and public spending (Gotell and Brodie, 1991, p. 62). It is hardly surprising then that, after the election of the federal Progressive Conservative party in 1984, women's organizations expended ever-increasing quantities of their political currency defending the federal state—more specifically, its postwar manifestation as a Keynesian welfare state—against the so-called Tory Agenda and the restructuring process.

Reading the Restructuring Process

Nevertheless, whether in the form of statistical data demonstrating the gendered foundations of restructuring or in the form of political protest, the conceptual and strategic reading we give the present era of restructuring is often inadequate. Feminists have tended to focus on, as Soja (1989) puts it, "the falling apart" and have not explored how "the building up again" proceeds unabated, often in the most subtle and seemingly innocent ways. In Foucault's terms, we have tended to interpret the events of the past decade as "evil" without recognizing that both the past and the present are dangerous in that they structure systems of domination and exclusion, albeit often quite differently. This inadequate reading of restructuring, I believe, most often takes one of three forms:

▶ *Liberal empiricism:* The fundamental assumption informing this approach is that providing state officials with "good" gender-sensitive research about the gendered impacts of restructuring will lead to policy reform aimed at correcting the negative effects.

▶ *Radical determinism:* This approach recognizes the gendered impacts of restructuring but argues that those impacts simply provide additional evidence of the perpetual and fundamental opposition between either the interests of capital and women, or women and men (Yeatman, 1990, p. 119; McDowell, 1991, p. 401).

▶ *Nostalgic welfarism:* This approach glorifies the postwar welfare state and reads any deviation from past experience as undesirable, disregarding that the welfare state also had negative consequences for women and other disadvantaged groups.

These readings of restructuring are inadequate on a number of counts. Liberal empiricism, for example, conveys the questionable assumption that unequal gender impacts are accidental rather than integral to the current round of restructuring. It also places the state outside the restructuring process, assuming that it can neutralize its gendered effects with the appropriate "facts" and political pressure. Radical determinism, in contrast, sees little hope for change because it envisions the state as always reinforcing, supporting, or acting on behalf of a unity of interests—for example, capital or men—that are outside the state system (Watson, 1990). It casts all women at all times and in all places as passive victims of the state. At the same time, it fails to recognize that not all women are disadvantaged by restructuring—or, at least, not to the same degree—and that the effects of restructuring can be quite different across, for example, racial and class groupings.

To avoid misinterpretation, I want to emphasize that my objections to nostalgic welfarism do not speak to the desirability and necessity of the collective provision of social welfare. In other words, I do not argue that we have no choice but to adjust to the leaner and meaner state that is currently being fashioned through a barrage of discursive practices, regulations, and public policies. My point is simply that the postwar welfare state was only one particular state form, one form of welfare provision, that arose out of very different historical circumstances and was creat-ed by different political actors with different political interests and alliances. As a reading of restructuring, then, nostalgic welfarism puts feminists in the paradoxical position of having to defend the same wel-fare state that they had previously, and with good reason, criticized for being an agent of social control and for being patriarchal, classist, and racist (Abbott and Wallace, 1992, p. 22). Increasingly, however, this reading is becoming less paradoxical than self-defeating. The postwar welfare state was always an ambiguous resource for women; even though it is now fading into history, it was never the endpoint in the evolution of state formation for women; rather, it was a short-lived and geographically isolated adaptation. Below, I argue that a feminist read-ing of restructuring must begin with the premise that this process simultaneously alters the economic, public, and domestic realms—the very constitution—of gendered political actors and, ultimately, the objects of feminist political struggle.

FEMINIST THEORIZING ABOUT THE STATE

Grand Theories

Feminist theorizing about the state has followed several different paths, all of which, some would argue, have ended in a conceptual cul-de-sac. Liberal feminists, for example, have been criticized for their optimistic depiction of the liberal democratic state as a potentially progressive and sovereign institution that, once "purged" of its sexism, is capable of legislating women's equality (Watson, 1990, p. 7). For these detrac-tors, public policy and law are incapable of realizing women's equality unless they are accompanied by a fundamental reorganization of soci-ety, including the public and private spheres and gender roles. At the same time, some socialist and radical feminist theories that character-ize the state as an agent of social control and patriarchy have been criti-cized for being overly deterministic and functional. These theories seem unable to account for why the state always acts in the interests of men, if indeed it does, or why it sometimes enacts reforms that appear to weaken the dominant patriarchal order (Gordon, 1990, p. 10). Moreover, this depiction of the state as a guarantor of patriarchal hege-mony tends to ignore the reality that public policies often have different consequences for different types of women. Similarly, public policies and state regulation may be contradictory or have the unintended effect of empowering women to take political action (Chunn, 1995, p. 177).

These concerns have led some feminists to abandon altogether the project of theorizing the state. Judith Allen, for example, discourages feminists from wasting any more time trying to construct "grand theories" of the state because, she argues, it is "a category of abstraction that is too aggregative, too unitary and too unspecific to be of much use in address-ing the disaggregated, diverse and specific (or local) sites that must be of most pressing concern to feminists." Indeed, she goes on to suggest that the state is not an "indigenous category" in feminist theory (1990, p. 22).

Allen's critique provides a new twist to a long-standing anti–statist tradition within feminist theory and practice. But do we risk too much when we choose to ignore or dismiss, in theory or in practice, the rele-vance of the state, especially during a period of fundamental restructur-ing? Although many feminist theories of the state appear fatally flawed, the fact remains that most feminist concerns—whether they relate to health, equity, or security—are necessarily state-centred (Brown, 1992). Can we really give up the important project of coming to a better understanding of the relationship between public policy and feminist goals of equality? When we stand on the outside looking in, don't we simply confirm the identities that the state imposes on us, including invisibility, rather than challenge them (Yeatman, 1993, pp. 231, 233)?

Rather than turning away from the state, then, feminists might be better advised to ask what it is about our thinking about the state that fails to capture our experience. What's wrong with thinking about the state, for example, as a thing, system, or subject (Brown, 1992, p. 12); as sovereign; as a place where power is centred; as situated above and acting on society; or as an agent of domination that reproduces the hegemony of a single interest, be it capital or patriarchy? What is it about these assumptions that has made the state "the major casualty of recent social theory" (Pringle and Watson, 1990, p. 54)?

The Welfare State

One could argue that the bell tolls for only certain strains of feminist theories of the state. In fact, these theories have focussed almost exclusively on the gendered underpinnings of the welfare state. Linda Gordon, for example, argues that feminist scholarship on the welfare state has moved through three discernible stages:

▶ *Discriminatory theories* demonstrated how welfare programs acted to reinforce sexist arrangements in domestic and public life.

▶ *Structural theories* emphasized how welfare policies functioned both to hold women in a subordinate position to men and as an broader agent of social control. A two-tier welfare system, which disadvan-taged women, also ensured women's economic dependence on men, and men's economic dependence on wages.

▶ *Women's political-activism and influence theories* have rejected the idea that all women are necessarily passive victims of the wel-fare state. Instead, these theories emphasize how they were active participants in the creation of that state and empowered by it (Gordon, 1990, pp. 18–23; Andrew, 1984).

The third type of theory elaborates on the "power resources" perspective on the welfare state, which emphasizes that "politics matter": the welfare state is not a monolithic agent of social control. Instead, social policy is seen to have both regulatory and emancipatory potential for women, even if the latter is unintentional (Orloff, 1993, p. 305). Frances Fox Piven is perhaps one of the most insistent in terms of the welfare state's emancipatory potential for women. Contrary to the deterministic characterization of the state as exercising social control over women and supplanting patriarchal relations of the family with a patriarchal relationship with the state, she argues that the flow of political power is not necessarily always unidirectional (1990, p. 255). She continues:

> Income supports, social services, and government employment partly offset the deteriorating position of women in the family and economy and have even given women a measure of protection and therefore power in the family and economy. In these ways the state is turning out to be the main recourse for women. (ibid., p. 254)

While many have applauded Fox Piven and like-minded feminists for resisting the all too frequent tendency to depict women as passive victims, the women's political activism approach also has its detractors. Wendy Brown, for example, argues that, although the welfare state may liberate a woman from the family, "she is immediately colonized and administered by one or more dimensions of masculinist state power" (1992, p. 30). Brown holds this view because she is wary of the immense regulatory capacities of the welfare state and because she sees that the state both reacts to and actively creates its subjects. She explains that the "state does not simply handle clients or employ staff." It also produces state subjects who are "bureaucratized, dependent, disciplined and gendered" (ibid., p. 30).

Brown argues that the welfare state is not a thing but, instead, a "multifaceted ensemble of power relations," an "unbounded terrain of powers and techniques," and "an ensemble of discourses, rules and practices" (ibid., p. 12). In the end, however, her analysis remains locked within Western feminist debates about the value of the welfare state for women and continues to depict it as responding to a unitary and ahistorical interest—"masculinist state power." I would suggest that many debates about the welfare state are simply that—debates about the welfare state—and may have little utility as a basis for understanding the emerging neoliberal state form.

State as Cultural Form

The tendency to view societal institutions as "reified monoliths" that perpetually victimize women has lost much of its force in the recent literature. Many social scientists now view societal institutions, including those within the state system, as social constructs that reflect the constraints of particular social structures and historical developments (Chunn, 1995, p. 177). A social-constructionist lens denies neither that the state is constantly implicated in the production and reproduction of power relations nor that its policies have real effects on the everyday lives of women. Further, it does not deny that the state can and does act instrumentally (too often, consistently) in the interests of some and not others. It does, however, challenge the way feminists have traditionally understood the dynamic among state power, gender identity, and gender relations (Brodie, 1994). As Orloff puts it, the new feminist thinking about the state emphasizes how public policy, in particular, "the character of public provision(,) affects women's material situations, shapes gender relationships, structures political conflict and participation, and contributes to the formation and mobilization of specific identities and interests" (1993, p. 303). In other words, women do not stand ahistorically outside a particular state formation but, instead, are historical products of public policy and other cultural forms.

The vast array of public policies and regulations that emanate from the state are not remote from women but, instead, help shape our life chances, our most intimate relationships, what we believe to be political, who we think we are, and how we make claims on the state and for what. Consequently, as Corrigan and Sayer forcefully argue, we must "grasp state forms culturally" (1985, p. 3). They suggest that the time-worn idea of the state as a coherent unity positioned instrumentally above society is "in large part an ideological construct, a fiction." While the institutions of government are real enough, the state–society relation is less directive than coterminous and discursive, embedded in our shared understandings what is natural, neutral, and universal. Corrigan and Sayer suggest that these shared understandings are anything but natural, neutral, and universal; rather, they are simply "impositional claims"—assertions about reality that are self-interested, biased, historically specific, and subject to political contestation. Nonetheless, they provide the cultural foundations for historically specific state forms. Different state forms, whether laissez-faire, welfare, or neoliberal, weave different meanings into the everyday. Among other things, these meanings are enshrined in law and public policy, embedded in institutions, and enforced through regulation and sanction (Corrigan and Sayer, 1985, pp. 2–7). States, first and foremost, "state": "They define, in great detail, acceptable forms and images of social activity and individual and collective identity; they regulate, in empirically specifiable ways ... social life. In this sense, 'the State' never stops talking" (ibid., p. 3).

Michel Foucault once suggested that "the state consists in the codification of a whole number of power relations" and that a "revolution is a different type of codification of these same relations" (Held et al., 1983, pp. 312–313). Canada is currently undergoing just such a revolution—one that is still incomplete and subject to contestation. It nonetheless seeks to recode the realm of the political, which the Keynesian welfare state "stated" in the postwar years with new shared understandings. The essays in this volume provide an initial examination of how the emerging new state form—the neoliberal state—is progressively recoding the terrain of the political, the workplace, and private life, and is thus reshaping gender relations and the everyday lives of Canadian women. Below, I suggest that this recoding or restating of the state–society relation is taking three principal forms:

▶ shrinking the realm of the state
▶ a redefinition of citizenship
▶ privatization and "refamilialization"

SHRINKING THE PUBLIC, EXPANDING THE PRIVATE

Market-Driven Adjustment

The emergence of the neoliberal state is being driven by what I term "restructuring discourse" (Brodie, 1994; 1995). It seeks to radically shrink the realm of political negotiation by increasing the autonomy of market forces and of the family. The central theme of restructuring discourse is that no political choices remain for shaping our collective lives and future other than to follow a market-driven approach to the globalization of the international economy. We are told that there is simply no escaping "adjustment," which restructuring discourse defines exclusively as reducing fiscal and regulatory burdens on industry and lowering expectations about the role of the state. As we noted earlier, this contention that there is no choice was the primary rationale offered to Canadians for entering both the Canada–U.S. and the North American free-trade agreements.

More recently, the no-choice theme has been applied to the ballooning deficit and government spending, particularly in the realm of social policy. The chief executive officer of the Canadian Imperial Bank of Commerce, who earns $1.5 million a year, provides an example of this discourse. Speaking about the deficit, he said, "the only policy that will work is spending cuts. Canada has only one choice, only one decision to make" (quoted in *Toronto Star*, September 16, 1994, p. A1).

According to the neoliberals, the state should neither protect domestic industry from global pressures nor provide a comprehensive social-welfare system for its citizens. In effect, this discourse attempts to decentre and displace the Keynesian welfare state with "hyper-liberal" impositional claims about self-regulating market forces and the primacy of the market in generating a new social order (Cox, 1991, p. 342; Drache and Gertler, 1991, p. 7). In the process, it elevates economics over politics and suggests this process is somehow inevitable, neutral, and beyond our control.

Of course, this market-driven approach to changes in the global economy is neither inevitable nor neutral. These are simply self-interested impositional claims that establish particular forms of domination and exclusions and, ultimately, must be contested as such. The international experience, for example, demonstrates that not all countries have adopted this strategy and that those which have are not faring particularly well in the new world order. And, as Isabella Bakker's chapter in this volume demonstrates, these macro-economic **stabilization policies** are not neutral but, instead, are placing an onerous burden on marginalized economic actors, especially women. The erosion of the welfare state and cuts in public-sector employment disproportionately affect women, effectively increasing their economic insecurity and their unpaid work in the family.

Judy Fudge's analysis (this volume) of how macro-economic policies are filtered through labour-market policy and labour relations strongly supports Bakker's arguments. She indicates that it now takes 65 to 80 hours of work each week for a family to earn what it typically took a single male breadwinner to earn in 45 hours in the 1970s. Women's labour-force participation, although increasing, continues to be characterized by female job ghettos, while the current trends toward smaller firms, smaller workplaces, and declining unionization have eroded women's working conditions, job security, and wages. If there has been any improvement in women's wages compared with men's in recent years, it is attributable to the fact that more men have been forced into "bad," "feminized" jobs and not to any real gains made by women. And this trend is likely to intensify in the future. As Patricia McDermott points out in this volume, the goals of pay and employment equity have been ineffective and probably will be one of the first casualties of the new order. Government social programs are being redesigned to promote equality of opportunity without conceding that some groups have been and continue to be disadvantaged and that such factors as pervasive racism, sexism, and homophobia make competition on a level playing field impossible. The federal government nonetheless suggests that creating "opportunity must be the watchword of our redesigned social security system" (Canada, 1994, p. 25). Concerns about equality of conditions appear to be a luxury of the past.

International Trading Agreements

Market-driven adjustment has not been gender-neutral, but the capacity for women to reverse these trends has been diminished by the shrinkage of political space. Restructuring discourse attempts both to depoliticize the market by representing it as natural and self-regulating and to close off spaces for political negotiation, perhaps most irreversibly through international trading agreements. These agreements are completely saturated with neoliberal assumptions and solutions that erode national sovereignty and the ability of governments to respond to the demands of the electorate. Changes in the regulation of international capitalism through the General Agreement on Tariffs and Trade (GATT) and regional treaties such as CUFTA, NAFTA, and the Single European Act effectively represent a "new constitutionalism" that defines and guarantees new rights to transnational capital—rights that often trump those of the citizens of liberal democracies such as Canada (Gill, 1992).

CUFTA, for example, specifically limits the terrain of the political by prohibiting governments from either favouring domestic producers or subsidizing national industry. NAFTA goes even farther by attempting to cap the domain of the state. It refers to the public sector as a "nonconforming" measure, limits the use of public corporations, and requires those remaining to change over to commercial operations and considerations (Cohen, 1993a). Implicit in these restrictions is the clear message that we have reached—indeed, surpassed—the appropriate boundary of state intervention and that restructuring demands retreat and attrition.

The constraints imposed on Canadian governments by international trading agreements obviously hold dangerous implications for women and for the achievement of women's equality as well as for all other subordinate groups. Such agreements can dictate how—indeed, whether or not—governments can initiate equity-based policies such as a national day-care program, incentives for women entrepreneurs, and protective regulation. Barbara Cameron's discussion of NAFTA and the new reproductive technologies in this volume explores how some of these constraints would play themselves out in the regulation of fertility. Thelma McCormack's essay outlines the many disagreements among women about the recommendations of the Royal Commission on the New Reproductive Technologies, which reported in 1992, setting out a strong moral argument for the non-commercialization of these technologies and for limiting women's fertility choices. But, as Cameron describes, even if there was widespread consensus among Canadians, and governmental resolve to regulate these new technologies, the terms of NAFTA might very well prohibit such regulations or make them too costly to consider. Moreover, Cameron suggests that governments in the future will be constrained from imposing a regulatory regime on new industries with as yet unimagined technologies.

Hollowing Out the Welfare State

The terrain of the political also has been eroded by the progressive "hollowing out" of the welfare state. Restructuring discourse is less concerned with the actual size of the welfare state than with its underlying ideals (Yeatman, 1990). During the past decade, "hardly a single federal social program has not been reduced or altered" (National Forum on Family Security, 1993, p. 8). These changes generally have been implemented through a series of budget cuts that critics have referred to as "social policy by stealth" (Cohen, 1993b, p. 267). This politics, which was perfected by the Mulroney government and subsequently embraced by the federal Liberals and most provincial governments, enables governments to enact without prior public consultation or participation immediate and significant changes in social policy by means of complex revisions of regulations and repeated budget cuts. The politics of stealth was used to put an end to the principle of universality in Canada's Old Age Security and Family Allowance programs and has severely restricted the provinces' capacity to finance social-welfare schemes. The Mulroney government unilaterally rewrote the terms of federal–provincial cost-sharing in the fields of social welfare, health care, and post-secondary education. In so doing, it effectively downloaded the fiscal crisis onto the provinces, which vary greatly in terms of capacity to cope.

Pat Armstrong's essay discusses how this downloading has put severe stress on the health-care system and the women who either work in it or are attended by it. Nurses are being deskilled in a leaner and meaner work environment, people in need of treatment are being **deinstitutionalized** in ever greater numbers, and the length of hospital stays is dropping dramatically. It is not uncommon, for example, for a mother to be sent home within hours of delivering her new baby. While this practice would appear to respond to the demands of the women's health-care movement that childbirth be demedicalized, at the same time, many of these women leave hospital without having been given sufficient instruction for the care of newborns and return to homes that have no support system in place.

All of these factors make it more difficult to be healthy. The discourse around health care is changing, putting greater emphasis on a woman's private responsibilities for her own health and for caring for the needs of family members. The health-care system, in other words, is being incrementally "privatized." Health is increasingly being seen as a "**lifestyle**" rather than a social issue, and health-care costs are being downloaded to the home and absorbed as part of women's unpaid labour. More important, this shift of the health-care burden onto women is being rationalized with specific reference to the progressive discourse of the women's health movement. The success of a new order often depends on its ability to incorporate criticisms of the old order, even if the outcomes are qualitatively different. The past calls of the women's health movement for a demedicalized and woman-friendly health-care model are being used to justify health-care cuts and the placing of more responsibility for health care on families and individual women.

Although many of these changes to the social safety net have occurred incrementally and almost invisibly, its redesign has been given a great deal of build-up and promotion. All Canadian women will be affected by these changes since old age, unemployment, and welfare benefits are also being reviewed. However, as Patricia Evans (this volume) points out, **single mothers** have been targeted in particular as a welfare "problem." The new welfare discourse privileges paid work over other activities such as caregiving, attempts to redefine the basis on which one is deemed to be deserving or undeserving of state assistance, and is aimed at breaking the cycle of so-called welfare dependency. Although the child-caring activities of single mothers were previously considered to be of overriding importance, effectively making them unemployable until their children reached school age, this is no longer the case. As Evans says, public policy is reshaping social identities of single mothers and their capacity to make claims on the state by redefining them as a welfare problem—as undeserving, employable, and dependent. A "fit" single mother is now a working mother.

REDEFINING CITIZENSHIP

The New Citizen

The current era of restructuring involves a complex displacement of state power and the political terrain once occupied by the welfare state. While the emerging neoliberal state maintains all the trappings of democracy and sovereignty, it nonetheless rests on impositional claims that prioritize the market over politics, limit the terrain of governmental intervention, and accord more value to the private than to the public (Jessop, 1993, p. 22). In the process, it nurtures new shared understandings of what it means to be a citizen and what the citizen can ask of the state. Although they varied considerably, postwar welfare states rested on a broad but ultimately fragile consensus about the rights of citizenship. The Keynesian notion of social citizenship conveyed the idea that poverty was not always an individual's fault, and that all citizens had the right to a basic standard of living. Moreover, it was assumed that the public could impose limits on the market, that people would not be forced to engage in market activities that denied their safety or dignity, and that the national community was responsible for the basic well-being of its individual members.

In Canada, this social citizenship was accompanied by an official policy of multiculturalism. This policy, as Christina Gabriel's essay shows, was designed to celebrate Canada's ethnic and racial diversity, while, at the same time, weaving a hierarchy of language, ethnicity, and race into Canada's social fabric. Gabriel demonstrates that official multicultural policy was both racist and gender-biased, allowing no political space for women to have a voice or representation within the designated multi-cultural communities. At the same time, the growing state apparatus was unable to incorporate the specific and different experiences of women of colour. Women of colour could not be slotted easily or neatly into the Canada's postwar citizenship matrix of multicultural policy, race-relations policy, and women's issues. Importantly, however, Gabriel's essay shows how the spaces created at the margins of the state apparatus provided a place for women of colour to contest their subordination and exclusion. She concludes that we need to restruc-ture the notion of citizenship to include difference and accommodate the intersection of race and gender.

However, it is precisely these postwar ideals of social citizenship and the accommodation of difference that are currently under attack in the new order. As the Canadian experience demonstrates, there has been a decided shift away from the idea of universal, publicly provided services and citizenship. The social safety net is poised for a major transforma-tion to make it fit with the market-based, self-reliant, and privatizing ideals of the new order. The federal government calls this planned reform "the most comprehensive reform of government policy in decades" (Canada, 1994, p. 10). In its discussion paper on the redesign-ing of the social safety net, it phrases this new meaning of citizenship unambiguously. "Improved government support," it suggests, "must be targeted at those who demonstrate a willingness and commitment to self-help". It is the primary task of the reform "to gear them more effec-tively towards helping individuals achieve the satisfaction and dignity of work" (ibid., pp. 25, 82).

The rights and securities universally guaranteed to citizens of the Keynesian welfare state are no longer rights, universal, or secure. The new ideal of the common good rests on market-oriented values such as self-reliance, efficiency, and competition. The new good citizen is one who recognizes the limits and liabilities of state provision and embraces the obligation to work longer and harder in order to become more self-reliant (Drache, 1992, p. 221). Moreover, as we shall see, there is little tolerance for making "special" claims on the basis of dif-ference or systemic discrimination.

The New Exclusions

As Gabriel points out, the postwar ideal of citizenship was far from all-encompassing. In many ways, the ideal citizen was the White male breadwinner. Those not fitting this stereotype, inlcuding women, single mothers, Native people, gay and lesbian couples, and immigrants, were excluded in different ways, from the full benefits of postwar social citizenship. The new order similarly sets up its own list of exclu-sions. First, the decline of universal social programs and the welfare state has created two categories of citizen—the "deserving" and the "undeserving." The idea here is that all able-bodied people are effectively "undeserving" of social assistance if they do not endeavour to retrain to compete in the job market or take some form of work to "top up" their social-assistance incomes and thus reduce the burden they impose on the state. Those who are unable to work, for whatever reason, or, as is more often the case, can't find a job, are thereby deemed lesser or undeserving citizens. Given that caregiving functions are being downloaded to the home and that there is still no national system of affordable child care, it is clear that women will be well represented among the ranks of "the undeserving."

Another potential source of exclusion arises from the idea of "targeting," which is fundamental to the new thinking about social-policy reform. As Evans explains, particular groups of women are being redefined through public policy as members of specially disadvantaged groups that require "targeted" programs to address their special needs (Yeatman, 1990, p. 134). The idea of targeting is entirely consistent with the hollowing-out of the welfare state. Its overt rationale is that, in an era of fiscal restraint, scarce resources are best targeted at those who need them the most. Thus, family allowance, a universal entitlement that constructed mothers as gendered citizens during the postwar years, has been transformed into a child tax credit available only to those defined as "deserving." Similarly, violence-against-women initiatives are structured to target those deemed to be members of high-risk groups—for example, aboriginal women, women of colour, immigrant women, and disabled women (see Gavigan and Levan, this volume).

As many of the essays in this volume point out, women's different experiences of oppression and the effects of racism and classism cannot be denied or ignored in the policy process or in feminist theorizing. Targeting, however, may simply have the effect of pathologizing difference instead of exposing the structural links among race, gender, poverty, and violence. It encourages us to point to single mothers as "the problem" with welfare or to aboriginal women as "the problem" in the growing incidence of violence against women. In the process, these women are disconnected from the structural biases that make their lives "different." They become arbitrary statistical and administrative categories that require some sort of therapeutic intervention to produce self-sufficient individuals (Brodie, 1995). At the same time, targeting makes invisible the problems shared by women who fall outside the identified groups. The potential exclusions, therefore, are double-sided—the targeted are pathologized as non-citizens, and the problems of non-targeted groups are rendered invisible.

In many ways, the growing distinction that restructuring discourse draws between the "ordinary" and the "special" is similar. The now popular designation of the women's movement as "a special interest group," for example, implies that its demands are not in the general interest.

"Special interest groups" don't speak for the "ordinary Canadian" but, instead, demand privileges that are unearned and violate the new norms of citizenship. The designation "special" is rapidly being cast over integral elements of our political community—people of colour, the working class, immigrant groups, lesbians and gays, the poor, and the First Nations. This designation effectively excludes them from the mythical "ideal" political community of ordinary Canadians and suggests that their demands for inclusion and equality are somehow outside of and antagonistic to the general interest. Since most of us can be considered special in one way or another, the ultimate function of this special/ordinary dichotomy is to suggest that we ought not to make demands on the state because ordinary people don't require state assistance and protection. It asks us to be silent about the very social designations that prevent, and will continue to prevent, our full inclusion in a community of citizens.

PRIVATIZATION, "REFAMILIALIZATION," AND CRIMINALIZATION

Privatization

Part III of this volume examines how the current era of restructuring is bringing changes to the regulation of the most intimate details of our lives. Most associate the process of restructuring with the ascendency of a market-driven economic development strategy, the globalization of production, the decline of public intervention in the economy and the erosion of the welfare state. But all of these changes are filtered through and enacted in our everyday lives—in systems of representation, cultural practices, social norms, and individual behaviours and attitudes (Harvey, 1989, p. 238). In fact, some social theorists suggest that major economic and political transformations, such as the one we are now experiencing, are unlikely to succeed unless individuals and groups are coerced or more subtly persuaded to act in ways consistent with the logic of the new governing order. Social crisis generally ensues unless there is a match between the new order and compatible norms of behaviour and representations of reality (Lipietz, 1987, Chap. 1). Public policies along with representations emanating from the mass media and other important social institutions are the key to the fit (or the discrepancy) between the emerging order and extant behaviours and beliefs. Combined, these forces perform the task of **moral regulation**—a process of "normalizing," "rendering natural," or "taking for granted" the impositional claims that provide the basic premises for a particular state form (Corrigan and Sayer, 1985, p. 4).

We have already encountered some elements of the new order of moral regulation. For example, the familiar claims that we have no choice, that it is imperative that we follow a market-driven development strategy, that we can identify the deserving and undeserving poor by their participation in the work force, that the problem of the deficit must be solved by cutting social spending—all of these are moral/political claims that seek to shape what we see as natural, neutral, and good.

The new moral order seeks to accord more value to the private than to the public and to the individual than to the collective, and to reassert that the family is the site for self-sufficiency and responsibility. These goals are being interwoven into a variety of policies and regulations aimed at privatizing those things and responsibilities that we once took for granted were part of the public realm. Critical governing instruments of the welfare state such as public corporations and social-welfare services are said to be "re"-privatized to the market and the home, thereby creating the illusion that they are being returned to some place in which they "naturally" belong. Moreover, once in their "natural" place, they are not governed by "unnatural" political practices. Privatization rests on the unverifiable impositional claim that services and assets created in the public sphere are now more efficiently delivered and maintained through market mechanisms. In the process, they are removed from the realm of political negotiation and subjected to market-oriented rather than political evaluative criteria (Yeatman, 1990, p. 173).

Privatization involves much more than simply removing things from the public basket and placing them on the market or in the home. The things moved are themselves transformed—a lesson we ignore only at great peril. As things are shifted from the public to the private, they become differently encoded, constructed, and regulated. Citizens with a right to health care, or just plain sick people, for example, become consumers of alternative medical-delivery systems even though the choices available are often non-existent, inappropriate, or dangerous. Similarly, deinstitutionalized mental patients become the responsibility of the family or, failing that, are attended to by social workers or by the police rather than by providers of mental-health care. In the process, they become something different—street people—with lost histories, different life chances, and different relations to the state's regulatory mechanisms. The underside of privatization is always rerepresentation and reregulation.

Refamilialization

It should come as no surprise that a dominant thread running through the moral regulation of the 1990s is the glorification and refamilialization of the family. The value accorded the private sphere of the family is particularly obtrusive in right-wing rhetoric, which blames the welfare state and feminism for the breakdown of the social fabric. More broadly, however, there is a growing consensus among policy-makers that families (whatever their form) should look after their own and that it is up to the neoliberal state to make sure that they do (Abbott and Wallace, 1992, p. 2).

This inflated valorization of the family is occurring on a number of different levels. Thelma McCormack's essay on the Royal Commission on New Reproductive Technologies demonstrates that the report's findings were grounded in moral arguments about the family rather than in technological imperatives or in providing women with real reproductive choice. Its findings reflect numerous cultural biases about the family, the gestational parent, and motherhood. Shelley Gavigan elaborates on this perspective by examining family ideology and the legal definition of "spouse," which limits options for women, especially immigrant women, and is seriously threatening for lesbian women. The ideology of the nuclear family provides the prism through which relationships are judged and socially valorized. Gavigan sees this prism as dangerous and regressive. As she argues, one's dignity and personal and economic security in the new order ought not to, and need not, depend upon being situated in or relegated to a familial relationship.

The question of the family is a complex and contradictory one for lesbians and gays, as Brenda Cossman's essay on the controversy over same-sex spousal benefits in Ontario points out. She discusses how Canadian society is now characterized by a diversity of family forms, including same-sex unions, but also how the traditional stereotype of the heterosexual nuclear family provides a strategic dilemma for lesbian couples. They are simultaneously both outside and inside the family. On the one hand, the hegemony of the traditional family form has been oppressive to women in general and lesbians specifically. It defines lesbian couples as deviant and outside the realm of normal family relations and privilege. On the other hand, while lesbians may strive against being assimilated under heterosexual family ideology, the fact remains that the family is assumed to be the most appropriate unit for the distribution of social benefits and rights. Lesbian couples and their children, in other words, lose a great deal in terms of economic rights, security, and benefits by their continued exclusion from government definitions of "family," which privilege a heterosexual union. Cossman describes the evolution of Ontario's same-sex legislation and discusses its ultimate defeat. For the time being, policy-makers have decided that lesbian couples, with or without children, are not families.

Criminalization

Lise Gotell's essay on the recent evolution of pornography policy in Canada also suggests that the increasingly restrictive regulation of this policy field was motivated by the Conservatives' "family values" platform and a concern to preserve the family. This moral stance against the explicit representation of human sexuality was based on the notion that, as Brian Mulroney put it, "our Canadian family is the cornerstone of all decent social initiatives" (quoted by Gotell). Gotell, however, suggests that there are other explanations for the increasing regulation and criminalization of sexual representation, especially lesbian and gay representations. An anti-pornography agenda allowed the government to build a diverse coalition of support among those, for example, moral conservatives and feminists, who view pornography as harmful to women without its having to expend any financial resources. The Conservatives' anti-pornography initiatives and the Supreme Court's decision in *Butler* are examples of how feminist rhetoric has been appropriated to legitimate and modernize what is really an old conservative moral agenda.

Gotell's essay also demonstrates the contradictory nature of feminist politics. While the Supreme Court embraced the notion that pornography is harmful to women, the charges ensuing from the decision have been levelled against lesbian and gay sexual representations instead of heterosexist ones. Moreover, anti-pornography initiatives allow the neoliberal state to step up its law-and-order agenda and appear to be concerned about popular anxieties without expending significant governmental resources for the very real problems that confront Canadian women.

Andrea Levan's analysis of the Canadian Panel on Violence Against Women supports this view. Responding to the public outrage following the Montreal Massacre, the Mulroney government appointed a $10-million panel to study the growing incidence of violence against women and to submit recommendations to the government. Levan's essay illustrates many of the dilemmas of feminist politics in the 1990s. The panel highlighted the question of participation in a lavish public spectacle at a time when the government was drastically cutting back its financial support of rape crisis centres and women's shelters. Another issue was the representation of difference, which ultimately led a number of important women's organizations to boycott the panel. In the end, the panel's report was ambiguous, unwelcome, and, for women in the shelter movement, an inexcusable misallocation of scarce government resources. Moreover, Levan suggests that the panel episode served to discredit the feminist movement and reinforce the government's resolve to treat the problem of violence as "inside the criminal justice system" and as an individual problem.

CONCLUSION

The essays in this book point to the emerging new order as fraught not only with new dangers for Canadian women, but also with contradictions. However, the essays also suggest that the response of the women's movement should be neither acquiescence nor resignation.

As Foucault suggested, recognizing the dangers in a new order should not lead "to apathy but rather to a hyper and pessimistic activism.... The ethical and political choices that we confront everyday consist in locating the main danger" (quoted in Fink-Eitel, 1992, p. 10). The current era of restructuring provides the women's movement with a fundamental challenge—to interrogate the new order's impositional claims and to understand the new cultural and political forms that it underwrites. More than this, it invites us to imagine alternatives and to build a new social consensus about a more equitable collective future.

REFERENCES

Abbott, Pamela, and Wallace, Claire. (1992). *The family and the new right.* Boulder, CO: Pluto Press.

Abele, Francis. (1992). The politics of competition. In Francis Abele (Ed.), *How Ottawa spends 1992–93.* Ottawa: Carleton University Press.

Allen, Judith. (1990). Does feminism need a theory of the state? In Sophie Watson (Ed.), *Playing the state: Australian feminist interventions.* London: Verso.

Andrew, Caroline. (1984, December). Women and the welfare state. *Canadian Journal of Political Science.*

Bakker, Isabella (Ed.) (1994). *Strategic silences.* London: Zed Books.

Brodie, Janine. (1990). *The political economy of Canadian regionalism.* Toronto: Harcourt, Brace, Jovanovich.

Brodie, Janine. (1992). The constitutional confidence game: The economic proposals and the politics of restructuring. Unpublished paper presented to the Department of Political Science, Carleton University.

Brodie, Janine. (1994). Shifting public spaces: A reconsideration of women and the state in the era of global restructuring. In Isabella Bakker (Ed.), *Strategic silences.* London: Zed Books.

Brodie, Janine. (1995). *Politics at the margins: Restructuring and the Canadian women's movement.* Halifax: Fernwood.

Brodie, Janine, and Jenson, Jane. (1995). Piercing the smokescreen: Stability and change in brokerage politics. In Alain Gagnon and Brian Tanguay, (Eds.), *Canadian political parties in transition* (2d ed.). Toronto: Nelson.

Brown, Wendy. (1992). Finding the man in the state. *Feminist Studies, 18,* 1.

Cameron, Duncan. (1989). Political discourse in the eighties. In Alain Gagnon and Brian Tanguay (Eds.), *Canadian political parties in transition* (2d ed.). Toronto: Nelson.

Canada. (1994). *Improving social security in Canada: A discussion paper.* Hull: Human Resources Development Canada.

Chunn, Dorothy. (1995). Feminism, law and public policy: Politicizing the personal. In Nancy Mandell and Ann Duffy (Eds.), *Canadian families: Diversity, conflict and change.* Toronto: Harcourt, Brace and Company.

Cohen, Marjorie Griffin. (1993a, December). Economic restructuring through trade: Implications for people. Paper presented at the Shastri Indo-Canadian Seminar on Economic Change and Economic Development, New Delhi.

Cohen, Marjorie Griffin. (1993b). Social policy and social services. In Ruth Roach Pierson, Marjorie Griffin Cohen, Paula Bourne, and Philinda Masters. *Canadian women's issues*, Vol. 1: *Strong voices*. Toronto: James Lorimer.

Cohen, Marjorie Griffin. (1994). Democracy and trade agreements: Challenges for disadvantaged women, minorities and states. Paper presented at Do Nation-States Have a Future conference, York University, Toronto.

Corrigan, Philip, and Sayer, Derek. (1985). *The great arch: English state formation as cultural revolution*. London: Basil Blackwell.

Cox, Robert. (1991). The global political economy and social choice. In Daniel Drache and Meric Gertler (Eds.), *The new era of global competition: State policy and market power*. Montreal and Kingston: McGill–Queen's University Press.

Drache, Daniel. (1992). Conclusion. In Daniel Drache (Ed.), *Getting on track: Social democratic strategies for Ontario*. Montreal and Kingston: McGill–Queen's University Press.

Drache, Daniel, and Gertler, Meric. (1991). Introduction. In Daniel Drache and Meric Gertler (Eds.), *The new era of global competition: State policy and market power*. Montreal and Kingston: McGill–Queen's University Press.

Elson, Dianne. (1992). From survival strategies to transformation strategies. In Lourdes Beneria and Shelley Feldman (Eds.), *Unequal burden: Economic crisis, personal poverty and women's work*. Boulder, CO: Westview Press.

Fink-Eitel, Hinrich. (1992). *Foucault: An introduction*. Philadelphia: Pennbridge Books.

Fox Piven, Frances. (1990). Ideology and the state: Women, power and the welfare state. In Linda Gordon (Ed.), *Women, the state, and welfare*. Madison: University of Wisconsin Press.

Friedman, Harriet. (1991). New wines, new bottles: The regulation of capital on a world scale. *Studies in Political Economy, 36*.

Fudge, Judy. (1989). The privatization of the costs of reproduction. *Canadian Journal of Women and the Law, 3*.

Gill, Stephen. (1992). The emerging world order and European change. In Ralph Miliband and Leo Panitch (Eds.), *New world order? Socialist register 1992*. London: Merlin.

Gordon, Linda. (1990). The new feminist scholarship on the welfare state. In Linda Gordon (Ed.), *Women, the state, and welfare*. Madison: University of Wisconsin Press.

Gotell, Lise, and Brodie, Janine. (1991). Women and parties: More than an issue of numbers. In Hugh Thorburn (Ed.), *Party politics in Canada*, (6th ed.) Toronto: Prentice-Hall.

Harvey, David. (1989). *The condition of postmodernity*. London: Basil Blackwell.

Held, David, *et al.* (Eds.). (1983). *States and societies*. Oxford: Open University Press.

Jessop, Bob. (1993). Toward a Schumpeterian workfare state? Preliminary remarks on post-Fordist political economy. *Studies in Political Economy, 40.*

Leger, Huguette, and Rebick, Judy. (1993). *The NAC voters' guide.* Hull: National Action Committee on the Status of Women.

Lipietz, Alain. (1987). *Mirages and miracles.* London: Verso Books.

McDowell, Linda. (1991). Life without father and Ford: The new gender order of post-Fordism. *Transnational Institute of British Geography, 16,* 400–419.

McFarland, Joan. (1993). Combining economic and social policy through work and welfare: The impact on women. Paper presented to the Economic Equity Workshop, Status of Women, Ottawa.

National Forum on Family Security. (1993). *Family security in insecure times.* Ottawa: Canadian Council on Social Development Publications.

Nicholson, Linda. (1992). Feminist theory: The private and the public. In Linda McDowell and Rosemary Pringle (Eds). *Defining women: Social institutions and gender divisions.* London: Polity Press.

Orloff, Ann Shola. (1993, June). Gender and the social rights of citizenship: The comparative analysis of gender relations and welfare states. *American Sociological Review, 58.*

Pierson, Ruth Roach; Cohen, Marjorie Griffin; Bourne, Paula; and Masters, Philinda. (1993). *Canadian women's issues,* Vol. 1: *Strong voices.* Toronto: James Lorimer.

Pringle, Rosemary, and Watson, Sophie. (1990). Fathers, brothers, and mates: The fraternal state in Australia. In Sophie Watson (Ed.), *Playing the state: Australian feminist interventions.* London: Verso.

Rebick, Judy. (1994). An Interview with Judy Rebick. *Studies in political economy,* 44.

Soja, Edward. (1989). *Postmodern geographies.* London: Verso.

Ursel, Jane. (1992). *Private lives, public policy: 100 years of state intervention in the family.* Toronto: Women's Press.

Watson, Sophie. (1990). The state of play: An introduction. In Sophie Watson (Ed.), *Playing the state: Australian feminist interventions.* London: Verso.

Wilson, Elizabeth. (1977). *Women and the welfare state.* London: Tavistock.

Wilson, Elizabeth. (1988). *Hallucinations: Life in the postmodern city.* London: Radius.

Yeatman, Anna. (1984). Despotism and civil society: The limits of patriarchal citizenship. In J.H. Stiehm (Ed.), *Women's view of the political world of men.* Dobbs Ferry, NY: Transnational Publishers.

Yeatman, Anna. (1990). *Bureaucrats, technocrats, femocrats: Essays on the contemporary Australian state.* Sydney: Allen and Unwin.

Yeatman, Anna. (1993). Voice and representation in the politics of difference. in Sneja Gunew and Anna Yeatman (Eds.), *Feminism and the politics of difference.* Halifax: Fernwood Publishing.

Yeatman, Anna. (1994). *Postmodern revisionings of the political.* New York: Routledge.

Young, Iris Marion. (1989). Polity and group difference: A critique of universal citizenship. *Ethics, 99.*

Young, Iris Marion. (1990). *Throwing like a girl and other essays in feminist philosophy and social theory.* Bloomington: Indiana University Press.

PART I

RESTRUCTURING

THE

ECONOMY

CHAPTER 1

Deconstructing Macro-economics Through a Feminist Lens

Isabella Bakker

> Feminist theory suggests that the definition (of economics) focusing on choice, which looks at human decision as radically separated from physical and social constraints, and the definition stressing material well-being, which ignores non-physical sources of human satisfaction, are not the only alternatives. Such a dichotomy merely reinforces the separation of humans from the world, the *res cogitans* from the *res extensa*. What is needed instead is a definition of economics that considers humans *in relation* to the world. (Nelson, 1994, p. 32)

State responses to restructuring are premised on notions of gender-neutrality or, at best, on an outdated gendered division of labour. Considerations of policies, their impacts in terms of resources, and the nature of the adjustment process are, according to mainstream economics, premised on aggregate, abstract, and spatially neutral formulations. Just as Harold Innis foresaw the spatial effects of Keynesian policies (Innis, 1956), feminist economists argue that macro-economic stabilization policies while appearing to be gender-neutral, put a disproportionate burden on marginalized citizens. In recent years, feminist economists have begun to challenge conventional approaches to structural change, and more broadly have rejected the claims that economics is universal, value-free scientific inquiry, pointing out, instead, that it is gendered discourse (Ferber and Nelson, 1993). In both **micro-economic** constructions that apply to the individual and the household (Folbre 1986, 1992; Sen 1990) and broader macro-economic inquiries (Elson, 1991; Bakker, 1994), feminist economists have exposed the "male bias" inherent in both economic theory and its effects.[1] Beyond the efforts to expose the **androcentric** bias in much of the writing about economics, some have argued for an economics that is simultaneously objective, post-modern, and more useful in implementing social change (Nelson, 1994).

In this essay, I suggest that the significance of recognizing gender for economic processes goes beyond questions of social justice. Ignoring gender relations in an analysis of economic restructuring and adjustment in the current period yields a distorted analysis. Some authors have argued convincingly that the current round of restructuring is extending rather than ameliorating the unequal division of labour and resources between the sexes. The dual pressures of women's increased labour-force participation and the simultaneous contraction of the Keynesian welfare state is, in Fraser's (1989) words, "reprivatizing" what were previously publicly provided services. The first section of this essay elaborates on these issues and situates them in the Canadian context. The second section looks at one area of economics, macro-economics, and several key areas of fiscal policy from the vantage point of gender. Markets and economic activity are seen as socially embedded and regulated[2]; that is, they are social constructions that rest on embedded norms of public and private, man and woman, economy and family. The laws of the market work through and within gendered and racially segmented structures. Macro-economics is androcentric because the male worker/consumer/citizen is often assumed to be the norm (i.e., the policy target). The interactions between paid and unpaid labour are left out of modelling considerations, as indeed are any observations from the "soft" disciplines (i.e., not math and statistics) about social networks and people's personal histories. Powerful cultural assumptions shared by a scientific community become difficult to contest through the more careful application of existing methods precisely because they are embedded in a system of shared meanings and values (Ferber and Nelson, 1993).

The conventional approach in economics is facilitated by how the macro level is conceived—that is, as dealing with aggregates and not talking about men or women. Instead, macro discussion is about the nation, growth, gross domestic product (GDP, the size of the economy), employment, and so on. Such a conceptualization implies a horizontal configuration of interests, that the well-being of the nation is shared by all its members. In this sense, the differential effects of policy are difficult to fit into the narrative of national economic well-being because a decline in inflation rates or a rise in GDP is assumed to benefit all, even those at the margin of the nation (Bergeron, 1993).

RESTRUCTURING DEFINED IN THE CANADIAN CONTEXT

In standard economic terms, structural change at the most basic level involves a change in the composition of something—for example, the economy, a sector, or a region or firm. Most conventional economic

analysts distinguish structural change in industrial structures from cycli-
cal shifts in the composition of output, employment, and trade. A standard account is offered by the Organization for Economic Cooperation
and Development (OECD), which isolates two aspects or dimensions of
structural change:

> Compositional structural change refers to changes in the industrial com-
> position or profile of an economy: changes in the output or employment
> shares accounted for by different industries, for example, or changes in
> the mix of factor inputs used by industries. Its main characteristic is that
> it examines individual industries; the capital and labour inputs they use;
> and the way in which industries are connected to one another, both
> domestically and internationally.... Institutional structural change is con-
> cerned with the behaviour of labour and financial markets, the traded
> goods market, and the operation of the public sector.... The characteris-
> tic of institutional structural change is that it examines broad markets
> not necessarily restricted to any one industry and is concerned with
> deviations from competitive market behaviour. (1992, pp. 167–168).

A broader conception sees restructuring as a series of cumulative
and conjunctural crises in the international division of labour and the
global distribution of economic and political power; in global finance;
in the functioning of national states that are losing economic and
political control of national economies; in the decline of the
Keynesian welfare state and the established social contracts among
labour, government, and business; and in the increasing exploitation
of marginal forms of labour performed by women, youth, and minorities (Bakker, 1994).

Beyond Keynesiansim: The Neoliberal Thrust

The current "restructuring" of the transitional features of capitalism of
the past two decades has manifested itself in a number of dramatic
changes in the structure of production and employment, and technology, and in the greater economic integration of the global economy.
These changes signal a break in the structural and institutional arrangements that characterized the postwar period of the Keynesian welfare
state (see Table 1.1). The relative decline in manufacturing and growth
of services in terms of employment are related changes that character-
ize the restructuring of production. The growing interdependence and
convergence of goods and services is part of this structural trend. The
structure and conditions of employment are also changing. For
instance, significant shifts have occurred in the occupational composition of employment across all sectors of the economy, especially
increases in professional, technical, clerical, and other specialized
occupations. In addition, the conditions of employment are changing,
with the trend toward greater reliance on part-time as opposed to full-
time employment and the move toward the **contingent work force**
and non-unionized labour.

TABLE 1.1
KEY FEATURES OF THE KEYNESIAN AND NEOLIBERAL STATES

	Keynesian State	Neoliberal State
Economic-Policy Emphasis	Legitimate role for government in the economy. Need for government intervention in times of recession and unemployment.	Reduce the role of government in economic management. Let the private sector (the "free market") guide economic policy.
	Should accumulate a surplus of funds in good times.	Move away from managing domestic economies to securing global markets.
	Emphasis is on keeping unemployment low.	Emphasis is on keeping inflation low.
Welfare State	Established to secure the continuity of income flows over the ups and downs of the economy on a universal basis.	Only most needy target groups such as the elderly poor should be covered (the "deserving").
	Taxes and expenditures financed out of an expanding economy. Workers' rising standard of living and rising profitability made the fiscal burden of the welfare state acceptable.	Emphasis on private provision of services, often through employment-based schemes.
	Social solutions to what are perceived to be socially determined problems.	Individual solutions to what are perceived to be individually determined problems.
Gender Order	Characterized by a gender division of labour, with women's primary role in the home and, secondarily, in the labour	Characterized by women's growing labour-force participation with some finding new opportunities in "good"

(continued)

(continued)

	Keynesian State	Neoliberal State
Gender Order	market. Their wages are supplementary to a family wage secured by the male breadwinner. Gender- (and race-) segmented labour markets.	jobs and the majority concentrated in part-time, less-secure jobs. As economies restructure, men are increasingly competing with women for the "bad" jobs. Increasing polarization among different groups of women. The stable nuclear-family model is gradually being replaced by more diverse family structures as divorce becomes more prevalent. Dual pressure of economic necessity and increasing individual responsibility for the sustenance of children and other family members.

Structural change, of course, is a constant in a dynamic economy. However, what is at issue here is state-managed structural change at the macro level of fiscal and monetary policy. To what extent do institutional relations that are not gender-ascriptive become gendered? Research in the developing countries, for example, has shown that liberal stabilization policies, those policies aimed at constraining aggregate demand through the use of traditional demand-side fiscal and monetary macro policy tools, have had disproportionately harsh effects on women and the poor, and, therefore, on human development overall (UNDP, 1992; Afshar and Dennis, 1992; Commonwealth Expert Group, 1989; Cornia, Jolly, and Stewart, 1987).

Only recently have analysts in the OECD countries begun to consider whether stabilization policies (directed at cuts in government spending on services, salaries, and investments) and structural adjustment initiatives, such as trade liberalization and the abolition of food subsidies, may deepen existing gender inequities in the paid and unpaid sectors of the economy. For example, the recasting of welfare-state services and benefits signals an assumption by the state that "the community" (read: women) will increasingly "take up the slack." This is evident in the movement toward community care for the elderly, the disabled, and the terminally ill. It is estimated that by the year 2006, people over age 65 will constitute 14 percent of the population in Canada, with the fastest-growing group being those over age 85 (Fair Tax Commission, 1992). At the same time, women's labour is becoming more important in the formal sphere of production, so fewer women are available to provide full-time care for frail elderly or disabled relatives. As Linda McDowell has pointed out: "This contradiction between restructuring in the spheres of reproduction and production has, so far, been contained by greater inputs of female labour to both spheres. But the consequent 'social speed up' is not infinitely extendible" (1991, p. 191).

A feminist political-economy intervention would add that this particular round of restructuring in the advanced industrial economies appears to be marked by a reinforcement (rather than a fundamental restructuring) of women's ambiguous place in the labour market. Research here in Canada (Connelly and MacDonald, 1990; Armstrong, 1993) and at the wider level of the European Community (1992) and the OECD (1993) supports this observation. In the Canadian case, women's progress is usually measured against a male standard. However, what appears to be a situation of greater economic equality between women and men actually reflects a decline in men's economic situation rather than real gains for women (Armstrong, 1993). This situation is more a result of restructuring than of direct competition from women:

> Restructuring is not only eliminating many men's jobs and creating many part-time or part-year ones, it is also transforming many of the full-time jobs that remain. Many of the "good jobs" are not so good any more. Hours and shift work have increased, and so has insecurity. Work is intensified, whether or not people have full-time or part-time employment. Those women who have moved into traditional male work frequently find that it has become more like traditional women's work and management strategies in all sectors frequently serve to reduce worker power while claiming the opposite.... Moreover, new state strategies are designed to cut jobs in the non-commercial services, in the areas where women have found their best jobs and where affirmative action has been the most successful. (Armstrong, 1993)

Convergence and Difference

In Canada as elsewhere, casualization (the trend towards more part-time or contractually limited work) and other structural adjustments in labour markets may be reducing the work conditions of many men to women's levels (Standing, 1989). In the European Community, two trends have characterized women's economic position over the 1980s: *uniformization and convergence and segmentation and differentiation.* Uniformization, or the narrowing of the formal gap between the kinds of work done by women and men, and the continuity in working career among women signal a convergence. However, this uniformization has not necessarily led to greater gender equality since structural change and economic crisis have reinforced inequalities between women and men in terms of pay, unemployment, and job precariousness and have widened differences among women (Commission of the European Communities, 1992, p. 55). This widening of differences, hastened by restructuring, means a greater classed and raced differentiation of resources among women competing in the market (Bakker, 1991).

This raises the issue of so-called flexibility in employment and male/female differences. As long as flexible employment is associated with marginalization of the work force (mostly women and ethnic minorities), there is a higher probability that these marginalized workers are bearing the brunt of the costs of structural change. And as long as social investment in reproduction is not recognized or granted sufficient priority, women will likely continue to bear this burden disproportionately, as reflected, in part, in their overrepresentation among involuntary part-time and discouraged workers. In this sense, women are providing the flexibility that allows men's working patterns to be less flexible (OECD, 1993). Women's lack of bargaining power within and outside the household limits their labour-market power and tends to bias their labour participation toward low-skill, part-time work.[3] At the same time, another implication of earnings, skill, and job polarization is that, as women continue to be drawn to either pole of employment (high wage or low wage), the disparity among them will increase—in other words, some will have more bargaining power and access to resources than will others.

Women are being drawn into the labour force in contradictory and complex ways. For some, such as those entering managerial and professional jobs, new opportunities are being created. For others, such as contingent workers, pre-existing patterns of exploitation based on gender and race are shaping their experience. This situation has economic as well as political implications. **Pay equity** (equal pay for work of equal value) and **employment equity** legislation, for example, assume a commonality of interests among women, but economic restructuring appears to be creating both material differences and skill divisions within female ranks. The increasing polarization or segmentation among women signals, for some authors, a class-based divergence of interests among women in the labour force (Blum, 1987).

This raises questions about the potential long-term implications of such trends for overall aggregate growth and development. A low-wage, low-skill strategy will not be effective in combatting increased international competition since low-wage industries will not survive when business relocates to developing countries (Schmid, 1993). Such a trend also raises concerns about traditional labour-market equity initiatives such as equal pay for work of equal value. Here the role of unions is important in resisting the divisions among workers resulting from restructuring of industries and work environments. New gender-based strategies are required to reach the vast majority of workers in most

OECD countries, who are not unionized. Aside from broader-based bargaining inside the labour movement, political campaigns around employment standards (see, for example, Ontario District Council of the ILGWU and INTERCEDE, 1993) and gender-sensitive strategies that take into account women's experiences of gender discrimination at work and within unions, and the connection between the household and the workplace, might begin to build a strategic institutional link between equity and economic restructuring (Briskin, 1993). Results-based equality rather than abstract equality is another strategy that recognizes that people are different in different ways. As Brenner notes: "If our goal is to enable everyone to have the same opportunity to participate, then it is necessary to accommodate people's differences, to denormalize the way institutions formulate their rules by revealing the plural circumstances that exist, or ought to exist, within them" (1993, p. 139).

DECONSTRUCTING MACRO-ECONOMICS THROUGH A FEMINIST LENS

This essay does not delve into the extensive feminist literature on the state, nor does it consider the issues raised by the "hollowing out" of the state in an era of global finance and production (Jessop, 1993). Rather, the focus is on critiquing the assumed gender-neutrality of market relationships and illustrating the new insights gained from a deconstruction of Canadian expenditure and taxation policy. Three arguments are made about macro-economics as seen through a feminist lens: (1) that markets are not gender-neutral institutions but are imbued with an androcentric bias; (2) that those members of society doing reproductive work are ultimately in a state of economic dependence; and (3) that the macro narrative is an aggregate based on assumptions about how human resources are produced, allocated, reproduced, and maintained.

Androcentric Markets

Most economic discourse is dominated by neoclassical conceptions of markets based on the assumption that markets function on the basis of perfect competition. As a result, economic analysis is rooted, from its basic theoretical assumptions, in a gender-neutral abstraction of markets. However, markets do have a gender dimension. A gender-relations[4] analysis focusses precisely on how market relationships that appear to be gender-neutral implicitly imply the male standpoint (Whitehead, 1979; Elson, 1992). As Elson puts the point:

> Being a worker, or a farmer, or an entrepreneur, does not overtly ascribe gender; but women and men have very different experiences as workers, farmers and entrepreneurs; and the supposedly gender-neutral

terms "worker", "farmer", "entrepreneur", are imbued with gender implications. In fact, the "worker" or "farmer" or "entrepreneur" is most often taken to be a man—creating male bias in both economic analysis and economic policy. (1992, p. 2)

This bias is circumscribed and shaped primarily by the ways in which a society organizes the interrelationships between paid work and raising children. Most people (mainly women) engaged in child rearing do not have an independent entitlement to resources and are dependent on others (family members, life partners) or welfare-state arrangements to meet their needs. Markets operate without recognizing that the unpaid work of reproduction and maintenance of human resources contributes to the realization of formal market relations. The current round of restructuring of state finances is reprivatizing many maintenance and caring activities that, through Keynesian welfare state interventions, had become public, state-sector responsibilities. Based on a more individualized notion of dependency, its social and structural foundations are increasingly being cast aside in favour of *individual* solutions to what are perceived to be *individually determined* problems (see Fraser and Gordon, 1994). This perception, in turn, is reinforced by the political view that the postwar welfare-state strategy is no longer viable since no common denominator of a race, class, and gender strategy exists (Williams, 1989).

A further obstacle faced by analysts wishing to link a gender-relations analysis to macro-economics is that macro policy is connected to our views of the nation. It is viewed as an aggregate, all-inclusive entity.[5] As Bergeron (1993) has noted, the "narrative of inclusivity impedes our awareness and examination of the oppression of those in the 'margins' of the nation." In this sense, a feminist approach to macro-economics can help us get at how the marginalized are affected via restructuring and the macro-level responses initiated by the state.

The analytical foundations of macro-economics are not linked to a gender-relations analysis. Emerging out of the postwar acceptance of Keynesian demand-oriented economic policies, macro-economics is preoccupied with aggregate measures of economic change such as output levels; their fluctuations and relationship to rates of growth, unemployment, and inflation; the budget surplus/deficit; levels of government expenditure and taxation; the changing balance between different sectors of the economy; and monetary and exchange-rate policy.

Despite the absence of "people" at the level of macro-economic theory and measurement, there are, nevertheless, built-in assumptions about the individual, who is, paradoxically, both a commodity and a rational economic person; the determinants of the level and pattern of economic activity; and human resources—how they are allocated to production, and how they are reproduced and maintained. These assumptions include seeing the reproduction and maintenance of human beings as outside economic inquiry, as automatic or "natural." Macro-economic policies assume that women's labour is infinitely elastic (able to stretch in times of restraint and contract in times of prosperity), and that switching of resources occurs because all factors have relatively equal mobility (Elson, 1987). In this sense, many of the costs and benefits of resource reallocations, and their asymmetrical impact on gender relations, are not fully accounted for by policy-makers. Furthermore, the interrelationship between market and non-market activity is left out of policy reform and planning.

What follows is an attempt to begin to map out several areas of macro-economic policy intervention from a gender-relations approach, a perspective that "gives voice" to the hidden assumptions behind macro-policy formulation. These examples are not comprehensive; instead, they are suggestive of the policy analysis yielded by an approach that takes into account the different starting positions of men and women vis-à-vis the paid and unpaid economies. A more comprehensive analysis would have to offer a more detailed listing of macro-economic policies, incorporate constructions of the masculine in the feminine (ideologies and theory) and disparities along racial and ethnic lines, and offer a more detailed look at the social forces and historical structures shaping gender outcomes.

TAXATION

The technical character of taxation, much like the domain of macro-economics, makes people disappear. Behavioural assumptions made about people are grounded in economics, where "women and their realities disappear in the face of general theoretical frameworks, methodological practices, and orthodoxies of objectivity in the [scholarly] disciplines" (Cassin, 1993, p. 109). At the aggregate level of total revenue raised, there are no obvious differentials by sex. However, the existing tax system contributes to, supports, and enforces the gendered division of unpaid labour (Lahey, 1985). Once taxes are subdivided into *direct* (income) and *indirect* (consumption, VAT), several effects along gender lines can be discerned. For example, the almost universal trend of adopting *value-added taxes* in the 1980s has been recognized as a regressive policy initiative from the vantage point of the poor and women, who, in global terms, constitute the majority of the poor. Consumption taxes disproportionately impact on the lower-income groups, who pay a larger chunk of their earnings through this tax. Also, indirect taxes are recognized as having a greater impact on women, who universally act as managers of the household consumption budget. Direct income taxes, in contrast, have a greater impact on men because of their greater access to employment and higher incomes (OECD, 1985). Evidence exists that overtaxation of women (as compared with men within the earnings categories of the income tax) will be intensified through recent tax reforms (Cassin, 1993, p. 114).

Wealth and Gender

Phillips (1993), in a study of tax policy and the gendered distribution of wealth in Canada, notes that additional insights can be gained by looking at the tax system through the lens of a "wealth-sensitive feminist analysis." Phillips argues that wealth inequalities—that is, inequalities in goods that can be exhanged for money such as stocks and shares—affect women's lives in qualitatively and quantitatively distinct ways. Tax incidence becomes even less progressive and more biased against women because income levels (almost always the sole indicator of ability to pay) ignore the social and economic benefits enjoyed by wealth holders:

> For example, income levels are used to set marginal rate brackets, to determine entitlement to the GST Credit, the Child Tax Credit and other concessions, and to establish thresholds for "clawing back" Old Age Security. Given that wealth is distributed much more unequally than income, all these components of the tax system may be seriously under-estimating the taxable capacity of the wealthy, and overestimating that of the poor. Similarly, by measuring the distribution of the tax burden according to income level only we minimize the degree of inequality among taxpayers, and therefore exaggerate the progressivity of the tax system. This has particular implications for women, who are disadvantaged relative to men in terms of wealth, as well as income. Using income as a proxy for ability to pay therefore obscures the full nature and extent of gender bias in the tax system. (1993)

Canada has no personal-wealth tax, unlike the United States and most other OECD countries. This exclusion of wealth from the tax base is not a gender-neutral policy since the ability to inherit and hold wealth free of tax primarily benefits men and helps to maintain economic inequities that sustain women's subordination. Furthermore, failure to redress wealth inequalities through the tax system are linked to a notion that the household is the natural and private sphere for women's support by male breadwinners. The notion in taxation and other state policies that income is pooled in households (thus denying public responsibility for women's welfare) needs to be explored through studies on intrafamily-distribution of resource allocations. Available evidence does point to a complex process of resource allocation within households, one not necessarily based on equal and altruistic principles. Evidence from developing countries is more plentiful and suggests that neither joint decision making nor equal sharing of resources within households is all that common (Dwyer and Bruce, 1988; Sen, 1990).

Fairness

The Working Group on Women and Taxation of the Ontario Fair Tax Commission has provided a useful set of guidelines for assessing the fairness of the current tax structure from a gender-aware perspective. Indeed, the questions posed by the Working Group may be as important as the answers they derived from the Ontario tax case since they can be applied in a systematic fashion to other tax jurisdictions. The impact of the tax system on women should be measured, according to the Working Group's report, on whether it increases economic inequality, reflects this inequality, or reduces it (Fair Tax Commission, 1992, p. 3). So, for example, women's primary responsibility for caregiving and their disproportionate share of unpaid household work "raises questions about the design of the provisions in the tax system that recognize unpaid work, the tax treatment of unpaid work, the impact of unpaid work on the design of subsidies for retirement savings, and the recognition of the unequal division of unpaid work between custodial and non-custodial parents in the tax treatment of these payments" (ibid., p. 5). To what extent should the tax system be used to give recognition to unpaid caregiving provided to the elderly or disabled dependents? This is particularly relevant in light of the shift to **deinstitutionalization** in long-term care, which adds such care to women's unpaid work in the home.

Tax on child-support payments is another policy area in which issues of tax fairness have arisen. From a gender-neutral perspective, this policy distinguishes between custodial and non-custodial households. In practice, women and children generally bear the financial consequences of separation and divorce with "a comparison of the financial circumstances of support payers and recipients show(ing) that support payments generally represent a smaller share of the income of payers than of recipients" (ibid.). Since the large majority of recipients are women, this means that, while men can deduct support payments from their taxes, the average custodial mother pays 30 percent of her child support (which, on average, is less than half of what it costs to raise a child) in income tax (Leger and Rebick, 1993). In addition, the deferred revenue to federal coffers is estimated at approximately $400 million annually (Fair Tax Commission, 1992).

EXPENDITURE

Assessing the impact of expenditure policies by gender is a highly complex task, given the vast range of programs, types of spending, and complexities introduced by the reform of trade regimes. From an exclusively macro-economic vantage point, the central concern is the impact of shifts in aggregate demand and the subsequent changes in output, employment, and prices. Undoubtedly, a larger or smaller deficit will work its way through the economy in ways that change not only the macro aggregates but also the relative economic status of different groups of men and women.

However, any effort to understand the way in which decisions to alter aggregate demand are not gender-neutral must go beyond the employment, output, and price effects. It must also contend with the highly differentiated impact that shifts in expenditure levels and program priorities have on women and men. The starting point for this more disaggregated analysis is naturally a taxonomy of state spending. Approaches to defining the different aspects of state expenditure range from modest accounting frameworks to full-fledged functional breakdowns. Four major government spending functions are usually isolated in the public-finance literature: (1) provision of "pure" public goods (defence, government administrative services); (2) provision of merit goods (education, health, housing); (3) income maintenance and other transfers; and (4) provision of general economic services (OECD, 1985; 1991). Table 1.2 shows the possible gendered effects of these expenditures, and below I offer a disaggregation of several of these expenditure categories; my intention is not to be comprehensive but rather to use examples to illustrate gender-awareness in analysis.

TABLE 1.2
GOVERNMENT EXPENDITURES AND RELATED GENDERED EFFECTS

Examples of Government Expenditures	Examples of Related Gendered Effects
a. Public-sector employment (spans all four areas of government expenditure.	a. Women in public-sector employment generally face better terms and conditions of work and remuneration than do those in the private sector; hence, macro policy initiatives that lead to cuts in public-sector employment and pay are particularly negative for the labour-market status and opportunities of women; cuts can also have spill-over effects in terms of shifting work to women in the private sphere (e.g., care of the sick and elderly).
b. Capital expenditures (economic services)	b. Capital expenditures and cuts have a disproportionate effect on men, given their generally above-average participation in these sectors, for example, construction.
c. Subsidies (economic services)	c. Subsidies can have a differential impact on the sexes, depending

(continued)

(continued)

Examples of Government Expenditures	Examples of Related Gendered Effects
c. Subsidies (economic services)	on what prices and goods are controlled (e.g., food and fuel) and which industries retain employment through the granting of subsidies (e.g., services, manufacturing).
d. Service delivery and goods provision (merit goods)	d. Service delivery in health, education, and training has been shown to have a male bias in client benefit; cutbacks in child care, and so on, transfer costs to women. Cuts in goods and services subsidized by the government (electricity, public transport, basic food stuffs) increase pressures on those who administer the household on a daily basis.
e. Transfers (income maintenance and other transfers)	e. The extent to which individual economic security depends on transfers (e.g., old age benefits versus private pensions) needs to be distinguished along gender lines; inequities may arise in transfers received with restriction of access, for example, having to work longer to get unemployment benefits.

Public Employment (Cuts Across All Four Government-Spending Functions)

Public-sector wages are an important instrument of macro-economic policy in the dual sense of setting the de facto standard for the private sector as a comparator and influencing the total demand for labour in the economy. Also, public-sector employment influences the level of aggregate demand, thereby acting as a built-in stabilizer. The OECD cites a strong correlation between women's labour-force activity and the size and growth of the public sector (OECD, 1993, p. 11). Cuts in public-sector expenditures may be particularly damaging to women's labour-market position, given that the public sector provides relatively better job opportunities and higher salaries for women than does the private sector. In the public sector, there is less vertical segregation (concentration of women in low positions) and greater horizontal occupational segregation (concentration of women in few occupations).

Also, the majority of public-sector jobs offer better employment protection and social security. However, recent developments in public-sector employment indicate a trend toward greater reliance on precarious part-time positions and lower wages compared with trends during the high-growth period of the public sector.

In Canada, public-sector retrenchment has occurred in the form of public-expenditure cuts in such areas as pay and employment. Additionally, deregulation and privatization have led to changes in the demand side of the labour market. While men have been most effected by deregulation, which has been most evident in transportation industries like trucking and airlines (where reductions in union wage premiums have tended to effect men working in those industries), women have been disproportionately affected by public-sector employment and wage cuts (Gunderson, Muszynski, and Keck, 1990). In Ontario, recent social contract "settlements" are likely to affect those with the least power. In the Ontario Public Service, most of the job losses will be experienced by "unclassified" workers (the majority of whom are women and minorities) who never obtained a formalized job status.

Another new direction in public-sector restructuring is the trend to home-based work. An example cited by those concerned about labour-flexibility policies predicated on existing structural labour-market inequalities is the Government of Canada's announced "Telework Policy." This 1992 policy signals the promotion and institutionalization of the more generalized trend toward home-based work in certain sectors. A recent study of home-work policy notes that the program appears, on the surface, to be appealing to workers on a number of levels (Leach, 1993). This program offers some workers the possibility of working at home as part of a three-year pilot project in order to offer increased worker flexibility and reduce overhead costs and traffic congestion and pollution. While the union representing these workers (Public Service Alliance of Canada) approaches home work with caution (citing no contract language covering workers at home in terms of health and safety concerns), some public-sector workers welcome the opportunity to work at home. They see it as a positive option because it involves less commuting time, more time to work, and a better balancing of work and family responsibilities (including care of children and the elderly). Leach contrasts the high hopes of public-sector workers with the actual experiences of industrial home-based workers to highlight potential shortcomings of the spatial relocation of public-sector work to the private sphere of the home. It remains an open question whether the situation of professional home-based workers and that of industrial home-based workers are strictly comparable. Industrial home-based workers and domestic workers are disproportionately immigrant and visible-minority women, who face more limited employment opportunities and, in the case of domestic workers, a tenuous employment status. Unlike other workers from abroad, domestic workers are denied landed-immigrant status upon entry into Canada. Nevertheless, comparative data do indicate a common set of constraints and pressures (increased stress, lengthening of the working day), a privatization of what were previously issues of public responsibility and debate, and a limit to the possibility of collective action on the part of an increasingly fragmented and isolated work force.

Capital Expenditures (Economic Services)

Capital expenditures are investments in fixed assets such as infrastructure, whereas operating expenditures are payments made to cover the operation and maintenance of current services. Salaries are the main component of operating costs, and therefore raise similar issues to those outlined above in reference to public-sector wages. The extent to which public-service cuts free up public money for building infrastructure at the expense of a more diverse work force in the public sector should be part of the policy-evaluation process. Capital expenditures tend to have a greater short-term positive impact on employment for men, given their employment concentration in construction, engineering, and other infrastructure-related trades.[6] For example, the recent $6-billion infrastructural investment initiative of the federal government or Ontario's announced expansion of the Metro Toronto Convention Centre, designed to signal to the public that government is taking the initiative in the job-creation field, does, of course, provide much-needed short-term employment and spin-off effects. However, such megaprojects not only disproportionately benefit male workers, but also reinforce a view of the typical worker in hard times that is at odds with reality. As of the 1991 census, women constituted 45 percent of the labour force, had a labour-force participation rate of 60 percent, and demonstrated greater continuous attachment to the labour force. Wives' earnings play an increasingly important role in family income, and the number of single female–headed households with dependents is also on the rise. According to the 1991 census, there were almost a million lone-parent families with dependent children (18 percent of them headed by men), a number that represents 13 percent of all families.

Capital-expenditure projects also reify a hierarchy of infrastructural investment, placing social infrastructure such as child care in a secondary position to physical, technological, educational, and informational infrastructure. Whether infrastructure is an investment or a cost needs to be considered when assessing capital projects such as roads (often defined as an investment) versus health and education (often considered primarily in cost terms). Child care, for instance, also creates spinoff effects in the form of employment, both for those working in the child-care sector and for those adults released into the labour force through the provision of this infrastructural service. One of the associated costs of underinvestment in child care has been to limit women's choices and remuneration in the labour force, forcing some women to withdraw from the labour force (although this option is becoming less feasible) or to work part-time.

Subsidies (Economic Services)

Subsidies are often categorized as compensatory and complementary. Compensatory subsidies are intended to cushion the social consequences of structural change, whereas complementary subsidies are actually put in place to help stimulate structural change, (Mosley and Schmid, 1992). A gender-aware approach to subsidies would look at the sectoral composition of subsidies, relating it to the gender-based composition of employment in that sector. Where is structural change being stimulated? in what regions? Who is being employed via the funding of subsidies? Where is structural change occurring? What kind of compensatory subsidies are in place? Who is benefiting? (For example, subsidizing the domestic aluminum or steel industries via cheap energy may benefit male workers in that industry.) Another example would be the much-lauded area of training: Are trainees receiving cash or are they being reimbursed through a tax subsidy? What are the differences in take-up rates between public vocational training and cash incentives to employers? Which industries and sectors benefit from training? What is the gender composition of these sectors and the training participation along gender lines?

Service Delivery (Merit Goods)

Service or program delivery, such as improving the level of human capital (through education, training, and health care) and technology, relates to the structural aspects of macro-economic policies. Cutbacks in the delivery of services are part of the effort to reduce government spending and deficits, and have been a feature of structural adjustment programs' attempt to free labour for the production of trade goods. However, such cuts have implications for both employment and unpaid domestic labour. Simply, if fewer of the services required for the sustenance of human resources are provided by the public sector, then someone has to make up for the shortfall to prevent a decline in overall levels of well-being.

Debates about the efficiency and cost-effectiveness of public-sector provision of goods and services, especially welfare-state merit goods and transfer payments, have dominated the discussion of restructuring of the public sector/private sector relationship in the OECD. This partly reflects the movement away from equity concerns to those of efficiency and competitiveness. However, pessimistic views of the welfare state's impact on international competitiveness and the necessary downward pressure on levels of social protection that such views prescribe, remain subjects of further empirical research and debate (Mosley and

Schmid, 1992). This is too large a discussion to cover here, but it should allow for a consideration of alternative regimes for the provision of public services.

A gender-aware approach to the restructuring of state-provided services would include alternatives from the viewpoint of the users of services and be directed at the goal of facilitating human-resource development. In other words, a primary consideration for the restructuring of public-sector services should be the extent to which such restructuring will ameliorate the burden put on women by their being asked to contribute before they are able to enter paid employment. For the economist Ingrid Palmer (1991), women's unpaid work in reproduction and family maintenance can be seen as a "tax" that women are required to pay before they can engage in income-generating activity. She argues that gender relations based on a hierarchy of resources and unequal terms of exchange between women and men lead to resource misallocations that can be viewed as "gender-based market distortions." She concludes that women do not enter the market with the same resources and mobility (i.e., they cannot compete equally) because of the reproductive labour tax and gender-based distortions in resource allocation. For women, access to markets is limited because of the reproduction tax imposed on women and because men have a dominant position in terms of participation in markets (Palmer, 1992, p. 74).

Micro studies that look at intra- and interhousehold changes are necessary to give a fuller picture of the gendered effects of macroeconomic policies. In addition, further empirical work is needed to fully reveal the state's role in shaping or reducing women's unpaid reproductive burden. As Diane Elson (1992) has recently pointed out, even a bias-free access to markets will be a limited initiative as the reproduction and maintenance of human resources are structured through unequal gender relations and cannot be directly responsive to market signals. Women with higher incomes can buy substitutes through other women's labour, but a broader strategy implies access to public-sector services that will lighten the burden of unpaid work (Elson, 1992). Johanna Brenner gives an example in the U.S. case of the differential experiences and resources of women workers in the market: "There are upscale and downscale versions of fast food and frozen food, childcare, healthcare and business wear. For example, fees at Harvard University's seven childcare centres average $750 a month, while the average clerical worker earns only $1,500" (1993, p. 116).

Transfers (Income Transfers and Benefits)

Income transfers are the major means by which governments attempt to meet their redistributive objectives (see Box 1.1). Demographic, fiscal, and political pressures influenced this area of spending througout the 1980s. The shift from equity to efficiency concerns plus the fiscal crisis of many OECD states have contributed to the process of restraint and restriction of eligibility to various transfer programs. The differentiated consequences for men and women of transfer changes would need to take into account all of these factors. The extent to which individual economic security depends on transfers (for example, old age benefits versus private pensions) also needs to be distinguished along gender lines. In Canada, elderly women are heavily dependent on government transfers with pension income from RPPs, RRSPs, and other types of pensions, accounting for an increasingly larger proportion of women's total income (up from 8.4 percent to 11.6 percent in 1988), yet still lagging well behind that of men (Galarneau, 1991).

From OECD research, we know that unemployment benefits and temporary sickness and maternity benefits increased little in real terms in the 1980s (OECD, 1991, p. 173). In some cases, unemployment benefits per recipient increased relative to GDP per head as eligibility was reduced. The European Community seems to confirm that there may be a gendered dimension to eligibility reductions. It is noted that, in 1989, for the whole of the European Community, 26 percent of female job seekers and 34 percent of male job seekers received unemployment benefits or welfare (Commission of the European Communities, 1992, p. 33).

In Canada, recent changes to the Unemployment Insurance Act (Bill C-21) are likely to have a disproportionate impact on women's coverage. The increase in the number of weeks of insurable employment required to qualify for unemployment insurance will especially disadvantage part-time workers (70 percent of whom are women) and those working in part-year jobs. Training is now funded through Unemployment Insurance (in 1991–92, 31.8 percent of participants were women) and the income support allowances for English as a Second Language training have been eliminated. The latter forced the closure of community-based training organizations whose programs were directed at the most employment-disadvantaged women (Leger and Rebick, 1993).

BOX 1.1

Four Major Categories of Transfers in the OECD

▶   old age and disability benefits

▶   unemployment benefits

▶   family allowances

▶   sickness and maternity benefits

MONETARY POLICIES AND TRADE REGIMES

M onetary policy is how government influences the rate of interest in order to regulate the level of investment, output, employment, and other macro-economic outcomes. A range of financial policies also influence the conditions of access to credit. There is a great deal of debate in the economics literature about the manner in which monetary-policy tools actually influence the economy. There are equally diverse opinions regarding the relationship between interest rates, one of the primary monetary targets, and investment. At a macro level, the impact of monetary policies on gender status and asymmetries is translated through the same aggregate variables as is fiscal policy. However, when considered in terms of the specific mechanisms used to conduct monetary policy, there are a wide range of distinct effects on women and men.

For example, monetary policy often targets exchange rates and is used by governments to promote (by reducing the value of the currency) or discourage (by pushing up the value of the currency) exports. Hence, it influences the level and type of domestic production activity and employment. The extent to which such shifts represent increased choice and enhanced bargaining power or an additional burden or restriction needs to be explored through case studies. The literature on structural adjustment in developing countries has explored some of the linkages.[7]

Monetary policy also targets interest rates, often with the aim of reducing inflation by making it more expensive to borrow money. Uncovering the gender dimensions of interest-rate targets involves an examination of the immediate effects of interest rates on different types of economic activities plus a careful consideration of the secondary consequences that attend changes in the cost of living. Non-production activity needs to be surveyed in relation to these secondary consequences since cost-cutting is often absorbed by women's increased labour in the household and in the caregiving sector. Low-income borrowers' disadvantaged position vis-à-vis credit markets, in terms of both insufficient collateral and the institutional procedures of credit-lending agencies, implies that changes in monetary policy are likely to have differential impacts on different groups of women and men.

Trade liberalization is another area of macro-economic policy that has been subject to a great deal of analysis and debate in the last few years. Space does not permit a consideration of this important area in this essay; however, some thoughtful work exists on the garment industry (for example, Vosko, 1993), and the Ontario Women's Directorate (1993) has completed an update of their earlier (1987) report on the Canada–U.S. Free Trade Agreement and women that tries to take into account North American Free Trade Agreement (NAFTA) legislation. The difficulty with much of the research on the likely effects of NAFTA is that few studies have focussed on the specific impacts of women relative to men (see Ontario Women's Directorate, 1993, for an overview). Carefully monitoring the gender-differentiated impacts of NAFTA is one necessary but insufficient starting point. A more fruitful approach may be one suggested by Marjorie Cohen (1994). She urges a broader focus on how the economic regulations inscribed within NAFTA will constrain government from acting on behalf of people's economic interests. This links debates about trade effects to broader concerns about the changing nature of citizenship.

CONCLUSION

A feminist economics builds on an analysis of differences among people and extends it to a discussion of the relationship between human needs and the goods and services traded in the market. At the epistemological level, feminist economics combines the social construction of science with the social construction of gender into what Ferber and Nelson (1993) have termed a "feminist constructionism." In this essay, I have tried to illustrate, through the example of several fiscal and monetary policies, how a gender-relations approach nuances both the evaluation of policy impacts and their potential effectiveness. The fact that macro-economic policies work through and within gendered structures and relations shapes the choices and the material conditions faced by different economic actors in the process of restructuring. The newly emerging order is creating increased autonomy for some and increasing economic insecurity for others. How state policies contribute to the entrenchment of these differences or how they may aid in surmounting them should be a central aspect of the discussion of macro-economic restructuring.

NOTES

1. An earlier version of this essay was presented at the Economic Equality Workshop, Status of Women Canada, Ottawa, November 29–30, 1993. Funding for this research was supported by the SSHRC Strategic Grants Division (#861-93-0120). Additional research assistance is acknowledged—thanks to Lois Harder and Christina Gabriel.

The term "male-bias" is from Elson and "indicates an orientation that tends to work to the benefit of men rather than women.... There is no implication that all men are necessarily male-biased;

nor that all men are better off than all women.... Male bias stems from a failure to take into account the asymmetry of gender relations; the fact that women as a gender are socially subordinated to men as a gender through both social structures and individual practices" (1991, p. 47).

2. The term "embedded" comes from anthropologist Karl Polyani in his *The Great Transformation* (Boston: Beacon, 1944). He argued that pre-capitalist economies were "embedded" in society—that is, people did not see economic activities as separate from other activities. Capitalism saw the economy as becoming "disembedded," as separate from society and more specialized.

3. Flexibility in men's jobs where collective-bargaining power exists (for example, the construction industry) protects industries from marginalization and part-time initiatives. Standing's (1992) notion of co-operative rather than subordinated flexibility that would "facilitate flexible work patterns on terms desired by workers" may be a good starting point for a broader, equity-based approach to flexibility.

4. Gender-relations analysis includes both men and women. "Gender relations" can be defined in terms of the interplay between historical practices that are distinguished according to masculine and feminine (theories and ideologies, including religious ideas), institutional practices (such as state and market), and material conditions (the nature and distribution of materials capabilities along gender lines). "Gender relations" are social constructions (social forces and historical structures) that differentiate and circumscribe material outcomes for women and men. This definition of gender relations recognizes that the interplay of race, class, and sexuality underpins the form and structure of actual gender relations.

5. All citizens, female and male, within the boundaries of the nation-state would, by definition, achieve the highest possible well-being. This narrative of inclusivity mirrors economists' treatments of the household as a black box, a natural and obvious social entity that yields mutually agreeable rewards and trade-offs.

6. In the longer term, infrastructure spending on schools, hospitals, transportation, water, and sewer systems can also have a profound effect on both women's tasks in the household sector and their labour-market position.

7. As Appleton (1991, p. 17) notes, "macroeconomic theory implies that even with a 'neutral' policy stance, structural adjustment will have systematially different effects on various sectors of the economy. It is well understood that the fall in domestic demand will

tend to cause a 'real depreciation'; that is, a fall in the relative price of 'non-tradeable', those goods which are sheltered from international competition. Furthermore, adjustment to temporary external shocks may have differential effects on capital and consumer good industries. Moreover, there may be changes in trade policy, altering the price of protected tradeables relative to those which are unprotected."

REFERENCES

Afshar, H., and Dennis, C. (1992). *Women and adjustment in the Third World.* London: Macmillan.

Appleton, S. (1991). Gender dimensions of structural adjustment: The role of economic theory and quantitative analysis. *IDS Bulletin, 22* (1).

Armstrong, P. (1993). *The feminization of the labour force: Harmonizing down in a global economy.* Paper prepared for the North–South Institute Conference on Structural Change and Gender Relations in the Era of Globalization, September 30–October 1.

Bakker, I. (1991). Pay equity and economic restructuring: The polarization of policy? In Judy Fudge and Patricia McDermott (Eds.), *Pay equity: A feminist assessment* (pp. 254–280). Toronto: University of Toronto Press.

Bakker, I. (1994). Introduction: Engendering macroeconomic policy reform in the era of global restructuring and adjustment. In I. Bakker (ed.), *The strategic silence: Gender and economic policy.* London: Zed Press.

Bergeron, S. (1993). *The gendered subject of macroeconomics.* Paper prepared for the conference Out of the Margins: Feminist Perspectives on Economic Theory, Amsterdam, June.

Blum, L. (1987). Possibilities and limits of the comparable worth movement. *Gender and Society, 1* (4).

Brenner, J. (1993). The best of times, the worst of times: U.S. feminism today. *NLR200* (July/August).

Briskin, L. (1993). Equity and economic restructuring in the Canadian labour movement. *Economic and industrial democracy.* forthcoming.

Cassin, A.M. (1993). Equitable and fair: Widening the circle. In A. Maslove (Ed.), *Fairness in taxation* (pp. 104–134). Toronto: University of Toronto Press.

Cohen, M. (1994). *Democracy and the future of nations: Challenges for minorities, women and the disadvantaged.* Paper prepared for the Harold Innis Centenary Celebration Workshop, Global Markets: Do Nation States Have a Future?, York University, Toronto, January 7–9.

Commission of the European Communities. (1992). *The position of women on the labour market.* Women of Europe Supplement 36. Brussels.

Commonwealth Expert Group on Women and Structural Adjustment. (1989). *Engendering adjustment for the 1990s.* London.

Connelly, P., and MacDonald, M. (1990). *Women and the labour force.* Ottawa: Statistics Canada.

Cornia, G.; Jolly, R.; and Stewart, F. (1987). *Adjustment with a human face.* Oxford: Clarendon Press.

Dwyer, D., and Bruce, J. (Eds.). (1988). *A home divided: Women and income in the Third World.* Stanford, CA: Stanford University Press.

Economic Council of Canada. (1990). *Good jobs/Bad jobs.* Ottawa.

Elson, D. (1987). *The impact of structural adjustment on women: Concepts and issues.* Discussion Papers in Development Studies, DP8801. Manchester: Department of Economics, University of Manchester.

Elson, D. (1991). *Male bias in the development process.* Manchester: Manchester University Press.

Elson, D. (1992). *Gender analysis and development economics.* Paper for the ESRC Development Economics Group, Annual Conference, Manchester.

European Network of Experts on the Situation of Women in the Labour Market. (1992, October). *Bulletin on women and employment in the EC.*

Fair Tax Commission of the Government of Ontario. (1992). *Working group report: Women and taxation.* Toronto: Government of Ontario.

Ferber, M. and Nelson, J. (Eds.). (1993). *Beyond economic man: Feminist theory and economics.* Chicago: University of Chicago Press.

Folbre, N. (1986). Cleaning house: New perspectives on households and economic development. *Journal of Development Economics, 22.*

Folbre, N. (1992). *Rotten kids, bad daddies, and public policy.* Paper prepared for presentation at the International Food Policy Research Institute–World Bank Conference on Intrahousehold Resource Allocation, Washington, DC, February 12–14.

Fraser, N. (1989). *Unruly practices: Power, discourse and gender in contemporary social theory.* Minneapolis: University of Minnesota Press.

Fraser N., and Gordon, L. (1994). A geneology of dependency: Tracing a keyword of the U.S. welfare state. *Signs, 19* (2).

Galarnau, Dianne. (1991). Women approaching retirement. *Perspectives.* Autumn.

Gunderson, M.L. Muszynski, and Keck, J. (1990). *Women and labour market poverty.* Ottawa: Canadian Advisory Council on the Status of Women.

Jessop, B. Towards a Schumpeterian workfare state? Preliminary remarks on post-Fordist political economy. *Studies in Political Economy,* No. 40, 1993.

Innis, Harold. (1956). *Canadian economic history.* Mary Innis (Ed.). Toronto: University of Toronto Press.

Lahey, K. (1985). The tax unit in income tax theory. In E. Diane Pask, Kathleen A. Mahoney, and Catherine A. Brown (Eds.), *Women, and the law and the economy.* Toronto: Butterworths.

Leach, B. (1993). *Behind closed doors: Homework policy and lost possibilities for change.* Paper prepared for the North-South Institute Conference on

Structural Change and Gender Relations in the Era of Globalization, September 30–October 1.

Leger, H. and Rebick, J. (1993). *The NAC voters' guide*. Hull: Voyageur Publishing.

McDowell, L. (1991). Life without father and Ford: The new gender order of post-Fordism. *Transnational Institute of British Geography*. 16.

Mosely, H. and Schmid, G. (1992). *Public services and competitiveness*. FS I 92-5. Berlin: Wissenschaftszentrum Berlin.

Nelson, J. (1994). *Feminist economics: What might it look like?* Paper prepared for the Conference Out of the Margin: Feminist Perspectives on Economic Theory, Amsterdam, June 2–5, 1993.

Nelson, J. (1993). The study of choice or the study of provisioning? Gender and the definition of economics. In Marianne Ferber and Julie Nelson (Eds.), *Beyond economic man: Feminist theory and economics*. Chicago: University of Chicago Press.

OECD. (1985). *OECD Economic Studies*, No. 4. Special Issue on the Growth of Government.

OECD. (1991). *Shaping structural change: The role of women*. Paris: OECD.

OECD. (1992). *Industrial policy in OECD countries, Annual Review 1992*. Paris: OECD.

OECD. (1993). *Women and structural change in the 1990s*. Paris: OECD. Report by Gunther Schmid.

Ontario District Council of the International Ladies' Garment Workers Union and INTERCEDE. (1993, February). *Meeting the needs of vulnerable workers: Proposals for improved employment legislation and access to collective bargaining for domestic workers and industrial homeworkers*. Toronto: INTERCEDE.

Ontario Women's Directorate. (1993). *The North American Free Trade Agreement: Implications for women*. Toronto: OWD.

Palmer, I. (1991). *Gender and population in the adjustment of African economies: Planning for change*. Geneva: ILO.

Phillips, L. (1993). *Tax policy and the gendered distribution of wealth*. Paper prepared for the North-South Institute Conference on Structural Change and Gender Relations in the Era of Globalization, September 30–October 1.

Sen, A.K. (1990). Gender and cooperative conflicts. In I. Tinker (Ed.), *Persistent inequalities: Women and world development*. New York: Oxford University Press.

Schmid, G. (1993). *Women and structural change in the 1990s*. Paris: OECD.

Standing, G. (1989). Global feminization through flexible labour. *World Development*. Vol. 17, no. 7.

Standing, G. (1992). Fragmented flexibility: Labour and the social dividend solution. In D. Drache, (Ed.), *Getting on track: Social democratic strategies for Ontario*. Montreal: McGill–Queen's University Press.

UNDP. (1992). *Human development report 1992*. New York: United Nations.

Vosko, L. (1993). *The last thread: An analysis of the apparel goods provisions in the NAFTA and the impact on women.* Ottawa: Canadian Centre for Policy Alternatives.

Whitehead, A. (1979). Some preliminary notes on the subordination of women. *IDS Bulletin,* Vol. 10, no. 3.

Williams, F. (1989). *Social policy: A critical introduction.* London: Polity Press.

SUGGESTED READING

Cohen, Marjorie. (1994). Women and economic policy. In Ruth Pierson and Marjorie Cohen, *Canadian Women's Issues.* Vol. 2: *Bold Visions.* Toronto: James Lorimer.

Elson, Diane. (1991). *Male bias in the development process.* Manchester: Manchester University Press.

Ferber, Marianne, and Nelson, Julie. (1993). *Beyond economic man: Feminist theory and economics.* Chicago: University of Chicago Press.

Folbre, Nancy. (1994). *Who pays for the kids? Gender and the structures of constraint.* New York and London: Routledge.

MacDonald, Martha. (1993). Becoming visible: Women and the economy. In G. Finn (Ed.), *Limited edition: Voices of women, voices of feminism.* Halifax: Fernwood Publishing.

QUESTIONS TO CONSIDER

1. What are the basic gender assumptions underlying conventional economic policies and models?

2. What are some possible gendered effects of restructuring in the area of: (i) government expenditures; (ii) taxation; (iii) monetary and trade policies?

3. In what ways do men and women share similar experiences coming out of the restructuring process? in what ways do their experiences differ?

CHAPTER 2

Fragmentation and Feminization: The Challenge of Equity for Labour-Relations Policy

Judy Fudge

The Canadian labour market is changing. Increasing numbers of people are employed in small firms that tend to pay lower wages and provide fewer benefits than do larger corporations. Union influence is declining as a growing proportion of jobs do not require organized labour. Despite the fact that women are almost as likely as men to be working at paid employment, women continue both to receive less pay and to be employed in female job ghettos. Wages are dropping, and jobs are becoming more insecure as part-time, temporary, and precarious employment expands and the number of full-time and relatively secure jobs contracts.

Macro-economic policies embraced by both the former Conservative and the existing Liberal federal governments have contributed to the change in the Canadian labour market. These policies include reducing the deficit, lowering interest rates, cutting social programs, and increasing competition. However, the impact of such policies on the labour market is not direct because macro-economic policies are filtered through another level of policies, those directed specifically at the labour market.

Labour-market policy is concerned with regulating the supply and demand of labour and includes training, labour adjustment (including unemployment insurance), immigration, labour relations, and employment regulations. My focus is on a particular aspect of labour-market policy— those legal instruments concerned with influencing the terms and conditions of employment by regulating the conduct of firms and trade unions in the labour market. This policy area is known as "labour relations."

Labour-relations policy is generally seen as gender-neutral; that is, the prevailing assumption is that labour-relations policy should neutrally reflect the choices of male and female workers, unions, and employers. However, governments have increasingly recognized that sex discrimination distorts the labour market. As a result, sex-specific legislation, such as laws governing maternity leave and equal pay for work of equal value, has been implemented. The idea is that women should have opportunities equal to those of men to compete in the labour market.

My aim in this essay is to identify and evaluate the underlying gendered assumptions or norms that shape key elements in labour-relations law and policy to see how they interact with the restructured labour market. Attention to the gendered dimension of labour-relations policy not only helps to explain why women workers in general have fared so much more poorly than men, but also suggests that an uncritical reliance on a form of employment that has historically been identified with men in order to develop labour policy does little to improve women workers' employment. The reason is that the current process of economic restructuring is also reconfiguring gender relations. Thus, in order to evaluate the impact of labour-relations policy on the kind of employment available to men and women workers, it is crucial to identify the gendered assumptions upon which the policy rests.

In this essay, I examine labour-relations law and policy in Ontario under the New Democratic Party government that was elected in 1990. I selected Ontario as the case study because its government has concentrated on four elements of labour-relations law—collective bargaining, employment standards, **pay equity**, and **employment equity**—as part of its "equity agenda" for women and other marginalized groups. The impact of these policies on women's employment is evaluated in this essay.

By emphasizing its commitment to equity in the labour market, the New Democratic Party (NDP) government hopes to persuade its democratic socialist and social democratic supporters that, despite its imposition of public-sector union wage concessions and public-service cutbacks, it has not adopted a neoconservative agenda. While its overwhelming preoccupation is with reducing the provincial deficit in order to attract private capital to the province, the government claims that its labour-relations law reforms, which were designed to reflect the changes in the labour market, will promote greater equity for women and other marginalized groups (*Globe and Mail*, December 30, 1993, pp. A1, and A7).

In this essay, I evaluate the Ontario NDP government's equity agenda in terms of its prospect for providing women workers with relatively secure and well-paid jobs. Equity as a regulative or normative ideal has two different (and often competing) political resonances:

▶ the traditional liberal understanding of equity as equality of opportunity; and

▶ the democratic socialist understanding of equity as substantive equality of condition.

I argue that, in the contemporary context of economic restructuring, the meaning of equity within the social democratic lexicon has lost its political resonance with substantive equality and has become exclusively identified with equality of opportunity. By failing to address central elements of the transformed labour market, its fragmentation and **feminization**, the NDP government's labour-relations policy ignores the fact that ever-increasing numbers of people in the province are forced to work at bad jobs for low wages. Equality of opportunity simply provides increasing numbers of workers in Ontario with the chance to compete for bad jobs.

THE CHANGING SHAPE OF THE CANADIAN LABOUR MARKET

Fragmentation

"Fragmentation" refers to the increasing segmentation of the labour market. Instead of picturing the labour market as open and competitive, it is more accurate to see it as separated into various different submarkets that recruit different kinds of workers for different jobs, firms, and industries in the economy. Factors that contribute to the greater fragmentation of the labour market are the changing size and shape of the firms providing jobs and the associated impact on the influence of trade unions.

Small Firms

Although there is no standard definition, small businesses are often identified by the number of people they employ. Usually a manufacturing enterprise is considered to be a "small business" if it has fewer than 100 employees. A small business in the service sector generally has fewer than 50 employees. Since the late 1970s, small businesses have been the key contributors to net job creation in Canada. Between 1979 and 1989, for example, businesses with fewer than 100 employees created just under 90 percent of all growth in employment in Canada (Manly and Martin, 1994, p. 3). Moreover, this figure does not include the profound increase in self-employment. Slightly more than half of all Canadians working in the private sector were either self-employed or working in businesses with fewer than 100 employees in 1991.

Both the former federal Conservative government and the new Liberal regime elected in 1993 have emphasized policies and platforms designed to facilitate the growth and survival of small businesses to strengthen the country's economic recovery. Other commentators, however, are not as optimistic about the employment opportunities offered by these firms (Brown, Hamilton, and Medoff, 1990). Over time, the death rate of smaller businesses makes the net contribution in job growth difficult to estimate. Jobs created in small firms tend to be less stable and durable, and pay lower wages than those created in large firms (Morissette, 1991, pp. 41–43). Under Canadian collective-bargaining law, it is extremely difficult to unionize small firms (O'Grady, 1992, p. 158), and many forms of legal regulation designed to improve the terms and conditions of employment simply do not apply to small firms (Armstrong and Armstrong, 1994, p. 27).

It is also unclear whether many of these small firms are, in fact, independent productive units. Often, small firms do not grow out of individual entrepreneurship but rather out of corporate restructuring. Many large corporations have reorganized in order to off-load production to smaller firms through a variety of complex contractual relations, including franchise arrangements, subcontracting pyramids, and supply agreements (Harrison, 1994, pp. 4–5). The incentive for large corporations to move from vertically integrated production and distribution into a network of small firms bound together by ties of ownership, contract, and authority is that, in law, the latter are treated as distinct legal entities—independent persons—instead of as part of an integrated production process. As a result, it is extremely difficult, given existing legal principles, to hold one member of the group responsible for the actions or omissions of other members. This legal fact allows economically dominant firms in the network to escape liability for their actions—even if these actions force small firms to push down wages, erode working conditions, or, in some instances, avoid statutory standards (Collins, 1990, p.737). For example, because McDonald's organizes its business through franchises that have relatively few employees, the corporation avoids a range of employment-related standards that are triggered by size of work force.

Small Workplaces

Further complicating any evaluation of firm size and its impact on conditions in the labour market is the fact that there is not necessarily a correlation between firm and workplace size. For the purposes of collective-bargaining law in Canada, the size of the workplace is the most significant factor. The general starting position is that certification (the legal process a union must undergo in order to represent a particular group of workers) and collective bargaining take place at the level of the workplace unless both the union and the employer agree to move the relationship to the level of the firm as a whole (O'Grady, 1992, pp. 157–158).

Since the late 1970s, Canada has witnessed a proliferation of small workplaces and a marked shift in employment to these establishments. In Ontario, for example, the proportion of workers employed in establishments with fewer than 20 workers increased from 16.28 percent in 1978 to 24.01 percent in 1986. This represents a shift of almost 8 percentage points in as many years (O'Grady, 1992, p. 159). Moreover, between 1976 and 1984, fully 87 percent of all jobs created in Canada were in establishments employing fewer than 20 people (Urban Dimensions Group, 1989, pp. 7–8). The extent to which small-establishment growth will continue is the subject of some debate. It is clear, however, that the shift to small workplaces has negative implications for Ontario workers. According to one Ontario study, "larger establishments are more likely to be subject to union organizing drives and collective bargaining" (Urban Dimension Group, 1989, pp. 28–29). Moreover, they are more likely to be subject to regulation by Ontario's anti-discrimination and employment law.

Declining Unionization

The diminishing size of the firm and the workplace has had a profound impact upon unionization in this country. Collective bargaining between workers and employers in privately owned workplaces is declining (O'Grady, 1992, p. 153). Moreover, public-sector unionism, which accounted for the greatest part of the increase in the number of union members as a proportion of workers during the 1960s and 1970s, stabilized throughout the 1980s, because public administration and education/health services, the two sectors with the highest percentage of unionized workers, are regarded as "saturated." As far as union membership is concerned, the suggestion is that further unionization is likely not possible and that present levels of union membership may even decline (White, 1993, p. 192). As governments across Canada decide to reduce their deficits through public-sector employment restraint and privatization, many currently unionized jobs are being threatened as well.

Structural shifts in employment from the goods-producing to the service sector explain only part of the decline in private-sector unionization. They cannot account for the entire decline since no segment of the private sector has escaped unscathed. Even within the traditional base of industrial unionism—large firms and workplaces within the manufacturing sector—evidence of the contraction in unionization is compelling (O'Grady, 1992, p. 153).

Declining unionization is also directly linked to the size of the workplace. In 1989, for example, the overall rate of unionization in Canada was 38 percent. In firms with fewer than 20 workers, however, only 13 percent of workers belonged to trade unions. In other words, the percentage of unionization rises as the size of firm increases, as Table 2.1 shows. Unless radical changes are made to Canadian collective-bargaining legislation, the proliferation of both small firms and small workplaces will be likely to erode further the proportion of unionized workers in the Canadian labour force.

TABLE 2.1
PERCENTAGE OF UNIONIZED WORKERS BY FIRM SIZE IN CANADA IN 1989

Size of Firm	% of Workers Unionized
20 – 99 workers	32
100 – 499 workers	50
500 and more workers	56

Source: White, J. (1993), p. 195. Patterns of unionization. In L. Briskin and P. Mc Dermott (Eds.), *Women challenging unions.* Toronto: University of Toronto Press. Reprinted with permission of the University of Toronto Press.

Feminization

Feminizing the Labour Force

Since the early 1940s, in Canada women's labour-force participation has increased threefold, with participation by married women with children representing the most dramatic increase (Armstrong and Armstrong, 1993, pp. 15–19; Phillips and Phillips, 1993, pp. 32–36). By the 1990s, six out of ten working-age women, as compared with seven out of ten working-age men, were in the labour force. As well, women's labour-force attachment has strengthened. Women work in the paid labour market for longer periods now than before. Thus, women's participation patterns and rates are increasingly approaching those of men (Phillips and Phillips, 1993, p. 35; see Box 2.1).

Despite their profound increase in numbers, women have remained largely segregated into female-dominated industries and occupations. Generally these so-called job ghettos are characterized by low pay, no career path, low status, and the absence of union representation

---

BOX 2.1

Feminization The process of economic restructuring that began in the mid-1970s and deepened throughout the 1980s has parallelled what has been termed the "feminization of labour." This "feminization" has been characterized by

▶   a feminization of the labour force (an increase in the number of working women) and

▶   the feminization of the labour market in terms of the types of jobs that are being created.

(Armstrong and Armstrong, 1993, pp. 28–41; Phillips and Phillips, 1993, pp. 60–61). Moreover, for every occupation group, for every age group, for part- and full-time workers, for every education level, and for every region in Canada, men received higher average earnings (Phillips and Phillips, 1993, p. 51). The result has been a gendered wage gap, with men earning considerably more than women. If all Canadian workers are considered, women were paid just 60 percent of what men were in 1990 (Armstrong and Armstrong, 1993, p. 41). Although there has been some improvement in relative wages for women in the last two decades, it is slow, and the dollar gap has continued to grow (Phillips and Phillips, 1993, p. 50).

In the manufacturing sector, women workers are clearly and con-sistently concentrated into smaller businesses, whereas men tend to populate the larger-sized firms (White, 1993, p. 195). White also found that, in personal/business services and in education/health services, women are also disproportionately found in small firms, although the trend was not as pronounced. In other industries, the association between gender and firm size is either negligible or inconsistent. However, across all industries, there is a significant dif-ference in the proportion of men and women in the smallest firms, those with fewer than 20 employees. Almost 31 percent of all women workers, in contrast to 25 percent of men, are employed in these firms. This finding is important because these small firms pay the lowest wages and provide the fewest benefits. Moreover, since only 13 percent of workers in firms with fewer than 20 employees are union members, this helps to explain why women's unionization rate in 1989 was 29 percent, in contrast to 38 percent among men (White, 1993, p. 192).

Feminizing Work

At the same time as women's labour-market participation has increased, so too has the proportion of non-standard forms of employment, otherwise referred to as bad, precarious, or casual jobs. **Non-standard employment**, which includes part-time, part-year, temporary help agency work, and own-account self-employment (where no workers are employed), deviates from the norm of full-time, full-year employment. The latter tends to be better paid and provide better benefits and job security (Economic Council of Canada, 1991, p. 13). Historically, women have been disproportion-ately represented in non-standard jobs. This is the second aspect of the feminization of labour.

In Canada, in the late 1980s, fully one-third of all jobs were non-stan-dard, with more than three-quarters of jobs in the service sector so char-acterized (Economic Council of Canada, 1991, pp. 81–82). Rather than eroding the traditional sexual division of labour, Canada's post-industrial labour market appears to be the site of its consolidation, and even growth (Boyd, Mulvihill, and Myles, 1991, p. 422).

Polarization and Harmonization

The upshot of the fragmentation and feminization of the labour market has been to bring women's labour-market profile closer to men's. According to Armstrong (in press), "if we look at such measures as participation rates, the proportion of women in traditional male work and in higher education, the gap in wages between men and women, and job tenure, female and male employment patterns have become increasingly similar." But simply because women's employment has moved closer to the male standard does not mean that women's labour-market position has substantially improved. This situation is attributable to the fact that the labour market is characterized by increasing polarization, or what the Economic Council of Canada called the "good jobs/bad jobs" phenomenon; the proportion of jobs characterized as middle in the economy has shrunk as job creation has shifted to both poles, with the largest proportion of jobs being created at the bottom end.

Consequently, what appears to be a situation of greater economic equality between women and men actually reflects a decline in men's situation rather than real gains for women. A recent Statistics Canada study concluded that times were tougher for working men in the 1980s than they were during the Great Depression of the 1930s (*Toronto Star*, March 30, 1994, p. C3). Moreover, this situation is more a result of restructuring than it is of direct competition from women. Women's and men's work have become more similar precisely because fewer people have a choice about what kinds of paid work they take. Increasingly, the only jobs available are bad jobs; thus, more men are doing work that has historically been associated with women. And while it is important to recognize that women's unionization rate overtook men's in the 1980s, it is little comfort for women to find that their influence is expanding in a labour movement that is stagnant or declining (White, 1993, p. 191).

At the same time as we see a harmonization between men's and women's work, we observe an increased polarization among women workers themselves (Cohen, 1992, p. 114; Armstrong, in press). Some women are moving into good jobs in managerial/administrative and professional occupations; however, a larger proportion are being recruited into the bad jobs at the bottom of the labour market. The increasing inequality among women becomes even more visible when full-time work is compared with part-time and temporary work across occupations. Thus, an uncritical reliance on a male standard to measure women's gains obscures both the extent to which men's employment has deteriorated throughout the 1980s and the degree to which gains enjoyed among women have been distributed unequally.

IMPLICATIONS FOR CANADIAN LABOUR-RELATIONS LAW AND POLICY

Restructuring

Since the mid-1970s the economies of Western industrialized countries, Canada's included, have undergone a restructuring that involves a shift from central elements of the **Fordist** postwar compromise. At the most general level, the Fordist model consists of mass production of consumer goods in huge vertically integrated firms for a mass consumer audience, and secure unionized employment for male workers in the industrial sector (Armstrong, 1993, p. 107). This current round of restructuring has been driven by a series of growing and historical crises in the international division of labour, a further shift in economic and political power in favour of transnational corporations and global finance, and the capacity of the governments to regulate business (see Bakker, this volume). To varying degrees, elected governments have adopted a range of macro-economic policies that are designed to attract private capital to invest in their economies. These include

▶ deficit containment,

▶ dampening inflation,

▶ reducing government spending in the social welfare field,

▶ privatization, and

▶ deregulation.

How macro-economic policies have affected the employment opportunities in different countries depends upon the combination of institutional structures that evolved in the postwar period, largely as a compromise between business and labour. National compromises range across a spectrum, which, at one end, heavily stressed individualism and self-reliance (the United States is at this end), and, at the other end, instituted government policies to provide a healthy social safety net (Germany is located here). Canada's place on this spectrum has been characterized as "permeable Fordism" because of its export-led economy and weak social safety net in comparison with those of Western Europe (Jenson, 1989, pp. 78–80).

GENDER AND THE POST-WAR COMPROMISE

One effect of the process of restructuring has been to render visible the norms or assumptions of the standard employment relationship (Muckenberger, 1989, p. 386). Gendered assumptions about the appropriate role of women in the labour market served to make the selective function of the standard employment relationship invisible, at worst, and unproblematic, at best (Fudge, 1993, p. 232). These assumptions have also profoundly influenced labour-market policy.

Segmentation

In the period immediately after the Second World War, the Canadian state brokered a compromise between capital and organized labour. This compromise basically permitted capital to protect its interest in maintaining and increasing profits through management of and control over the labour process, rather than by engaging in direct confrontation with organized labour over the issue of wages. Capital's goal was to contain unionism and control the costs of labour. Segmentation of the labour market served both of these goals. Through segmentation, capital could concede higher wages to organized workers and, at the same time, preserve a large category of unorganized low-wage workers. The segmentation strategy combined with the expansion of the service sector dramatically increased the demand for low-wage, semiskilled workers. As Ursel observes, "women constituted the largest pool of such labour in Canada and were, therefore, a key component in the segmentation strategy of capital" (1992, p. 239).

Despite the dramatic increase in women's labour-market participation during the Second World War, the federal government's postwar labour-market policy reflected the view that women's place was primarily in the home. The husband was viewed as the chief wage earner (Porter, 1993, p. 114). In other words, this policy was explicitly gendered, as it was designed to reduce women's, especially married women's, attachment to the labour force. Day cares were closed, civil service regulations barring women from federal government work were renewed, and the income tax was amended to create a disincentive for married women to work for pay (Porter, 1993, pp. 114–115). In an effort to steer them from the relatively well-paid jobs they had enjoyed during the war, women were encouraged to undertake training in such areas as domestic service, household management, waitressing, and hairdressing.

The Unemployment Insurance Act, which was crucial in shaping Canada's postwar compromise, was inscribed with gender. Pierson found that the contribution and benefit structure of the 1940 act reproduced sexually unequal wage hierarchies and provided that women's principal access to benefits was indirect, through the dependents' allowance

(1986, pp. 93–95). Moreover, after the war, Canada's full-employment policy was specifically limited to men. As Porter recounts, "the state was involved in rebuilding a particular type of labour market structure which involved women moving from relatively highly-paid and highly-skilled wartime manufacturing jobs into part-time and insecure jobs in the low-paid manufacturing and growing service sectors" (1993, p. 115).

In part, the postwar institutional compromise was premised on the assumption that the labour market was unfragmented. This assumption was false. In Canada, the labour market has always been highly segmented, both on gender and on racial/ethnic lines (Phillips and Phillips, 1993, pp. 76–83). At the most general level, the Canadian labour market has always been divided into a primary (or core) sector amd a secondary (or peripheral) sector. From the end of the Second World War, the key factor distinguishing the two sectors was firm size. Large companies, which provide relatively well-paid and secure jobs, comprise the primary labour market, whereas small firms, which provide precarious jobs, are found on the periphery. The existence of this fragmentation in the labour market was ignored in labour policy because the incumbents in the peripheral labour market were women and new immigrants. Since women's participation in the labour market was temporary and contingent, usually confined to the time in women's lives when their family responsibilities were the lightest, it did not matter that women's employment and income were precarious. Women's paid labour, precisely because it was considered secondary, did not disrupt the norm of the standard worker as a man with a dependent family. The postwar compromise was built upon and reinforced this particular family form and organization of patriarchal relations.

Women's participation in the labour market increased in the 1960s as the public and private service sectors expanded, but this did not disrupt the sexual division of labour. In fact, it intensified the segregation of women into secondary and low-wage jobs. However, the restructuring that began in the mid-1970s has challenged the representation of the standard worker as a man earning enough to support his dependent family by working full-time and with job security in industry. By the late 1980s, it took between 65 and 80 hours of work each week for a family to earn what it took a single breadwinner—typically, a man—to earn in a 45-hour work week in the 1970s (*Globe and Mail*, January 3, 1992, pp. A1, A5). Women's paid work can no longer be dismissed as economically marginal. The restructuring of the labour market has not been gender-neutral.

COLLECTIVE-BARGAINING LEGISLATION

Collective bargaining was a key institution embedded in the postwar compromise. A central element of the Canadian legislative scheme was the highly regulated certification procedure through which unions have had to navigate in order to present workers' demands to their employers. Although gender-neutral on its face, in operation collective-bargaining legislation was (and remains) highly gendered. In fact, it has entrenched and reinforced a labour market divided by gender. Collective-bargaining legislation was never designed to extend the scope of unionization beyond core industries, which included the mass-production industrial, resource-extraction, construction, and transportation sectors. All of these sectors in the Canadian economy have been populated by men (Fudge, 1993, p. 243). Thus, in its very conception, collective bargaining was never intended to extend to the sectors where women worked.

During the postwar reconstruction, large companies in the primary sector had a vested interest in stable labour supplies. In exchange for restrictions on unions' ability to disrupt production, core industries, in general, offered unionized jobs with training opportunities, internal job ladders, and job security. Moreover, these jobs structured and drew upon a primary labour market composed of skilled, unionized, and white male labour. The immediate postwar demand for a family wage was met through the provision of family allowances directly to women in their role of nurturers in the domestic realm (Ursel, 1992, pp. 158–194). One of the consequences of this compromise was that industrial unions displayed little interest in organizing or protecting women (Glasbeek, 1993, p. 251).

In contrast, small competitive companies in the secondary sector offered non-unionized jobs, with little training or promotional opportunity and minimal job security (Ursel, 1992, p. 239). This periphery was recruited from the secondary labour market, which attracted unskilled, marginal labour, identified with women and immigrants.

Collective-bargaining legislation empowered labour-relations boards across the country to determine which groups of workers could join together for the purpose of collective bargaining. By selecting the appropriate bargaining unit, the board determines both the constituency within which a union needs to establish majority support and the group of employees that can engage in collective action. By linking union organization for the purpose of collective bargaining to the worksite through the certification procedure, labour-relations boards largely ensured that workers in the peripheral labour market, who were mostly women, would not benefit from unionization. Because women were employed in different firms and different occupations than men, bargaining-unit determination reflects the segregated labour market (Fudge, 1993, p. 236).

The boards' bargaining-unit policy made it extremely difficult for workers in small workplaces in a competitive sector to wield enough bargaining power to secure a collective agreement. What this meant was that workers in the secondary sector, who were mainly women, never enjoyed the benefit of collective bargaining. In the 1950s and 1960s, organized labour did not have a strategy that could effectively counteract the segmenting trends in the labour force. The wage gap between unionized and non-unionized sectors increased, unionized occupations decreased, and non-unionized occupations proliferated (Ursel, 1992, p. 242).

In the 1960s, collective-bargaining rights were extended to workers in the public sector. This change both dramatically increased the numbers of unionized workers and had a profound impact upon the unionization of women. Organized labour, stalled at less than a third of the non-agricultural work force as late as 1966, grew to more than 40 percent during the next ten years. Furthermore, the organization of government employees accounted for the largest increase in unionization of women, a 160 percent increase for women compared with a 40 percent increase for men (White, 1980, p. 22).

By the mid-1980s, it was clear that collective bargaining was being progressively confined to the public sector, to the regulated private sector, and to a narrowing base in industry and construction (O'Grady, 1992, p. 155). The barriers that are built into the labour-relations system inhibit the extension of unionization and collective bargaining to workers in small workplaces in competitive sectors and workers in non-standard forms of employment. As increasing numbers of women entered the labour market, they were recruited into those jobs that were hard, if not impossible, to organize under the existing collective-bargaining law. Thus, collective-bargaining law reinforced a highly gendered and fragmented labour market with the result that women in the private sector were denied the benefits of collective action.

EMPLOYMENT-STANDARDS LEGISLATION

Unlike collective-bargaining legislation, which was gender-neutral on its face, the first minimum-wage legislation in Canada was explicitly gendered. After the First World War, women workers and women's organizations in British Columbia, Saskatchewan, Manitoba, and Ontario managed to secure the introduction of legislation that imposed a minimum wage for women and child workers only (Russell, 1991; McCallum, 1986). While business generally opposed wage-setting by the state, it was prepared to accept minimum wages for women and children as the price for labour harmony. Adult male workers were excluded from the legislation. Instead of unionizing women workers, trade unions showed their support for women in their struggle to improve their working conditions by endorsing minimum wages for women.

Minimum-wage legislation signalled a public recognition of the fact that women were workers. At the same time, however, the minimum wages that were established effectively entrenched a gendered division of labour. The family form underlying the postwar compromise and regulated through legislation assigned reproductive tasks to married women in households and the best wage opportunities to men in paid employment (Russell, 1991, p. 87). Minimum wages in the four provinces were explicitly designed to provide a woman with a subsistence living in the event that she was entirely self-supporting and had no dependants. This benchmark excluded women who were not dependent upon men but who supported dependants. It assumed a definition of family that invoked male headship, despite the fact that there were numerous women workers who either supported dependants or were unmarried, or both (Russell, 1991, p. 85; McCallum, 1986, p. 32).

By the 1960s, minimum-standards legislation applied equally to men and women. Despite the fact that this legislation was gender-neutral, it maintained its secondary and subordinate character. Now every jurisdiction in Canada has comprehensive employment-standards legislation that provides a range of statutory entitlements. These include minimum wages, maximum hours of work, overtime rates, maternity and parental leave, mass-termination notice, and vacations and holidays to both male and female workers. However, these standards are low, riddled with exemptions, and ineffectively enforced. The prevailing assumption is that collective-bargaining legislation is the primary, and preferred, mechanism for regulating the terms and conditions of labour, and that employment-standards legislation is simply an adjunct to that process (Fudge, 1991a, p. 4).

The fact that the majority of workers who have relied upon employment standards have been women, young workers, or recent immigrants explains why there is little pressure to improve the legislation (Fudge, 1991b, p. 78). It was never part of the general consensus that they would derive the benefit of full employment, collective bargaining, or the family wage. This was the preserve of male workers in the primary sector. The fragmented nature of collective bargaining in Canada had a direct bearing on the precarious nature of employment in the secondary labour market. This form of organization probably gives unions more control over the labour process, thereby enabling them to secure better terms and conditions for their members. Nevertheless, a consequence of a fragmented structure is "to expose the remaining parts of the employment system to unregulated terms and conditions of employment" (Rubery, 1988, p. 271). Collective bargaining was confined to the male-dominated primary sector, exposing women to poor regulation in the more competitive and vulnerable labour markets. In part, the inequality in the labour market was tolerated as it reflected and reinforced unequal gender relations.

THE EQUITY AGENDA IN ONTARIO

Business Opposition

The New Democratic Party government elected in Ontario in 1990 managed to avoid any real political fallout when its raised the minimum wage, loosened the qualifications for maternity leave, and introduced parental leave, as part of its "Agenda for People" (see Box 2.2). But it faced a backlash when it sought to hold directors and officers of bankrupt companies liable for employees' wages. The spectre of the government bringing actions against directors and officials on behalf of workers who were owed wages mobilized the business community. Business was content to see the government provide a fund for compensating employees in the event of employer bankruptcy, but it did not want to see those people responsible for running the corporation held personally liable for any risks. Thus, the government stepped in to provide workers with a maximum entitlement under the publicly financed wage-protection fund and let the human beings running the corporation off the hook.

In retrospect, the furore over directors' liability was minor in contrast with the outcry business orchestrated against proposals for reform of the collective-bargaining law. To help sell its reform agenda, the government embarked on a lengthy consultation process. In the daily press, the debate over labour-law reform was framed as big unions attempting to persuade their friends in government to tip the law so that it would favour workers.

The government sold its labour-law reform package by sounding the themes of partnership with business and increased equity. Collective bargaining was characterized as providing workers with greater input into the business, which was important if there was to be a long-lasting

---

BOX 2.2

The Equity Agenda in Ontario As Ontario's economy stalled in a deep recession, in October 1990 its citizens elected their first New Democratic Party (NDP) government. With close ties to organized labour, the NDP ran its election campaign on the basis of its "Agenda for People." Key elements in that platform were designed to promote greater equity in the labour market and workplace. In its first throne speech, the government promised to:

▶   amend the labour-relations legislation to make it easier for workers to unionize

▶   improve some central employment standards

▶   ensure that workers enjoyed at least some of the wages owing to them by bankrupt employers

▶   extend pay equity to women in female-dominated workplaces

▶   introduce employment-equity legislation. (*Globe and Mail*, November 21, 1990, pp. A1, A8)

and mutually beneficial relationship. Identifying the changing nature of the work force, the workplace, and jobs, the government claimed that labour law needed to be overhauled if the increasing numbers of women and visible-minority workers were to enjoy the benefits of collective bargaining.

After a long battle, legislation was finally enacted that tipped the balance of power slightly more in favour of labour. Labour-relations boards were given greater powers to stop employers from interfering with the formation of trade unions and could, under a narrow range of circumstances, join together bargaining units, and employers were prohibited from hiring replacement workers during a strike (Panitch and Swartz, 1993, pp. 163–169). Organized labour had been demanding most of these changes for decades.

Despite the uproar created by the business community, it is unlikely that the reform package will significantly halt the decline in unionization in Ontario. Contrary to the government's claims, the legislation still continues to ignore the most significant trends in the labour market, especially the proliferation of small, hard-to-organize workplaces and the increase in non-standard forms of employment. The reform package was designed for a 1970s labour market rather than the polarized one of the 1990s.

Implementing Equity

Instead of directly addressing the changing quality of jobs, what the Ontario government has done is to move along the most explicit part of its equity agenda—extending pay equity to female-dominated institutions and introducing new employment equity legislation. Pay and employment equity have been part of the NDP's political platform since the Royal Commission on Equality and Employment introduced "equity" into political debate in 1985. The main focus of the commission was employment equity, but it also set the framework for the development of pay equity legislation in Canada in the 1980s. For example, it recommended proactive legislative strategies to implement **affirmative action** and equal pay for work of equal value. It also shifted "the definition of both issues to an equity framework that called for policies that would recognize what was fair to employers as well as the rights of women and other disadvantaged groups" (Findlay, 1991, p. 94).

Both pay and employment equity deal with occupational segregation on the basis of gender. They differ, however, in their approach and solutions (see Table 2.2).

While pay and employment equity embody different techniques for ending discriminatory employment practices, they share similar assumptions. This is not surprising, given that both were driven by the NDP, which was concerned to eradicate particular forms of discrimination in

TABLE 2.2
PAY AND EMPLOYMENT EQUITY

Pay Equity	Employment Equity
Pay equity is narrowly targeted to end wage discrimination on the basis of sex through comparisons of male- and female-dominated jobs. The only effect it could have on occupational segregation is to create an incentive for men to enter into jobs traditionally associated with women by improving the remuneration for such jobs.	Employment equity is more ambitious in that its goal is to end the underrepresentation of women as well as aboriginal people, people with disabilities, and members of visible minorities in certain sectors of employment. It imposes a legal obligation on individual employers to eliminate any barriers to the employment of the designated groups in their enterprises. The purpose of employment equity is to ensure that an organization's work force is representative of the working-age population in which it is located.

the workplace. Both concentrate their efforts upon the rationalization of practices within an individual workplace. Moreover, both pieces of legislation received support from a coalition of groups and, initially, drew outrage from business interests. The government was, in both cases, forced to persuade the opponents of the equity initiatives that they would neither interfere with business's right to manage nor compromise its profits.

PAY EQUITY LEGISLATION

In 1987, the Liberal government of Ontario introduced the Pay Equity Act (RSO 1990, c. P7). This legislation was the centrepiece of the Liberal–NDP Accord of 1985. In it, the NDP agreed to support the minority Liberals in exchange for a commitment to introduce elements of the social democrats' legislative agenda. The major proponent of pay equity was the Equal Pay Coalition, an umbrella organization for women's groups and trade unions that had long advocated equal pay for work of equal value (Cuneo, 1990, p. 9). By the time the legislation was in draft form, the Liberals had fought another election and, this time, had won. Then, business opposition to pay equity was unleashed.

The Pay Equity Act was intended to "redress gender discrimination in the composition of employees employed in female job classes in Ontario" (RSO 1990, c. P7). The path-breaking aspect of the Ontario legislation was that it applied to both public and private sectors.

Establishments with fewer than 10 employees, however, were not subject to pay equity legislation, and those establishments with fewer than 100 employees had less onerous obligations. While simple in conception, the pay equity legislation rests upon a number of seemingly technical decisions. And, it is here that Cuneo argues that "devices were set up in the legislation whereby pay equity would not cost employers any more in terms of labour expenditures than they would otherwise have to bear in the absence of pay equity" (1991, p. 56).

The Ontario legislation imposes an obligation upon employers to make comparisons between female-dominated and male-dominated job classes within the same establishment. These job classes are first identified, then assigned a value based upon a job-comparison system. This system considers four factors:

▶ skill

▶ effort

▶ responsibility

▶ working conditions

The comparison must be gender-neutral. This requirement in the job-comparison system was designed to counteract the use of traditional job-evaluation techniques, which have tended to reproduce, rather than overcome, sex-based wage discrimination. To be entitled to a pay equity wage adjustment, the incumbents in a female job class must find an appropriate comparator—a male job class with the same or less value that receives higher wages. Where there is more than one possible male comparator, the pay equity adjustment is based on the comparator with the lowest wage rate. Where there are no comparators of equal or less value, there is no pay equity. Any substantial wage adjustment made necessary by pay equity is to be paid out gradually. The legislation specifies that the maximum adjustment an employer is obliged to make is 1 percent of the previous year's payroll.

The Plan's Flaws

From the outset, it was obvious that pay equity would not work for those women most in need of it. Pay equity was designed to combat the undercompensation effect of gender-based occupational segregation. But where occupational segregation is most extreme, it is impossible to locate a male comparator. Almost 50 percent of the women in workplaces covered by the Pay Equity Act are unable to claim pay equity adjustments under it (Findlay, 1991, p. 81). In recognition of this, the Liberals included a provision that required the Pay Equity Commission, the agency authorized to administer the scheme, to conduct a study of female-dominated job sectors in which there are no male-dominated job classes on which pay equity comparisons could be based. The commission also was required to report to the Minister of Labour with recommendations for redressing such discrimination.

The commission conducted its study in two stages. In the first, it outlined the scope of the problem in nine predominantly female sectors and identified five options that would relieve wage discrimination. In the second stage, the options were tested, and four of them were recommended by the commission to the Minister of Labour. To deal with female-dominated establishments in the broader public sector, such as day cares, the commission recommended the proxy-establishment approach. This method whereby female job classes in the "seeker " establishment were compared with male job classes in an establishment external to it was seen as the best solution.

The Liberal government rejected the commission's recommendation for proxy comparisons in the broader public sector. The reason it offered was that this method was inconsistent with a basic principle underlying the act, which explicitly states "that work traditionally performed by women be paid the same as work traditionally performed by men that is of *comparable value to the employer in the employer's establishment*" (Findlay, 1991, p. 82). To remedy the problem of there being no direct male comparators for a female job class, the Liberals accepted the commission's recommendation that the proportional-value method of comparison be made applicable to public-sector employers and to private-sector employers with more than 100 employees.

At the same time as the debate over the preferred mechanism for extending pay equity to predominantly female establishments was under way, profound limitations built into the very structure of the legislation began to be identified. Key structural elements of the act, such as how to identify the employer and what constitutes a gender-neutral job-comparison system, were undefined. The result was that any controversy would have to be resolved through lengthy and expensive litigation. Moreover, by confining pay equity to a single employer's establishment, the legislation ignored that aspect of the gendered wage gap attributable to the fact that women are employed in establishments or sectors where men are not. The estimates of what portion of the 40-percentage-point earnings differential would be closed by the pay equity initiative varied widely—from a high of 15 points to a low of 2 to 3 percentage points (Fudge and McDermott, 1991, p. 282). What is clear, however, is that pay equity was never designed to close the entire wage gap.

For the majority of women workers in Ontario the ability of pay equity to increase their wages depends upon a number of factors (see Box 2.3).

BOX 2.3

Factors Involved in Wage Determination

▶ the sector in which women workers are employed

▶ whether or not women workers are unionized

▶ the existence of an appropriate male job class as a comparator

▶ the size of their employer's work force

▶ whether or not workers are employed on a casual or temporary contract basis

---

And it is precisely these factors, listed in Box 2.3, which strongly correlate with low pay, that the Pay Equity Act is not able to remedy (Fudge and McDermott, 1991, p. 283). Because women are situated in different positions in the labour market, the range of pay equity adjustments under the Ontario legislation will vary widely across industries and between establishments. Women who are employed in occupations with formal accreditation and who are represented by strong female-dominated unions are likely to do best under the scheme. Unorganized women in the private sector, particularly those working for small firms, will obtain little, if any, benefit at all. In the end, then, pay equity will intensify wage polarization among women workers themselves.

The legislation does not require employers to file their pay equity plans with the commission. There is, therefore, simply no way of telling which women workers in the province are receiving pay equity adjustments or how much they have received. This self-regulation approach to the implementation of pay equity represents a profound flaw in the legislation. Unless a union representing women workers, or the women themselves, complain, there is no way to ensure that the pay equity process has been completed.

A study conducted by the Pay Equity Commission in late 1990 and early 1991 indicated that only 50 percent of the employers required to do so had, in fact, posted pay equity plans. In 1990, the total pay equity adjustments in the public sector amounted to 2.2 percent of the previous year's payroll. The average adjustment in the private sector, however, was well below the limit of 1 percent of the annual payroll (McColgan, 1993).

Pay Equity and Restructuring

The limited potential of the Ontario Pay Equity Act to improve the wages of women workers in the province is further undermined by the process of economic restructuring, the deregulation of labour markets, and heightened competition and technological change (Bakker, 1991, pp. 278–279).

The decline in firm and establishment size, the growth in the contingent work force, skills diversification, and the polarization of the labour market limits pay equity to a smaller and smaller segment of the work force. As Bakker puts it, "the question for policy makers now is how pay equity can be adapted to take account of these trends" (1991, p. 254).

Although reforming pay equity was a major element in the NDP's successful electoral platform in 1990, it did not address the crucial question of the changing labour market. Instead, it limited its initiative to introducing the proportional value for the private, broader public and public sectors, and the proxy comparison for the broader public sector. The government claimed that this would extend pay equity to 420 000 women who would otherwise be excluded. By legislating cross-establishment comparisons in the broader public sector, the NDP government went farther than the Liberals had. However, citing current economic constraints, the minister responsible for the legislation stated that it was necessary to extend the timelines for achieving pay equity in the public sector. This move cast doubt on the NDP's commitment to improve wages for the thousands of women receiving low pay in the broader public sector.

The significance of the proxy method in alleviating the wage gap in the broader public sector will depend upon the size of the pay equity fund that the government is prepared to provide. Financially strapped publicly funded agencies simply do not have the resources to make pay equity wage adjustments and continue to provide the full range of services. Unless the government decides to finance these increases, the proxy-comparison method will introduce "another round of relatively futile exercises in which overextended workers expend much energy and expense to define pay equity adjustments that would, in most cases, force employers to cut services or increase clients' fees" (Findlay, 1991, p. 83).

The NDP's amendments to the Pay Equity Act ignores both the fragmentation and the polarization of the labour market. The gendered wage gap has declined. This does not mean, however, that women's wages have improved. Instead, the shrinkage in the gendered wage gap is attributable to the fact that men's wages have declined. Pay equity cannot help the growing contingent work force employed in their homes, in small establishments, or on a temporary basis. The problem is that the pay equity legislation reflects rather than mediates crucial elements in the labour market that result in women's low pay. The NDP government's legislation has done little to recognize or ameliorate these broader effects.

EMPLOYMENT EQUITY LEGISLATION

During the third reading of Bill 79, the Employment Equity Act, Elaine Ziemba, the Minister of Citizenship, announced that "the purpose of this legislation is to provide equality of opportunity and equitable treatment for groups in our society who have, for far too long, faced barriers to their equal participation in the workplace" (Legislative Assembly of Ontario, 1993, p. 4803; see Box 2.4).

The groups identified suffer the highest levels of unemployment and underemployment; in other words, these groups are trapped in low-paying jobs and are underrepresented in positions of authority. The goal of the legislation is to identify and eliminate systemic barriers to the equal representation for these groups within Ontario workplaces by placing a positive obligation on employers to develop and implement employment equity plans.

One of the underlying motivations for employment equity is the changing demographics of the province's work force. It is estimated that, shortly after the turn of the century, 62 percent of the work force and more than 80 percent of new labour-market entrants will be from the four equity-seeking groups (Office of the Employment Equity Commissioner, 1992, p. 4). Organizations representing women, visible minorities, disabled people, and aboriginal people demanded a more far-reaching solution to the problem of systemic discrimination in employment than the individual complaint mechanism provided in the Human Rights Code. In responding to these demands for equity, the government had to reassure those people who had something to lose from the implementation of employment equity. It needed to ensure both that unions and employers were on side.

The government attempted to do this by establishing the Office of the Employment Equity Commissioner. It was mandated to conduct a lengthy series of consultations to determine the shape of employment equity. Throughout the consultations, the government was careful to emphasize that employment equity was designed to allow working people to compete on an equal footing. It simply meant fairness and equal opportunity, not reverse discrimination. The government sold employment equity as opening doors for all workers rather than closing doors to the dominant groups. Sounding a recurring theme in submissions made by business, Manulife Financial declared that "employment equity is not only a legal, social and moral obligation. It is also a

---

BOX 2.4

Employment Equity Employment equity applies to four designated groups:

▸   aboriginal people

▸   people with disabilities

▸   members of visible minorities

▸   women

common-sense business policy designed to increase productivity, improve our ability to attract and retain talented employees and enhance our position in both domestic and international markets" (Office of the Employment Equity Commission, 1992, p. 34).

Balancing Competing Claims

In drafting the legislation, the NDP government had to balance the interests of employers, unions, and designated groups. Not surprisingly, employers preferred employer-determined goals and timetables over fixed standards imposed by government regulation. They were also concerned that small businesses were exempted from onerous obligations. Business wanted the requirements for planning and goal-setting to take into account downsizing, the flattening of organizational structures, and low employee turnover, as well as shifts in the economy, the labour force, and individual business environments. Unions were concerned to preserve seniority, which they considered a fundamental principle in the labour movement. Meanwhile, equity seekers wanted mandatory legislation with both qualitative and numerical goals for each workplace. The precise measures advocated, however, depended upon the particular needs and history of the each of the four designated groups. The government constructed a carefully fashioned compromise that was designed to ensure partnership among the various interests around the implementation of employment equity (see Box 2.5).

The plan must contain measures that provide for the elimination of any identified barriers and the creation of positive measures regarding recruitment, hiring, retention, treatment, and promotion of the four designated groups. The plan must include measures designed to accommodate designated groups, numerical goals for each of the designated groups in each occupational group in the workplace, and specific goals and timetables relating to these measures. The numerical goals, which

---

BOX 2.5

The Employment Equity Act The Employment Equity Act (SO 1993, c. 35), which came into effect in 1994, imposes three general obligations on employers:

▸ to assess the existing employment levels of the designated groups within each organization by conducting a work force survey

▸ to conduct a qualitative assessment of workplace barriers by reviewing employment policies and practices

▸ to prepare an employment equity plan (Waldorf, 1994)

were one of the most contentious elements of the legislation, require employers to establish timetables in order to achieve a representative workplace. These goals, reflecting the working-age population of the designated groups in that particular geographic area, must be set for each occupational category and location. In situations where an employer's work force is unionized, bargaining agents are required to assist their employer in developing and implementing an employment equity plan for their workplace.

In addition to setting out the obligations imposed upon employers and trade unions, the legislation sets out a mechanism for enforcing these duties. In this respect, the Employment Equity Act addresses many of the problems identified under the Pay Equity Act. Employers are required to file summaries of their equity plan with the Employment Equity Commission, which, in turn, has the authority to conduct an audit of the employer's plan. Thus, unlike pay equity, employment equity allows for third-party monitoring. Moreover, it specifically permits individual employees to file a complaint regarding employment equity, even if their union has endorsed the equity plan. This is an important mechanism that pay equity fails to provide. And unlike the case under the Pay Equity Act, if the Employment Equity Tribunal, which is charged with adjudicating any disputes under the legislation, finds that an employer has failed to meet its obligations, it can order the employer to create an employment equity fund and appoint an administrator. The administrator is responsible for developing, implementing, reviewing, and revising the employment equity plan, all at the employer's expense.

Employers' Flexibility

The employment equity legislation looks much stronger on its face than the Pay Equity Act. Nevertheless, it is important to note that the key technical details of scheme are contained in the regulations. Survey requirements are specified in the draft regulations, as are the employment policies and practices that must be assessed, the barriers that must be eliminated, and the measures that must be taken to achieve employment equity. While the legislation appears to impose rather onerous obligations on employers to introduce measures to accommodate members of designated groups, broad scope is given to employers to select the measures they find appropriate (Waldorf, 1994).

No specific measures are imposed upon employers. Instead, the regulation directs the employer to select some combination of measures that would eliminate barriers and achieve designated group compensation (Ontario Regulation 390/94, s.17(2)). Similarly, the standard that the numerical goals and timetables must meet is one of reasonableness: they must be "reasonable progress toward achieving compliance with the principles of employment equity" (Employment Equity Act, SO 1993, c.35, s.13).

The Employment Equity Act applies to the entire public sector, employers in the broader public sector with 10 or more employees, and private-sector employers with 50 or more employees (Employment Equity Act, s.7). Small employers, however, have less onerous obligations than their larger counterparts. The former are defined as employers in the broader public sector that have fewer than 50 employees or private-sector employers that have fewer than 100 employees (Regulation, s.11). The work-force surveys conducted by smaller employers need not be as detailed as those required of larger employers, nor are small employers obliged to develop numerical goals for their organizations for each of the occupational categories.

Employers are given a great deal of discretion in implementing employment equity. For example, even when there is evidence in a complaint that an employer has not honoured its obligations under the legislation, the tribunal will not necessarily make a finding of non-compliance. So long as the employer has designed a plan that would, if implemented, "constitute reasonable progress toward" realizing employment equity and has made "all reasonable efforts" to implement its plan and achieve its goals, it has not violated the legislation (Employment Equity Act, ss.12, 28(2); Waldorf, 1994). Moreover, the legislation addresses unions' concern that employment equity not be used to undermine the principle of seniority. It makes it clear that seniority rights for layoffs or a recall to work after layoff are not considered to be barriers to equity. Other seniority rights are not to be considered barriers unless a board of inquiry, under the Ontario Human Rights Code, decides that a particular seniority right discriminates against members of a designated group.

One of the most striking aspects of the Employment Equity Act is its failure to provide for any serious conflict of interest among employers, unions, and designated groups on the way to achieving employment equity. However, from the government's perspective, this is not a failure, since it does not perceive the existence of any serious conflict of interest between these groups (Waldorf, 1994). The NDP government places employment equity in the context of economic renewal. From its perspective, "in tough economic times, it makes sense for every employer to run as productive an operation as possible. Employment equity will help tap sources of ability and talent that have been held in check by discrimination" (Ontario Ministry of Citizenship, 1993, p. 2). Employment equity is portrayed as actually assisting in the economic rationalization of business practices. Equality of opportunity, rather than equality of condition, is the operative premise of the legislation (Employment Equity Act, s.11(3), (4)).

Employment Equity and Restructuring

It is precisely the current legislation's emphasis on equality of opportunity that undermines its ability to improve substantially the working conditions of women and other designated groups. Employment equity will do nothing to halt the shrinkage in the share of employment in large firms and the increase in non-standard employment. The chief problem with the legislation is that it ignores the fragmentation and feminization of the labour market.

The most optimistic prognosis for the labour market is that employment in large firms will expand slightly as the economy recovers. This means that employment equity will take some years to effect the composition of the work force in large firms. The assumption is that, as older workers leave standard jobs in large firms, they will be replaced by workers from the equity target groups. Meanwhile, the removal of barriers to training and promotion within an employer's work force should foster the upward mobility of those members of designated groups who already are employed. To the extent that employment equity is successful in these respects, we should see an increasing polarization within the labour markets of the designated groups. But employment equity will do nothing for the vast majority of equity seekers who are likely to find employment in small firms that fall outside of the scope of the legislation. While the act applies to approximately 75 percent of Ontario's work force, it does not apply to those employees in small workplaces who are most in need of it. This is particularly troubling since the share of employment in small firms is growing. And it is precisely these firms that are characterized by low wage rates, little chance for promotion, and few, if any, benefits. More troubling, employment equity will do nothing for the workers who will be confined to non-standard work—the fastest growing form of employment. The problem is that the legislation ignores the overall deterioration in the conditions of and payment for work.

CONCLUSION

Since its election, the NDP government in Ontario has been preoccupied with the project of economic renewal. That this is the case is not surprising, given that the social democratic party achieved its first electoral victory in Ontario as the province's economy plunged into the depths of its worst recession. By towing the line on government spending and demonstrating its willingness to get tough with public-sector unions, the NDP government has sought to persuade private investors that the province's economy is a good risk. In this way, it hopes to generate sufficient private investment to create enough jobs to put the thousands of unemployed people in the province back to work.

What distinguishes the NDP government of Ontario from its neoconservative counterparts elsewhere has been its emphasis on a social-equity agenda. But the government has not explicitly articulated what it means by "social equity." It has largely ceded the battle over the appropriate role of the state in directing the economy to the private sector. In doing so, it has promoted an understanding of equity that is almost exclusively identified with equality of opportunity. The decisions of private investors to maximize their profits will shape the labour market. To the extent that firms choose to organize production in ways that lower the costs of labour, the Ontario government has decided not intervene. Despite the opportunity to do so, it has failed either to make it significantly easier to unionize small workplaces or to impose effective regulatory standards upon non-standard employment. Instead, it has focussed on introducing legislation designed to equalize opportunities for employment for equity seekers at a time when the condition of employment for the majority of people is declining.

Equality of opportunity for women, who have historically been denied access to good jobs, is an important goal. However, a preoccupation with equalizing employment opportunities at the same time as the labour market is deteriorating for the majority of working people does nothing to resolve the underlying distributional problem. Put simply, the majority of jobs being created today are bad jobs. At best, pay and employment equity will intensify the polarization of the labour market for women and other equity seekers. Women, aboriginal people, people with disabilities, and members of visible minorities who are fortunate enough either to be employed or find employment in the public sector or large firms may well benefit from pay and employment equity. But, as we have seen, the extent to which they will be able to do so depends upon a range of factors beyond their control. For the majority of workers who are entering the current labour market, equality of opportunity simply means the opportunity to work at jobs that are hard to unionize, pay little, and provide even less in the way of benefits.

Attention to the gendered dimension of both employment and labour-market policy is crucial at the present time, when the male standard of employment is in decline. The restructuring of the labour market, its fragmentation and feminization, has not been gender-neutral. As a consequence, gender relations are also being restructured. It is crucial to recognize this because "it is only by understanding the extent to which a new set of gendered relations are at the heart of restructured economies that we can begin to comprehend that restructuring ... and the space there is within it for generating equality" (Jenson, 1993, p. 1). Gender-sensitive policy analysis suggests that it is necessary to invigorate the political meaning of equity to include concerns about the type of employment opportunities being created for women and all marginalized groups.

REFERENCES

Armstrong, P., and Armstrong, H. (1994). *The double ghetto* (3d ed.). Toronto: McClelland and Stewart.

Armstrong, P. (in press). The feminization of the labour force: Harmonizing down in a global economy. In I. Bakker (Ed.), *Changing space, gender and economic restructuring*.

Armstrong, H. (1993). The Re-organization of work. In W.R. Hanna and C. Cockerton (Eds.), *Humanities: Self, society and culture* (4th ed.) (pp. 102–109). Toronto: Thompson Educational Press.

Bakker, I. (1991). Pay equity and economic restructuring: The polarization of policy. In J. Fudge and P. McDermott (Eds.), *Just wages*, (pp. 253–280). Toronto: University of Toronto Press.

Boyd, M.; Mulvihill, M.; and Myles, J. (1991). Gender, power and post-industrialism. *Canadian Review of Sociology and Anthropology, 28*(4), 406–436.

Brown, C.; Hamilton, J.; and Medoff, J. (1990). *Employers large and small.* Cambridge, MA: Harvard University Press.

Cohen, M. (1992). The feminization of the labour market: Prospects for the 1990s. In D. Drache (Ed.), *Getting on track* (pp. 105–123). Montreal and Kingston: McGill–Queen's University Press.

Collins, H. (1990). Ascription of legal responsibility to groups in complex patterns of economic integration. *Modern Law Review, 53* (6), 731–744.

Cuneo, C. (1990). *Pay equity.* Toronto: Oxford University Press.

Cuneo, C. (1991). The state of pay equity: Mediating gender and class through political parties in Ontario. In J. Fudge and P. McDermott (Eds.), *Just wages* (pp. 33–59). Toronto: University of Toronto Press.

Economic Council of Canada. (1990). *Good jobs, bad jobs.* Ottawa: Minister of Supply and Services.

Economic Council of Canada. (1991). *Employment in the service economy.* Ottawa: Minister of Supply and Services.

Findlay, S. (1991). Making sense of pay equity: Issues for a feminist political practice. In J. Fudge and P. McDermott (Eds.), *Just wages* (pp. 81–109). Toronto: University of Toronto Press.

Fudge, J. (1991a). *Labour law's little sister: The Employment Standards Act and the feminization of labour.* Ottawa: Canadian Centre for Policy Alternatives.

Fudge, J. (1991b). Reconceiving employment standards legislation: Labour law's little sister and the feminization of labour. *Journal of Law and Social Policy, 7*, 73–89.

Fudge, J. (1993). The gendered dimension of labour law: Why women need inclusive unionism and broader-based bargaining. In L. Briskin and P. McDermott (Eds.), *Women challenging unions,* (pp. 231–248). Toronto: University of Toronto Press.

Fudge, J., and McDermott, P. (1991). Pay equity in a declining economy. In J. Fudge and P. McDermott (Eds.), *Just wages,* (pp. 281–288). Toronto: University of Toronto Press.

Glasbeek, H. (1993). Agenda for Canadian labour law reform: A little liberal law, much more democratic socialist politics. *Osgoode Hall Law Journal, 31*(2), 233–263.

Harrison, B. (1994). The myth of small firms as the predominant job generators. *Economic Development Quarterly, 8*(1), 3–18.

Jenson, J. (1989). "Different" but not "exceptional": Canada's permeable Fordism. *Canadian Review of Sociology and Anthropology, 26*(1), 69–94.

Jenson, J. (1993, February). Part-time employment and women: A range of strategies. Paper presented at the Economic Equality Workshop, sponsored by the Status of Women Canada, Ottawa.

Legislative Assembly of Ontario, 3rd Session, 35th Parliament (1993, December). *Hansard.* Ottawa: Queen's Printer.

Manley, J. (The Minister of Industry), and Martin, P. (The Minister of Finance). (1994). *Growing small businesses.* Ottawa: Industry Canada.

McCallum, M. (1986). Keeping women in their place: The minimum wage in Canada. *Labour/Le Travail, 17,* 29–56.

McColgan, A. (1993). Legislation pay equity? Lessons from Canada. *Industrial Law Journal, 22*(4), 269–286.

Morissette, R. (1991). Are jobs in large firms better jobs? *Perspectives on Labour and Income in Canada,* 40–50.

Muckenberger, U. (1989). Non-standard forms of work and the role of change in labour and social security regulation. *International Journal of the Sociology of Law, 17,* 381–402.

O'Grady, J. (1992). Beyond the Wagner Act. In D. Drache (Ed.), *Getting on track* (pp. 153–169). Montreal and Kingston: McGill–Queen's University Press.

Office of the Employment Equity Commissioner. (1992). Opening doors: A report on the employment equity consultations. Ontario: Queen's Printer.

Ontario Ministry of Citizenship. (1993, December). *Questions and answers on the Employment Equity Act.* Toronto.

Panitch, L., and Swartz, D. (1993). *The assault on trade union freedoms: From wage controls to social contract.* Toronto: Garamond.

Phillips, P., and Phillips, E. (1993). *Women & work* (rev. ed.). Toronto: James Lorimer.

Pierson, R. (1986). *They're still women after all: The Second World War and Canadian womanhood.* Toronto: McClelland and Stewart.

Porter, A. (1993). Women and income security in the post-war period: The case of unemployment insurance, 1945–1962. *Labour/Le Travail, 31,* 111–144.

Rubery, J. (1988). Women and recession: A comparative perspective. In J. Rubery (Ed.), *Women and Recession* (pp. 253–286). London: Routledge and Kegan Paul.

Russell, R. (1991). A fair or minimum wage? Women workers, the state, and the origins of wage regulation in Western Canada. *Labour/Le Travail, 28*, 59–88.

Urban Dimensions Group (1989). *Growth of the contingent workforce in Ontario: Structural trends, statistical dimensions and policy implications.* Toronto: Ontario Women's Directorate.

Ursel, J. (1992). *Private lives, public policy: 100 years of state intervention in the family.* Toronto: Women's Press.

Waldorf, L. (1994). *Ontario's equity laws: What remains of the pursuit of economic justice after workplace harmonization?* Manuscript submitted for publication.

White, J. (1980). *Women and unions.* Ottawa: The Canadian Advisory Council on the Status of Women.

White, J. (1993). Patterns of unionization. In L. Briskin and P. McDermott (Eds.), *Women challenging unions* (pp. 191–206). Toronto: University of Toronto Press.

SUGGESTED READING

Armstrong, Pat, and Armstrong, Hugh. (1994). *The double ghetto* (3d ed.), Toronto: McClelland and Stewart.

Duffy, Ann, and Pupo, Norene. (1992). *Part-time paradox: Connecting gender, work and family.* Toronto: McClelland and Stewart.

Economic Council of Canada. (1990). *Good jobs, bad jobs.* Ottawa: Minister of Supply and Services.

Phillips, Paul, and Phillips, Erin. (1993). *Women and work.* Toronto: James Lorimer.

Ursel, Jane. (1992). *Private lives, public policy: 100 years of state intervention in the family.* Toronto: Women's Press.

QUESTIONS TO CONSIDER

1. What is the difference between equality of opportunity and equality of condition? How has this difference effected employment equity legislation? Why?

2. What is meant by the "feminization" of the labour market? Centre your discussion around the problems of occupational segregation, the polarization of the labour market, and the uneven impacts for women.

3. During the current era of restructuring, there has been a steady growth in the number of small businesses in Canada. What implications does this have for women workers? Why?

CHAPTER 3

Pay and Employment Equity: Why Separate Policies?

Patricia McDermott

The undervaluation of women's work and discrimination in employment practices have been on the Canadian public-policy agenda for decades. Yet, despite the interdependent nature of these persistent features of our labour market, they have been structured by the state as separate social problems that require distinct solutions. Policies related to **pay equity** are aimed at the wage gap between men and women, while those related to **employment equity** seek to redress discriminatory employment practices, especially hiring, promotion, and retention. Both remedial legislation and feminist organizing have been shaped by this dichotomy.

Even though not reflected in policy practices, these phenomena are inherently interrelated. The significantly lower pay of female workers, demonstrated by a long-standing wage gap in Canada of between 30 and 35 percent, is directly related to the dramatic occupational segregation of women and men in the workplace. Nevertheless, in Canada, as elsewhere, policy-makers have treated these issues as distinct. For example, the United States, Australia, New Zealand, and many members states of the European Union have put in place separate legislative initiatives and separate government-sponsored programs to address systemic inequity in employment opportunity and discriminatory pay practices. In the United States, the "comparable worth" movement for equal pay for work of equal value was shaped by the parameters of the 1963 Equal Pay Act, while **affirmative action** programs, aimed as well at racial discrimination, were fought for and implemented under the Title VII amendment to the U.S. Civil Rights Act (1964). A similar development occurred in Britain, where the government responded to the problem of unequal pay by passing the 1979 Equal Pay Act and addressed employment equity issues under the Anti-Discrimination Act of 1975.

The province of Ontario offers a unique setting in which to assess how these two equity goals have operated separately; in this jurisdiction, in recent years, two, arguably quite advanced, statutes have been passed to redress the issues of gender-based pay inequality, as well as discrimination in employment opportunities. The Pay Equity Act, which came into force 1988, has been heralded as the most advanced pay-discrimination legislation in the world (*New York Times*, July 27, 1989). In 1994, the Ontario legislature also passed the Employment Equity Act, again one of the first "proactive" statutes in any industrialized nation aimed at eliminating barriers to hiring and promotion for four "designated groups," including women, that have historically experienced discriminatory employment practices.

This essay attempts to answer several questions. How have the solutions to these interrelated problems been shaped as separate? Second, has this two-pronged approach helped further the goal of improving the position of women in terms of pay and employment equality? Would combining these two policies have been more beneficial? It is, of course, always easier to speculate, after the fact, on how things could have been done differently; however, the persistent and universal nature of the separation of these two related goals deserves careful study because, as I will argue, this separation in itself could become a barrier to equality for women.

A HISTORICAL LOOK AT THE ISSUES IN CANADA

The historical roots of the concept of pay equity go back to a much more straightforward concept that remained on the Canadian public-policy agenda well into the 1950s—namely, the concept of "equal pay for equal work." The earliest public concern about the lower wages of women workers came initially from craft unions. In the 1880s several male-dominated craft unions moved from what they had consistently demanded until that time—a "family wage" for male breadwinners—to advocate equal pay for equal work for women. The motivation for this move, according to Canadian historian Leo Johnson, is quite suspect. The apparent change of strategy on the part of these unionists clearly came less from concern about unequal pay for women workers than from the fear that the established practice of paying women less for the same work would clearly operate to erode male wages. As Johnson notes of male trade unionists in nineteenth-century Ontario:

> The initial reaction of the male workers to the employment of women and children had been to oppose equal wages for them.... Finally cooler heads among the craft workers began to prevail. Rather than opposing equal wages for women, they believed that men should make equal

> wages for women a key demand. Women ..., they argued, were naturally inferior workers and to enforce lower wages for them simply had the effect of making their labour competitive to that of men. If employers were required to pay equal wages for women ... the result would ultimately exclude women from the labour market. (1974, p. 29)

This demand for equal wages for women doing the same work as men has historically been accompanied by a series of protective legislative measures around issues such as hours of work (including restrictions on shift work), restrictions on weight to be lifted, and prohibitions regarding the type of work women could do, such as mining. These protective measures both discouraged employers from hiring women and further entrenched the gendered segmentation of the labour market. The passage of such legislation as the Factory, Shops and Mining Operations Act required special regulations, facilities, and hours, and involved additional surveillance from factory inspectors. As Jane Ursel has argued, the "creation of legal distinctions between male and female labour created economic and political disincentives for employers tempted to extend the use of cheap female labour into traditionally 'male' occupations" (1984, p. 541).

What was the result of these trends? Women primarily tended to continue doing different work from that done by men. "Women's work" has come to be characterized culturally as easier, less demanding, and less skilled—in other words, it has been undervalued. It should also be noted that increased interest in protective legislation for women resurfaced when men returning from both World Wars wanted to reclaim their jobs. As part of the war effort, women had flooded into these so-called "non-traditional" occupational areas, such as construction, mining, agriculture, and especially manufacturing—a historical fact often overlooked when the gendered segmentation of the labour market is analyzed (Department of Labour, 1959, p. 5) Thus, from at least the 1880s in Ontario, the two issues of unequal pay and the gendered segmentation of the labour market were closely intertwined. Male workers have promoted equal pay for women to perpetuate a segmented labour market and their economically advantageous position within it.

THE ROOTS OF PAY EQUITY LEGISLATION

The best way to describe the history of legislation in Canada that is directed at reducing the persistent gender-based wage gap is to discuss the three trends in legislative reform, (see Box 3.1).

The Universal Declaration of Human Rights adopted by the General Assembly of the United Nations in 1948 stated that "everyone, without any discrimination, has the right to equal pay for equal work" (s. 23.2). This principle was eventually formulated by the International Labour

---

BOX 3.1

Three Trends in Legislative Reform

▶   the initial "equal pay for equal work" approach, which is also referred to as "equal work" legislation

▶   the subsequent "equal pay for work of equal value" initiative, or "equal value" legislation

▶   the recent wave of "pay equity" legislation introduced, to date, in five Canadian jurisdictions (McDermott, 1993)

Office, an agency of the United Nations, as "equal pay for work of equal value in the case of men and women" and was enshrined as Convention 100. Member states of the United Nations were asked to become signatories to this convention in 1951. Canada became a signatory nation but responded with only a half-measure—namely, a coast-to-coast wave of "equal pay for equal work" legislation, clearly not comparable to the equal-value standard. These provisions were "complaint-based," meaning that they required employees to initiate actions against their employers, a feature that has greatly diminished the effectiveness of equal pay legislation. Moreover, until the mid-1970s, equal-pay complaints could be made only if the jobs being compared were identical. In 1970, a court decision in Ontario found that female nurses' aides and male hospital orderlies, although not doing exactly the same jobs, were performing "substantially the same work" within the meaning of the statute (*R.* v. *Howard*, Exp. Toronto (Metro) (1970), 13 D.L.R. (3d) 451). This decision resulted in the legislative standard in Ontario, and eventually in other provinces, becoming "equal pay for *substantially* the same work" (Employment Standards Act, s. 33.1).

Although this standard broadened the scope of the equal-pay remedy, the method of determining what would be considered "substantially equal" remained quite restrictive. Basically, the jobs done by women and men had to involve substantially the same skill, effort, responsibility, and working conditions. These four factors, it should be mentioned, are the universally accepted standard used to assess the value of work. Thus, even though "substantially the same" measure was employed, a job done by a woman that involved, say, more skill but less responsibility than a similar job done by a man, would not trigger remedial action. The jobs had to be found equivalent on each factor and not on the overall evaluation score.

The equal pay provisions throughout Canada have also included exemptions such as merit systems, which allow an employer to justify a pay differential that would otherwise be found discriminatory under the legislation. The restrictive method of defining "substantially the same," the complaint-based structure of the legislation, and the exemptions have operated to make Canadian equal pay laws relatively ineffective, even in the limited areas where men and women do the same type of work. The major reason why equal pay laws have not been able to reduce the wage gap in any significant way, however, is the high degree of gender segregation of the labour market. The increasing realization that, on the whole, men and women tend to do different work, in largely different sectors of the economy, has generated a push for "equal value" legislation that would redress systemic wage discrimination by ensuring that pay for "women's work" is based on what that work is worth, both to the employer and to society.

Only three Canadian jurisdictions—those of the federal government, the province of Quebec, and the Yukon Territory—introduced "equal pay for work of equal *value*" legislation in the late 1970s. Again, the method of comparing jobs has involved a job-evaluation process that uses the four standard factors noted above. The *total* evaluation score, however, and not the rating for each factor, is compared. Since equivalency for each factor is not necessary, as it is under the "equal work" standard, *completely different* jobs can be compared. This ability to compare so-called apples and oranges represents the most significant feature of the move from "equal work" to "equal value" legislation.

The federal government's equal-value scheme, codified in federal human-rights legislation (s. 11 of the Canadian Human Rights Code), introduced the closely related concepts of "occupational groups" and "gender predominance" into its provisions. Rooted in the notion of "systemic discrimination," both requirements that a complaint be remedied for a homogeneous occupational group and that the group have a majority of female incumbents set the stage for future "proactive" pay equity legislation. In essence, the gender-predominance concept acknowledges the reality that a highly segregated labour force is at the heart of wage discrimination. It is here that one clearly sees how interrelated discriminatory pay and employment practices are; yet, this legislation is aimed only at the wage component of discrimination.

It should be noted that the "equal value" legislation is still complaint-based and contains a list of exemptions, similar to those found in the "equal work" provisions, that can be used to justify an arguably discriminatory wage practice. For example, if the women workers in a factory are on a piece-rate wage system and the male workers, despite their doing jobs of equal value, are not on a piece-rate system, a claim for unfair wages cannot be made. In over a decade and a half, the equal-value provisions have not proved effective in significantly narrowing the wage gap. In the federal arena, for example, the Canadian Human Rights Commission has handled only approximately a dozen "equal value" cases since the provisions came into force in 1978. Although these cases have resulted in some significant wage increases for those involved, the activity under this initiative is unlikely to bring about a significant reduction in the wage gap for federally regulated employees covered by the provisions. The recent trend among equal-pay advocates and some policy-makers is to move to a *proactive* pay equity model that shifts the onus for eliminating discriminatory pay practices onto the employer rather than placing the burden solely on employees, who tend to be reluctant to bring a complaint against their employer.

The first Canadian jurisdiction to pass a proactive Pay Equity Act was Manitoba (1984); Ontario, Prince Edward Island, New Brunswick, and Nova Scotia followed over the next four years. Basically, Canadian proactive systems, patterned after legislative schemes in the United States, particularly Minnesota's, operate by evaluating all "female- and male-dominated jobs" (a term defined in each act) and comparing them to ensure that the workers in the female and male jobs are being paid according to the same measure of value. In other words, if, after an evaluation process, a female job is found to have the same value as a comparable male job, and the pay for the female job is lower, pay equity legislation would require that the wages for the female job be raised to equal those of the male. Thus, proactive pay equity differs in a fundamental way from "equal work" and "equal value" legislation, both of which are complaint-based. Under pay equity legislation, employees do not have to initiate complaints; rather, it is the responsibility of employers to demonstrate that they are not engaged in discriminatory pay practices.

Given the complex nature of statutory pay equity schemes, it is difficult to describe the legislation briefly. Suffice it to say that the wage adjustments actually delivered under pay equity implementation exercises are often very disappointing indeed, because of how the legislation is structured. For example, since the pay equity legislation in Canada is focussed solely on gender and not race, the "male comparator" selected for an undervalued female job class could represent a male job class whose wages are low because of discrimination on the basis of race or ethnicity. Rather than addressing the inequity of both the occupational segregation and the undervaluation for both men and women in all racial and ethnic groups, the current legislation creates an artificial world in which it is assumed all men, despite their race or ethnicity, are paid significantly more than women.

The Ontario Pay Equity Act, it should be mentioned, is unique in Canada in that it covers both public- and private-sector employers (all the other proactive statutes apply only to public-sector employers). The Ontario act is, unfortunately, also unique for the low standard of equity it delivers. For instance, if a female-dominated job class in the job-comparison scheme is seeking a male comparator of equal value, and if there is more than one male comparator available, the female job class receives the lowest wage of all the possible male comparators. This one fact alone highlights the problem of not introducing basic concepts of discriminatory treatment of those groups, who, as noted above, receive lower wages precisely because of their race or ethnicity.

THE ROOTS OF EMPLOYMENT EQUITY LEGISLATION

The legislative origins of employment equity law in Canada are based primarily in American case law, launched under the Title VII amendment to the U.S. Civil Rights Act, as mentioned earlier. Indeed, the most important decision for the development of Canadian legislation and employment equity programs is the American case *Griggs* v. *Duke Power Co.* (401 U.S., 424 [1971]), which went all the way to the U.S. Supreme Court. This case was a godsend to those advocating the need for affirmative-action measures. It was about a group of Black male workers who were hired by the Duke Power Company in North Carolina. This company was found to have engaged in discriminatory behaviour against its Black employees. For instance, Black workers were never promoted beyond the lowest-paid department in the firm. The aptitude tests that they were required to write were found to be discriminatory for disadvantaged Black employees, given the well-documented inequities Blacks face in the educational system in the area and, indeed, throughout the United States.

One of the most important principles set out in the *Griggs* decision was that of "bona fide occupational qualification." It was found that the aptitude tests used by Duke Power did not, in fact, measure success on the jobs in question but were merely, found the Supreme Court, "built-in headwinds" to prevent a fair and open competition for hiring and promotion. Undoubtedly, the most important finding in the *Griggs* case, however, was that, for the first time ever, a senior court in a common-law jurisdiction found that the employer did not have to engage consciously in wilful discrimination to be held accountable. Even when discriminatory behaviour was deemed unintentional, the outcomes of any such actions could still be discrimination. Thus, the legal stage was set for the fundamental and critical legal concept of "systemic discrimination."

It was not long after the *Griggs* decision that a Canadian women's organization, Action Travail des Femmes, launched a similar case against the Canadian National Railway, claiming systemic barriers to the higher-paid, so-called non-traditional trade jobs in CN's car-maintenance yards. In an uncannily similar set of facts, involving some of the same mechanical aptitude tests as figured in the *Griggs* case, the Supreme Court of Canada followed the same judicial reasoning and found CN to have engaged in discriminatory employment practices—whether intentionally or otherwise. The Court fashioned a remedy that set a standard for Canadian employment equity initiatives for a decade to come.

The company was to take concrete steps to attract female applicants. Job advertisements were to be placed in women's as well as men's washrooms in the company buildings. Women applicants who approached the firm were to be systematically encouraged to consider these jobs, rather than being discouraged from applying for them. Candidates were to be evaluated only on the basis of bona fide occupational requirements and were not to be administered tests that were unrelated to job performance and that disadvantaged women, who tended to have less "mechanical" training than men and whose physical strength, on average, tended also to be less than men's. In other words, the Court was saying that it was allright to test for physical strength as long as those currently doing the job were required to have a specific level of strength. The judgement also required CN to hire a number of female workers that was equal to those doing non-traditional work in the surrounding labour market.

The CN case clearly contributed to the introduction of the 1986 Employment Equity Act that covers employers in the federal jurisdiction—about 10 percent of the Canadian work force. This act has been greatly criticized since its introduction for "having no teeth." Basically, this statute requires that federally regulated employers collect work force data once a year on the four designated groups (disabled persons, aboriginal persons, visible minorities, and women) and file it with the federal government. The scheme is essentially "self-regulating," with each employer deciding its own goals and targets. There are few penalties possible under the act, and those sanctions available are rarely imposed. The federal government also introduced a non-statutorily based federal contractors' compliance program, which requires an employer wanting to do business with the federal government (for contracts valued at more than $200 000) to be "in compliance" with the goals of the employment equity program.

The federal Employment Equity Act and the contractors' compliance program have been most effective in getting employers to collect data about their hiring, retention, and promotion of employees from the four designated groups; however, it is unclear whether these initiatives have been effective in increasing representation. Since the legislation and the program were introduced during a recession, economic hardship was regularly used as an excuse by employers who had made little progress toward even their own, often modest, self-designed and -imposed targets.

Like the federal statute, Ontario's recently passed (1994) Employment Equity Act also refers to the four designated groups as a core operational concept. It should be noted that the Ontario act uses the category "racial minority," while the federal statute employs the term "visible minority." The Ontario act is somewhat more aggressive in terms of placing the onus on employers to remove barriers to the hiring and promotion of the designated groups, and also stipulates some monetary sanctions.

Again, like the federal legislation, the Ontario act essentially requires that employers collect data and monitor their own progress in the advancement of each designated group within each category. There is no direct mention of wages in the statute.

HOW DID THESE INITIATIVES GET SEPARATED?

When one looks back at the history of pay and employment equity legislation, it is difficult to see just how and why these two policy initiatives became separated. From the vantage point of Canada in the 1990s, it appears that the early employment equity legislation, especially at the federal level, was greatly influenced by the affirmative action programs so popular in the United States, especially for Black workers. These programs were directly linked to the civil-rights movement and began to flourish after the landmark case of *Griggs* in 1971, launched, as discussed earlier, under Title VII of the Civil Rights Act. Indeed, throughout the 1970s in the United States, the term "affirmative action" was much more closely affiliated with race than with gender. The legal notion of "systemic discrimination" was subsequently adopted by women's groups in both the United States and Canada. Indeed, as was discussed, the *CN* case in Canada was, over a decade later, almost an exact replica of the *Griggs* case, except discrimination against women instead of Blacks was proved. Thus, although early employment equity initiatives in Canada had primarily focussed on gender, race had always been affiliated with such programs. Also, the federal employment equity legislation was drafted after the Canadian Charter of Rights and Freedoms, which acknowledged Canada as a multicultural nation, came into force in 1981. Therefore, it is not surprising that the legislation introduced the concept of designated groups, based, in part, on race.

Since the early focus on employment equity legislation patterned itself after the U.S. model, the goal of the legislation was primarily about *integration* of Blacks and Whites—not just at work, as was the focus of the *Griggs* case, but in housing and educational institutions as well. The Canadian feminist organization Action Travail des Femmes, which launched the *CN* case, similarly focussed on integration of women into men's jobs. These jobs were known to be far better paid, although, it was beginning to be acknowledged, not necessarily as highly skilled as had been formerly assumed. Indeed, the *CN* case details some of the supposed "requirements" for the CN jobs, which the Supreme Court of Canada found not to be "bona fide occupational qualifications."

In postwar Europe, the focus on equality was on wages. For example, as noted earlier, the International Labour Office (ILO), a United Nations agency mandated to issue international labour standards after the Second World War, emphasized pay, not anti-discrimination, initiatives. This is not to say that employment equity received no attention in European countries. Britain, for example, passed the Anti-Discrimination Act in 1975, but again, as in Canada in the 1970s, the initial focus of "positive action" programs (the British term for "affirmative action") was gender not race.

As noted earlier, the ILO's universal declarations on equal pay for work of equal value played an important role in shaping the direction of equality legislation around unequal wages in Canada throughout the 1950s—in the shape of the half-hearted "equal pay for equal work" provisions passed into provincial employment-standards legislation. Thus, it may be that originators of the policy initiatives adopted in Canada—the United States, for employment equity, and Europe, for pay equity—shaped the primary focus of these schemes in Canada.

The separation of these two policy initiatives, however, was in some ways, unconscious. In the early 1980s, the policy separation of pay and employment equity, at least in Ontario, for example, was not conceptually clear or complete. The Abella Commission on Equality in Employment blurred the line between "employment equity," the new term coined by the commission, and what was still called at the time "equal pay." Indeed, the commission saw "equal pay as an integral element in the implementation of employment equity" (Abella, 1984, p. 232). However, the commission's thrust, which clearly influenced the shape of the federal Employment Equity Act passed in 1986, was the implementation of a program based on the hiring and promotion of designated groups and not the pay of these groups. The targets and goals emphasized under such schemes solely related to hiring and promotion and not to unfair wage practices.

WHY NOT COMBINE THESE SOCIAL GOALS?

As mentioned earlier, pay equity legislation in Ontario can potentially deliver to women a wage adjustment that is seriously depressed, since the comparator could be a group of male workers who are underpaid because of race or ethnicity. Also, what about female job classes for whom the wage scale is even more depressed because workers who comprise those job classes are primarily racial- or ethnic-minority women? Why should they be compared with their similarly disadvantaged brothers? And what about the underpaid men? Why should discriminatory wage legislation leave them out in the cold? Clearly something is wrong here. Many U.S. comparable-worth exercises factored in race as an obvious element in the calculation of the undervaluation of women's work, and many U.S. pay-equity exercises included racial groups in the process. That the Ontario Pay Equity Act did not indicates a clear lack of commitment to both reduce the gender-based wage gap and redress discriminatory wage practices for both male and female workers of all races, ethnicities, and abilities. The act, a compromise from the outset, was clearly designed to spare employers the full impact of equity legislation.

At a practical, implementation level, a strong argument could be made that the same job-information data are being collected, especially with regard to female job classes, over and over again. This is a time-consuming and costly exercise. At the very least, Ontario's Employment Equity Act should have been designed to build on a pay equity exercise. Once you see clusters of women in the lowest pay ranks of an organization's hierarchical structure, and also find that their jobs are more valuable, insofar as more skill and responsibility are involved than they are being paid for, why does this group need to find a male comparator? Instead, ideal legislation would move their wages up in relation to those of other employees, male or female, *and* then start an employment equity exercise.

Furthermore, how can the barriers to obviously underutilized groups be remedied? How can more women from these groups enter the higher levels of the organization's occupational structure more quickly? What kind of training do they need to access the organization's currently higher-paying jobs? If a female-dominated group is lucky enough to receive a pay adjustment under Ontario's Pay Equity Act, why should they stay stuck at the bottom of the organization's structure?

The gendered nature of "women's work" is also a very revealing phenomenon. Characteristically, women's jobs are the low-paid ones, at the bottom of both the wage and the occupational structures of a firm. They are often dead-end jobs that offer little in terms of advancement or training opportunities. They also have an uncanny similarity to the work women do at home. One could compellingly argue that this is no coincidence, if the goal is to make a patriarchal societal system function smoothly. Little girls are socialized to work at taking care of and serving people, cleaning, cooking, and engaging in repetitive, "never-ending" work typical of that done in the home. Thus, they need no "training" in the world of wage labour. Their skills for such work are "innate"—a classic argument in the theoretical understanding of how women's work becomes socially undervalued. Women are thus paid less for this work and, it could be argued, made more dependent on male wages in the home. This situation also feeds into unequal power relationships on the domestic front, whereby the male breadwinner's job is more important, and accommodations—such as who has use of the car, whose commuting time should be factored into relocation decisions, and who should stay home when the children are ill—can flow from the fact that one person makes significantly more money than another. Thus, lower pay can function to keep women, as much as possible, tied to the home, carrying out traditional domestic duties and engaged in "secondary" wage earning, which can result in their having less power over an array of fundamental decisions within the home.

The argument that a segmented labour market and the wage gap support the patriarchal family structure is also reflected in the reality of the workplace. Women do different, supposedly less valuable, work, from that done by men. Thus, men and women do not work together. They are literally kept separate and apart in many workplaces, and throughout much of the labour market. Thus, when a phenomenon like sexual harassment in the workplace is analyzed in this broader context, it can be seen as a tool for literally "keeping women in their place"— separate, doing different and underpaid work. If they venture into a male terrain, they could be harassed as a reminder that they have ventured into territory in which they do not belong.

The tendency to see unequal pay and discriminatory employment practices as two separate problems, operates to blur the reality of what is occurring and makes the solutions fragmented and less effective. The insistence on separating these issues also makes even those who advocate the advancement of women's equality structure their demands in less powerful ways. A good example of this is the well-known *Sears* case in the United States: the American Equal Opportunities Commission launched the case against the retail giant Sears because the largely female retail clerks who worked at Sears had unequal access to the much-better-paid commissioned salespersons jobs, dominated by men.

At first glance *Sears* looks primarily like an employment equity case—a group of women at the bottom of the system trying to get access to a better job, in terms of career advancement and, of course, pay. A closer examination, one that would involve a careful study of the duties of both the retail clerks and the commissioned sales personnel, however, would reveal that the jobs are virtually the same. A case could even be made that the women retail clerks work harder; carry more responsibility for customer "goodwill" for the organization; and, in terms of the dollars brought into the corporation, do work that is of more value to Sears. Ironically, the men sold many so-called big-ticket items that probably could be sold more effectively by women, who, because of their traditional domestic responsibilities, are likely to have more comprehensive "product knowledge" about "big-ticket" merchandise, such as refrigerators, stoves, carpeting, and furniture, than would male commissioned sales personnel.

So why did Sears not want a significant proportion of women in commissioned sales? The decision clearly had nothing to do with this essentially identical work being more skilled, complex, or difficult, but had a great deal to do with Sears's corporate strategy of having men dominate the upper levels of the corporate hierarchy. If they kept the pool of commissioned sales personnel largely male and then drew their management trainees from it, the logic emerges as flawless. Thus, the "employment equity" aspect of the *Sears* case becomes understandable. The women face a barrier to equal access to better-paying jobs because of the corporate desire to maintain a largely male management cadre. We cannot, however, forget that the jobs in the management ranks are not only higher paid, but truly "better" jobs, involving more skill and responsibility. These are the jobs that the women sales clerks are really being prevented from achieving. No experience in commissioned sales could be seen as an unfair barrier to achieving a management position. An employment equity solution would involve Sears removing this discriminatory barrier, accepting similar retail work as appropriate work experience, and recruiting a proportionate number of retail clerks into management-training positions.

It also has to be kept in mind that the work done by the primarily female retail clerks was actually of equal value when compared with that of the male-dominated commissioned sales positions; thus, this is an interrelated "equal pay for work of equal value" case. If women retail clerks are doing as valuable work in terms of skill and responsibility as the men in commissioned sales, why not *pay* them more? Why should the women retail clerks have to move across the aisle from Linens to Appliances to double their salary when the work they are doing in Linens is just as valuable?

The *Griggs* case was not simply about Black workers getting out of the lowest-paid department in the Duke Power Company and into jobs with more responsibilities and skills, but also about getting into better-paying jobs. Similarly, the *CN* case was not just about women getting into the car-maintenance yards, but about making more money. Employment equity concerns have to be assessed in the context of unequal wages. Why accept that an employer has "made progress" in hiring and promotion goals unless the measure of success is directly tied to wages? What is the point, other than defeating the purpose of equity legislation, of creating a new management category and paying those in it the same amount or only marginally more than they were making previously? What of the employer who hires members of the designated groups who, because of systemic discrimination, will work for less? Should this practice be rewarded by a government employment equity agency? Again, wage data have to be factored into how we measure success.

CONCLUSION

This essay has argued that employment and pay equity legislation have to operate together to be effective. I have also suggested that the separation of these two goals, to the extent that it obfuscates the role that both unequal pay and the gendered segmentation of the labour market play in strengthening our patriarchal system, harms the pursuit of full equality for women workers. Sometimes it is difficult to see how legislation could have been structured differently to deliver a much higher degree of equality. In the Ontario context, the Pay Equity and Employment Equity acts came to us already shaped by politics or compromise. It is important to realize that putting these two concepts together makes them not only a powerful explanatory device, but a tool that would decrease the possibility that equality will slip through the cracks, as it so often does in the arena of equity litigation and lobbying.

REFERENCES

Abella, Judge Rosalie Silberman, Commissioner. (1984). *Equality in employment: A royal commission report*, Vol. 1. Ottawa: Supply and Services.

Department of Labour. (1959). *Equal pay for equal work: The growth of an idea*. Ottawa: Labour Canada.

Johnson, Leo. (1974). The political economy of Ontario women in the nineteenth century. In J. Acton, P. Goldsmith, and B. Shepard (Eds.), *Women at work in Ontario*. Toronto: Women's Press.

McDermott, Patricia. (1993). Equal pay in Canada. In F. Eyraud (Ed.), *Equal pay protection in industrialized market economies: In search of greater effectiveness*. Geneva: International Labour Office.

Ursel, Jane. (1984). The state and the maintenance of patriarchy: A case study of the family, labour and welfare legislation in Canada. In J. Dickinson and B. Russell (Eds.), *Family economy and the state: The social reproduction process under capitalism*. Toronto: Garamond Press.

SUGGESTED READING

Abella, Judge Rosalie Silberman, Commissioner. (1984). *Equality in employment: A royal commission report*. Ottawa: Supply and Services.

McDermott, Patricia. (1993). Equal pay in Canada. In F. Eyraud (Ed.), *Equal pay protection in industrialized market economies: In search of greater effectiveness*. Geneva: International Labour Office.

QUESTIONS TO CONSIDER

1. Why have pay equity and employment equity been pursued as distinct rather than interrelated policy goals in Canada? How are women workers adversely affected by having two separate policy regimes to regulate sex discrimination in the workplace?

2. Discuss the differences among pay equity, equal pay, and employment equity as they are defined by federal and provincial legislation in Canada.

3. Which women workers would benefit most, and how, from combining pay and employment equity policies into a single regulatory strategy?

CHAPTER 4

Brave New Worlds for Women: NAFTA and New Reproductive Technologies

Barbara Cameron

The Royal Commission on New Reproductive Technologies (NRT) submitted its report to a newly elected Liberal government on November 15, 1993, in which it proposed a strong system for regulating the industries affiliated with NRTs (Canada, Royal Commission, 1993). A month and a half later, despite concern expressed by many Canadians that the free-trade agreement among Canada, the United States, and Mexico would severely limit the sovereignty of the Canadian state, the Liberal government allowed the North American Free Trade Agreement (NAFTA) to come into effect. In designing their regulatory system for commercial activity related to NRTs, the commissioners apparently had not considered the relevance of NAFTA, which is essentially a set of rules specifying what governments in Canada, the United States, and Mexico may and may not do to regulate business. The commission's failure to consider the constraints imposed on Canadian governments by this new international agreement, I argue here, make it highly unlikely that the recommendations of the royal commission will be adopted.

The recommendations of the Royal Commission on New Reproductive Technologies provide a useful case study for exploring how NAFTA constrains the action of the Canadian state in an area of importance to all Canadians, and to Canadian women in particular. Unlike many policy areas where Canadian opinion is divided on whether the state should intervene to limit the market, in the area of reproduction the royal commission's researchers found a consensus among Canadians that commercialization is not acceptable and that regulatory measures by the state are essential. Furthermore, the philosophy underlying the report of the royal commission about the appropriate roles for the state in regulating the private market contrasts sharply with that of the NAFTA (see McCormack, this volume). Put simply, the recommendations do not fit easily within the regulatory framework imposed on national states by NAFTA. Finally, new reproductive technologies are an emerging area for state regulation and were probably not anticipated by the drafters of NAFTA, even though NAFTA establishes the ground rules for regulating not only existing but any future economic activity. An examination of the implications of NAFTA for new reproductive technologies suggests some of the issues Canadians will face as new industries emerge based on some future, as yet unimagined technologies.

This essay explores the implications of the NAFTA for regulating commercial activities related to the new reproductive technologies and argues that NAFTA restricts in important ways the capacity of the Canadian state to act to prohibit or restrict these activities in ways that reflect the wishes of Canadians. It begins with an overview of the commercial potential of the new reproductive technologies and the possible opportunities for trade in goods and services related to them. It then outlines the regulatory framework proposed by the Royal Commission on New Reproductive Technologies and explores the compatibility of these recommendations with the provisions of the North American Free Trade Agreement. Finally, it draws conclusions, based on this case study, about the implications of NAFTA for the capacity of the women's movement in Canada to use the state to protect and advance the interests of women.

OLD AND NEW REPRODUCTIVE GOODS AND SERVICES

The term "reproductive technologies" is used to refer to the knowledge, techniques, practices, and procedures that involve intervention in human reproduction or arise out of the capacity for such intervention. "Old" reproductive technologies include the accumulated knowledge about reproduction, the drugs and techniques used in the birth process, and the ovulation-prevention drugs and other devices used in birth control. The designation "new" is commonly reserved for the recently discovered or perfected techniques and procedures for intervening in human reproduction to assist fertility or to preserve or alter in some way human reproductive material, such as the sperm or zygotes (fertilized eggs).

The distinction between "old" and "new" reproductive technologies is somewhat artificial. Underlying both fertility-inducing and fertility-prevention drugs is a scientific understanding of the two hormones estrogen and progesterone. Both were discovered in the 1930s and, in that decade, estrogen was first synthesized, and progesterone extracted. Assisted insemination in human beings has been practised in North

America since at least 1884 (Canada, Royal Commission, 1993, p. 4). The first successful insemination of a woman with semen that had been frozen in liquid nitrogen and then thawed occurred in the 1940s. The first recorded in-vitro fertilization was performed by a researcher at Harvard in 1944. Up until the 1960s, research on human eggs was carried out with eggs retrieved from ovaries removed during hysterectomies. But, in the 1960s, laparoscopy was developed, which enabled researchers to see the uterus and **fallopian tubes** and to retrieve eggs directly from the former. In 1967, ovulation-inducing drugs that could be used to increase the number of eggs available during a menstrual cycle became generally available. In the early 1970s, the first retrieval, culture, and fertilization of human eggs was achieved, and, in 1978, the first human baby, Louise Brown, developed as a result of the fertilization of the ovum outside her mother's body, was born in England. The new applications of these technologies result from lower costs of production, techniques that improve the success rates for assisted insemination, and changing social attitudes about the appropriateness of intervening in reproduction.

The term "new reproductive technologies" is used in this chapter, as it is in the report of the royal commission, to apply to those technologies related to assisted human insemination as well as to those genuinely new technologies related to gene therapy, genetic alteration, the use of fetal tissue, and **prenatal diagnosis** and therapy. The main new reproductive technologies are described in Box 4.1.

NRT technologies give rise to new goods and services that may be sold on the market. Drugs, of course, have been commodities for some time, and new fertility drugs expand the markets for pharmaceutical companies. However, the idea that human sperm, ova, zygotes, or fetal tissue are commercial products to be sold on the market departs from previous thinking and practices in the reproductive health system. The technology of cryopreservation, which allows sperm and zygotes (but not the unfertilized ova) to be preserved for extended periods of time outside the human body, is the basis for an industry in collecting, storing, and distributing these "products."

Research institutes, often affiliated with pharmaceutical companies, become purchasers of fetal tissue and of zygotes, with the goal of discovering profitable cures for diseases. The perfection of procedures related to assisted insemination and artificial insemination give rise to medical facilities that specialize in the provision of these services. Prenatal diagnosis and laboratory tests, often related to these services, lead to the expansion of medical laboratories. Donor insemination makes possible surrogate motherhood, which provides the basis for related legal and medical services. A biotechnology industry has emerged to produce health-care goods, including fertility-testing kits, products for diagnosing and treating sexually transmitted diseases, pregnancy-detection kits, and genetic probes used in paternity

---

BOX 4.1

The New Reproductive Technologies

▶   *Cryopreservation:* a technique for preserving sperm and zygotes (fertilized ova) by freezing them in liquid nitrogen and then thawing for future use. This makes possible the delinking of reproduction and intercourse, permitting fertilization of the egg outside the body, or the fertilization of an egg inside the woman's body but without intercourse. Technology has not extended preservation through this method to the human egg.

▶   *In-vitro fertilization or assisted insemination:* techniques for fertilization of the egg other than through intercourse.

▶   *Fertility drugs:* based on the synthesis or the extraction of naturally occurring hormones. These drugs make possible control over ovulation and the production of multiple eggs. These are essential for fertilization of the egg by artificial means. The two most common fertility drugs in Canada are clomiphene and human menopausal gonadotropin (or hMG).

▶   *Pre-natal procedures:* techniques for detecting characteristics of the embryo or fetus (well-known prenatal diagnostic methods, such as ultrasound scanning and amniocentesis) that make possible the early detection of the characteristics of a fetus, including its sex.

▶   *Genetics procedures:* techniques for altering the structure of particular genes, including gene therapy (which is directed at curing a disease resulting from a defective gene) and genetic engineering (which involves isolating genes, replicating them outside of their cells, and altering their structure and their relationships to the rest of the genetic material, as in cloning).

---

suits. A medical-devices industry produces the specialized equipment used in tests to measure hormone levels, ultrasound equipment, and equipment for use in in-vitro fertilization.

THE NRT INDUSTRIES IN CANADA

Marketing NRTs

The goods and services associated with the new reproductive technologies may be produced or delivered according to a market or a non-market model. In a market model, NRT goods and services are treated as appropriate subjects for commercial exploitation, with perhaps somewhat more stringent regulation than other industries. In a non-market model, they are treated as part of a non-profit, publicly run health system.

The Canadian system of production and delivery of NRTs has developed as a mixture of the commercial and public/non-profit. For the most part, the non-commercial elements of the system have been an outgrowth of the public nature of much of our medical-care system and the fact that the commercial potential of some of these technologies has only now become apparent. Although, thus far, the NRT industries have evolved along a "mixed-market model," characterized by both commercial and public/non-profit elements, if the state does not intervene to regulate these new industries, the production and distribution of these products and services will be left almost entirely to the market-based commercial arena.

In order to provide a sense of the major players and the linkages between the "suppliers" and the major producers or service delivers within these industries, an overview follows of what might be called the "fertility industry" and of other NRT industries.

The market for the fertility industry is couples and individuals who, for physical or social reasons (for example, the lack of a partner of the opposite sex), experience difficulty conceiving without some form of medical or legal assistance. The "customers" or "clients" are **infertile** couples, single infertile women, or men or women without reproductive partners. The services that they seek include:

▶ assisted insemination (AI); and

▶ in-vitro fertilization (IVF) or preconception arrangements (surrogate motherhood). In Canada, in 1991, about 3400 women used AI services (more than any other infertility treatment) and 2495 women used IVF services (Canada, Royal Commission, 1993, pp. 434, 707).

Sperm Banks

In some AI cases, the "supplier" of the sperm is the male partner in the couple seeking the service; in other cases, the supplier is either an individual known to those seeking the service or to their physician, or a facility that specializes in the collection, storage, and distribution of human sperm. In the case of in-vitro fertilization, both the egg and sperm may be supplied by the couple seeking the service or by other another woman and man.

Two types of sperm banks exist in Canada: public and commercial. Public sperm banks, affiliated with hospitals or universities, account for eleven of the fifteen sperm banks in the country. The other four sperm banks—Repromed (Toronto); Gamete Service (Toronto); University of Calgary; and L'Institut de Médecine de la Reproduction de Montréal Inc.— are commercially operated. In addition, several U.S. commercial sperm banks ship sperm into Canada (Canada, Royal Commission, 1993, p. 707).

The economics of a commercial sperm-bank operation are as follows: the donor is paid $75 for one donation of eight to ten units, which are then sold to doctors at a per-unit price of $100 to $150. Therefore, a $75 investment generates $1000 or more, out of which the clinic pays for testing the sperm, freezing and thawing it, record keeping, and distribution. In addition, the physician who makes the purchase from the sperm bank may mark up the cost in setting the selling price to the client. The total value of Canadian commercial trade in human sperm is not known (ibid., pp. 707–708).

Fertility Drugs

The largest, most economically powerful players in the fertility industry are the multinational pharmaceutical companies that supply the ovulation-inducing (fertility) and other drugs required for the assisted-insemination and in-vitro fertilization procedures. At present in Canada, one corporation—Servono Canada, whose parent company is the Switzerland-based Ares-Serono Group—accounts for three-quarters of the sales of fertility drugs. Less than 1 percent of the research budget of the Ares-Serono Group is spent in Canada (Canada, Royal Commission, 1993, p. 705). Other corporations that sell fertility drugs in Canada are Merrill Dow, Ayers, and Sandoz; none of the Canadian-owned generic pharmaceutical companies currently produce fertility drugs. As of 1993, the market for fertility drugs accounted for about $16 million out of the $4.2-billion pharmaceutical market in Canada (ibid., p. 700), and the Canadian market for fertility drugs is estimated to be about 3.2 percent of the total world market (ibid., p. 705).

Assisted Insemination and In-Vitro Fertilization

The assisted insemination (AI) and in-vitro fertilization (IVF) services are delivered in publicly or privately owned clinics. In 1991, in Canada, 24 clinics provided AI procedures, 9 of them teaching hospitals and 5 other types of hospitals or private clinics (Canada, Royal Commission, 1993, p. 434). At that time, 17 clinics performed IVF procedures, 4 operating commercially and 13 affiliated with a university or teaching hospital. Three of the privately owned clinics—Toronto Fertility Sterility Institute, C.A.R.E. Centre (Mississauga, Ontario), and IVF Canada (Scarborough, Ontario)—were owned and operated by physicians; the other commercial clinic—Institut de Médecine de la Reproduction de Montréal (IMRM)—was owned by local business interests. In 1991, one-quarter (640 out of 2495) of all IVF patients dealt with private clinics (ibid., p. 707).

Coverage of the costs related to AI and IVF procedures also reflect a mixture of market and non-market principles. Assisted insemination was covered under medicare in five Canadian provinces in 1991; in-vitro fertilization was covered only in Ontario (ibid., p. 434). Where the procedures are not covered by medicare, the "consumer" is charged for them. However, as the royal commission pointed out, these rates are in fact highly subsidized by the publicly operated medical system, since the fees charged do not cover the costs associated with the frequent premature and multiple births and chronic disease or disability in children resulting from IVF pregnancies. The commission maintained that, if all the costs related to IVF were assumed by the privately operated clinics, the fees they would have to charge would be much higher than the market would bear. The commission expressed particular concern about the subsidy the public system pays to the physician-owned clinics, where the professional recommending a procedure also stands to gain financially from performing it (ibid., p. 562).

In situations where the procedures are covered by medicare, the person receiving the services will still incur substantial costs for those goods and services provided on the market model. In Ontario, where IVF is partially covered by medicare, research conducted for the royal commission found that the cost to the patient for such expenses as drugs and travel was $1575.05, and the cost to the public medical insurance plan was $3891.35 for one round of IVF treatment (ibid, p. 523).[1] Some provinces cover the cost of the assisted-insemination procedure but not the cost of cryopreservation and the donor sperm (ibid., p. 434).

Surrogate Motherhood

Another service offered by the fertility industry is surrogate motherhood, an arrangement whereby a woman agrees to conceive and bear a child with the understanding that the child will be raised by someone else. This service may be a commercial or a non-profit arrangement. A commercial arrangement will typically involve the woman who will bear the child, the couple or the individual planning to raise the child, a lawyer who draws up the preconception agreement between the surrogate and the parent(s), and the physician who carries out the procedure and provides medical care during pregnancy and delivery.

In most cases, the procedure used is assisted insemination, with the sperm provided by the male in the couple planning to raise the child and the ovum supplied by the surrogate mother. However, in some cases, IVF is used, with both the sperm and the ovum coming from the couple planning to raise the child. The lawyers or the physicians may also act as brokers, charging a fee not only for their professional services but also for bringing together the potential surrogate mother and those seeking the service. In Canada, such arrangements would be subsidized by the public medical insurance system, as is any assisted insemination, IVF, or regular pregnancy.

The only information available in Canada about the extent of commercial preconception arrangements comes from a 1988 study for the

Law Reform Commission of Canada. This study examined 118 cases of preconception arrangements involving Canadians. Of these, 42 took place in Canada, and the other 76 involved U.S. agencies. In 13 cases involving U.S. agencies, Canadian women served as the gestational mother; in 62 cases, Canadians were the commissioning couple; and in one case, a Canadian single man received a child (Royal Commission, 1993, p. 665). The royal commission found no evidence of commercial brokers operating in Canada, but found that, in the United States, some lawyers and doctors operated practices entirely devoted to preconception arrangements, and a range of profit-making organizations have emerged to facilitate them (ibid., p. 663).

Genetics Testing

In addition to the fertility industry, another industry affiliated with the new reproductive technologies—the genetics-testing industry—has developed and shows significant growth potential. Currently, in Canada, this industry primarily offers prenatal diagnostic services (PDN), which consist of tests intended to determine whether or not a fetus has a congenital anomaly or genetic disease. The most common of these services include the following: amniocentesis, which tests the amniotic fluid for fetal abnormalities such as Down's Syndrome; choriconic villus sampling (CVS), which both tests fetal tissue for fetal abnormalities in biochemical makeup and determines the sex of the fetus; targeted ultrasound, which uses sound waves to produce images of the fetus; and maternal serum alpha-fetoprotein (MSAFP), a test on maternal blood carried out around the sixteenth week of pregnancy (Canada, Royal Commission, 1993, p. 1163). The greatest potential for growth in this industry lies not with PND but with the development of gene-probe technology that will make it possible to test adults for the presence of genes related to certain multifactoral diseases such as auto-immune disorder, neurological disorders, blood diseases, and cancers. The market for this service is thought to be very large in the United States, where many employers continue to pay the costs of private medical insurance for their employees (ibid., p. 702).

The primary deliverers of prenatal diagnostic services in Canada are the genetics centres, which are affiliated with publicly run institutions, and the medical laboratories associated with them (ibid., pp. 756–769). In 1991, there were 22 genetics centres, all of them in hospitals in urban centres. Sixteen of these were in university medical centres or tertiary-care hospitals associated with university medical centres, and 6 were in large community hospitals. There were also 35 formal outreach sites associated with the genetics centres. In 1990, 22 000 women were referred for prenatal diagnostic services at genetics centres. In Canada, $100 million is spent annually on ultrasound tests; in 1990, 37 163 women were screened for MSAFP through labs associated with genetics centres.

In addition to the services offered by genetics centres, there is a growth in PND services being provided by physicians in private practice and by private medical laboratories. The services provided by physicians include taking blood samples for MSAFP screening, performing routine ultrasounds in their offices, and referring patients to a local facility for routine ultrasounds (ibid., p. 767). The amount of PND testing taking place in private facilities is increasing; for example, in Ontario, in 1989, more than 25 percent of MSAFP testing was done in private laboratories (ibid., p. 820).

Reproductive Products

New reproductive technologies have led to the expansion of the medical-devices industry in Canada. Eighty percent of the medical devices sold in the $2.5-billion Canadian market are imported. Most of the firms in the market are foreign-owned (mainly U.S.) multinational corporations, some of them subsidiaries of pharmaceutical companies. Medical devices related to NRTs account for a small proportion of the market and consist mainly of diagnostic-test materials and equipment used in laboratory testing to measure hormone levels as well as ultrasound and specialized equipment for use in IVF and other forms of assisted conception. Currently, sales of test materials in Canada amount to $350 million annually; sales of ultrasound equipment $50 million annually; and sales of devices for assisted-conception procedures $250 000 (Canada, Royal Commission, 1993, pp. 704–705).

Products related to reproductive health care are provided by biotechnology companies, another industry related to the new reproductive technologies. These include diagnostic and therapeutic products related to sexually transmitted diseases, pregnancy-detection and -assessment products, and hormone-testing products (including fertility-testing kits). The royal commission estimated that 7 of the 90 biotechnology firms in Canada that could be identified as active in health care are involved the area of reproductive health (ibid., p. 701). One of the companies owns the rights to the gene-probe technology used in paternity tests and another is trying to license the probe for the cystic fibrosis gene. The Canadian NRT biotechnology industry is small, and the Canadian market for many products will be serviced by foreign manufacturers.

Biotechnology

Another potentially significant area of economic activity related to new reproductive technologies is research carried out by biotechnology companies; pharmaceutical companies; and public research institutions, particularly universities. Internationally, research is being conducted using human embryos and sperm and fetal tissues for such purposes as finding cures for diseases such as Parkinson's and Alzheimer's, identifying genes linked to particular disorders, and finding new methods of fertility control. The royal commission found that little or no research on human embryos or fetal research was being conducted by biotechnology or pharmaceutical companies in Canada. A survey undertaken by the commission, however, found that future research by pharmaceutical companies on human embryos and fetal tissue was a possibility in Canada (1993, pp. 981, 623).

THE ROYAL COMMISSION'S REGULATORY FRAMEWORK

A fundamental principle underlying the regulatory approach recommended by the Royal Commission on New Reproductive Technologies is the "principle of the non-commercialization of reproduction." This principle involves opposition to commercialization, meaning "activities involving the exchange of money or goods and intended to generate a profit or benefit for those engaging in this exchange," and to commodification, which is "the treatment of human beings or body tissues and substances as commodities—as means to an end, not as ends in themselves" (Canada, Royal Commission, 1993, p. 55). The argument supporting the principle of the non-commercialization of reproduction was put forward in strong moral language:

> Commissioners believe it is fundamentally wrong for decisions about human reproduction to be determined by a profit motive—introducing a profit motive to the sphere of reproduction is contrary to basic values and disregards the importance of the role of reproduction and its significance in our lives as human beings. Commodifyng human beings and their bodies for commercial gain is unacceptable because this instrumentalization is injurious to human dignity and ultimately dehumanizing. We therefore consider commercialization of reproductive materials and reproductive services to be inappropriate. (ibid., pp. 56, 57)

Under the approach adopted by the royal commission, activities such as assisted conception and surrogacy are not, in and of themselves, a problem. What requires government regulation is the commercialization of these activities. The regulatory framework they propose consists of two main elements: criminalization and mandatory licensing. Criminalization would prohibit certain commercial activities under threat of criminal sanction. Mandatory licensing would be used to regulate the non-profit delivery of reproductive services, as well as certain activities related to the new reproductive technologies permitted to operate on a commercial basis. The commercial activities which would be prohibited under threat of criminal sanction include those listed in Box 4.2.

BOX 4.2

Prohibited Areas of Commercialization

▶ the sale of human eggs, sperm, zygotes, fetuses, and fetal tissue

▶ advertising for, or acting as an intermediary to bring about, a preconception agreement (i.e., an agreement to act as a surrogate mother)

▶ receiving payment or any financial or commercial benefit for acting as
   an intermediary

▶ making payment for a preconception arrangement

▶ any research involving the genetic alteration of human zygotes or
   embryos related to ectogenesis, cloning, animal/human hybrids, or
   the transfer of human zygotes to another species, or the maturation
   and fertilization of eggs obtained from a human fetus (Canada, Royal
   Commission, 1993, p. 1022)

One implication of the approach recommended by the royal commission is that some commercial activities in Canada would have to be
removed from the market to the public or non-profit sphere. The existing commercial sperm banks would have to become non-profit institutions or cease operating. In addition, the sale of sperm to individual
Canadians, physicians, and clinics by commercial sperm banks in other
countries would have to be prohibited (ibid., p. 448). The privately
owned clinics offering assisted-conception services would have to operate on a non-profit basis or close. Canadians could no longer participate
in commercial surrogacy arrangements based in Canada or involving
individuals or organizations outside Canada. The future development of
sex-selection clinics (including commercial clinics) would be precluded
by the recommendations of the royal commission.

In areas where the royal commission would permit commercial activity, it recommends greater government regulation of the private market
through a mandatory licensing system. It does not recommend that
physicians be prohibited from offering ultrasound procedures. However,
it does call on provincial governments to ensure that the physicians
ordering the tests are not those who provide them (ibid., p. 818). All
facilities, including physicians' practices, offering ultrasound would be
licensed and monitored. While not requiring that medical laboratories
carrying out tests related to NRTs be non-profit, the royal commission
does recommend that all such labs operate in connection with the public and non-profit genetic centres and that provincial governments
refuse to provide reimbursement for MSAFP services conducted in other
facilities (ibid., p. 821).

Similarly, the commission does not require that all research be conducted in a non-profit facility, but recommends that facilities conducting

NRT research be licensed, and the research monitored. With respect to embryo research, it recommends that only research directed at understanding human health, not commercial gain, be licensed (ibid., p. 1030). It proposes that patents related to innovative medical treatments, and to human ova, sperm, zygotes, embryos, and fetuses not be issued; however, it is somewhat more equivocal about NRT-related gene probes and medical devices (ibid., p. 721). Rather than making a firm recommendation on whether patents are to be issued to human-cells lines, a potentially expensive and profitable line of research for pharmaceutical companies, the royal commission argues that further study of the issue of intellectual-property protection in the area of NRTs is necessary (ibid., p. 723).

At the centre of the mandatory licensing system would be a national reproductive technologies commission, appointed, like other federal regulatory bodies, by the governor-in-council. The mandate of the national commission would be to ensure that new reproductive technologies are developed and applied in the national interest (ibid., p. 1023). The national commission would operate through six subcommittees. With the exception of the Infertility Prevention Subcommittee, whose mandate centres on public and professional education, these subcommittees would be responsible for issuing licences and monitoring the observance of guidelines. The royal commission recommended that women should normally make up one-half of the members of the National Reproductive Technologies Commission and each of its subcommittees (ibid.).

The mandatory licensing and monitoring responsibilities of the five subcommittees related to regulating commercial activities arising from new reproductive technologies are briefly summarized in Box 4.3.

NAFTA AND THE REGULATION OF NRTS

The economic model that underlies the North American Free Trade Agreement (NAFTA) assumes a decidedly different role for government in the regulation of business from the approach taken in the report of the Royal Commission on New Reproductive Technologies. The provisions of NAFTA are based on the premise that the state's role in interfering with the market is confined primarily to setting standards with respect to health and safety, consumer protection, and the environment. The possibility of state-owned enterprises or state-recognized monopolies and state-run social services is allowed by NAFTA, but only when very specific conditions are present. State-owned or -recognized monopolies are to be operated "solely in accordance with commercial considerations in its purchase or sale of the monopoly good in the relevant market" (NAFTA, article 1502 3(b)). Under NAFTA, governments

---

BOX 4.3

Regulatory Subcommittees Proposed by the Commission

▶ *Assisted insemination subcommittee* would be responsible for administering separate licences for the following three services: the collection of sperm; the storage and distribution of sperm; and the provision of assisted-insemination services. The subcommittee would also set the standards and guidelines to be adopted as conditions of licences and for monitoring developments in the field of assisted insemination. (Canada, Royal Commission, 1993, pp. 1025–1027)

▶ *Assisted conception subcommittee* would set the standards and guidelines that would be the condition for the compulsory licensing of any physician, any centre, or any other individual or facility related to assisted conception. Such services include the fertilization of the egg outside the woman's body and the transfer of the embryo either to the woman who was the source of the egg for the embryo or to another woman. (ibid., p. 1027)

▶ *Embryo research subcommittee* would be responsible for licensing facilities engaged in research using human zygotes, or developing standards and guidelines to be adopted as conditions of licence, and for monitoring developments in this area. (ibid., p. 1029)

▶ *Prenatal diagnosis and genetics subcommittee* would have responsibility for licensing facilities providing prenatal-diagnosis services and for developing standards and guidelines to be adopted as a condition of licence and monitoring developments. In addition to licensing facilities and monitoring activities related to prenatal diagnostic services, this subcommittee would monitor gene-therapy developments related to reproduction. (ibid., pp. 1031–1032)

▶ *Fetal tissue subcommittee* would monitor the supply and use of fetal tissue, develop standards and guidelines to govern the issuing of licences, and oversee the licensing program for any physician, centre, clinic, or other individual or facility providing fetal tissue for research. (ibid., p. 1033)

---

are permitted to provide services such as law enforcement, correctional services, income security or insurance, social security or insurance, social welfare, public education, public training, and health and child care, but only in a manner that treats foreign service deliverers in the same way as domestic ones (article 1201 3(b)). The one major exception to the market-driven model on which NAFTA is based is the protectionist provisions for intellectual-property rights, which have the effect of granting a monopoly for a period of twenty years to those corporations holding patents on inventions.

The American Model

The economic model behind NAFTA is essentially that of the U.S. economy, and the practices of the U.S. government are taken as the norm. Government behaviour that departs from this norm is permitted in the agreement, but only when presented as an exception to the rule. The agreement is structured so that the market-drive provisions are included in the body of the text, and the exceptions, which permit a more interventionist role for the state, are usually included in annexes to chapters or to the agreement as a whole. Very often, the restrictions on the market that countries are maintaining are explicitly subject to ongoing negotiation.

The effect of basing NAFTA on the U.S. economic model is to limit the sovereignty of the Canadian and Mexican states much more than that of the United States. While all three national governments are equally bound by the provisions of NAFTA, in many instances only the Canadian or the Mexican state has a history of using the measures prohibited by the agreement. Like virtually all other countries in the world except the United States, Canada and Mexico have placed restrictions on foreign investment in their countries. They also have relied on an active role for the state in either owning or regulating service industries, such as banking and telecommunications, considered vital to national sovereignty. NAFTA explicitly limits the measures that states may use in these and other areas. The underlying assumptions are that the extension of market relations in virtually all areas of human activity is desirable and that the limitation of market activity by the state is not.

Morals versus Markets

The argument of the Royal Commission on New Reproductive Technologies is a moral one. It is not based primarily on health considerations or consumer protection, which are considered "legitimate objectives" of government regulation within NAFTA. As defined in Chapter 9 of NAFTA, "legitimate objectives" include safety; protection of human, animal, or plant life or health, the environment, or consumers; and sustainable development (NAFTA, article 915). Instead, the commissioners maintain that the commodification of the human body and commercialization of reproductive materials and services are immoral. Implicit in their position is the view that there are certain moral limits on the extension of market relations. They are saying that such activities as in-vitro fertilization, fertilization by a donor sperm, and even surrogacy are morally acceptable, but payment for these services are not. The notion that some activities are morally acceptable but payment for them is not would be familiar to Americans with respect to such matters as prostitution. However, the exchange on the market of goods and services arising from new reproductive technologies has been considered by U.S. law and practice to be appropriate.

In a situation where the United States treats NRT goods and services as commodities to be offered for sale, what are the possibilities within NAFTA for the Canadian government to decide to remove them from the sphere of market activity? The reality is that the provisions of NAFTA offer very few opportunities for the Canadian government to impose such restrictions without risking legal challenges by U.S.-based business interests and the possibility of retaliatory trade measures by the U.S. government. (Such retaliatory measures would not invariably be taken by the U.S. government, but they would remain an option.)

The prohibition of market activity in an area not universally recognized as inappropriate for market relations is treated by NAFTA as a "non-conforming measure." The agreement makes it possible for the three signatory governments to "grandparent" existing non-conforming measures by listing them in Annex I. It also makes it possible for governments to reserve existing and future government measures for coverage by NAFTA, provided these are listed in Annex II to the agreement. It also allows countries to designate, in Annex III, the areas reserved solely for state rather than private market activity, but only Mexico took advantage of this opportunity.

Canada has not specifically exempted NRT goods and services from the provisions of the agreement, although Canada's reservation on social services might have some application. Indeed, as they are currently provided in Canada, NRT goods and services are not "non-conforming." The private market is allowed to operate in the sale of sperm and surrogacy services and in private clinics specializing in in-vitro fertilization and other assisted-insemination procedures. Implementing the recommendations of the royal commission would mean that some goods and services currently on the market would be removed and placed exclusively in the non-profit and public sphere. NAFTA permits such a change but is designed to discourage any such incursions into the sphere of market activity by making them as costly as possible.

Constraints on the State

Three sections of NAFTA are relevant to any extension of the role of state or of not-for-profit institutions: article 1110 in the investment chapter, which covers expropriation and compensation; article 1502 in the chapter on "competition policy, monopolies, and state enterprises"; and Annex 2004 to the chapter on dispute-settlement procedures, which deals with "nullification and impairment." These articles are described in Box 4.4.

Measures that remove certain activities from the private market might well be considered "tantamount to nationalization," and a government that adopts such measures would be required to compensate

---

BOX 4.4

The New Rules Imposed by NAFTA

▶ Article 1110 makes it a violation of the agreement for a state to "directly or indirectly nationalize an investment of an investor of another Party in its territory or *take a measure tantamount to national-ization or expropriation* of such an investment," except under certain conditions. These conditions permit such action "for a public pur-pose" and upon payment of compensation at fair market value.

▶ Article 1502 permits a state to designate a monopoly, which means to allow a government agency or a private consortium to be the sole provider or purchaser of a good or service. However, a government must ensure that any such monopoly "acts solely *in accordance with commercial considerations* in its purchase or sale of the monopoly good or service in the relevant market, including with regard to price, quality, availability, marketability, transportation and other terms and conditions or purchase or sale." The definitions at the end of Chapter 15 make it clear that this means in a way "consistent with normal business practices of privately-held enterprises in the relevant busi-ness or industry."

▶ Annex 2004 gives a party to the agreement access to the dispute-settlement procedure if any benefit it expected to enjoy under the trade in goods, cross-border trade in services, intellectual property, and other provisions of the agreement is "nullified or impaired as a result of the application of any measure that is not inconsistent with this Agreement." In other words, the offending measure could be in keeping with the agreement but interfere with benefits one of the par-ties thought it would enjoy.

---

any provider of these goods and services based in one of the other two signatory countries. The "nullification and impairment" clause might be cited by companies not currently operating in the Canadian market who could argue that they expected to have the opportunity to access that market under the agreement and therefore would suffer a loss as a result of restrictions on commercial operations imposed by the Canadian government. They might use this section to claim compensa-tion for expected future benefits. Should the Canadian government decide to designate one agency, whether privately or publicly run, as the sole collector, storer, and distributor of sperm—as it does, for example, with the Red Cross for blood—then the monopoly provision would apply. If sperm were designated a "monopoly good," as blood currently is, then NAFTA directs that the government must ensure that it is purchased and sold at a price comparable to market rates.

Intellectual Property

The provisions in the Intellectual Property chapter of NAFTA governing patents provide another example of the differences between the philosophy of the royal commission and that of the free-trade agreement. One of the recommendations of the royal commission is that human ova, sperm, zygotes, embryos, and fetuses that have been genetically altered not be considered to be intellectual property. The argument of the commissioners is that these entities have the potential for human life and "inherent in the moral point of view and respect for human life is abhorrence of the recognition of property interests of one human being in another" (Canada, Royal Commission, 1993, p. 722). NAFTA recognizes the right of a state to exclude an innovation from patentability, but on the condition that

> preventing in its territory the commercial exploitation of the inventions is necessary to protect *ordre public* or morality, including to protect human, animal or plant life or health and to avoid serious prejudice to the environment, *provided that the exclusion is not based solely on the ground that the Party prohibits commercial exploitation in its territory of the subject matter of the patent.* (article 1709 (2); emphasis added)

The final clause of this article means that NAFTA does not recognize opposition to commercial exploitation as a moral ground for excluding an innovation from the protection of intellectual-property rights. In doing so, it rejects the entire moral basis of the regulatory framework proposed by the Royal Commission on New Reproductive Technologies.

NAFTA does allow a state to exclude from patentability diagnostic, therapeutic, and surgical methods for the treatment of human beings. This was a provision of the Canadian Patent Act at the time that NAFTA came into effect and is a recommendation of the royal commission with respect to reproductive medical treatments. However, NAFTA also requires a government to extend patent protection for a period of twenty years from the filing of an application, and excludes the past practice of the Canadian government of allowing a generic-drug industry to produce a pharmaceutical product at greatly reduced prices (NAFTA, article 1709 (12)).

Standards

Under NAFTA, the Canadian government would still retain the right to impose standards that must be met by the producers of good and services entering the Canadian market. Chapter 9 of the agreement identifies safety; the protection of human, animal, or plant life or health, the environment, or consumers; and sustainable development as "legitimate objectives" of standards-related measures (NAFTA, article 915). So, for example, a fertility drug deemed unsafe could be excluded from the Canadian market. However, Chapter 9 also sets out in considerable detail procedures to bring about a harmonization of the standards of the three countries. Basically, a country is required to treat the standards established by one of the other countries as equivalent to its own unless it can demonstrate that they are not (article 906). In addition, the agreement requires that each government provide "Inquiry Points" for the other governments or "interested persons" "to answer all reasonable inquiries ... and to provide relevant documents or information" regarding any existing or proposed standards-related measure at all levels of government (article 910). Under NAFTA, "persons" refers not only to individuals but also to corporations. The likely effect of this will be to provide powerful corporate interests, such as the U.S.-based multinational pharmaceutical companies, with guaranteed access points to influence the standards-setting process of foreign governments.

Reservations

As indicated earlier, the Canadian government did place a reservation in Annex II to NAFTA with respect to social services. This reservation is directed at excluding existing and future measures of Canadian governments related to certain public and social services from coverage by important clauses of NAFTA. This reservation is worded as follows:

> Canada reserves the right to adopt or maintain any measure with respect to the provision of public law enforcement and correctional services, and the following services *to the extent that they are social services established or maintained for a public purpose*: income security or insurance, social security or insurance, social welfare, public education, public training, health and child care. (NAFTA, Annex II, p. II-C-9; emphasis added)

While this reservation appears to be fairly comprehensive, there are some difficulties in applying it to goods and services related to new reproductive technologies.

An important problem with this reservation is the phrase "to the extent that they are social services established or maintained for a public purpose." Nowhere in the agreement is the term "social services" defined, and there is some uncertainty about what would fall under this rubric. The phrase "to the extent" implies that there are degrees of social services and that, at some unspecified point, a social service becomes something else—presumably a service delivered on the private market. This ambiguity could become quite important as provincial governments trim their deficits by removing more and more health services from coverage by medicare. In-vitro fertilization is currently covered to a limited extent only in Ontario. If a service is not covered by Canada's public medical insurance program, can it still be considered a "social service"? Since services related to NRTs are highly discretionary and sought by only a small minority of the population, a strong argument can be made that they are not social at all but, rather, private and individual.

Even without the ambiguity surrounding the definition of "social service," there is a problem with the scope of the reservation in Annex II.

It does exclude certain public and social services from the "national treatment" provisions of the Investment and Cross-Border Trade in Services chapters of NAFTA or from the requirement that providers of cross-border services be permitted to have a "local presence" in the Canadian market, such as a sales office. It also allows the government to introduce measures with respect to the nationality of the board of directors and management of these services. However, Annex II does not apply to the monopolies (NAFTA, article 1502) and the expropriation and compensation (article 1110) provisions examined above. This means that the "right to adopt or maintain any measure" related to social services does not include the right to remove a good or service from the private market into the public or non-profit sphere without paying market-value compensation to U.S.- or Mexico-based providers of these goods and services.

There is, of course, no certainty that the Canadian government will move in the direction proposed by the Royal Commission on New Reproductive Technologies or of the more restrictive regulatory regime being promoted by women's organizations. If the Canadian government does not remove reproductive goods and services from the market, it will be bound by NAFTA to treat U.S.- and Mexico-based providers of these goods and services in the same way it does Canadian providers. This is the implication of the "national treatment" clause, which covers goods, services, and capital, and is a fundamental principle of the agreement. A consequence of this principle is that private U.S. clinics could operate in Canada as long as Canadian private clinics are allowed to operate. Under the Investment chapter of the agreement, the Canadian government would be prevented from insisting that the managers of these clinics be Canadian (article 1107). Furthermore, under the Cross-Border Trade in Services provisions of NAFTA (Chapter 12), the Canadian government would be obligated to allow U.S. suppliers of good or services to set up an office or other "local presence" in Canada (article 1205) to solicit business. The only way the Canadian government could escape coverage by the "national treatment," "local presence," and "management" provisions of the agreement would be to convince the U.S. and Mexican governments that reproductive goods and services were protected under the social services (particularly health care) reservation in Annex II. As discussed earlier, this claim might be difficult to defend successfully.

CONCLUSION

Using the case of new reproductive technologies, this essay has shown that NAFTA contains provisions that can be used to limit the capacity of a member state of NAFTA to regulate commercial activity within its territory. These provisions essentially establish a set of rights for foreign commercial interests that wish to challenge some regulatory measure established by one of the NAFTA states. They would be activated in much the same way that the rights guaranteed under Canada's Charter of Rights and Freedoms are—namely, by a challenge to a state measure lodged by a private interest—except that, under NAFTA, only corporate rights are guaranteed. For that reason, NAFTA may be seen as a "charter of rights for corporations." Whether or not these rights would be invoked, however, depends on the level of knowledge and organization of the commercial interests affected by particular state regulatory measures. As this essay has shown, commercial interests affiliated with the new reproductive technologies are in a position to demand that the rights guaranteed to them under NAFTA be respected.

The free-trade strategy in Canada has often been defended as a way to establish a "level playing field" for trade. As this essay has shown, the effect of NAFTA is, instead, to tilt the balance of power farther away from those who favour state regulation of business and more toward those who favour deregulation. The women's movement in Canada has a strong tradition of advocating state regulation of commercial activities, through measures such as **pay equity** and **employment equity** legislation. Indeed, the criticism by the National Action Committee on the Status of Women of the regulatory proposals in the report of the Royal Commission on New Reproductive Technologies is that they are too weak, and provide for too little democratic accountability. Yet, compared with the restrictions on corporations under NAFTA, the proposals of the royal commission are quite strong.

The lesson to be learned from this case study is not that populist organizations, such as the National Action Committee on the Status of Women, can do nothing in the face of NAFTA. Indeed, with new reproductive technologies, there is a strong argument to be made that organizations should push as hard as possible, and as quickly as possible, for effective state regulation. The commercial interests based on NRTs will become stronger, not weaker, as time passes. Even when the competing interest is already politically sophisticated and well organized around trade issues, as the multinational pharmaceutical companies are, organizations would be well advised to pursue their demands for state regulation. As the example of new reproductive technologies shows, NAFTA has potentially negative implications in areas unimagined by most Canadians. Challenging NAFTA on issues that command a strong base of public support is one way to bring these implications home to Canadians, and to raise in a very practical way the question of whether or not the limitations NAFTA places on the Canadian state fit with the vision of democracy shared by most Canadians.

NOTES

1. In 1994, the Ontario government delisted IVF treatment, except in cases where there is complete bilateral blockage of the fallopian tubes. In such cases, women are eligible for only three cycles of treatment.

REFERENCES

Canada. Royal Commission on New Reproductive Technologies. (1993). *Proceed with care: Final report of the Royal Commission on New Reproductive Technologies*, 3 vols. Ottawa: Canada Communications Group.

SUGGESTED READING

Canada. Royal Commission on New Reproductive Technologies. (1993). *Proceed with care: The final report of the Royal Commission on New Reproductive Technologies*, 3 vols. Ottawa: Canada Communications Group.

McCormack, Thelma. Chapter 8 in this volume.

QUESTIONS TO CONSIDER

1. The Royal Commission on New Reproductive Technologies argued for government regulation of these technologies in order to maintain the decommercialization of human reproduction. How does this view differ from the philosophy underlying NAFTA?

2. Identify the areas under NAFTA that specifically undermine the ability of Canadian governments to regulate.

3. How could Canadian governments regulate the new reproductive technologies within the constraints imposed by NAFTA? Is the regulation of NRTs necessary or desirable for women?

PART **II**

RESTRUCTURING
THE
STATE

Unravelling the Safety Net: Transformations in Health Care and Their Impact on Women

Pat Armstrong

In a meeting I attended recently, a senior bureaucrat in the Health ministry referenced Ivan Illich to justify dramatic reductions in hospitals stays. The radical critique of institutional care and allopathic (that is, conventional) medicine developed twenty years ago in Illich's books *Medical Nemesis* (1975) and *Limits of Medicine* (1976) was being used to elicit our support for the current transformations in health care. I was particularly struck by this reference because it illustrated so clearly what I argue in this essay—namely, that progressive discourse is generally used to legitimate regressive practices in health-care reform. I want to explore both what might today be called "the appropriation of voice" and what, in the 1960s, was called the differences between "the rhetoric and the reality," particularly in terms of how these relate to women and their health-care work.

PROGRESSIVE DISCOURSES AND PRACTICES

The Women's Health Movement

Although, twenty years ago, Illich was a very visible critic of modern Western approaches to health care, in Canada, much of the challenging of theory and practices of medicine was being done by women. What is often called "the women's health movement" became visible in the 1960s, through both publications by women and women's interventions in health care.

Given that only women get pregnant, it is not surprising that the women's health movement emerged primarily around issues related to contraception and childbirth. In the late 1960s, for example, a group of women formed the Montreal Health Press and published a book on birth control that was "part of a movement for reproductive freedom" (Cherniak, 1990, p. 3). Such a publication may seem unremarkable today, but when the group was formed it was illegal to distribute such information. By publishing on newsprint and distributing the booklets free of charge, Montreal Health Press put into the hands of thousands of women information on how women's bodies worked and on how to prevent pregnancy. The very process of creating and distributing the booklets was an empowering one.

Across the country, women demanded the right to control their own bodies through access to abortion and birth control. They also attacked the transformation of childbirth into a single medical event that was to be managed by doctors and treated with drugs and technology (Armstrong 1993b; Pierson 1993). This medicalization of childbirth was criticized on the grounds that it not only made women powerless in the process, but also risked their health. Women called for a new emphasis on developing continuous social support for pregnant women rather than on providing intermittent medical care focussed primarily on the birth process. They argued that babies should not be automatically separated from their mothers after birth and that mothers should not be automatically separated from their homes and friends. And they produced a great deal of evidence to support their claims that health care too often threatened women's health while eliminating women's traditional practices (Cooperstock, 1977; Romalis, 1982).

Gradually, these women began to question all of the assumptions central to the delivery of health-care services (Kleiber and Light, 1978; McDonnell and Valverde, 1985; Smith and David, 1975). In Vancouver, for example, "in the fall of 1971, a group of young women met to discuss their own health care needs and their dissatisfaction with the health care system" (Kleiber and Light, 1978, p. 9). By 1973, this small self-help group had joined with others operating an abortion referral system, trained themselves in alternative techniques, and formed the Vancouver Women's Health Collective to provide "health education and preventative care for women" (ibid.).

They were concerned that health care as practised in Canada in the postwar period had become increasingly doctor- and hospital-centred. In this system, it was assumed that doctors are experts who objectively diagnose and treat on the basis of scientifically established procedures applied to individual women in order to cure them. And sensible women would simply obey. The women's health movement sought to challenge the authority, expertise, and practice of doctors. Instead, they worked together to "equip women to participate in decisions regarding their health care" and to "develop an understanding of quality health care so that women would expect and demand such care" (Hall, 1974, p. 33).

Self-help, social and emotional support, and prevention were stressed as critical to health. Rejecting the medical model that viewed patients as a collection of parts to be fixed, they promoted an emphasis on caring for the whole person and on developing "optimal health potential" (ibid.). The dangers of various treatments and procedures were exposed, as were the biases in many doctors' approaches to women (Smith and David 1975). Like Illich, these women revealed the problems with and limits of institutional care. They called for more community involvement in decisions made about such care. They fought for the empowerment of patients, for alternatives to the dominant form of medicine, and for the integration into the community of those unnecessarily institutionalized.

In developing their critiques, the women's health movement increasingly broadened their notion of health and of prevention (see Box 5.1). Like the reformers of the last century, they began to examine how social structures, social relations, and economic conditions influenced health (Cook and Michinson, 1976, pp. 203–205). Their research made it clear that prevention was more about conditions and relations than about personal choices and practices (Chenier, 1982; MacLeod, 1980; National Council of Welfare, 1979; Rosenberg, 1990). Women's groups' efforts were directed increasingly at altering the social and economic policies and practices that made it difficult for women to achieve, maintain, or return to health.

Unions and Health Care

At the same time as women's groups were developing a critique of the health-care system from the outside, women working within the system

---

BOX 5.1

Shifting Trends in Women's Groups Women's groups began focussing more and more on what might be summarized as a concern with food, clothing, shelter, jobs and joy. The major elements of this shift of focus were:

▶ the feminization of poverty

▶ violence against women

▶ health hazards at work

▶ unemployment

▶ the organization of work

▶ housing and job security in and out of the household

were getting organized into unions (Armstrong, 1993a; Day, 1993; White, 1986). The postwar period witnessed an enormous expansion in institutional care, an expansion that reflected the introduction of government-funded hospital care, the new approaches to care, and the new technologies (Armstrong, 1993b; Naylor, 1986; Taylor, 1987). Between 1951 and 1971, the number of women employed in health and welfare work increased more than threefold, to almost 400 000 (Statistics Canada, 1978, Table 4). And a growing number of the women doing health-care work were married and relatively permanent members of the labour force. For example, in 1971, the average age for nurses was 34, and the overwhelming majority were married (Statistics Canada 1975, Table 8). Although nurses had long sought better conditions, more control, and decent pay, the major impetus for unionization came when large numbers of them came together for long periods of time in big hospitals.

These health-care workers, like the women outside the system, wanted more power. They sought to gain this power, in part, by limiting the rights of doctors to control the work of others employed in the system. They also struggled to carve out special areas of work for themselves, and this often meant emphasizing a different kind of health care. For instance, nurses were pivotal in introducing a new model called "primary care" in the 1970s. In theory at least, primary care meant "accountability to the patient and family ... autonomy ... co-ordination of care, which promotes consistency and harmony; and the comprehensiveness of care, or total patient care" (MacPhail, 1988, p. 180).

The discourse of women's groups was similar in many ways to that of other reformers. But, unlike Illich's work, it stressed the particular impact on and interests of women, as well as women's traditional approaches to caring work. It was not, however, without contradictions. The emphasis on women's shared health concerns often meant that the interests of the White, middle-class, Canadian-born women, who dominated the movement, were given precedence. And the struggle for monopoly over specific aspects of caring work often meant that the health-care hierarchy was reinforced while women doing health-care work were divided from one another.

Nevertheless, women's groups have made some important gains. Abortions are no longer illegal or so difficult to obtain. There is better access to birth control, and childbirth is more under women's control. Midwives can now practice legally in Ontario, and pregnancy is to be treated by them as a natural process that continues over time and involves an array of family and friends. Domestic violence is no longer publicly acceptable or conveniently hidden. Although women's groups have fewer success stories around poverty and employment, they have made some important gains in terms of access to better jobs and better pay, and in terms of the punishment of sexual harassers. Hospital workers, in particular, earned the right to say no to the doctors, and to receive decent wages. But women's greatest success has been in terms of the discourse. Indeed, the whole talk in the new state-sponsored investigation of health is focussed on prevention rather than cure, on community rather than on institution, and on empowerment rather than medical authority. But the triumph of this discourse has not necessarily meant better times for women. Below, I explore how this discourse is being increasingly used against women and, in the process, risking their health.

THE NEW RHETORIC IN HEALTH

Looking Outside the Health-Care System

Like Illich and the women's health movement, the *Summary of the Report of the British Columbia Royal Commission on Health Care and Costs* (British Columbia Royal Commission on Health Care and Costs, 1991, p. 13) maintains that the "traditional focus of our health care system is the curing of illness and not the prevention of disease." It goes on to say that "it is time to change this focus.... If British Columbians are to improve the quality and healthy duration of their lives, they must *pay more attention to areas outside of the health care field.*" They must pay more attention because "health is also influenced by early childhood experiences, the nature and availability of housing, an individual's employment status, hazards in the workplace and environmental pollutants, family and community support and self-esteem" (ibid.)

Similarly, *Nurturing Health*, a report prepared by the Ontario Premier's Council on Health Strategy (1991a), makes it clear that research data show that other factors are more important determinants of health than the formal health-care system. And it recognizes that this does not simply mean an improvement in individual lifestyle. Rather, lifestyles themselves are seen as "strongly influenced by the social environment," and population health as linked to economic health. Moreover, according to the report, "social and physical environments— as manifested in the places people work and live, their education, income and social supports—have a major impact on people's health" (Ontario Premier's Council on Health Strategy, 1991a, n.p.).

Reports in both provinces were also concerned about empowerment. "Enabling people to make their own health care decisions is indeed healthy public policy," says the British Columbia report (1991, p. 13), while another report from the Ontario Premier's Council talks about the need for the active participation of citizens in the "decisions that affect their health" (1991, n.p.). It is not only individuals who need to be empowered, according to these reports. They speak of empowering communities and health-care workers as part of a new strategy to achieve well-being for all and to redesign the health-care system. Part of the strategy for empowerment is the increased emphasis on "community settings" for health care (Ontario Premier's Council on Health Strategy, 1991c, p. 3), on bringing care "closer to home" (British Columbia, 1991, p. 6).

In many ways, these reports can be seen as a victory for health reformers. Those critiques that had been dismissed a couple of decades ago as radical departures from accepted practice are now referenced as the basis for provincial reports. The discourse that once was shared by a few outside the system is being paid for and distributed by the state. In fact, many health reformers contributed to the reports. But the practices justified on the basis of these ideas is far from that envisioned by the women's health movement, by other reformers, or even perhaps by those writing the reports.

THE REALITY OF STATE
HEALTH-CARE PRACTICES

In order to examine the differences between the talk about health reform and state practices, it is important to understand that the determinants of health as set out in these reports have three basic, and overlapping, components. One component is the health-care delivery system. Since at least the Second World War, that system has been primarily, though not exclusively, designed to cure through intervention. The second component is made up of the individual practices known as **lifestyle in health care**. The third component consists of the social and economic structures, relations, and conditions that set the context for both prevention and cure.

As the reports, and the reformers, point out, the most critical component in the determinants of health is the third one. Indeed, it is integral to the other two. However, the three components are often treated as separate aspects of health, so it is useful for analytic purposes to do the same here.

Lifestyles

Yoga and Yogurt

The talk of self-help and prevention that was common in the women's health movement was quickly taken up by the state. In 1974, when many feminist groups were beginning to intervene directly in issues related to health-care delivery, the federal government published *A New Perspective on the Health of Canadians* (Lalonde, 1974). Widely referenced as the Lalonde Report, it called on individuals to take responsibility for their own health. Stressing the "decisions by individuals which have repercussions on their health," the document blamed the ill for "behaviour and living habits which adversely affect health" (1974, p. 34). Similarly, almost a decade later, Statistics Canada's *Perspective on Health* identified the "determinants of health status" (listed in Box 5.2). The terminology shifted from the prevention of disease or injury to the promotion of health. This shift was supposed to reflect a move away from a curative approach. By 1993, state-sponsored health-promotion surveys had broadened the factors of lifestyle that are taken into account by including questions on issues such as social support and "family functioning." The emphasis on individual practices remained very strong, however (Stephens & Graham, 1993).

Carrots and Condoms

What I have called "the yoga and yogurt approach" to health became broadened, and some larger "environmental" and social aspects have been addressed. But the new strategy can mainly be described as "the carrots and condoms approach," with the focus still on individual choices rather than on the economic and social factors that limit choices and make some choices meaningless.

Smoking is an example. This is one area where states have gone beyond the lifestyle approach. Most of the anti-smoking effort, however, has been directed at personal behaviour change, even though the most effective strategies undertaken so far have been to forbid smoking in certain areas and to raise the cost of cigarettes. And, recently, we have seen states at both the federal and the provincial level give in to pressure—supported by the cigarette manufacturers—to lower taxes, in spite of the clear evidence of health risk not only to smokers but to non-smokers as

---

BOX 5.2

Statistics Canada's Determinants of Health Status

▶ tobacco

▶ alcohol

▶ activity and fitness

▶ drugs used illegally, taken in certain combinations, or mixed with alcohol

▶ traffic accidents

▶ "lifestyles" and preventive health practices such as pap smears and breast self-examination as "determinants of health status" (Abelson, Paddon and Strohmenger, 1983, p. 35)

well. Although there is also evidence indicating that stresses resulting from work environments and poverty encourage smoking, there has been virtually no effort directed at these causes of lifestyle practices (Karasek and Theorell, 1990, p. 8). Similarly, states have put up signs in washrooms warning pregnant women not to drink alcohol, despite the fact that there is no clear evidence indicating that a drink or two will harm the fetus. But little attention has been paid to the stresses that encourage people to drink in the first place.

There are clear advantages to an emphasis on personal behaviour change for governments. First, it is a relatively low-cost strategy that has support from a broad spectrum of publics. Second, although cigarette and alcohol manufacturers have complained, this lifestyle approach leaves corporations relatively free of state interference and creates new markets for those selling, among other things, low-fat yogurt and high-fibre cereals. Third, it creates the appearance of government action on health promotion while placing the responsibility for health firmly elsewhere.

For women, in contrast, this emphasis on lifestyle has clear disadvantages. First, information about the benefits of eating bran and reducing cholesterol levels is directed at women, since they are held responsible for family health practices. Second, this approach of blaming individuals for their own health problems contributes directly to the perpetuation of health practices that have been detrimental to women. For example, approximately 75 percent of those prescribed the anti-depressant Prozac are women (Hurst, 1994, p. F3). A medical doctor who has written about the drug describes it as a "feminist drug, liberating and empowering," suggesting that women need chemical support in order to act like men. While appropriating the language of the women's movement (cited in ibid.). It is primarily women who have been prescribed drugs as a treatment for stress and who have had their problems diagnosed as psychological—practices that are reinforced by the lifestyle approach to health (McDonnell, 1986). Finally, health promotion in which the components of good health are defined as achievable through personal behaviour does little about the major determinants of health and justifies the shift in the health-care workload to women. Not only are services being downloaded onto women in the home, but women are also expected to provide the social support, especially by promoting a functional family, that has been identified as crucial for health.

HEALTH CARE AND DELIVERY

Deinstitutionalization

Like the women's health movement, the various provincial reports have questioned the effectiveness of institutional care, challenged the notion that it it the best way to provide services, and called for the empowerment of both patients and health-care workers. The Nova Scotia Provincial Health Council, for example, maintained that "spending more money has not led to major improvements in health." It also complained that "health care providers and the public have few chances to participate in health planning" (1992, p. 5).

About the same time as the women's health movement was emerging and Lalonde was promoting prevention, Health ministries and health councils began a strategy of **deinstitutionalization**, closing institutional beds and moving residents into the "community." The first patients to be deinstitutionalized were those in mental-health centres. This movement out of institutions was often supported by those within and outside such institutions. Both professionals working in the field and patients' rights advocates argued that "adequate psychological and social treatment cannot and is not being provided by the staff available" in institutions (Roberts, quoted in Simmons, 1990, p. 126).

Moreover, they argued that living outside institutions would contribute to "the empowerment of service consumers in defining and resolving their problems" (Dickinson, 1994, p. 471). States used the same kinds of language to justify the dramatic reductions in psychiatric hospital beds. Defending the closures in 1975, the Ontario Minister of Health said, "It has been accepted that those people should be back in the community for their own sake" (quoted in Simmons, 1990, p. 161). In the most recent government documents on mental health, the continuing practice of deinstitutionalization is talked about in terms of the "need to promote opportunities for self-help; and consumer and family participation in the mental health system" (MacNaughton, 1992, p. 7).

After the move to deinstitutionalize the psychiatric patients, the same approach was adopted toward institutions for the disabled and the elderly (Chappell, 1993). As was the case with the lifestyle approach, recent initiatives have been based on a broadening of the old deinstitutionalization strategy and on some new language to explain the approach. Backed by research that indicated that most people preferred to remain out of institutions as long as possible, the various ministries and institutions have launched programs both to keep such people out of institutions and to release many of those who have been institutionalized. The Ontario Ministry of Health, for example, explained its program for seniors, the physically disabled, and those with special needs in terms of support for consumers "who choose to remain as long as possible in the familiar surroundings of their homes or with families" (Ontario Ministry of Health, 1993, p. 7).

At the same time, hospital stays for those undergoing specific treatments or surgery have been dramatically reduced. Mothers giving birth usually stay less than 24 hours, and women having hysterectomies may be sent home the next day. More and more treatment is provided on an outpatient basis. As is the case with other forms of deinstitutionalization, these strategies, too, are justified on the basis of previously rejected radical talk. Now, there is increasing discussion of problems with physician autonomy, with past medical practices, and with the effectiveness of new technologies. This discussion uses much of the language and research of the women's health movement.

Physicians' Autonomy

The British Columbia report, for example, says that the physician is no longer "the only person qualified to decide on what treatment or studies are appropriate for a patient" (British Columbia Royal Commission on Health Care and Costs, 1991, p. 8). Various policy initiatives have stressed the variations in surgical rates and medical practices that suggest medicine is not simply that application of scientific knowledge (Lomas, 1990). A recently released book, published by the C.D. Howe Institute, says: "Suggestions that as much as 30 to 40 per cent of health care spending goes to pay for inappropriate procedures are widely quoted in the public debate." Moreover, it suggests that "the system requires little rigorous evidence that a new technology is effective before allowing, even encouraging, its widespread adoption and use" (Blomqvist, quoted in Priest, 1994, p. A19). Similarly, in his book on new management strategies, the administrator of a major Ontario hospital cites a study indicating that only 15 to 20 percent of medical practice has been scientifically established as effective and another that suggests heart bypass surgery is of dubious benefit (Hassen, 1993, pp. 78–80).

Directly related to these critiques of past practices is the introduction of new management strategies often lumped together as **total quality management**. This approach "includes team work in everything; customer or patient satisfaction; ... employee empowerment; automation, innovation by everybody, management through vision and values; strategic choices; developing core competencies and focusing on the interdependencies of organizations" (Ontario Premier's Council on Health Strategy, 1991, p. 6). In an endorsement that appears on the back cover of Hassen's book on total quality management, Ontario's former Health minister claims the administrator "shows how hospitals can achieve results through the active involvement, ownership and commitment of people in their work." According to Toronto's Women's College Hospital, "the key to the program, which shifts the focus from the traditional top-down management style to a much more bottom-up and across structure, is 100 per cent employee involvement.... The idea of being constantly in touch with your customer, consumer or community is a discipline that is extremely important, so you don't waste resources that aren't needed" (Dimers, 1992, p. 11). Although initially developed for private-sector production, "total quality management, Hassen claims, "may be more natural to health care than even to industry or business because the practices of the majority of health care professionals are value-based in concepts of service, care, and compassion for the sick and injured" (1993, p. 63).

A DIFFERENT REALITY

Increasing Women's Workload

All this talk about employee and customer empowerment, about considering whole people with psychosocial needs, about community care and family choices, about critically assessing institutional care and physicians' autonomy has led to some improvements in health care. But, for the most part, the rhetoric has been used to justify a reality that differs significantly from that the language implies. Strategies introduced in the name of total quality management and deinstitutionalization are not, for the most part, improving women's health or work.

Deinstitutionalization can, as a study of one supported housing project for people with long-term psychiatric problems indicates, encourage the development of skills, personal growth, and independence (Boydell and Everett, 1992). But developed primarily as a cost-cutting strategy, deinstitutionalization has mainly meant more work for women and fewer choices for both those giving and those receiving care (Armstrong, 1993b; Chappell, 1993).

As Chappell points out, a "typical response to escalating costs is to close long-term hospital beds without any expansion to home care programs" (1993, p. 46). Although many of the elderly and disabled who remain outside institutions or who are sent home from institutions can cope with some demands of daily life, many require some assistance. As more of the chronically ill are deinstitutionalized, and as hospitals stays are shortened, however, the care requirements of those sent home both expand and change. More and more of those sent home require considerable nursing care that involves very intimate, time-consuming tasks and considerable skill.

And most of this care is provided by women, even though the overwhelming majority of women today are in the labour force. There can be no question that the women at home full-time do the caring work. Indeed, Statistics Canada's General Social Survey indicates that "women performed about the same proportion of caring activities whatever their labour force status" (Dowler, Jordon-Simpson, and Adams, 1992, p. 130). Moreover, women already are "consistently more time stressed than men, regardless of age or stage in life" (Frederick, 1993, p. 7). This is, in large part, because they now provide a great deal of caring work. Increasing deinstitutionalization, without the provision of alternative services, will put women under more stress and further limit

their choices (Armstrong, 1993b). Even if some more money is directed toward expanding current kinds of home care, it will still mean that
"caregivers have little say. They must adjust to the system if they want
the older persons in their care to receive the services" (Chappell, 1993,
p. 48). An American survey indicates that many women who must take
over care of the elderly have to switch from full- to part-time paid work
or give up their labour-force job entirely (Dowler, Jordon-Simpson, and
Adams, 1992, p. 132). There is every reason to believe this also would
be the case in Canada.

Quality of Care

It is not only the women who provide care who are given fewer choices.
Women are also the majority of those receiving care. Many of those
sent closer to home do not want their most intimate needs attended to
by a close female relative. Some may fear that their female relative
lacks the skills or capacity to provide care; others may worry about the
extra work burden the caring work places on a female relative. Many
may not be appropriately provided for, and may end up back in the
institution they left. One American study, for example, indicates that as
many as one in four elderly patients sent home may receive inadequate
care from friends or relatives (*Today's Seniors*, 1994, p. 29). Although
Canadian institutions offer more services than do their U.S. counterparts, with deinstitutionalization we are increasingly harmonizing down
to the U.S. model. In the process, women find themselves with less
power and poorer health.

The rhetoric of community involvement in designing and implementing this movement back to the community has not been realized in
practice either. In Aronson's study of government-initiated consumer
participation processes, for example, the response to one elderly
women's suggestion for a small supported housing arrangement
revealed that "impractical dreaming about living arrangements not
presently attainable administratively or beyond the bounds of the insti-
tutional-community dichotomy embedded in the reforms could not be
accommodated" (1993, p. 371). Aronson concluded, on the basis of
her study, that public consultation on long-term care reform represented data collection more than democracy. It was "analogous to seeking
data on customer preferences for use in product development" (ibid.,
p. 374). This is not what the women's health movement meant about
choice and empowerment!

Controlling Women Workers

Similarly, total quality management (TQM) strategies have not meant
empowerment for the women who form the overwhelming majority of
those who work in the health-care system. As Richardson points out in
the report on TQM she prepared for the United Nurses of Alberta, the

main goal of this management strategy is the control of variation and of workers (1993, p. 46). The continuous quality improvement is primarily about getting more work done by fewer people. It requires the breakdown of jobs into measurable functions, and the careful recording of tasks, which allow not only for the increased monitoring of workers, but also for the transfer of tasks from the more highly trained to the less highly trained.

Richardson offers the example of one Edmonton hospital that distributed a paper full of the new talk of vision and empowerment, mission, and values. But "embedded in the seductive language was the announcement that 78 registered nurses and 76 licensed practical nurses would be laid off and that 74 nursing attendants would be hired to replace them. This is a classic example of how TQM programs result in de-skilling, job losses and management by stress" (1993, p. 49).

Our research with Ontario hospital workers suggested that the team concept of TQM actually served to undermine women's traditional ways of co-operating with each other (Armstrong et al., 1994). One clerical worker explained that, "before, where somebody would finish the work and say, 'Okay, what have you got to do? And I'll help you with that', they won't now. They don't want to get involved. Besides not having the time, if they did have the time, they won't (offer to help) in any case because it's their job and they can't afford to take any more on. But in case something gets to be theirs, they don't want to take it on. And it's turning co-workers against each other. Whereas before they worked as a unit, now they're turning against each other" (ibid., p. 22).

According to these women, new management strategies gave them less control over their shifts, less choice about when to change patients' beds or diapers, and more reporting and other work to do. Although the new data-control systems were introduced as a means of demonstrating how overworked they were, women quickly found that the data were used instead to expand their workloads. As one RNA explained, "They told us that if we do the numbers properly they could say ... according to these numbers you need an extra half person and you can have it because it says so in the numbers. An so I was actually quite pleased at first. Finally it's going to show what we do in a day. But it didn't happen" (ibid., p. 24). What did happen was that the formula was changed to indicate they could further cut staff.

Patient Power

All these changes mean there is less power for the patients as well. There are patients' rights programs in place, and these create the impression of empowerment. But hospital stays have been shortened so much that, as one dietary worker put it, "they're not in there long enough to complain" (Armstrong et al., 1993, p. 8). Patients are more often asked about whether or not they want surgery, and about what treatment they prefer. Often, though, the information is not provided in a manner that makes the choice real. As one RNA explained, "The doctors are in and out. They hardly ever spend the time, a minute, with them. Like you're having half your lung out. Do you know what that means?" (ibid., p. 7). Or they are provided with the information in such a way that there are no choices to make. A study of an "educational device" designed to assist women decide whether or not to have radiation after breast surgery found that 34 out of 37 "chose" radiation, suggesting that information was presented in a way that left women few choices to make (Sutherland and Till, 1994).

In addition to promising empowerment, the talk of TQM also raises questions about the efficacy of acute-care procedures and calls for a new focus on quality care. Yet these new management strategies not only deny empowerment to the women who work in the health-care system, they also prevent them from focussing on caring for the whole person. The pressure to work harder and faster, and the allocation of workers on the basis of easily measured tasks, means that women barely have time to provide basic services for patients. It also means they have no time to provide other kinds of support, even though the reports justifying the reforms maintain that such support is critical to health. As one RNA put it, "We have no patience for the patients." According to another, "nurses are so scared of losing their jobs now that there's so much tension on the floors now, and you even ... people on the same shifts fighting against each other.... I think everybody's on edge, very testy. I find the patients have suffered, but the patients have become more demanding ... because what's happening is we've cut back. And we've cut back on the quality of things and on the amount of stuff we get. And what happens is when a patient come in, they say 'Don't we get this anymore?' 'And why are you not here?' Well, we don't get it anymore, we cannot supply that anymore" (Armstrong et al., 1993, p. 10).

One clerical worker nicely summed up in what she saw as the new hospital care: "We process people just ... like in a chocolate factory" (Armstrong et al., 1993, p. 4). And this increasing emphasis on tasks and on discharging people as quickly as possible coincides with a time when patients are more likely to be far from supportive relatives and to be undergoing very complex and life-threatening procedures.

Cuts and Chemicals

The new work organization has increased the focus on what I call "the cuts and chemicals approach" to health, rather than support caring for the whole person. There has been an intensification of treatment and intervention, whereas more and more of the diagnosis and monitoring are done by technology. At the same time, less and less effort is devoted to health promotion within the hospital, promotion that all the talk says is so critical to health. Although the discourse about the determinants of health is unanimous in the view that food and shelter and security are critical to maintaining health and resisting disease, hospitals are busy cutting back on cleaning, on food preparation and delivery, and on job security for health-care workers.

Laundry, housekeeping, and dietary services within hospitals are being redefined as "hotel services," signalling a move to private-sector practices. Yet hospitals have quite special cleaning, laundry, and dietary needs because patients have lower immunity, because some of the "dirt" is dangerous, and because patients have particular dietary requirements.

Moreover, the women who do these services define themselves as health-care workers, and the move to hotel approaches significantly undermines the basis for their job satisfaction and work commitment (White, 1990). Job satisfaction, the research cited in the new discourse claims, is critical to well-being. When combined with the threat of layoff, these strategies can serve to make the women who work in the health-care system ill.

Although justified in the language of the women's health movement, deinstitutionalization, for the most part, has not transferred care to supportive communities where people can determine their lives. The movement out of institutions was primarily justified in terms of an implicit criticism of those institutions. Yet new strategies have mostly meant and intensification of old practices, and less of the old services rather than new kinds of care.

SOCIAL AND ECONOMIC CONDITIONS AND RELATIONS

The discourse in and out of the state consistently identifies social and economic conditions and relations as the key determinants of health. Indeed, cutbacks have been justified on the basis of this agreement, for it is argued that health cannot be further improved by investing in health-care services, given that the main health determinants are found elsewhere. But, at the same time as Canadian governments are busy dismantling the health-care system, they are also dismantling the supports for healthy living.

Social-Security Cuts

The most obvious move in this direction is the onslaught on the social-security system. Many social-security programs are women's programs. Universal family allowance payments were payable to women. When universality was replaced by income as the basis for payments, it was women who lost the automatic right to the allowance. This "targeting" of programs to "those in need" was the first step away from guaranteeing social security as a right and toward granting social security as a privilege to the deserving poor.

Women are also the majority of those on welfare, and here, too, we have seen an increasing emphasis on targeting "the deserving poor." Among those over eighteen years of age, 59 percent of the poor are women (National Council of Welfare, 1993a, p. 24). Women who are single parents are particularly at risk, with more than 60 percent of them falling below the poverty line in 1991 (ibid., p. 22). And aboriginal women are even more at risk of being poor, single parents (Lindsay, 1992, p. 14). Other unattached women under age 65 had poverty rates close to 40 percent. The incomes of many are "abysmally low," and most welfare payments do not even bring incomes up to what Statistics Canada describes as the poverty line (National Council of Welfare, 1993b, p. 24). "The only 'discretion' many welfare recipients have is whether to live in substandard housing to save money on rent or how to cut back on food when the money starts running short toward the end of the month" (ibid.).

Given that women are the majority of those receiving welfare, cutbacks on welfare payments, new surveillance rules, and workfare programs have a major impact on women and make it even more difficult for them to be healthy. In New Brunswick's new work and welfare program, for example, single parents are the target population, and women make up three-quarters of those participating (McFarland, 1993, p. 14). But being targeted does not necessarily mean women's conditions are significantly improved. Women on the program were "dissatisfied with their financial situation. They claimed they were getting less on the program than they would have been getting on social assistance, despite what they had been promised ... they felt they had not been given all the necessary information when they entered the program. They put it in terms of being 'lied to' and being 'treated like guinea pigs for the civil servants to experiment on'" (ibid., p. 16).

Work-Force Participation

Employment does not necessarily solve women's financial problems either. Women are the majority of those who earn minimum wage, and a woman employed full-time on minimum wage still falls below the poverty line. In 1992, 17 percent of women employed full-time, full-year earned less than the $15 000 Statistics Canada set as the poverty line for a single person that year (National Council of Welfare, 1993b). When these and other women become unemployed, they are less likely than men to be eligible for unemployment insurance or to be able to collect enough money from UI to live above the poverty line.

Women also are less likely than men to have pensions from paid work, both because fewer of them have held labour-force jobs and because women's labour-force jobs are less likely to include pensions. This means that women are more dependent than men on state pensions, and on income supplements to these pensions. Indeed, these pensions have largely accounted for the slow decline in poverty rates for elderly women.

Women's wages, benefits, and working conditions are more likely than those of men to be protected only by the minimum standards set by states (see Fudge, this volume). But what we are seeing is a withdrawal of states from the regulation of industries, a refusal to raise minimum wages, and cutbacks in social-security programs. Such policies make it even more difficult for women to be healthy.

At the same time, states have been withdrawing funding from women's shelters, from women's health magazines, and from women's self-help groups. Money also has been withdrawn from programs designed to defend women's rights before courts and human-rights tribunals. All these policies make it increasingly difficult for women to have access to the food, clothing, shelter, and employment that are recognized to be the determinants of health and said to be the focus of health-promotion strategies.

CONCLUSION

There has been a great deal of talk about health as the product of forces outside the health-care system. This talk has provided the justification for huge cutbacks in health-care services that have thrown many women out of paid work, threatened the jobs of others, and increased the household burden of many. While the talk has also included a critique of the acute-care hospital system and the physician-centred approach to care, many of the new managerial strategies have primarily served to intensify the focus on treatment and cure. And although there is much talk of empowerment for workers and patients, many of those in and out of the system have less power. Most consultations with consumers mean little more than being surveyed by the manufacturer about brand preference. Meanwhile, states are reducing the capacity of women to remain healthy by dismantling social-security programs, by deregulating industries, and by moving away from an equity agenda.

REFERENCES

Abelson, Janet; Paddon, Peter; and Strohmenger, Claude. (1983). *Perspectives on health*. Ottawa: Minister of Supply and Services Canada.

Armstrong, Pat. (1993a). Women's health care work: Nursing in context. In Pat Armstrong, Jacqueline Choinière, and Elaine Day, *Vital signs: Nursing in transition* (pp. 17–58). Toronto: Garamond.

Armstrong, Pat. (1993b). *Closer to home: More work for mother.* Paper distributed by the British Columbia Hospital Employees Union.

Armstrong, Pat; Choinière, Jacqueline; Feldberg, Gina; and White, Jerry. (1994). *Voices from the ward.* Paper distributed by York University Centre for Health Studies and the Ontario Council of Hospital Unions.

Aronson, Jane. (1993). Giving consumers a say in policy development: Influencing policy or just being heard? *Canadian Public Policy, 14* (4): 367–378.

Boydell, Katherine, and Everett, Barbara. (1992). What makes a house a home? An evaluation of a supported housing project for individuals with long-term psychiatric backgrounds. *Canadian Journal of Community Mental Health, 10* (1): 109–123.

British Columbia, Royal Commission on Health Care and Costs. (1991). *Closer to home: A summary report.* Victoria: Royal Commission on Health Care and Costs.

Chappell, Neena. (1993). Implications of shifting health care policy for caregiving in Canada. *Journal of Aging and Social Policy, 5*(1/2): 39–55.

Chenier, Nancy Miller. (1982). *Reproductive hazards at work.* Ottawa: Canadian Advisory Council on the Status of Women.

Cook, Ramsey and Mitchinson, Wendy (Eds.). (1976). *The proper sphere.* Toronto: Oxford University Press.

Cooperstock, Ruth. (1977). *The epidemiology of psychotropic drug use in Canada today.* Paper presented at World Congress on Mental Health, Vancouver, August.

Day, Elaine. (1993). The unionization of nurses. In Pat Armstrong, Jaqueline Choinière, and Elaine Day, *Vital signs: Nursing in transition* (pp. 89–223). Toronto: Garamond.

Dickinson, Harley. (1994). Mental health policy in Canada: What's the problem? In B. Singh Bolaria and Harley Dickinson (Eds.), *Health, illness and health care in Canada.* (2nd ed.). Toronto: Harcourt Brace.

Dimers, Sara. (1992). Total quality management—A strategy for success. Women's College Hospital, *Housecall*: 10–11.

Dowler, Judith; Jordon-Simpson, Deborah; and Adams, Owen. (1992). *Health Reports, 4* (2): 125–136.

Epp, Jake. (1988). *Mental health for Canadians: Striking a balance.* Ottawa: Health and Welfare Canada.

Frederick, Judith. (1993). Are you time crunched? *Canadian Social Trends,* pp. 6–9.

Hall, Audrey. (1974). A self-help clinic for women. In Ruth Roach Pierson, Marjorie Griffin Cohen, Paula Bourne, and Philinda Masters, *Canadian women's issues* (pp. 180–82). Toronto: James Lorimer and Company.

Hassen, Philip. (1993). *Rx for hospitals: New hope for medicare.* Toronto: Stoddart.

Hurst, Lynda. (1994). The lure of instant therapy. *The Toronto Star.* March 27, F3.

Illich, Iwon. (1975). *Medical nemeses; The exploration of health.* London: Colder and Boyars.

Illich, Iwon. (1976). *Limits to medicine*. London: Penguin Books.

Kleiber, Nancy and Light, Linda. (1978). *Caring for ourselves: An alternative structure for health care*. Vancouver: Public Health.

Lalonde, M. (1974). *A new perspective on the health of Canadians*. Ottawa: Queen's Printer.

Lindsay, Colin. (1992). *Lone-parent families in Canada* (Cat. no. 89-522). Ottawa: Ministry of Industry, Science and Technology.

Lomas, Jonathon. (1990). Finding audiences, changing beliefs: The structure of research use in Canadian health policy. *Journal of Health Politics, Policy and Law* (15): 525–542.

MacDougall, Heather. (1990). *Activists and advocates*. Toronto: Dundurn Press.

MacLeod, Linda. (1980). *Wife battering in Canada: The vicious circle*. Ottawa: Minister of Supply and Services Canada for the Canadian Advisory Council on the Status of Women.

MacPhail, Jannetta. (1988). Organizing for nursing care: Primary nursing, traditional approaches, or both? In Janet Kerr and Jannetta MacPhail (Eds.), *Canadian Nursing, Issues and Perspectives* (pp. 177–86). Toronto: McGraw-Hill-Ryerson.

McDonnell, Kathleen (Ed.). (1986). *Adverse effects: Women and the pharmaceutical industry*. Toronto: Women's Press.

McDonnell, Kathleen and Valverde, Mariana. (1985). *The healthsharing book*. Toronto: Women's Press.

McFarland, Joan. (1993). Combining Economic and Social Policy Through Work and Welfare: The Impact on Women. Paper presented to the Economic Equality Workshop. Ottawa, November.

McNaughton, Eric. (1992). Canadian mental health policy: The emergent picture. *Canada's Mental Health*, March 3–10.

Montreal Health Press. (1990 [1968]). *Birth control handbook*. Montreal: Montreal Health Press.

National Council of Welfare. (1993a). *Poverty profile: Update for 1991*. Ottawa: National Council of Welfare.

National Council of Welfare (1993b). *Welfare incomes, 1992*. A Report of the National Council of Welfare. Ottawa: National Council of Welfare.

National Council of Welfare. (1979). *Women and poverty*. Ottawa: National Council of Welfare.

Naylor, David. (1986). *Private practice: Public payment*. McGill-Queen's University Press.

Nova Scotia Provincial Health Council. (1992). *Toward achieving Nova Scotia's health goals: An initial plan of action for health care reform*. Halifax: Nova Scotia Provincial Health Council.

Ontario Ministry of Health. (1993). *Building partnerships in long term care: A new way to plan, manage and deliver services and community support*. Toronto: Ontario Ministry of Health.

Ontario, Premier's Council on Health Strategy. (1991a). *Nurturing health: A framework in the determinants of health*. Toronto: Premier's Council on Health Strategy.

Ontario, Premier's Council on Health Strategy. (1991b). *A vision of health: Health goals for Ontario.* Toronto: Premier's Council on Health Strategy.

Pierson, Ruth Roach. (1993). The politics of the body. In Ruth Roach Pierson, Marjorie Griffin Cohen, Paula Bourne, and Philinda Masters, *Canadian women's issues* (pp. 98–185). Toronto: James Lorimer and Company.

Priest, Lisa. (1994). Well-off should repay medical costs, new book says. *The Toronto Star*, March 29, A19.

Richardson, Trudy. (1993). *Total quality management programs: More work for less pay.* Edmonton: United Nurses of Alberta.

Romalis, Shelly. (1982). *Childbirth: Alternatives to medical control.* Austin: The University of Texas Press.

Rosenberg, Harriet. (1990). The home is a workplace. In Meg Luxton, Harriet Rosenberg, and Sedef Arat-Koc, *Through a kitchen window* (pp. 57–80). Toronto: Garamond.

Simmons, Harvey. (1990). *Unbalanced: Mental health policy in Ontario; 1930–1989.* Toronto: Wall and Thompson.

Smith, Dorothy and David, Sara. (1975). *Women look at psychiatry.* Vancouver: Press Gang.

Statistics Canada. (1978). *1971 census: Economic characteristics industry trends 1951–1971* (Cat. no. 94-793). Ottawa: Minister of Industry, Trade and Commerce.

Statistics Canada. (1975). *1971 census: Occupations* (Cat no. 94-723, Vol III, Part 2). Ottawa: Minister of Industry, Trade and Commerce.

Stephens, T. and Graham, D. (1993). *Canada's health promotion survey.* Ottawa: Health and Welfare, Canada.

Sutherland, H.J. and Till, J.E. (1994). Quality of Life and Decision-making at Micro, Meso and Macro Levels. Paper delivered at Health and Behaviour 1994 Conference. Queen's University, Kingston, May.

Taylor, Malcolm. (1987). *Health insurance and Canadian public policy.* Montreal: McGill-Queen's University Press.

Today's Seniors. (1994). Family care may not be enough for elderly patients.

White, Jerry. (1990). *Hospital strike.* Toronto: Thompson.

White, Julie. (1986). *Women and unions.* Ottawa: Canadian Advisory Council on the Status of Women.

SUGGESTED READING

Armstrong, Pat; Armstrong, Hugh; Choinière, Jacqueline; Feldberg, Gina; and White, Jerry. (1994). *Take care: Warning signals for the Canadian health system.* Toronto: Garamond.

Baines, Carol; Evans, Patricia; and Neysmith, Sheila. (Eds.). (1991). *Women's caring: Feminist perspectives on social welfare.* Toronto: McClelland and Stewart.

Kleiber, Nancy, and Light, Linda. (1978). *Caring for ourselves: An alternative structure for health care.* Vancouver: Public Health.

Lomas, Jonathan. (1990). Finding audiences, changing beliefs: The structure of research use in Canadian health policy. *Journal of Health Politics, Policy and Law, 15,* 525–542.

Pierson, Ruth Roach. (1993). The politics of the body. In Ruth Roach Pierson, Marjorie Griffin Cohen, Paula Bourne, and Philinda Masters, *Canadian women's issues* (pp. 98–185). Toronto: James Lorimer.

Sherwin, Susan. (1992). *No longer patient: Feminist ethics & health care.* Philadelphia: Temple University Press.

QUESTIONS TO CONSIDER

1. What problems are created by running the health-care system like a business?

2. Why should women be concerned about deinstitutionalization?

3. Why is health care a woman's issue?

4. Identify the major characteristics of a woman-designed health-care system.

5. Have differences among women been taken into account by the women's health movement?

CHAPTER 6

Single Mothers and Ontario's Welfare Policy: Restructuring the Debate

Patricia Evans

The gendered division of labour, and the relationship between women's work at home and in the labour market, have been central concerns for feminists. Campaigns for **pay equity** and to improve child care attest to the importance many feminists place on the potential of government action to alter women's position in the family and the labour market. However, there has been generally less attention paid to the situation of women who are especially vulnerable to state regulation in each of these important arenas. These are the women who are rearing children on their own and require **social assistance** to support their families—roughly 40 percent of Canada's **single mothers**.[1] They are increasingly viewed as "employable." In terms of social assistance, this status typically has meant lower levels of benefits and greater scrutiny of continuing eligibility than apply to the more "deserving." The changing terms and conditions that surround a single mother's receipt of social assistance reflect society's shifting expectations of women at home and in the economy and reveal, in particularly sharp focus, the relationship between women and what we conventionally term the "welfare state."

Over the last twenty years, the "work versus welfare" debate has increasingly focussed on single mothers. This discourse has resonated somewhat differently across the English-speaking countries, but the central policy question is similar: On what terms does the single mother receive financial support from the state? In particular, what expectations of employment are attached to welfare benefits for single mothers? And the responses to these questions are converging, along with the implicit and explicit expectations of paid work, to make the single mother's entitlement to social assistance more conditional.

The issue of employment, welfare, and the single mother is receiving considerable attention in the public arena, as social-assistance programs are being redesigned to tie them more closely to work-related activities. It also raises issues for feminists who hold a diversity of views on the nature and causes of women's subordination in paid and unpaid labour. This essay explores the work/welfare debate with an examination of both the public discourse and the concerns it raises for feminists. The first section focusses on the public debate by exploring the changing equation of women, work, and welfare over time; the second section discusses recent proposals for welfare reform in Ontario; and the final section considers the issues that this debate raises for feminists.

WAGES AND WELFARE: THE CHANGING POLICY EQUATION

The changing perspectives surrounding single mothers, wages, and welfare are reflected in the shifts in public policy, shifts that make social-assistance policies increasingly oriented to paid work (see Box 6.1). This discussion highlights some of these important developments. While the focus is Canadian, and on Ontario in particular, the trends across English-speaking countries are clear. They are all concerned to move single mothers from the welfare caseloads into the labour market. While the policy interest in moving single mothers from welfare to work appeared first in the United States, where it continues to be pursued most aggressively, a major preoccupation with social assistance in Britain and Australia, and even more so in Canada, has been the "problem" of the single mother (Evans, 1992; 1993).

Canadian social-assistance policy has always been ambivalent about whether, and to what extent, single mothers should be expected to take up paid work. Policies and practices have never entirely exempted the single mother from an expectation of employment, nor have they rigorously enforced a work requirement as a condition of eligibility. Nonetheless, the emphasis on the single mother as "mother" and as "worker" has shifted over time, as the following discussion of Ontario

---

BOX 6.1

Mileposts in Social Assistance for Single Mothers

1916	Manitoba introduces Canada's first mother's pension
1966	Canada Assistance Plan adopted
1979	Ontario Work Incentive (WIN) Program adopted
1982	Ontario Employment Supports Initiative (ESI) Program adopted
1988	Ontario Social Assistance Review Committee established
1990s	Ontario and federal government welfare-policy review

policy illustrates. Ontario's policies are of interest for at least two reasons: (1) its policies affect more single mothers than any other province; and (2) as a traditionally prosperous province, its potential to implement its prefered options is greater than that of poorer provinces.

Single Mothers in Ontario

Although policy in Ontario has never viewed the single mother exclusively as either mother or worker, it is still possible to distinguish three broad policy orientations. While the orientations do differ, their chronological parameters are less precise and should be regarded as general timelines only. In the first period, from the 1920s to the end of the 1950s, the policy emphasis was on single mothers primarily as mothers rather than as workers. Beginning early in the 1960s, and continuing until the mid-1980s, policy reflected the view of single mothers as both mothers and workers, and the discourse, although not the reality, embodied notions of opportunity and choice. The third, and current, period begins in 1988, when a single mother's entitlement to income support begins to erode and she is increasingly viewed as a worker, and *not* a mother. It is important to note that this categorization differentiates the policy orientations, not the orientations of the single mothers themselves. Although it is often not recognized, single mothers on social assistance have had, and continue to have, considerable involvement in the paid labour force (Hurl, 1989; Evans, 1984).

Mothers, *Not* Workers

The policy perspective toward single mothers during the first time period was as mothers, not workers, or at least not full-time waged workers. In 1916, Manitoba introduced the first Canadian "mothers' pension" or "allowance," which provided a small, but regular monthly benefit to "needy" single mothers who met the stringent eligibility criteria. These criteria could restrict the benefit, as did the 1920 Ontario legislation, to widows or wives of permanently incapacitated husbands who were also British subjects and judged to be "fit and proper" persons. Mothers in receipt of the original mothers' pensions or allowances were encouraged—indeed, often expected—to supplement the low level of the mothers' pension or allowance with income from boarders, taking in laundry or sewing, and other "hearth-bound" activities (Little, 1994; Strong-Boag, 1979). But single mothers during this period were not generally expected, and at times were not allowed, to participate in the formal labour market. Full-time employment was viewed as incompatible with their duty to their children. This is completely consistent with the "breadwinner" model of the family. It served to support these women "as a reserve army of labour characterized by seasonal, part-time, service and small-business work with few if any benefits" (Little, 1994, p. 12).

The Second World War increased the interest in employment for the single mother, but this interest was to be short-lived. During the war, single mothers, along with their married counterparts, were encouraged to respond to the wartime demand for labour. A demonstration of patriotism was also required at the end of the war, but women were then expected to vacate their jobs to make room for the returning soldiers. Policy in the postwar period did embody an increasing assumption that single mothers should supplement their benefit with part-time work (Little, 1994), but the benefit was also supposed to replace the need for full-time employment. Although the expectations on single mothers were never completely separated from the needs of the labour market, with the exception of the war years, waged work was *not* a significant expectation of single mothers on social assistance during this period.

Workers *and* Mothers

In 1960, a modification made in the social-assistance regulations marked what Lorna Hurl terms the "first formal preference for work over welfare" (1989, p. 24). The change permitted the Ontario welfare authorities to deny beneifts to an applicant, or cancel benefits in the case of a recipient, if suitable employment was deemed to be available. Despite the fact that this regulation has rarely, if ever, been invoked, it did mark the beginning of a period when the single mother was viewed as both mother *and* worker, and policies began explicitly to encourage not only the single mother's labour-force participation, but also her transition from welfare to work. The passage of the Canada Assistance Plan in 1966 provided for federal cost-sharing and prompted an expansion of employment services, and these had a distinctly individualizing and rehabilitative flavour. A 1968–69 annual report from the Department of Family and Social Services, for example, noted that workers were to assist recipients "in achieving economic independence and more effective functioning in society" (cited in Hurl, 1989, p. 24). The requisite "good" behaviour of the single mother, an integral part of the welfare "bargain," gradually shifted the focus from mothering and morality to labour-force participation.

Explicit interest in moving single mothers into paid work made its appearance in Ontario in the 1960s. This interest became much more prevalent in the 1970s, when a variety of provincial initiatives were implemented to increase the financial rewards of paid employment. Regulatory changes were made to allow single mothers to retain a small, but increased portion of part-time earnings. The major initiative in this period, however, was the Ontario Work Incentive (WIN) Program of 1979 that was designed to promote the single mother's transition from social assistance to full-time employment. The WIN Program offered a wage supplement and permitted single mothers to retain some social assistance–related benefits. However, its failure to address the affordability and accessibility of child care, the meagre supplement levels, and the lack of available information about the program meant that this much-heralded "reform" never involved more than 3 percent of single mothers on social assistance (Evans, 1988). In 1982, the province introduced the Employment Supports Initiative (ESI), which provided pre-employment programs such as life skills and job counselling as well as information and referral to training and education programs. With ESI, the province shifted the definition of the "problem" from low wages to inadequate preparation for employment. Despite a new emphasis on full-time employment, the prevailing perspective during this period is of the single mother as mother *and* worker, and the decision about paid work, at least in principle, was voluntary.

Workers, *Not* Mothers

In the third period, the continuing ambivalence about employment expectations for single mothers appears to crystallize into a greater tendency to view them *as* workers, *not* mothers. This first becomes explicit in 1988, when the Social Assistance Review Committee, established by the Liberal government, headed by David Peterson, delivered its report (Ontario, Social Assistance Review Committee, 1988). This report, generally regarded fairly favourably by the anti-poverty forces, was called *Transitions*. As its title suggests, it underlined the importance of work incentives, training, and employment planning for individuals on social assistance. Within this framework, contingent support was given to the at-home role for single mothers. The report recommended that "single parents," the gender-neutral term used to refer to a distinctly gendered type of family, should be exempted from the requirement to register for the proposed, but never implemented, Employment Opportunities Program. The rationale was that parents were in the best position to make decisions that so fundamentally affect the care of their children. However, the report also noted that, if enough single parents did not make the "right" decision, that is, did not join the work force, then the status of their exemption should be reconsidered.

One of the report's more progressive recommendations became the STEP program. It was designed to increase the amount of earnings social-assistance recipients could retain. This program has been cut back since its introduction, because of rising costs and concern about the growing gap between the incomes of the working poor who received welfare and those who did not. It was thought that it encouraged women to stay on provincial social assistance rather than to leave the caseload (Ontario, Ontario Social Assistance Reform Project, 1993). In the current period, then, the trend toward viewing single mothers as workers is increasing, and we see the first explicit expression that this might have to take priority over their role as mothers. Recent proposals to restructure Ontario's social assistance system (ibid.) suggest a further weakening of a single mother's entitlement to social assistance based on her child-rearing responsibilities. Although Alberta has held explicit expectations of employment for single mothers for some time, it is now an NDP government that appears to be increasing the work-related obligations for single mothers on social assistance.

PUBLIC POLICY AND ONTARIO'S PROPOSALS

Although the discussion in this essay centres on Ontario, the themes that accompany the push to restructure social programs reverberate at the federal and the international level. While the pressures of globalization, free trade, and economic restructuring are typically invoked to suggest that social spending needs to be reduced, others suggest that they reinforce the need for greater government involvement and stronger social programs (for a good discussion, see Muszynski, 1994). However, Canada seems poised to follow the United States in reducing welfare benefits and other forms of wage and social protection. The current federal review of social programs, for example, is almost certain to result in further reductions to Unemployment Insurance and to lessen the requirements on provinces to adhere to the current limited federal standards regarding needs-tested assistance. These changes will further erode the already deteriorating position of women both as consumers and as employees of a declining welfare state (Luxton and Reiter, 1993). In addition to the pressures of globalization and unemployment, there are also specific factors in Ontario's policy environment that help to "target" single mothers for social-assistance reform in Ontario (see Box 6.2). There are three that are particularly important.

The Welfare Discourse: Ontario's "Reforms"

This is the background against which the Ontario government, other provincial governments, the federal government, and the governments of other countries are re-examining their social-assistance policies. Ontario's proposals are of particular interest because they represent the most specific and broadly based plan to overhaul a provincial social-assistance system that has been espoused thus far.

The Minister of Community and Social Services announced the objectives of the proposed social-assistance reform in the white paper *Turning Point* (Ontario, 1993, p. i): "Our goals are straightforward: we want to assist people in moving as quickly as possible back to work, we want to provide long-term support to those who are unable to work,

BOX 6.2

Reasons for Targeting Single Mothers

1. *Provincial spending on social assistance:* Since 1988–89, the costs of social assistance have almost tripled (*Globe and Mail*, July 9, 1993). This rise is attributable, in part, to a significant increase in the numbers on social assistance as a result of the recession of the 1990s. However, the federal "cap on CAP" has placed, for the first time since the inception of the Canada Assistance Plan in 1966, a ceiling on the federal contribution to the costs of social assistance. This has increased the province's portion from 50 to 72 percent of the total bill and represents an estimated loss of 6.7 billion in federal revenue. (Ontario, 1993)

2. *Labour-force participation:* A further factor that has contributed to defining single mothers as "employable" is the continuing rise in the labour-force participation rates among women with children, who are now more likely to be in paid work than are single mothers (Dooley, 1993). Women in two-parent families do not necessarily view their employment decisions as reflecting much "choice."

3. *Increasing imbalance between wages and welfare:* Social-assistance rates are based on need, and so reflect family size. Wages do not take family size into account, and the relative value of the provincial minimum wage declined by 18 percent between 1975 and 1990 (Ontario, 1993). In addition, globalization and free trade have meant that the jobs that do exist are increasingly bifurcated into the short-term, part-time, and low-wage sector, and the high-paying, high-skill sector. The tax burden on low-income families has also increased significantly in recent years (Battle, 1990). These trends, coupled with recent increases in Ontario social-assistance benefits, have resulted in a growing disparity between level of benefits and income from low-wage employment. The National Council of Welfare (1993, Table 11), for example, estimates that a single mother with one child on Ontario Family Benefits receives $4685 more per year than she would receive in take-home pay from full-time work at the minimum wage.[2]

and we want to help families to raise their children without having to rely on welfare."

In one sentence, the minister managed to address the major themes that constitute the current welfare discourse:

▶ the privileging of market work over other kinds of activities

▶ the increasing distinction between the "deserving" and the "undeserving"

▶ the problem of welfare "dependency."

These themes, translated into Ontario's proposals, do not bode well for a large number of single mothers. The proposed changes would create three separate benefits; for the purposes of this discussion, however, the first two are most relevant.

Ontario Adult Benefit (OAB)

This program would provide a basic benefit to cover the costs of food, clothing, and shelter. There is no mention of "adequacy" and, in order to ensure that work incentives are maintained, the levels of benefit are to be tied explicitly to the provincial minimum wage. An additional supplement to the basic OAB benefit is available to the small proportion of the caseload who are over 65 and to the larger group of individuals with disabilities. Single mothers are not included in this supplement, which signals a distinct demotion in the social-assistance ranks. Under the current two-tiered system, single mothers, together with individuals with disabilities and the elderly, receive Family Benefits. Total Family Benefits payments, intended for long-term recipients, are larger than those for General Welfare Assistance. The latter program is directed to the "employables" whose need for assistance is assumed to be short-term. A supplement for single mothers was not mentioned in the White Paper. However, the first page of the discussion paper that followed the White Paper mentioned "sole parent supplement," although it was never referred to again (Ontario, Social Assistance Reform Project, 1993). If, as seems possible, all references to the supplement were supposed to be omitted in the final version, this would appear a particularly graphic illustration of policy ambivalence toward a single mother's "worthiness."

Joblink

This back-to-work program includes three streams: intensive job search, education and training, and subsidized employment (termed "job creation"). Individuals admitted to JOBLINK are entitled to a benefit called the "Employment and Training Allowance" (ETA) that includes an amount equal to the basic OAB benefit, an additional flat-rate training allowance, and access to other benefits based on a "menu" of special needs, such as child care and travel. The ministry never indicated the amount of the supplemental training allowance, but one estimate placed it at $450 per month (*Toronto Star*, January 4, 1994, p. 1).

Participation in JOBLINK is voluntary, but once an agreed-upon employment plan is in place, those who fail to fulfil the conditions of the job search, training or education, or job-placement requirements will be returned to OAB. JOBLINK is planned to provide places for approximately one out of every four potential participants. Despite a general perception that individuals on social assistance must participate in employment programs, the ministry has asked for guidance from community groups as to how these scarce places might be fairly rationed. As is true of the vast majority of employment programs, the problem is too many participants, not too few. The Ontario reforms create a three-tier hierarchy: those who are entitled to a long-term supplement; those who are labour-market bound and receive a JOBLINK place; and those who are "left over" and relegated to the lowest tier. This third group includes those individuals whose category of need does not entitle them to a long-term supplement. It is not clear if single mothers will receive a long-term supplement, but it is clear that lack of space will prevent many from participating in JOBLINK.

Ontario Child Income Program (OCIP)

This program replaces the children's portion of the social-assistance benefit with a separate benefit that would also be available to the children of the working poor. There are a number of positive aspects to this change, including extending financial help to low-income families who are not on social assistance. However, there are also concerns. Depending on the level and structure of the benefit, some social-assistance families could be worse off. In addition, separating out the children's benefit may make it politically easier to lower the level of the adult rate and could further jeopardize adequacy in social-assistance rates.

The provincial government recently announced that spending cuts have forced them to put OAB and OCIP on temporary hold. JOBLINK will continue, although the cancellation of the provincial plan to expand child care will make it even more difficult for some single mothers to participate. Nonetheless, the government has found sufficient resources to hire 270 individuals to scrutinize all the files of Family Benefits recipients, despite the lack of evidence that fraud is a significant problem (*Globe and Mail*, March 30, 1994, p. A4).

THE COSTS OF SOCIAL-WELFARE REFORM

In broad outline, Ontario's welfare proposals seem relatively benign compared with recent policies in Aid to Families with Dependent Children (AFDC), the U.S. social-assistance program directed largely to single mothers (see Box 6.3).

As well, the expectations of employment for single mothers on social assistance are more explicit and restrictive in some provinces. In Alberta, for example, a single mother is now entitled to stay at home only until her youngest child is six months old. The Ontario government has discussed the possibility of making entitlement to social assistance conditional for some groups of single mothers, but to date this has not occurred.

BOX 6.3

Social-Welfare Reform in the United States   Changes in some states south of the border include:

▶   no additional payments for children born to single mothers who are already on AFDC;

▶   single mothers under age 18 are not eligible for AFDC unless they are attending school;

▶   the Clinton government is considering taxing welfare and food stamps and mandating work–for–welfare programs after two years of AFDC receipt. (*New York Times*, February 13, 1994, p. 1)

Despite the fact that, in relation to these examples, the Ontario proposals seem relatively benign, they are not. Furthermore, they raise particular dilemmas and challenges for feminists that the more blatant work requirements of social assistance do not.

Undeserving Mothers

Single mothers, as a group, are being redefined as the "undeserving." The failure to include single mothers in the proposed Long Term Income Supplement that was to be available to the elderly and those with disabilities—a demotion in the ranks of "deservingness"—is likely to increase the vulnerability of working mothers. One of the factors that explains why single mothers in Britain have been relatively sheltered from employment targeting is that the social-assistance program they rely upon also includes a large component of the elderly poor. In the United States, in contrast, single mothers have been highly visible, and extremely vulnerable, in the AFDC program, which is composed almost entirely of single mothers (Evans, 1992). The Ontario proposals seemed poised ultimately to translate into lower levels of benefits and increasing stigma for those who are not able to participate in JOBLINK. And, because the number of spaces is limited, many single mothers will be affected.

Compartmentalizing Mothers

As a group, single mothers are increasingly divided between those who are labour-market bound and those who are not. This distinction may make enormous sense to the policy-makers, but it makes much less sense to single mothers that their lives are frequently character-ized by entries and exits into the labour market, determined by the demand for labour and the needs of their children. As one response to these proposals suggested: "Sometimes they stop working because they are laid off or their contract ends. Often, they stop working because they decide that their children need them at home, or they are fired because of extra sick leave taken to care for a child. They may also quit because they are worn out trying to juggle their two jobs" (Stairs, 1994).

Access to JOBLINK raises additional concerns. While job-search expenses for participants are covered (occasional babysitting, transportation, clothing and grooming costs), it is highly unlikely that all those searching for employment can be accommodated in JOBLINK. It is not clear, however, that all single mothers who are job-hunting will receive JOBLINK job search-related benefits. In addition, if access to JOBLINK is not on a "first come, first served" basis, how will spaces be rationed? Will those single mothers who are perceived to have the most obstacles to employment be viewed as "too costly" an investment, and increasingly be left behind their more advantaged counterparts?

Waged work and immediate and direct preparation for paid employment appear to be the only activities supported in these proposals. Post-secondary education is explicitly excluded, and there is no indication that self-employment initiatives or community volunteer activities are eligible for the Employment and Training Allowance (Social Planning Council, 1993).

Few Government Obligations

For those participating in JOBLINK, there are clear expectations of the participant, but not of the government. When women take up subsidized employment slots, what are the working conditions? The government has been silent about any obligation, on its part, to ensure that workplaces and jobs meet employment standards and occupational health and safety regulations. There appears to be very little government accountability to ensure that job preparation and training programs result, at the end of the day, in reasonable employment. The record of these programs is not good (Lord, 1994; Porter, 1991; Evans, 1993).

Absence of Choice

The absence of a mandated requirement is not the equivalent of choice. Although the NDP government seriously considered mandating participation in JOBLINK for certain groups of participants, including single mothers with children over age 12 (Social Planning Council, 1993), in the end it opted for a voluntary program. However, if the gap between the general benefit levels and ETA is significant, the choice becomes illusory. Individuals not in job training are implicitly penalized for non-participation.

FEMINIST PERSPECTIVES ON WORK AND WELFARE

W hat do these proposals tell us about gender relations and the state, at least in this pivotal arena? There seems to be an increasing bifurcation between the construction of the problems of "ordinary" employed women and that of poor women. At a time when there is increasing attention, at least in principle, to the systemic discrimination women face in the labour market, the issue is defined very differently within social assistance, where the perception is that single mothers on social assistance are poor because they lack adequate education and training, and the "problem" with welfare is that it provides inadequate financial incentives. This perception is clearly distorted. Isolating the employment problems of women on welfare from other women ignores the realities of the lives of many women on social assistance as they cycle on and off welfare, frequently in synchronization with the rhythms of the low-wage and insecure labour market.

The problems of low-income single mothers are largely framed within the narrow confines of a human-capital approach to the labour market, which assumes an important connection between wages and individual levels of education, training, and work experience. This approach causes a disruption, rather than a conjunction, of the issues of women's poverty and labour-market discrimination. Policy is poised to redefine the work/welfare issue for single mothers based on a male model. The association between the rewards that an individual receives in the labour market and the quality of his or her "human capital" may not be clear and direct for many men (especially those disadvantaged by race and class), but it fits much less comfortably with the systemic discrimination women face in the labour market. The reason why only one out of ten single fathers lives in poverty in comparison with almost half of single mothers cannot be explained by differences in education (Evans, 1991). There is an irony that welfare policy is becoming increasingly gender-blind at a time when gender consciousness is supposed to be on the rise.

The work/welfare debate raises some difficulties and dilemmas for feminists. While there is broad-based agreement that it is essential that single mothers on social assistance have opportunities to participate in the labour market, there is less consensus about the relative merits of income from social assistance versus income from paid work. Feminists are not entirely exempt from the general public's fundamental ambivalence "about whether public support of single mothers is better or worse than sending mothers into the labor force" (Gordon, 1990, p. 11). Feminist ambivalence derives from two interrelated sources: (1) views about the nature of the welfare state; and (2) views about women's work caring for children and others. This ambivalence has weakened our preparedness *and* our ability to deal with some fundamental contradictions. Principally, we should endorse strong income-support programs at the same time that we recognize that these very programs, because of their failure to address structural inequalities, may also help to institutionalize women's poverty. The next sections of this essay discuss these areas of ambivalence for feminists.

Feminist Gaze on the Welfare State

In the first wave of feminism, the creation of the welfare state was generally regarded as positive and liberating for women. The second wave has been more critical. Feminists have unravelled the ways in which social-welfare provisions help to support both capitalism and patriarchy, offered important insights into the discriminatory nature of state provisions, and pointed to the powerful forces of social control. Income support from the state has often been characterized as "public patriarchy" (see Hernes, 1987). The tendency either to praise the welfare state for its liberating potential *or* to condemn it for reinforcing male dominance through its support for particular family forms is giving way to more nuanced perspectives. These underscore the contradictory effects of the welfare state on the lives of women, effects that are increasingly viewed as neither completely positive nor completely negative. Recent perspectives, for example, suggest that welfare-state policies emerge from the compromises that reflect and mediate political and social conflict (Dahl, 1990). More attention is also given to women's agency as they negotiate welfare provisions (Gordon, 1990), and the potential of the state to serve as an important political resource and potential ally (Piven, 1990; Orloff, 1993). In addition, the overarching notion of "the state" is being replaced by a differentiated understanding of its many and layered parts (Pringle and Watson, 1992; Allen, 1990).

Ann Shola Orloff (1993) points out that the feminist controversy over the fundamental factors that underlie women's oppression is greater than the mainstream welfare-state debates about the roots of class oppression. An important arena of diverse perspectives centres on the nature and consequences of women's caring; this is particularly relevant because of the theoretical and practical dilemmas it highlights in the issue of single mothers, paid work, and welfare.

Feminist Gaze on Women's Caring

Feminists have differed in the "lens" they bring to women's traditional role in providing care for others. For some, "social reproduction," or the work women do in providing for and nurturing others, is viewed primarily as functional for patriarchy or capitalism, or both (see, for example, Ursel, 1992). This has led, at times, to what Gillian Pascall (1986, pp. 21–22) refers to as "an economistic tendency to see the human results of reproduction solely as labourers in the capitalists' vineyard." This arguably reductionist perspective of women's work in the home is countered by those who emphasize an "ethic of care," suggesting the significance and importance of the relational, as well as the instrumental aspects of the work involved in tending others. This standpoint, in turn, is justifiably criticized for celebrating the very aspects of women's lives that lie at the root of their subordination. Many feminists, aware of the history of the negative effects of protective legislation, are understandably reluctant to "valorize" women's caring responsibilities (McCormack, 1991).

So it is generally agreed that women's hidden work in the household needs to become more visible. But there is considerable diversity in the ways that feminists understand the nature of this work. This is reflected in a disarray of terminology. The terms "domestic labour" and "social reproduction" are often rejected because they suggest that women's caring work is confined to the private sphere (Leira, 1992). But to refer to women's "caring" is also problematic because it conjures up images of love and affection and may "romanticize women's adaptations to powerlessness" (Fraser and Gordon, 1994). This perspective can easily obscure the onerous nature of the work and the costs it imposes on women. "Compulsory altruism," a term coined by Hilary Land and Hilary Rose (1985), may more accurately capture the nature of much of this work, and the significant constraints on women's freedom to refuse to undertake it. In general, however, a dilemma has emerged whereby an equality that obscures the realities of the work women do in looking after others comes up against a difference that cannot promote equality.

The two strategies that have been identified for achieving economic independence for women are described in Box 6.4. The second of these has characterized second-wave feminism, at times with an assumption that it is sufficient. This has meant that we have focussed on access to jobs, the creation of more woman-sensitive employment programs, and child care, and there has been a reluctance to provide active support for women's at-home position. As understandable as this reluctance is, it has also meant less sensitivity to the erosion of the claims of the non-employed, poor, single mother. It may be better to live with the tension between an "equality" and "protection" than to resolve it in favour of one or the other. In commenting on the 1988 U.S. welfare reforms that reinforced the work-conditioning aspects of AFDC, Gordon suggests that they resulted from "an alliance between those who believe that employment and reliance on wages is on the whole strengthening to women and those who would use employment as a punishment for deviant women" (1990, p. 38). It is important that feminists are not silent partners in such an alliance.

BOX 6.4

Two Strategies for Achieving Women's Economic Independence
Over time, two major strategies have been identified in the central feminist project of achieving women's economic independence:

▶   ensuring that women who care for children in the home have access to adequate incomes

▶   increasing access to adequately paid work and the services that make this possible. (Orloff, 1993)

Restructuring the Debate

If the feminist project is to reintegrate the single mother on social assistance back into the mainstream of concern about women's economic independence, there are a number of challenges to be confronted. And, perhaps most important in meeting these challenges is to learn to live more comfortably with tensions and dualities, rather than accepting the dichotomies of prevailing discourse: dependence/independence; paid work/welfare; equality/protection. What are these challenges?

Dependence or Independence

First, we must avoid the trap of viewing welfare as "dependency." While recognizing that income from employment may be preferable, in a number of respects, to income from social assistance, it is important not to view welfare receipt as simply a transition from private to public patriarchy. To do so suggests an implicit acceptance that a dependency relationship exists, and an agreement with the goal of "independence" along with its equation with waged work. To claim that "welfare mothers ought to work," as Nancy Fraser and Linda Gordon (1994) point out, is to define work only in terms of paid labour, and to identify child rearing as non-work. Ironically, the socially constructed "dependency" of women results from *giving* care, whereas, for others, relationships of dependency flow from *receiving* care (Graham, 1983). Similarly, the "independence" of men is often achieved and aided by the so-called dependent status of a woman. Diana Pearce comments: "as long as we accept the denigration of women who take care of dependent children as 'dependent', and as long as the welfare problem is termed one of 'dependency' then the policy choices are constrained to a set of equally impossible choices for the single mother" (1990, p. 275).

A rejection of the notion of welfare dependency diversifies the interpretation of the strategic interests of single mothers beyond child-care and employment programs, although these are critical services. But it does remind us that "the struggle over the value of caring work for making claims on the welfare state continues, even if we reject maternalist postures of the past" (Orloff, 1993, p. 322). This suggests that we must be as concerned to ensure that the already low levels of social-assistance benefits do not fall even farther beneath the poverty line in order to provide incentives for those entering the waged labour force. Working for "benchmarks" with which to gauge and track benefit adequacy and maintaining a needs-based, rather than a work-conditioned, approach to social assistance then take their place as important feminist goals, along with access to child care, appropriate training opportunities, and adequately paid employment.

Paid Work or Welfare

The distinction between "independence" and "dependence" extends into a false dichotomy between paid work and "welfare." This dichotomy fails to resonate with the lives of many low-income single mothers, who move in and out of the low-wage labour market, and it has also helped to separate the problems of low-income single mothers from the broader issues of gender divisions in the labour market and in the household. Many countries have been more prepared to acknowledge the interrelationship between household and workplace disadvantage through universal child-care provision, flexible and generous parental leaves, and child allowances. While these policies may more effectively compensate, rather than redress, the gendered divisions in the household and workplace, they do result in significant improvements to the economic situation of single mothers. Relatively few single mothers in Sweden have recourse to social assistance (Kamerman and Kahn, 1989), and their economic disadvantage, in comparison with two-parent families, is also small (Hauser and Fischer, 1990; Wong, Garfinkel, and McLanahan, 1993). In contrast, the lack of policy response in the English-speaking countries to the workplace/family dynamic that jeopardizes women as a whole, also results in a high degree of economic vulnerability for single mothers.

CONCLUSION

The ideal is not to move everyone into the labour market, ignoring the activities, critically important for society and community, of other types of work that need to be done and valued. Nor is it to glorify the work that women traditionally have been assigned, helping to curtail their participation in other spheres. The challenge lies in "overcoming not only arbitrary divisions of labor but also arbitrary divisions of labor's meaning" (Fraser and Gordon, 1994, p. 25). Ultimately, policies must support a sharing of paid and unpaid labour between women and men, and acknowlege the public, as well as the private, nature of this responsibility. As Dahl notes:

> The quest to let women's reality count on a par with men in social planning, means to adjust the law to citizen's lives such as it is shared *between* the market and the family; to recognize the necessity of time-sharing between the *two* productive spheres, and to give value to new combinations of work within and outside the market, both among different groups of citizens and over individual lifespans. (1990, p. 15)

This long-range vision is not on the immediate horizon, but it does suggest some criteria to use in evaluating the proposals for welfare reform that are proliferating at the federal and provincial levels of government. Is the legitimacy of income support recognized for single mothers through a commitment to benefit adequacy and an absence of work-conditioning? In addition to the need for affordable and accessible child care and training for *good* jobs, do the proposals reinforce discrimination in the labour market by relegating women to low-paid and insecure employment? And, finally, is there action directed to increasing jobs? Without this recognition, women will continue to be compartmentalized into those "on welfare" and those "in work," the "problems" of single mothers constructed as separate and distinct from "other" women, and single mothers subjected to increasingly punitive measures.

NOTES

1. This estimate is based on the 1990 figure of 778 395 single mothers in Canada (Vanier Institute of the Family, 1994) and a reported 310 380 single "parents" on the provincial social assistance caseloads in March 1990 (calculated from tables in Health and Welfare Canada, 1991). These will be almost entirely women. It is important to note that these "point in time" figures will underestimate the proportion of those who, at some time while they were single mothers, received social assistance.

2. In the summer of 1993, this issue received considerable publicity when an Ontario civil servant gave up her $41 000 job to go on to Ontario Family Benefits because she claimed (erroneously) that she would be only $20 a month worse off (see Martin, 1994; *Globe and Mail*, August 25, 1993, p. A4).

REFERENCES

Allen, Judith. (1990). Does feminism need a theory of "The State"? In Sophie Watson (Ed.), *Playing the state* (pp. 21–37). London: Verso.

Battle, Ken. (1990). Clawback: The demise of the universality in the Canadian welfare state. In Ian Taylor (Ed.), *Social effects of free market policies* (pp. 269–296). New York: St. Martin's Press.

Dahl, Tove Stang. (1990). *Bargaining for welfare: Control, class, and gender.* Paper given at the International Symposium on the Functions of Law in the Development of Welfare Societies, Oslo, August.

Dooley, Martin D. (1993). Recent changes in the economic welfare of lone mother families in Canada: The roles of market work, earnings and transfers. In Joe Hudson and Burt Galaway (Eds.), *Single parent families: Perspectives on research and policy* (pp. 115–131). Toronto: Thompson Educational Publishing.

Evans, Patricia M. (1984). Work and welfare: A profile of low-income single mothers. *Canadian Social Work Review,* 81–96.

Evans, Patricia M. (1988). Work incentives and the single mother: Dilemmas of reform. *Canadian Public Policy, 14* (2), 125–136.

Evans, Patricia M. (1991). Sexual division of poverty: Consequences of gendered caring. In Carol Baines, Patricia Evans, and Sheila Neysmith (Eds.), *Women's caring: Feminist perspectives on social welfare* (pp. 169–203). Toronto: McClelland and Stewart.

Evans, Patricia M. (1992). Targeting single mothers for employment: Comparisons from the United States, Britain, and Canada. *Social Service Review, 66* (3), 378–398.

Evans, Patricia M. (1993). From workfare to the social contract: Implications for Canada of recent US welfare reforms. *Canadian Public Policy, 19* (1), 54–67.

Fraser, Nancy, and Gordon, Linda. (1994). "Dependency" demystified: Inscriptions of power in a keyword of the welfare state. *Social Politics, 1* (1), 4–31.

Gordon, Linda. (1990). The new feminist scholarship on the welfare state. In Linda Gordon (Ed.), *Women, the state, and welfare* (pp. 9–35). Madison: University of Wisconsin Press.

Graham, Hilary. (1983). Caring: A labour of love. In Janet Finch and Dulcie Groves (Eds.), *A labour of love: Women, work and caring.* London: Routledge and Kegan Paul.

Hauser, Richard. and Fischer, Ingo. (1990). Economic well-being among one-parent families. In Timothy M. Smeeding, Michael O'Higgins, and Lee Rainwater (Eds.), *Poverty, inequality and income distribution in comparative perspective* (pp. 126–157). Washington, DC: Urban Institute.

Health and Welfare Canada. (1991). *Inventory of income security programs in Canada: July 1990.* Ottawa: Minister of Supply and Services.

Hernes, Helga Maria. (1987). Women and the welfare state: The transition from private to public dependence. In Anne Showstack Sasson (Ed.), *Women and the state* (pp. 72–92). London: Unwin Hyman.

Hurl, Lorna F. (1989). The nature of policy dynamics: Patterns of change and stability in a social assistance programme. Paper presented at the 4th National Conference on Social Welfare Policy, Toronto, October.

Kamerman, Sheila B., and Kahn, Alfred J. (1989). Single-parent, female-headed families in Western Europe: Change and response. *International Social Security Review, 42* (1), 3–34.

Land, Hilary, and Rose, Hilary. (1985). Compulsory altruism for some or an altruistic society for all? In P. Bean, J. Ferris, and D. Whynes (Eds.), *In defense of welfare*. London: Tavistock.

Leira, Arnlaug. (1992). *Welfare states and working mothers: The Scandinavian experience*. Cambridge: Cambridge University Press.

Little, Margaret Hillyard. (1994). *No car, no radio, no liquor permit: The moral regulation of single mothers in Ontario, 1920–1993*. Unpublished dissertation, Department of Political Science, York University.

Lord, Stella. (1994). Social assistance and "Employability" for single mothers in Nova Scotia. In Andrew F. Johnson, Stephen McBride, and Patrick J. Smith (Eds.), *Continuities and discontinuities: The political economy of social welfare and labour market policy in Canada* (pp. 191–206). Toronto: University of Toronto Press.

Luxton, Meg, and Reiter, Ester. (1993). Double, double, toil and trouble ... Canadian women's experience of work and family, 1980–1993. In Sheila Shaver (Ed.), *Gender, citizenship and the labour market: The Australian and Canadian welfare states*. SPRC Reports and Proceedings No. 109, (pp. 71–92). Social Policy Research Centre, Sydney: University of New South Wales.

Martin, Sandra. (1994, January). The making of an angry woman. *Toronto Life*, pp. 56–62.

McCormack, Thelma. (1991). *Politics and the hidden injuries of gender: Feminism and the making of the welfare state*. Ottawa: Canadian Research Institute for the Advance of Women.

Muszynski, Leon. (1994). Defending the welfare state and labour market polity. In Andrew F. Johnson, Stephen McBride, and Patrick J. Smith (Eds.), *Continuities and discontinuities: The political economy of social welfare and labour market policy in Canada* (pp. 306–326). Toronto: University of Toronto Press.

National Council of Welfare. (1992). *Welfare reform*. Ottawa: National Council of Welfare.

National Council of Welfare. (1993). *Incentives and disincentives to work*. Ottawa: National Council of Welfare.

Ontario. (1993). *Turning point*. Toronto: Ontario Ministry of Community and Social Services.

Ontario, Social Assistance Reform Project. (1993). *Proposed design features of the Ontario Adult Benefit (OAB)*. Discussion Paper no. 2. Ontario: Ministry of Community and Social Services.

Ontario, Social Assistance Review Committee. (1988). *Transitions*. Toronto: Queen's Printer.

Orloff, Ann Shola. (1993). Gender and the social rights of citizenship: The comparative analysis of gender relations and welfare states. *American Sociological Review, 58*, 303–328.

Pascall, Gillian. (1986). *Social policy: A feminist analysis*. London: Tavistock.

Pearce, Diana. (1990). Welfare is not *for* women: Why the war on poverty cannot conquer the feminization of poverty. In Linda Gordon (Ed.), *Women, the state, and welfare* (pp. 265–279). Madison: University of Wisconsin Press.

Piven, Frances Fox. (1990). Ideology and the state: Women, power, and the welfare state. In Linda Gordon (Ed.), *Women, the state and welfare* (pp. 250–264). Madison: University of Wisconsin Press.

Porter, Errol. (1991). *Long-term effects of three employment programs for social assistance recipients*. Toronto: Ontario Ministry of Community and Social Services, Research and Program Evaluation.

Pringle, Rosemary, and Watson, Sophie. (1992). "Women's Interests" and the post-structuralist state. In Michele Barrett and Anne Phillips (Eds.), *Destabilizing theory: Contemporary feminist debates* (pp. 53–73). Stanford, Ca: Stanford University Press.

Social Planning Council of Metropolitan Toronto.(1993). Welfare reform in Ontario: Turning POINT or Turning BACK? *Social Infopac, 12, 3*.

Stairs Felicite. (1994). Sole support mothers and the choice to go after paid work, Discussion Paper #5, Women Reforming Social Assistance. Sault Ste. Marie: Algoma Legal Clinic.

Strong-Boag, Veronica. (1979). "Wages for Housework": The beginnings of social security in Canada. *Journal of Canadian Studies, 14* (1), 24–34.

Ursel, Jane. (1992). *Private lives, public policy: 100 years of state intervention in the family*. Toronto: Women's Press.

Vanier Institute of the Family. (1994). *Profiling Canada's families*. Ottawa: Vanier Institute of the Family.

Wong, Yin-Ling Irene; Garfinkel, Irwin; and McLanahan, Sara. (1993). Single-mother families in eight countries: Economic status and social policy. *Social Service Review*, 177–197.

SUGGESTED READING

Evans, Patricia M. (1991). Sexual division of poverty: Consequences of gendered caring. In C. Baines, P. Evans, and S. Neysmith (Eds.), *Women's caring: Feminist perspectives on social welfare* (pp. 169–203). Toronto: McClelland and Stewart.

Fraser, Nancy, and Gordon, Linda. (1994). "Dependency" demystified: Inscriptions of power in a keyword of the welfare state. *Social Politics, 1* (1), 4–31.

Lord, Stella. (1994). Social assistance and "Employability" for single mothers in Nova Scotia. In Andrew F. Johnson, Stephen McBride, and Patrick J. Smith (Eds.), *Continuities and discontinuities: The political economy of social welfare and labour market policy in Canada* (pp. 191–206). Toronto: University of Toronto Press.

Piven, Frances Fox. (1990). Ideology and the state: Women, power, and the welfare state. In L. Gordon (Ed.), *Women, the state and welfare* (pp. 250–264). Madison: University of Wisconsin Press.

QUESTIONS TO CONSIDER

1. Does social-assistance policy toward single mothers support the argument that, for women, the welfare state contains both progressive and regressive elements? Why or why not?

2. The Ontario minister who introduced the package of reforms to social assistance commented that "we want to assist people in moving as quickly as possible back to work, we want to provide long-term support to those who are unable to work, and we want to help families to raise their children without having to rely on welfare." What are the assumptions that underpin these goals? Are they problematic for women? if so, in what way?

3. How might a feminist perspective reconstruct conventional notions of "dependence" and "independence"?

CHAPTER 7

One or the Other? "Race," Gender, and the Limits of Official Multiculturalism

Christina Gabriel

Official multiculturalism in Canada has become the source of considerable debate and tension.[1] On the one hand, it functions as the official expression of one of the myths of Canadian nationalism—the proof of our famed tolerance and the openness of our political community. On the other hand, it is increasingly being attacked as the cause of many of Canada's "problems" by people who fear the loss of "traditional" Canadian values and by others who charge that it is pandering to the demands of "special interests." Despite this debate and the fact that multiculturalism policy has significant impact and consequences for women, particularly women of colour,[2] there has been relatively little Canadian feminist analysis of official multiculturalism policy—an omission attributable, in part, to the fact that the terrain of this debate is seldom, if ever, viewed as gendered.

This essay offers a preliminary exploration of the interplay among the dynamics of gender, "race,"[3] and pluralism within the context of liberal democracy through the lens of official multiculturalism policy. It opens with a consideration of the conceptual location of multiculturalism within broader debates on citizenship. Next, it traces the evolution of the multiculturalism policy from being an unqualified celebration of culture toward becoming an acknowledgement—of sorts—of racism as a fact of life in Canadian society. This section is further developed with a specific focus on the contradictory and oft neglected gendered implications of this policy. Lastly, I consider how women of colour have sought political representation by invoking multiculturalism.

The encounters of women of colour with state institutions have often centred around issues of political representation and access to state-provided services. As such, they are part of the struggle against the multiple marginalization many of these women experience in Canadian society. This particular experience has been conceptualized by

Crenshaw, in reference to African-American women, as "intersectional."
She argues:

> Intersectionality captures the way in which the particular location of
> black women in dominant American social relations is unique and in
> some senses unassimilable into the discursive paradigms of gender and
> race domination. One commonly noted aspect of this location is that
> black women are in a sense doubly burdened, subject in some ways to
> the dominating practices of both a sexual hierarchy and a racial one.
> (1992, p. 404)

This dynamic, I argue, finds expression in the policy and practice of
official multiculturalism and in the structured complicity of state institutions. This complicity makes it very difficult, but not impossible, for
women of colour to demand recognition of their particular status at the
crossroads of gender and racial hierarchy. Various state policies and
offices have, more often than not, implicitly framed the issue of sexism
in terms of White women and racism in terms of visible-minority men.
This has more often led to the erasure of the intersectional experience
of women of colour.

CITIZENSHIP AND ISSUES OF REPRESENTATION

Over the last twenty years, liberal democracies have been prob-
lematized in new ways from the perspective of representation.
Liberal political discourse has been predicated on a universalistic
notion of citizenship. This notion has been challenged by a number of
"excluded" groups, such as women, people of colour, gays and lesbians, and people with disabilities. Each of these groups is contesting
its marginality. Increasingly, there is little consensus regarding a framework of representation, or how group interests are translated into policy outputs. In short, notions of citizenship are increasingly being debat-
ed, albeit from radically different perspectives, by feminists, socialists,
and the New Right, among others. At one and the same moment, citizenship has become the discourse in which problems are raised and
the means by which, once reformulated, the problem of representation
is "solved."

The Challenge of "Difference"

Changes in the world order, economic integration, and the international
division of labour have contributed to the massive migrations of people
from country to country. Among the most significant of these migrations has been that of people from the south to the north. As a result,
contemporary post-industrial societies are characterized by groups with

different ethnic and cultural identities from those of members of the so-called majority. These differences challenge traditional universalizing conceptions of citizenship, giving rise to new debates about what it means to be, for example, Canadian, English, French, or German. At the crux of these debates are two questions:

▶ Do we all need to share a common conception of national culture?

▶ Is such a common conception even possible in societies where some groups are socially and economically privileged?

Cultural identity and cultural exclusion find expression in many forms. This discussion foregrounds those of gender and "race." In racialized contexts, systemic socio-economic and ideological processes position "minority" populations on the margins. In Canada, official-multiculturalism policy is one response to address the way in which our society has become pluralized. Whether it can address the exclusion of certain groups from social and economic life while promoting tolerance is debatable. Nevertheless, multiculturalism—for better or worse—is inexorably tied to the concept of identity and citizenship policy. Changing conceptions of the community and who belongs to it inform both the way in which Canadians define themselves as a nation and their relations with one another and the state.

Boundaries of Citizenship

In Canada, officially at least, citizenship recognizes pluralism and the need to remove systemic barriers to individual advancement based on ethnic and racial background. Multicultural policy precludes cultural assimilation's being the "official" criterion that determines membership in the political community. This official endorsement of difference, however, has been the source of considerable tension.

Citizenship claims are made and contested on the basis of three specific and related axes. The first of these centres on who belongs and who is excluded from a particular community. Historically, various attempts have been made to restrict citizenship to certain groups and to exclude other groups entirely. The second and related axis of citizenship is a reciprocal notion of the rights and entitlements of the individual and, by corollary, the scope and nature of these social goods. The final axis is defined by questions of how these rights become a meaningful reality in practice (Hall and Held, 1989).

These questions were central to the work of T.H. Marshall. In particular, Marshall was concerned with how the formal political rights of liberal democracy could be reconciled with the social inequalities generated by a capitalist economic system. For Marshall, the postwar redistributive welfare state was one mechanism for addressing barriers to full membership and participation in the political community (see Box 7.1) (Turner, 1986).

BOX 7.1

Marshall's Classic View of Postwar Citizenship

▶   *Civil Rights:* rights necessary for individual freedom such as liberty; freedom of speech, thought, and faith; the right to own property and to conclude valid contracts; and the right to justice

▶   *Political Rights:* rights to participate in the exercise of political power as a member of a body invested with political authority or as an elector of the members of such a body

▶   *Social Rights:* the whole range, from the right to a modicum of economic welfare and security to the right to share to the full in the social heritage and to live the life of a civilized being according to the standards prevailing in the society. (Marshall, 1983, p. 249)

In Marshall's assessment of citizenship, the working class was cut off from a common culture and prevented from accessing a common civilization (Kymlicka, 1992). In his view, the expansion of social rights through the welfare state provided a means to make civil and political rights more meaningful. In this conceptualization, questions of class subordination became the foremost form of exclusion. And the issues of class have traditionally dominated debates about citizenship in the postwar period.

However, cultural identity and cultural exclusion take many forms, not just those of class. People of colour, women, people with disabilities, and gay men and lesbians have been excluded from the political community "not because of socio-economic status but because of their socio-cultural identity—their 'difference'" (Kymlicka, 1992, p. 26). Similarly, Yeatman argues that this concept of social citizenship itself is constructed on the assumption of a community whose members and groups share a common culture or idea about civilization. Thus, it constructs some groups as "other" because they occupy a disadvantaged position outside the norm. The terms "special-needs groups" and "minorities" to denote the status of such groups underscores the assimilationist ideal embodied within social citizenship more generally (Yeatman, 1994, p. 86). Because of its premises, Marshall's concept of social citizenship will not ensure that these groups transcend their marginality.

The prevailing postwar view of citizenship is, nevertheless, being challenged. Difference and subordinate status has become the basis of mobilization and claims for entitlement by those oppositional groups who have been systematically excluded from the political community. Feminists, for example, have highlighted not only how patriarchy has excluded women from the community but also the ways in which it has included them (Pateman, 1992). Gays and lesbians have mobilized to demand that same-sex couples receive the same rights and obligations as common-law couples of opposite sexes (see Cossman, this volume). Together, these groups, among others, are articulating broader conceptions of citizenship that are sensitive to issues of membership, expanding claims and rights to new areas and putting the complex notion of group identity—however defined—and its relation to the broader community on the agenda. Ironically, they make this challenge at a time when the welfare state itself is being restructured. It is also a time when the New Right is attempting to promulgate a narrower vision of citizenship that does not address any of the social dimensions of rights.

ALTERNATIVE VISIONS OF CITIZENSHIP

I f citizenship is to have any relevance to groups that have been systematically excluded, we need to think of ways that it can be reformulated. One reformulation, that advocated by cultural pluralists, supports the politics of identity and suggests various forms of differentiated citizenship in which group differences are valued and supported (Kymlicka, 1992, p. 28). Martin draws a useful distinction between demands for cultural pluralism and more radical versions of pluralism that call for "structural pluralism." The former embodies a recognition that cultural diversity is valuable and should be accorded public status and dignity. At its most minimal, this variant of cultural pluralism finds expression in avowals of cultural tolerance and the claims that groups should have distinct representation in politics and service delivery. In contrast, structural pluralism, or "differentiated citizenship," calls for recognition of group differences to be the basis for the allocation of social and economic resources and institutional reorganization in the areas of law, education, health, and language policy (Martin, 1991, p. 114). Official multiculturalism, as it currently stands in Canada, embodies the milder variant of cultural pluralism.

Feminist philosopher Iris Marion Young offers the most systematic theoretical elaboration of "differentiated citizenship." She begins from the position that a unitary conception of citizenship is unjust:

> In a society where some groups are privileged while others are oppressed, insisting that as citizens, persons should leave behind their particular affiliations and experiences to adopt a general point of view, serves only to reinforce that privilege, for the perspectives and interests of the privileged will tend to dominate this unified public, marginalizing or silencing those of other groups. (1990a, p. 120)

In the place of a universalistic notion of citizenship, Young calls for the adoption of a more heterogenous and differentiated concept. Within this framework, group representation becomes a method to "promote just outcomes within democratic decision making process" (ibid., p. 125). This process would be facilitated by institutional mechanisms and public resources for the effective recognition of oppressed and disadvantaged groups in three areas of activity (see Box 7.2).

I have highlighted this idea of differentiated citizenship because it offers an alternative to the dominant conception of universal citizenship. And Canadian multiculturalism policy, beset with contradictions and ambiguities, is a policy area that offers a starting point for this project to be undertaken. However, the future direction of citizenship policy in Canada, the debate concerning the parameters of official multiculturalism, and which disadvantaged groups may or may not benefit will largely be determined by political struggles. It is within such struggles that strong feminist representation is crucial if multicultural policy is to address the marginalization of women of colour.

OFFICIAL MULTICULTURALISM

The Symbolic Order

The policy of official multiculturalism was proclaimed by the Canadian government on October 8, 1971. On that day, Prime Minister Trudeau announced:

> A policy of multiculturalism within a bilingual framework commends itself to the government as the most suitable means of assuring the cultural freedom of Canadians. Such a policy should help break down discriminatory attitudes and cultural jealousies, national unity, if it is to mean anything in a deeply personal sense, must be founded on confidence in one's own individual identity. (quoted in Fleras and Elliott, 1992, p. 281)

BOX 7.2

Three Axes of a Differentiated Citizenship

▶   *Self-organization of group members* so that they gain a sense of collective empowerment and a reflexive understanding of their collective experience and interests in the contexts of the society

▶   *Voicing a group's analysis* of how social-policy proposals affect them and generating policy proposals themselves, in institutionalized contexts where decision makers are obliged to show they have taken these perspectives into consideration

▶   *Having veto power* regarding specific politics that affect the group directly—for example, reproductive rights for women, or use of reservation lands for U.S. Native peoples. (Young, 1990a, p. 124)

This policy (see Box 7.3) signalled that the federal government's approach to the issue of diversity—however defined—would be informed by an integrationist approach. In principle, this means that groups would participate as full equals in society and not have to forgo cultural distinctiveness. Thus, multiculturalism marked a rupture with past practices that had unashamedly espoused assimilation—practices that were an integral part of Canadian immigration policy. Until the late 1960s, selection criteria were premised on a policy of "preferred nationalities"—British subjects, followed by people from northwestern Europe (Frideres,1992 p. 48). In Canada, assimilation meant Anglo conformity, or the adoption of British cultural patterns and practices. While these two approaches, assimilation and integration, can be presented as analytically distinct, it should be noted that official multiculturalism policy reflects both tendencies. As Fleras and Elliott have noted, "in practice, integration and assimilation are operationally difficult to separate since the final product is unmistakably dominant-group in appearance" (1992, p. 316).

The key public message in the new policy was that no one culture would be elevated as official. All cultures were legitimate and to be valued. But the policy implicitly prioritized an English/French dualism insofar as multiculturalism was tied securely to a bilingual framework. The policy did not support the creation of separate organizations or institutions at odds with English or French structures. Instead, minority groups were encouraged to retain aspects of their culture, if they chose to, and to seek full participation in existing mainstream institutions and structures.

BOX 7.3

Multiculturalism's Four Organizing Principles

▶ First, resources permitting, the government will seek to assist all Canadian cultural groups that have demonstrated a desire and effort to continue to develop a capacity to grow and contribute to Canada, and a clear need for assistance, the small and weak groups no less than the strong and highly organized.

▶ Second, the government will assist members of all cultural groups to overcome the barriers to full participation in Canadian society.

▶ Third, the government will promote creative encounters and interchange among all Canadian cultural groups in the interest of national unity.

▶ Fourth, the government will continue to assist immigrants to acquire at least one of Canada's official languages in order to become full participants in Canadian society. (Fleras and Elliott, 1992, p. 282)

The priority given to English and French reflects the fact that multiculturalism emerged within the context of the Royal Commission on Bilingualism and Biculturalism. In part, it was a response to the demands by those groups, neither French or English, who wanted the national myth of "founding races" to reflect their contribution. As a result, multiculturalism, as initially framed, was directed at European immigrant groups and their needs in relation to cultural preservation and sharing. There was an emphasis on the arts, folk festivals, and ethnic-history projects. It has been argued that the 1971 policy marked an important restructuring of the symbolic order (Breton, 1986; Stasiulis, 1988; Fleras and Elliott, 1992). However, the four organizing objectives of the policy, as Kobayashi noted, were characterized by a general tendency to avoid "reference to economic or political factors, to programmes that would bring about social change beyond the confines of designated groups or to the issues of racism and other forms of discrimination." For these reasons, she argues that the political discourse of official multiculturalism hardly represented a radical challenge to the status quo, and certainly provided no means of changing it (1993, p. 217).

The policy, in fact, also privileged English/French dualism. This bias is underscored by the fact that recognition was given to the linguistic rights of only these two groups. Consequently, "this implies the linguistic assimilation of members of their groups into one or other of the two official language communities" (Stasiulis, 1988, p. 86). While culture and nationalism are not based solely on language, language is inexorably bound up with their authenticity and preservation. Despite its subsequent piecemeal policy, in response to pressures from minority groups, the federal government's support for official language instruction far exceeds that for third-language training (ibid., p. 88). In the absence of effective resourcing, it is very likely that many collectivities will be unable to preserve their language and will be indirectly pressured to assimilate.

The Limits of an Integrationist Model

Many of the initial limitations and subsequent difficulties of official multiculturalism policy in Canada can be traced back to the 1971 policy and its integrationist or liberal premises. The policy is as notable for what it doesn't say as for what it does say. Terms such as "cultural diversity," "integration," and "tolerance" mark its direction. Yet, these terms remain vague and unspecified. Canadian novelist Neil Bissoondath has remarked that "the act, activist in spirit, magnanimous in accommodation, curiously excludes any ultimate vision of the kind of society it wishes to create. It never addresses the question of the nature of a multicultural society, what such a society is and what it means." He asks: "How far do we go as a country in encouraging and promoting cultural difference? How far is far enough, how far is too far?" (*Globe and*

Mail, January 28, 1993). In terms of gender, for example, is the commitment to multiculturalism at odds with the gender interests of women within minority communities? How will this tension be mediated, and what will be the standard by which it is measured? Will it be problematic if the standard proves to be "Canadian" culture and norms?

The integrationist approach creates a particular dynamic between minority groups and mainstream society. Specifically, it constructs cultural difference almost entirely from the perspective of the former and asks how the latter can be more tolerant and respectful (Parekh, 1990, p. 67). In Canada, multiculturalism emerged, in part, because of the activism of ethnocultural groups. The government's response recognized that these cultures are an important resource and that their preservation is valuable. It has been singularly unsuccessful, however, in its attempt to demonstrate this value to mainstream groups. As a result, the view that the entire moral burden of tolerance is borne by the majority groups has become hegemonic. It finds expression in the party platform of the Reform Party, which calls for an end to official multiculturalism. Its supporters argue that "Canada is being stolen from us. It's being stolen by Quebeckers, by Ottawa bureaucrats and by ethnics who won't join the mainstream" (Gardiner, 1991, quoted in Keohone, 1992, p. 20). Increasingly, more and more Canadians are coming to believe that they are too tolerant. One study reported 72 percent of Canadians believe different ethnic and racial groups should try to adapt to Canadian society (*Toronto Star*, December 13, 1993).

Thus, as long as official multiculturalism is confined to, or perceived to be a policy directed at, "new" Canadians or "minorities," some disadvantaged groups will be forced to bear responsibility for their own problems. In the case of racism, people of colour, because of their "visibility," "culture," or "concentration," will be constructed as problems. Thus, in different ways, the racism of mainstream society is conciliated and not challenged.

The notion of culture in the integrationist approach, and, by extension, in multiculturalism policy, is problematic for a number of reasons. Culture, as a social form, is taken as natural, static, and unchanging. By default, the majority culture is taken as given in this strategy. As Parekh argues:

> It confines minority cultures to the private realm and hands over the public realm of common culture to the majority. The minorities are free to cherish their differences, but as far as the shared public realm is concerned they are required to accept, and become integrated into, the common culture more or less as it is. The liberal response thus does little more than carve out a precarious area of diversity on the margins of a predominantly assimilationist structure. (1990, p. 67)

In addition, the public representation of culture within multiculturalism is situated in past practices and traditions. Culture becomes the fixed signifier of country of origin, ethnicity, "race," and religion. Yet, culture is constantly being negotiated, mediated, and contested. The very process of migration, for example, "is often a rupture, a displacement; and return is always to a different place." Migration also encounters processes of industrialization and urbanization, "reducing the space where cultural practices could be maintained" (Pettman, 1992, p. 118). Hybridity characterizes the cultural landscapes of many industrial societies.

Official multiculturalism tends to treat cultural groups as homogeneous and essentialized categories. In doing so, it neglects the historical and political differences between groups. It also ignores the fact that, within groups, there are differences based on, among other things, class, gender, ability, and sexual orientation. This narrow treatment of culture underscores the inability of the integrationist approach, and, by extension, multiculturalism, to speak to the broader sociopolitical dynamics of "race" and gender. In its initial incarnation, multiculturalism identified language as the most important means to ensure meaningful participation in society by minority groups. The pervasiveness of racial and gender oppression in politics, the labour market, society, and forms of cultural life remained largely unrecognized and uncontested.

A Shift in Focus

By the 1980s, a number of factors forced the federal government to re-examine the efficacy of the program. It had become apparent that official multiculturalism policy, as initially conceived, was unable to address a range of concerns. Changing immigration patterns further highlighted the fact that the policy did not necessarily speak to the concerns of people of colour. Racist practices dictated that the experience of many new immigrants from the south, as well as people who had been in Canada for generations, would be fundamentally different from European immigrants. The concerns of the former revolved around systemic discrimination not just on the basis of language, but also in the areas of employment, housing, and education. In response, the government introduced a new policy with a clearer direction and focus, the 1988 Canadian Multicultural Act.

As a result, official multiculturalism evolved from a singular focus on folklore and heritage issues to a more *tentative* focus on social-equality rights (Kobayashi, 1993). The 1988 policy attempted to balance its earlier vision, focus on cultural maintenance and social integration, and meet new concerns by emphasizing equality measures. The policy focus shifted to the following priorities:

- race relations
- multiculturalism in the economy
- multiculturalism in education
- immigrant and visible-minority women
- multiculturalism in broadcasting

The fact that the boundaries of the policy were pushed in these directions reflects the successful mobilization of many ethnocultural groups.

Gender Implications of Multiculturalism

The question remains: Can multiculturalism policy address the "intersectional" experience of women of colour by confronting both racism and sexism? The 1988 policy identifies both race relations and immigrant and visible minority women as "priorities" of Multiculturalism Canada. This formulation, in and of itself, raises reservations about the ability of the policy to speak to the concerns of women of colour since, in focussing on cultural, ethnic, racial, religious, and linguistic groups, there is an overwhelming tendency for gender to be subsumed by group identity. Consequently, while women may be identified as a priority and may be empirically present in statistics, their concerns are not always addressed. Gender inequality, in relation to male power, whether intragroup or intergroup, seems to be neglected. Similarly, given the fact that multiculturalism neglects the gendered nature of culture, it also, by corollary, neglects the fact that racism is experienced differently by men and women.

Where women are specifically identified within the policy, they are usually constructed as the "problem" or "issue" that must be addressed. In 1982, the secretary of state said in the document *Multiculturalism—Priorities*: "Immigrant women are isolated both within their own and the larger society, often as a result of limiting cultural traditions and lack of basic life skills, particularly official language acquisition" (quoted in Das Gupta, 1994, p. 72). Das Gupta's assessment of this document leads her to conclude that it was premised on a "blame the victim" scenario. In other words, the exclusion of immigrant women from Canadian society is attributed to cultural deficiencies, ignorance, and the sexism of their own communities. This invidious process "removes the focus of analysis away from power inequalities existing in society which deny women in general, and immigrant women in particular, equal opportunities in life" (ibid., p. 73).

Critics of cultural pluralism frequently invoke the category "women" as a means to advance their arguments. On behalf of immigrant women, a number of cultural and/or family practices are scrutinized and are often found wanting when compared with a "universal" ideal. Martin's assessment of Australian multiculturalism provides an interesting case in point. She argues that "substantial aspects of Anglo-Australian culture, and a (male) Anglo-Australian national character" form the basis of a "good society." As a result, cultural practices are judged from the viewpoint of an "ideal anglo perspective" and are often deemed backward (1991, p. 121). Martin makes two observations of particular relevance for a gendered assessment of Canadian multiculturalism, both about calls for limiting cultural pluralism because of the implications the policy has for some groups of women:

▶ the deployment of the rhetoric of "progress" by dominant cultures (has been used) to justify the colonialization of subordinate cultures and the domination of colonized men

▶ the use of women to spell out the limits of tolerance in a culturally diverse society is not prompted by any interest in female inequality and certainly not by any interest in female oppression itself ... rather it is overridingly about treating women—wives, mothers, and daughters—decently, as a norm of conduct governing the ranking of men. (ibid., pp. 121–122)

This allows the issue of patriarchy in dominant societal practices related to the family to escape scrutiny because, by implication, women of dominant groups are already treated decently and do not experience sexism.

Cultural pluralism and multiculturalism do have the potential to preserve and exalt practices and or customs that may have negative consequences for women. However, as a political project, cultural pluralism is not inherently reactionary any more than it is inherently oppositional. For example, in criticizing multiculturalism, it has been suggested that ethnocultural organizations, in Canada "waste their energies and resources in espousing foreign causes, internal bickering and enforcing an outmoded fundamentalist code of behaviour" (Kumar and Bennett, 1991, p. 14). However, as Women against Fundamentalism, in Britain, has argued, it is not multiculturalism per se that is complicit with fundamentalism but a "particular essentialism and ungendered representation of culture which authorizes as spokesmen older and more conservative men and the failure to recognize that communities are subject to unequal power and contests for control from both without and within" (Pettman, 1992, p. 119).

Multiculturalism's critics fail to recognize that cultural practices, such as those that appear to oppress women, are always being challenged. Essentialist notions of culture can be manipulated to reinforce many oppressive power structures. The perils of official multiculturalism are situated in its unquestioned celebration of authenticity and its static notion of culture. The real issue for women is to interrogate and expose those who are constructing particular interests in the name of the community.

AN ONTARIO CASE STUDY

Not only has the migration of peoples from the Third World to Canada added new dimensions to the policy of multiculturalism, but its impact has been geographically uneven. In the postwar period, Montreal, Toronto, and Vancouver received heavy inflows of immigrants from the Third World. Ontario, in particular, received 52.4 percent of all immigrants coming into Canada in 1993. Twenty-eight percent of these new immigrants chose to settle in Toronto (Citizenship and Immigration Canada, 1994, p. 4). Not surprisingly, the province is also the home of the country's major national ethnic organizations. Ontario, in particular, will continue to face major challenges with respect to multicultural policy.

Women of colour have mobilized around the policy and practice of multiculturalism in Ontario, demanding recognition of their particular intersectional status at the crossroads of gender and race. This Ontario case study offers a particular example, in microcosm, of the problematic nature of the state's relationship with particular groups of women.

In the period between 1979 and 1990, women of colour struggled to be recognized and to put their issues on the provincial agenda. The stated goals of the province's 1987 Multiculturalism Strategy and Race Relations Policy—namely, a commitment to representation and access to government services—were one means by which women of colour contested their subordination and exclusion. However, these struggles took place on the margins of the state apparatus, in the advocacy offices of the Ontario Women's Directorate (OWD) and the Race Relations Directorate (RRD), and their impact on other political and bureaucratic arenas of the state is the subject of debate. These advocacy offices also appeared to have mutually exclusive mandates that could not address the "intersectional" social location of women of colour.

Thus, while the provincial state did appear to respond to some of the concerns of women of colour, it did so in ways that tended to reflect and reinforce their position of multiple marginality within broader society.

Ontario's Multiculturalism Strategy

The province of Ontario responded to the federal government's 1971 initiative by establishing the Advisory Council on Multicultural Issues. In 1977, it unveiled an official policy that recognized the presence of increased immigration by supporting the cultural endeavours of various groups. In 1987, the Ontario Liberal government further strengthened the province's commitment to multiculturalism when it announced its multiculturalism strategy. The policy states "that government, its ministries, boards and agencies are committed to equality of opportunity, full participation and responsible citizenship for all Ontarians regardless of cultural heritage or race" (Ontario Ministry of Citizenship, 1989, p. 1).

The strategy was to work in conjunction with the government's new 1986 race relations policy. And, while nominally separate, the two initiatives were intimately linked. According to the Ministry of Citizenship, "the policies share a commitment to equal access and participation for all Ontarians regardless of culture or race. In many cases, an initiative undertaken for one policy also supports the objective of the other." It continued to argue that "while its important to understand the conceptual relationship linking multiculturalism and race relations, we must not lose sight of the fact that action to identify and resolve existing needs and barriers to access of cultural and racial minorities is our prime goal" (1989, p. 42).

The government also provided institutional support in the form of the Race Relations Directorate within the Ministry of Citizenship. Its stated purpose was to develop policies and programs to promote harmonious race relations in the province. The 1987 Ontario multiculturalism strategy was marked by a commitment to both culture and equality. In addition, the focus on "diversity" reflected an attempt by the province to broaden the vision of multiculturalism as a policy for all its people rather than just ethnic minorities. "The dual focus on culture and equality put Ontario multiculturalism in step with comparable race relations initiatives at the Federal level" (Fleras and Elliott, 1992, p. 81). However, insofar as the developments in Ontario tended to reflect those at the federal level, they embodied many of the contradictions and problems outlined above.

Encounters with the Provincial State

Strong grass-roots mobilization brouth the particular situation of women of colour to the fore in the late 1970s and 1980s. As a result of this activism, "immigrant women" became a focus of concern for state officials, which generated a series of contradictory outcomes. First, women of colour were "targeted" and made eligible for grants set up for community research and projects. However, as Wallis, Gilles, and Hernandez explain, this targeting "takes away power from immigrant and visible minority women themselves. As 'targets' racial minority women become objectified; things are done for them: their own power is devalued" (1988, p. 45). As an "issue" or "target" throughout this period, women of colour were also often marginalized through a particular process of consultation that was by no means an extension of local democracy. Examples of this process include formal consultation mechanisms, task forces, conferences, seminars, workshops, and more ad hoc mechanisms such as meetings with bureaucrats and ministers. Again and again, similar issues of concern were raised, reiterated, researched, and revisited.

An early example of this type of consultation was the 1979 Joint Task Force on Immigrant Women. This initiative was sponsored by the Ontario Advisory Council on Multiculturalism in association with the Ontario Status of Women Council. And it has been argued that, since the former agency had lead responsibility, the "provincial government was considering immigrant women's issues from the perspective of multiculturalism, not gender" (ibid.).

The 1979 task force was the epitome of what Roxanna Ng has referred to as the legal, social, and labour market construction of immigrant women. She points out:

> In everyday life, only certain groups of women are seen to be "immigrant women" by other members of society. They are women of colour, including women from southern Europe and the Third World; women who do not speak English or who speak English with an accent (other than British or American).... In other words, the common usage of the term presupposes class and racist biases. (1988, p. 185)

The report of the joint task force is remarkable insofar as it made little or no mention of the systemic racism and sexism endemic to Canadian society. Instead, it tended to pathologize women of colour within the category of "immigrant women" by focussing on their perceived inadequacies or cultural deficiencies to account for the failure of some groups of women to integrate into the mainstream. For example, in the report's section on employment, the suggestion is made that immigrant women "are often ignorant of the rights due to them" under existing employment standards provisions and are "incapacitated by their lack of English" (Ontario Ministry of Culture and Recreation, 1979, p. 10). It further argues that an immigrant woman's disadvantage in, for example, the hiring process is attributable "in many cases" to an "unawareness of how to present herself, lack of work experience, lack of confidence due to different cultural background, etc." (ibid., p. 13). Among the many solutions proposed to this particular problem was increased community funding to encourage organizations to initiate programs involving job counselling, job training, and grooming hints.

Of course, all women of colour are not new arrivals, and many speak one of the two, if not both, official languages fluently. Yet, many continue to experience racism whether or not they are first- , second- , or third-generation Canadians. The focus on "immigrant women" and issues of settlement and adaptation tended to obscure the needs and concerns of many women of colour. In an effort to respond to this omission, the province, through its Race Relations Division and the Ontario Women's Directorate, initiated another process of consultation—community outreach—in 1982. The process culminated in a provincial conference on racism, sexism, and work the following year for "The Visible Minority Woman." At that time, the commissioner for Race Relations told the more than 400 participants that visible-minority women share problems with other groups of women. But "they have a special problem of their own, ie. their visibility. Because of that they suffer from racism and sexism" (Ontario Women's Directorate, 1983, p. 9).

Further, the chairperson of the Advisory Council on Multiculturalism and Citizenship suggest that "visible minority communities were distinguishable by race and colour, physiognomy and, sometimes, by accent" (ibid., p. 14). These comments are highlighted because they are indicative of the broader process alluded to above. Women of colour appear to be construed at one and the same time as victim and problem because of their "visibility." "Race" is treated as an unproblematic category that is somehow constituted by nature as opposed to being socially constructed. Racism and sexism were also largely conceptualized as separate and distinct.

The 1983 conference was important, however, insofar as it attracted 400 women of diverse backgrounds from across the province. One of its outcomes was the founding of the Coalition of Visible Minority Women (CVMW). This group has proved to be a strong advocate for immigrant and racial-minority women. Conference participants also made more than 100 recommendations related to policy and program development. Many of these can be grouped in the areas of language training, employment equity, training and accreditation, and access to health, social services, and child care.

The years following the 1983 Conference on Visible Minority Women were characterized by the failure of the provincial government to respond to any of its recommendations and resolutions. In 1986, the Coalition of Visible Minority Women, working with the Ontario Advisory Council for Women's Issues (OACWI), sought to make the government more accountable. Together, they met with Ian Scott, Minister Responsible for Women's Issues, and put forward a series of proposals (see Box 7.4 for details). Of this meeting, Carmencita Hernandez, a member of the coalition, wrote:

> Though it was the beginning of a dialogue between government and community, women were sobered by the meeting. After presenting their brief, they came to realize that there was no policy regarding visible minority women. As women, we were not targeted by policies and programs of the OWD; as visible minorities, we were lumped together with men by the Race Relations Directorate. (1988, p. 159)

The Ontario Women's Directorate, working with the Ministry of Citizenship and Culture (MCC) and the Race Relations Directorate, co-ordinated five regional workshops to be held across the province in an attempt to respond to some of the proposals. These 1987 workshops focussed on government policies and services relevant to visible-minority and immigrant women. A total of 109 recommendations were generated, but they differed little from those of the 1983 conference. One year later, women were once again were asking the government for follow-up action.

The province's Multiculturalism Strategy and Race Relations Policy became the area in which women of colour directed their focus. A number of groups, including the National Organization of Immigrant and Visible Minority Women (NOIVMWC), the Congress of Black Women, the Canadian Ethnocultural Council Women's Committee, the Chinese Canadian National Council on Women's Issues Committee, and the Coalition of Visible Minority Women, met with the Minister

---

BOX 7.4

Selected CVMW/OACWI 1986 Proposals

▶ Interministerial committee made up of staff from OWD and Race Relations Directorate to identify priorities for action by all departments

▶ Follow-up and implementation of recommendations from the 1983 Conference on Visible Minority Women

▶ Establish a formal relationship between OWD and the Race Relations Directorate

▶ Review all cabinet submissions for impact on visible-minority women

▶ Increase representation of visible-minority women on a number of agencies, boards, and commissions. (Ontario Advisory Council on Women's Issues, 1988, p.4)

Responsible for Women's Issues. They were specifically concerned that neither the multiculturalism strategy nor the province's race-relations policy had any clear guidelines to ensure full equality for women of colour.

NOIVMWC emphasized that "immigrant and visible minority women are doubly disadvantaged by race and gender" and this "combined discrimination permeates on both personal and institutional levels" (1988, p. 1). Akua Benjamin, from the Congress of Black Women, told the Minister of Citizenship and the Minister Responsible for Women's Issues that

> in the course of advancing the status of culturally and racially diverse population of Ontario as well as in the course of advancing the status of women, immigrant and visible minority women should not be left behind, neglected or ignored. We are not asking for special treatment. Within the struggle for equality, equality for one group is not the same as for another, simply because we are not all at the same starting line. (ibid., p. 17)

Groups also made these recommendations:

▶ The Ministry of Citizenship (MCC), the Race Relations Directorate (RRD) and the Ontario Women's Directorate (OWD) should collectively set a role model to line ministries to shape and promote immigrant and visible-minority women's issues.

▶ A team approach should be developed among these three departments to ensure a consistent and comprehensive approach toward immigrant and visible-minority women in the Multiculturalism Strategy and Race Relations Policy.

▶ MCC and RRD should assign a specific staff person to deal with immigrant and visible-minority women's issues, preferably of immigrant and/or visible minority background with an understanding of the community needs and sensitivity to minority women's issues.

▶ Appropriate resources should be allocated to these responsibilities. (ibid.)

There was a clear recognition that only through "structural changes within the government bureaucracy would immigrant and visible minority women have a focus and status within the Multiculturalism strategy and the Race Relations Policy" (ibid., p. 2). In making these recommendations, the NOIVMWC was moving toward a model, albeit limited, of group representation within the decision-making process.

In the period between 1979 and 1990, women of colour sought to redefine the ways in which they were included and excluded from decision-making processes. In doing so, they raised the issue of institutional sexism and racism, and their particular position of multiple marginality. Their concerted efforts had some results. They managed to have some of their members appointed to the province's advisory councils. Within the Ontario Women's Directorate, there is a designated staff person whose primary responsibility is immigrant and racial-minority women's issues. In 1988, the government established a women's subcommittee to the Cabinet Committee on Race Relations. Its purpose was "to ensure full integration of women's issues within government initiatives, specifically the Multiculturalism Strategy and Race Relations Policy" (Ontario Women's Directorate, 1989). The women's subcommittee lasted only from January 1989 to June 1990. Its review of the gender component in the multiculturalism strategy was somewhat summarily curtailed by the 1990 provincial election. The fact that this subcommittee did not survive the change of government is indicative of the fragile nature of the initiative itself.

The Structural Complicity of the State

The responses of the province of Ontario to the issues of women of colour were ad hoc, in part because state practice forced women of colour into institutional exile. They couldn't be slotted easily or neatly into the structural matrix of race-relations policy or women's issues. This position has been aptly described as "a political vacuum of erasure and contradiction maintained by the almost routine polarization of 'blacks' and women into separate and competing camps" (Crenshaw, 1992, p. 403). This dynamic found institutional expression within the state bureaucracies of the Race Relations Directorate (now the Ontario Anti-Racism Secretariat [OARs]) and the Ontario Women's Directorate (OWD). It served to establish a set of formidable limiting conditions that made political advances slow at best.

Initial attempts to respond to the needs and mobilization by women of colour, such as the 1983 Conference on Visible Minority Woman, were very much top-down affairs. For example, while state officials struck a committee of community-based activists to advise in the planning process of the 1983 conference, the committee's participation was limited to selection of cultural events and food. Committee members were not taken seriously (Hernandez, 1988, p. 159). If the participation of women of colour had been more meaningful at the planning stage, the intersection between racism and sexism would have been much clearer. Instead, the 1983 conference highlighted "visibility" as a key unifying factor. Women of colour, it was assumed, were more interested in issues of "race" than gender.

In a similar vein, throughout the 1980s, the logic prevailed that either immigrant and visible-minority communities were genderless or women within these communities would not have particular needs or concerns. Thus, on the one hand, women of colour were informed by the Minister Responsible for Women's Issues that he wanted "to deal with race-related issues in the wider context of *all* visible minority Ontarians—not just women" (Ontario Advisory Council on Women's Issues, 1988, p. 5). Similarly, the Minister of Citizenship responded to their concerns by saying, "it is seen as counterproductive to target programs for particular disadvantaged groups, e.g. isolating visible minority and immigrant women rather than addressing the needs of visible minorities and newcomers" (National Organization of Immigrant and Visible Minority Women, 1988). But, during this same period, women of colour were also being informed that, as all women in Ontario make strides, they, too, will gain. There was a general failure to perceive the particular position of women of colour, and this failure was compounded by the fact that no one ministry spoke to their concerns.

Throughout this period, groups such as the Coalition for Visible Minority Women and NOIVMWC emphasized that their issues should be promoted across the government. "Immigrant and visible minority women's issues should not be ghettoized within specific advocacy organizations for women or racial minorities" (ibid.). Despite their efforts, advocacy organizations remain the main mechanism of representation for disadvantaged groups. For women of colour, this remains problematic as they often fall between the mandates of those advocacy offices promoting gender and racial equality.

CONCLUSION

Official multiculturalism policy was the outcome of a particular struggle for representation and, since 1971, has helped to define the terms and conditions of this struggle. In general, the policy has evolved from a celebration of folklore and heritage issues to a more explicit focus on such issues as systemic discrimination. As such, the initiative should not be either dismissed too quickly as tokenistic or celebrated as the "right" solution.

The outcome of struggles for political representation and, by corallary, a recognition of group difference, as the case of women in Ontario demonstrated, will be marked by advances and setbacks that are not necessarily predictable. Positive outcomes or gains, however, are often very fragile, given the marginal status of groups advancing claims of "difference" and the strength of forces resistant to them.

The current policy and practice of multiculturalism policy, as the case in Ontario illustrates, is limited in its ability to address the specific intersectional location of women of colour. However, its federal evolution since 1971 underscores its ability to act as a resource for groups to challenge the terms of citizenship. As such, multiculturalism has the potential to form the basis of a more dynamic notion of citizenship and a new model for group representation.

NOTES

I would like to thank Janine Brodie and William Walters for their comments on the draft of this essay.

1. Drawn from the work of Chandra Mohanty (1991), the term "women of colour" is used throughout this essay. It is not synonymous with "non-white" or the Canadian state's term "visible minority." Rather, it refers to a group of women whose potential political alliances are determined by a common context of struggle—their "oppositional political relation to sexist, racist and imperialist structures" (Mohanty, 1991, p. 7). It is important to underscore that this alliance is not based on geographic location or racial identifications. In emphasizing a common context of struggle, this term also recognizes that women of colour are a very heterogeneous constituency and have different histories, backgrounds, and cultures.

2. "Race" is a concept that is socially and historically constructed. Its social meaning is constantly being challenged and transformed through political struggles. "Any number of markers—colour, physiognomy, culture, gene pools—may be summoned as signifiers of 'race.' Certain forms of racism will highlight biological characteristics as indicators of supposed 'racial' difference. Other forms may single out cultural differences as the basis of presumed impervious racial boundaries between groups.... Racism constructs 'racial' difference" (Brah, 1993, p. 11).

REFERENCES

Brah, Avtar. (1993). Re-framing Europe: En-gendered racisms, ethnicities and nationalisms in contemporary Western Europe. In *Feminist Review, 45*.

Breton, Raymond. (1986). Multiculturalism and Canadian nation building. In A. Cairns and C. Williams (Eds.), *The politics of gender, ethnicity and language in Canada*, Vol. 34, Royal Commission on Economic Union and Development Prospects for Canada. Toronto: University of Toronto Press.

Citizenship and Immigration Canada. (1994). *Facts and figures: Overview of immigration*. Ottawa: Supply and Services.

Crenshaw, Kimberle. (1992). Whose story is it, anyway? Feminist and antiracist appropriations of Anita Hill. In Toni Morrison, (Ed.) *Race-ing justice, En-gendering power*. New York: Pantheon Books.

Das Gupta, Tania. (1994). Multicultural policy: A terrain of struggle for immigrant women. *Canadian Women's Studies, 14* (2).

Fleras, Augie and Elliott, Jean Leonard. (1992). *Multiculturalism in Canada*. Scarborough: Nelson Canada.

Frideres, James. (1992). Changing Definitions of Ethnicity in Canada. In Satzewich.

Gardiner, W. Reform Party convention, Markham, Apr. 16 1991.

Hall, Stuart, and Held, David. (1989). Citizens and citizenship. In Stuart Hall and Martin Jacques, *New Times*. New York: Verso.

Hernandez, Carmencita. (1988). The coalition of visible minority women. In Frank Cunningham et. al. *Social movements/social change*. Toronto: Between the Lines Press.

Keohone, Kieran. (1992). Symptoms of Canada. *CineAction, 28*.

Kobayashi, Audrey. (1993). Multiculturalism: Representing a Canadian institution. In David Ley and James Duncan (Eds.), *Place, culture, representation*. London: Routledge.

Kumar, Prem, and Bennett, Pearl. (1991). Minority report. *Policy Options, 12* (9).

Kymlicka, Will. (1992). Recent work in citizenship theory". Ottawa: Multiculturalism and Citizenship Canada.

Marshall, T.H. (1983). Citizenship and social class. In David Held et. al. *States and societies*. London: Open University.

Martin, Jeannie. (1991). Multiculturalism and feminism. In Gill Bottomley, Marie de Lepervanche, and Jeannie Martin, *Intersexions*. Sydney: Allen and Unwin.

Mohanty, Chandra. (1991). Cartographies of struggle: Third World women and the politics of feminism. In C. Mohanty et al. *Third World and the politics of feminism*. Bloomington: Indiana University Press.

National Organization of Immigrant and Visible Minority Women. (1988). Brief to the Minister of Citizenship, Gerry Phillips and Minister Responsible for Women's Issues, Greg Sorbara.

National Organization of Immigrant and Visible Minority Women, Ontario Region. *Communique* Vol. II, No. 3.

Ng, Roxanna. (1988). Immigrant women and institutional racism. In S. Burt et al. *Changing patterns*. Toronto: McClelland and Stewart.

Ontario Advisory Council on Women's Issues. (1988). Submission to the Ontario Cabinet Committee on Race Relations regarding an overview of the status of program initiatives in relation to visible minority women.

Ontario, Ministry of Citizenship. (1989). Looking back, reaching forward. A multiculturalism strategy workshop. Workshop Proceedings, December 1.

Ontario Ministry of Culture and Recreation. (1979). *Report of Joint Task Force on Immigrant Women*. September.

Ontario Women's Directorate (OWD) and Ministry of Citizenship (MCC) (1987). "Report on the 1987 Community Workshops with Visible Minority and Immigrant Women."

Ontario Women's Directorate. (1983). *Proceedings of the Visible Minority Woman Conference on Racism, Sexism and Work, September 30–October 2.*

Ontario Women's Directorate. (1989). *Government initiatives relating to immigrant and visible minority women*. July.

Ontario Women's Directorate. Provincial Secretariat for Social Development. (1982). "The Government of Ontario Response to the Report 'The Immigrant Woman in Canada: A Right to Recognition.'"

Parekh, Bhikhu. (1990). Britain and the social logic of pluralism. In B. Parekh, *Britain, a plural society: Report of a seminar*. London: Commission for Racial Equality.

Pateman, Carole. (1992). *Promise and paradox: Women and democratic citizenship*. Second York Lecture In Political Science. Toronto: York University.

Pettman, Jan. (1992). *Living in the margins*. Sydney: Allen and Unwin.

Stasiulis, Daiva. (1988). The symbolic mosaic reaffirmed: Multiculturalism policy. In Katherine Graham (Ed.), *How Ottawa spends 1988/1989*. Ottawa: Carleton University Press.

Turner, Bryan. (1986). *Citizenship and Capitalism*. London: Allen and Unwin.

Yeatman, Anna. (1994). *Postmodern revisionings of the political*. New York: Routledge.

Young, Iris Marion. (1990a). Polity and group difference. In *Throwing like a girl and other essays in feminist philosophy and social theory*. Bloomington: Indiana University Press.

Young, Iris Marion. (1990b). Social movements and the politics of difference. In *Justice and the politics of difference*. Princeton, NJ: Princeton University Press.

Wallis, Maria; Gilles, Wenona; and Hernandez, Carmencita. (1988). Defining issues on our terms: Gender, race and the state—Interviews with racial minority women. *Resources for Feminist Research, 17* (3).

SUGGESTED READING

Das Gupta, Tania. (1994). Multicultural policy: A terrain of struggle for immigrant women. *Canadian Women's Studies, 14* (2).

Kobayashi, Audrey. (1993). Multiculturalism: Representing a Canadian institution. In James Duncan and David Ley (Eds.), *Place, culture, representation*. London: Routledge.

Young, Iris Marion. (1990). Polity and group difference. In *Throwing like a girl and other essays in feminist philosophy and social theory*. Bloomington: Indiana University Press.

QUESTIONS TO CONSIDER

1. Is it necessary, or even desirable, for citizens to share a common conception of culture? Is this possible in societies in which some groups are socially and economically privileged?

2. Is a commitment to cultural pluralism compatible with women's equality rights?

3. Given the current shift in official multiculturalism policy toward social equality, can it address the exclusion of certain groups, such as women of colour, from social life?

RESTRUCTURING PRIVATE LIFE

CHAPTER 8

Reproductive Technologies: Rights, Choice, and Coercion

Thelma McCormack

This essay examines the emergence and treatment of new reproductive technologies (NRTs) as a policy field in Canadian politics. The Canadian state has always been actively involved in the regulation of women's reproduction. These regulations, in turn, have had a profound impact on the everyday lives of Canadian women, their life "choices," and, indeed, their sexuality. Until recently, the politics of reproduction has revolved almost exclusively around issues of contraception and the right of women to terminate an unwanted pregnancy. The abortion issue certainly has not disappeared. The physical and psychological danger to people who carry out abortions, to women who voluntarily terminate pregnancies, and to all who support them is as great today as it was twenty years ago. Reproductive choice, therefore, continues to be an important issue for individual women and the women's movement. The scope of the reproductive-policy field, however, has been magnified in recent decades by the emergence of a variety of new reproductive technologies, a group of procedures to help men and women overcome problems of **infertility**, to allow men and women alternatives to coital conception, and to assist those who have some reason to be concerned about genetic anomalies to reduce the risk. Reproductive technologies have a long history, but they have now become wedded to the technological revolution. We are at the dawn of a new era when it will no longer matter how women become pregnant. Women will choose whether or not to become pregnant, and this decision will no longer be inflected by guilt or a sense of inadequacy. In this regard, NRTs potentially represent an enormous step forward in the psychosexual and reproductive history of women. However, the promise of reproductive choice offered by NRTs is being constrained and limited on the terrain of politics.

This essay reviews and critiques the findings of the Royal Commission on New Reproductive Technologies. I examine three sections of its

1993 report, *Proceed with Care*, to illustrate some of its problematic assumptions and assertions. These sections include the commission's treatment of surrogacy, which reflects serious cultural biases about the family and restores an earlier **essentialism** about the gestational parent; **prenatal diagnosis**, which opens the door again to a notion of the fetus as a person; and, finally, the question of fetal tissue, which raises questions of access. I begin, however, with a historical survey of approaches to infertility.

A BRIEF HISTORY OF INFERTILITY

A Male Problem

Through human history, infertility and its supposed cures have been the subject of much controversy and intervention. In biblical times, for example, infertility was understood as a consequence for men who disobeyed God. Women were passive partners who carried the seed but were not responsible for it. The three best-known examples of infertility in biblical literature are Sarah, wife of Abraham; Rebecca, wife of Isaac; and Rachel, wife of Jacob (Gold, 1988). Each of the women was initially unable to bear children. Their infertility, however, was not a judgement on them or on their behaviour but on their husbands, who had, in some way, displeased God. Infertility, in other words, existed in women to test men and their relationship with God.

A Male and Female Problem

Later in social history, folk medicine presented a different picture of infertility, indicating that it might be either male or female. Indeed, tests were devised to determine who was responsible, as were cures for both sexes. In the seventeenth century, *The Experienced Midwife* advised couples that, if they wanted to know whether the infertility was his or hers, they should "sprinkle the man's urine upon a lettuce leaf and the women's upon another, and that which dies away first is unfruitful" (quoted in Guttmacher, 1953, pp. 253–254). Another test would not only diagnose fertility but also predict the sex of the child "Wheat and spelt; let the woman water them daily with her urine.... If both grow she will bear; if the wheat grows it will be a boy; if the spelt grows, it will be a girl. If neither grows, she will not bear" (ibid., p. 253).

A Female Problem

Starting in the seventeenth century, when conception was better understood, particularly ovulation, the focus on infertility began to shift to women. When it did, the sexual pleasure of women was deemed essential for fertility (Eccles, 1982). According to these texts, a man must arouse a woman so that she would, upon reaching orgasm, open up to receive the male seed. Infertility, then, could be the outcome of either his impotence or his ineptitude. More interesting, however, are the cures that the folk literature prescribed. Mandrake roots, mistletoe, and willow branches under or beside the bed were commonly used. Intercourse under a tree also was recommended for overcoming a woman's sterility (Kennet, 1976). Garlic and Spanish Fly were thought to increase the efficiency of sperm. Concoctions made of spiders or other animal substances were also recommended (Guttmacher, 1953).

By the nineteenth century, herbs and spells were being replaced by mechanical inventions—crude reproductive technologies by today's standards. For example, a Dr. Graham developed a "celestial or Magnetico-Electrico bed," where, for a fee, infertile couples could spend the night. This bed, supported by six massive brass pillars, covered with Saxon blue and purple satin, and perfumed with Arabian spices, was developed on the premise that "the barren must certainly become fruitful when they are powerfully agitated in the delights of love" (Camp, 1973, p. 29). It was a short step from the electric celestial bed with music to the waterbed and piped-in Musak and, farther down the line, to the new reproductive technologies.

By the twentieth century, infertility had become medicalized and defined primarily as a female disorder. Freud and psychiatry dominated the first half of the century, and they were responsible for the radical transition in perspectives on infertility from biology and sexology to the motivation for motherhood. If women were not having babies, there must be an unconscious desire not to. The dominant figure in this research was Helene Deutsch, who provided the most extensive typology of the motivation of women who were unable to bear children (Deutsch, 1945). She started with the assumption that all women naturally want, expect, and need to experience motherhood. Denial or rejection of motherhood, therefore, was a psychological flaw, symptomatic of problems around sexuality and sexual identity.

We could further explore the history of infertility treatments. The purpose of this brief review, however, is to indicate how infertility became gendered. What began as a male problem in the earliest forms of patriarchal society became degendered when women were active as midwives and healers and when the treatments were more magical than medical, more herbal than technological. It was regendered in the age of science and technology, and when men controlled the professions. The report of the Royal Commission on the New Reproductive Technologies continues in this tradition. Although the commission was headed by a woman, the report, *Proceed with Care*, is not written from the perspective of women's reproductive history. Instead, it is a story of technology and what may or may not be its consequences. The report is imbued with assumptions about technological and biological determinism, as were many of the briefs presented to the commission. As is true of science fiction, the ones who believe it most are the ones who write it and, in doing so, convince themselves that fiction is fact.

THE ROYAL COMMISSION ON NEW REPRODUCTIVE TECHNOLOGIES

No royal commission in recent years has had a more troubled and vexatious history than the Royal Commission on New Reproductive Technologies (RCNRT). Its beginning in 1989 was marked by highly publicized controversies between the chairperson, Dr. Patricia A. Baird, a pediatrician and professor of medical genetics, and several members of the commission, including Maureen McTeer, a lawyer and wife of former Conservative prime minister Joe Clark. When the dissident group resigned in protest and began action to unseat the chairperson, she terminated their appointments and replaced them with others. This move was not unreasonable, but it did fan the flames of controversy.

The Royal Commission on New Reproductive Technologies was not the first governmental inquiry on this subject. Earlier, an Ontario commission had examined the social and legal issues arising from these new technologies (Ontario Law Reform Commission, 1985). The Warnock Commission in Britain preceded it (Warnock, 1984). In addition, business people and economists have watched the growth of biotechnology companies, which do everything from genetic diagnostics to marketing CAT-scan equipment. As well, academics and bioethicists, and think-tanks such as the Hastings Institute, had been reflecting on the clinical use of the new knowledge and research protocols. There was something intriguing about these new technologies that made it possible for a woman to conceive without coital intercourse. NRTs are not quite as spectacular as immaculate conception, but they are about as close as we are likely to get. And, many find these developments disturbing, if not undesirable. The Vatican, for one, completely rejects the use of NRTs to achieve fertility. It has issued a text stating that the Roman Catholic Church opposes any form of procreation outside of the "natural" form of sexual intercourse between a lawful husband and wife (Congregation for the Doctrine of Faith, 1987).

New reproductive technologies as well as the political infighting of the royal commission were steeped in controversy. It is hardly surprising then that, despite various forms of damage control, the commission and its discontents were never far from media attention, including the eve of the publication of its report, when a campaign was mounted to discredit its findings (Lippman, 1994). What intrigued the media, of

course, was a "story," a narrative about three groups of women competing for the public agenda. The first group was Dr. Baird and her commissioners; the second was mainstream feminists who wanted the
commission to give legitimacy to their opposition to any further development of use of reproductive technology; and the third was the
women who were clients and believed that they had a right to have children despite the bad hand they had been dealt by nature. Canadian
public opinion was closer to that of the third group. The briefs presented to the royal commission, however, came mostly from the second,
while the research agenda reflected Dr. Baird's special interest in science policy and regulation.[1]

Three Reference Points

The report's findings were informed by three overriding guidelines:

▶ the ethics of care
▶ the appropriate use of resources
▶ the rejection of a politics of rights

The Ethics of Care

The ethics-of-care conflict between Dr. Baird and her critics was political. Many were afraid that Dr. Baird, who is a research scientist, would
look upon reproductive technologies as if they were routine, value-free
developments in science. They also feared that she and her colleagues
on the commission would not evaluate NRTs from what the dissident
group considered the more critical feminist or ethical perspective. As it
turned out, the misgivings of Dr. Baird's critics proved to be false. Early
in the report, the commission established its claim to the moral high
ground. Its recommendations, the report claimed, are based on an
"ethic of care." Inspired by Carol Gilligan's work on gender differences
in moral behaviour, the "ethic of care" included "individual autonomy,
equality, respect for human life and dignity, protection of the vulnerable, non-commercialization of reproduction, appropriate use of
resources, accountability, and balancing of individual and collective
interests" (Report, 1993, p. 53). This grab bag of concerns hardly constitutes a coherent ethical theory, but it was an alternative to the older
and self-regulatory "professional ethic."

   The report implements its "ethic of care" by limiting choice for
Canadian women. Society has a collective responsibility to women, it
says, "which may require limiting choices by individual women if these
choices promote harmful social perceptions of womanhood or detrimental attitudes toward women as a group." Accordingly, it criminal-
izes surrogacy on the grounds that it is a commodification of human
life (ibid., Chap. 23). It also effectively bans sex selection because it

reinforces gender stereotypes (ibid., Chap. 28). And it removes all services through the private sector that could give upper- and middle-class
women a special advantage. Unless the services are covered by provincial health plans, they will not be available.

There is, then, a strong theme of social responsibility and a feminist
sensibility in the recommendations. Cumulatively, they dispel some of
the fears related to genetic engineering and defuse some of the
alarmist rhetoric that has surrounded it. Overall, the report brings to
the issues of reproduction a gendered set of criteria. These criteria are
different, on the one hand, from a purely scientific perspective that
looks primarily at the growth of knowledge, and, on the other hand,
from the perspective of bedside bioethics.

All of this, however, is cold comfort to women who are unable to
conceive and who found the report largely unresponsive to their needs.
What should have been a privileged voice in the report was barely audi-
ble. Indeed, the commission even questioned the status of this group
of women as legitimate stakeholders. Ironically, if these women had
defined themselves as disabled or challenged, the discourse might
have been different. Meantime, the government of Ontario, acting on
the recommendations in the report, moved quickly to delist in-vitro fertilization except under special conditions.[2] Infertile women who are in
child-bearing years had hoped for proactive support from the commissioners and a validation of their claims. Instead, they were held to a
stricter standard than their counterparts for whom fecundity had
become a burden and who were terminating pregnancies or seeking
tubal ligations to end any further child bearing. OHIP has not reduced
these services. Thus, the report succeeded in demystifying genetic
engineering, but largely at the expense of infertile women.

Appropriate Use of Resources

The second principle the commission adopted was more worldly, having less to do with the ethic of social care than with the economy of
health care. It recommended that all procedures had to be justified as
an "appropriate use of resources." Any new or experimental measures
of "unproven benefit" would be eliminated. This hard line, which
requires the physician to use only "evidence-based" treatments, would
reduce not only the number of services available, limiting them only to
those with a medical basis, but also the overall cost. Unless women can
show, for example, that their **fallopian tubes** are blocked "resulting
from disease, defect, or surgical sterilization," they would not be eligible for in-vitro fertilization (IVF) (Report, 1993, p. 526). Moreover, under
no circumstances would IVF be available to post-menopausal women,
who are normally infertile. Thus, any progress we may have made in
developing a more holistic model of medicine, a unified concept of
mind and body, is sacrificed by the report in order to contain costs and

to make certain that other, more urgent services are maintained. Of course, this leaves open the possibility that some forms of treatment would be acceptable if the costs came down or the economy went up.

The stress on the health-care system, its costs and allocation of services, is based on the assumption of a steadily rising demand curve for infertility treatments. There is, however, no evidence from previous population studies to support this expectation. Under ordinary circumstances, couples consider whether or not to go ahead with reproductive technologies and run the risk of no pregnancy, or, conversely, multiple births. Either outcome could be unwelcome and act as a damper on demand.

Couples who accept the odds but are unable to meet the standards of eligibility might turn to the private sector for a physician who would provide the service, but if the commission's recommendations are accepted, that possibility would be cut off. A private system, the report says, uses publicly funded resources but delivers its services only to those best able to pay (see Cameron, this volume). Accordingly, it recommended that there be no services except those offered through medicare and accessible to all. What the commissioners intended was to create a level playing field, but, as it turns out, it is a level playing field with almost nothing on it!

The Politics of Rights

Finally, the report takes on the politics of rights, claiming that "some have argued that the Charter can be interpreted as imposing an affirmative duty on the state to make new reproductive technologies available, so that those who are unable to become parents in the usual way can enjoy the same reproductive 'rights' as other members of society" (1993, p. 64). But "it is highly unlikely," the report says, "that the Courts would uphold such claims, given the broader social interest in providing basic health care for all Canadians and the existence of finite resources with which to do so" (ibid.). This dismissal of court-enforced reproductive rights simply brushed aside what are important rights-based questions raised by NRTs.

A distinction is sometimes made between individual and collective rights, between local and universal rights, between group and human rights. "Group rights" are those claimed, for example, by aboriginal people; "local rights" are community rights; "collective rights" are related to environmental law or social insurance. We have been primarily concerned with group rights as women, and with individual rights, as matters of discrimination. There are times when all of these conflict, and they may get resolved in the courts, in the legislatures, or on the street. But, for feminists, it is both incorrect and unnecessary to create a conflict or contradiction between pro-choice and structural equality (Lippman, 1994).

Choice

Throughout the debate on NRTs, key feminists in the Canadian women's movement, the National Action Committee on the Status of Women (NAC), and, ultimately, the royal commission, argued that the collective rights of women to be protected from the potentially harmful effects of new technologies outweighed any rights that infertile women might claim to use these technologies. This dichotomy, however, erodes a feminist conception of choice on a number of grounds. First, it confuses the social psychology of decision making with the entrenchment of rights (Rebick, 1994). Anyone who has ever worked in an abortion clinic knows that the reasons people have for seeking abortions are a mix of good and bad, wise and unwise, rational and irrational. But the motives people have are irrelevant. We operationalize freedom by having a choice at the institutional level and the chance to grow from the knowledge in retrospect, that our choices, may have been wrong. *La volonté* is the heart and soul, the core and pragmatic test of freedom.

Second, the dichotomy assumes that there is a trade-off between equality rights and autonomy rights (the right to exercise choice). Constitutional lawyers make this assumption, but, for feminists, the distinction is not divisive; each is as contingent on the other as mind is on body (Dworkin, 1977). Even in classical liberal theory, *cum* John Stuart Mill, there is a dialectical tension, rather than a forced choice, between individual and collective rights. To separate them analytically is to change the meaning of equality to some form of mechanical fairness. For feminists, however, equality is a transformative concept that refers to quality of life as well as equality of opportunity or equality of condition. The right to procreate and the right to terminate a pregnancy are autonomy rights that, with equality rights, are collective. There is no real conflict between autonomy rights and social justice, despite the words and games of constitutional lawyers.

Third, this forced distinction between individual and collective rights suggests that only fertile women ultimately can have a choice. The distinction rests on a double standard that accepts choice for abortion and contraception, yet rejects it for procreation. There is no mystery in this double standard. It reflects the **anti-natalism** of modernization theory and imperialist policies. Encouraging people to have smaller families has been seen as necessary for economic growth and development. But reproduction is not split in biology or in social life, and it ought to be our task to challenge this double standard. In other words, the primary distinction should be between those who choose to have children and those who choose not to, and not between fertile and infertile women.

To summarize, these three reference points—the ethic of care, the appropriate use of resources, and the politics of collective rights—belie any claims that the report would be objective, neutral, or even-handed.

Its parameters were set by including a chapter on adoption and none on abortion and contraception, although the latter two involve reproductive technology and the former does not. The omission of abortion and contraception raises a number of questions. Was the commission unwilling to apply its framework to abortion and contraception? Is it consciously splitting reproductive freedom into two sections: one logic for abortion and contraception, and another for assisted conception? Just as puzzling is the discussion of adoption, where the commissioners disregarded their own guidelines by accepting a dual public and private system, and recognizing that fees for private adoptions can be greater than those involved in surrogacy. Considering, too, the controversies over interracial and transnational adoptions, it is strange that the report says nothing about the ethics of Canadians adopting babies from Latin America and South East Asia (1993, Chap. 16).

The guidelines, then, are permeable and may be used selectively. On paper, however, they satisfy conservative no-growth economists who feel the health-care system is already stretched to its limits; please mainstream feminists who want to protect women from the abuses of medical technology, untested medications, and male-dominated medical institutions; and give some assurance to humanists and religious groups who fear the secularization and commercialization of reproduction.

Three Examples

I now want to turn to three concrete cases that demonstrate some of the problems with the commission's report. The first is the surrogacy question, which reveals the cultural biases of the report; the second is prenatal diagnosis, where abortion rights and reproductive technologies intersect; and the third is the uses of fetal tissue, the source of which is abortion, and the cash nexus.

Surrogacy

Nothing is more contentious among feminists and bioethicists than surrogacy or preconception arrangements whereby a woman or infertile couple simply contracts another woman to bear a child. What makes it a flashpoint is not the technology. In most cases, it is relatively simple, and its success rate tends to be high. Usually, the surrogate mother is fertilized through in-vitro fertilization with the male partner's sperm (see also Cameron, this volume). Biological questions involving surrogacy, however, are overshadowed by non-technical ones. What makes surrogacy special are:

▶ the legal problems (custody);

▶ the social status of the gestational and adoptive mothers; and

▶ questions about values (the meaning of motherhood).

The Royal Commission on the New Reproductive Technologies was not the first Canadian agency to examine the surrogacy issue. In 1985, the Ontario Law Reform Commission recommended that surrogacy be permitted, but emphasized the importance of preconception agreements and other regulations so as to avoid later misunderstandings and abuse. Similarly, the British Human Fertilization and Embryology Authority Act recommended that surrogacy be permitted, but only after permission of the licensing authority was given, and only after it has been ascertained that it was not for reasons of convenience (Morgan and Lee, 1991).

Yet, all of these reports reflect the ambivalence we have in bourgeois society about the presence of an outsider, a stranger, a third party in an intimate dyadic relationship. We shrink from the idea of an impersonal contract where there should be trust and erotic passion, and a monetary exchange based on "buyer beware" where there should be a spontaneous relationship. We deplore the cash nexus that renders all relationships guarded, fragmented, and impersonal. Possessive individualism may have weakened elsewhere in the welfare society but remains well and truly entrenched in family attitudes. Different people find surrogacy wrong for different reasons, but many find it acceptable subject to certain conditions. Public opinion was not as opposed to surrogacy as many of the briefs the commission received suggested. "Canadians," it said, "do not wish to close the door on preconception arrangements" (Report, 1993, p. 681). In addition, the commission found there were no agencies that provide the service in Canada, and if there had been, they "would probably be deemed illegal under provincial adoption laws" (ibid., p. 706).

The commission not only closed the door on surrogacy—it slammed it. Recommendation 199, which makes surrogacy a criminal offence, directed the federal government to legislate against it in the strongest possible way and to leave no loopholes:

> to prohibit advertising for or acting as an intermediary to bring about a preconception arrangement, and to prohibit receiving payment or any financial or commercial benefit for acting as an intermediary, under threat of criminal sanction. It should also legislate to prohibit making payment for a preconception arrangement, under threat of criminal sanction. (ibid., p. 690)

Further, the commission recommended that provincial colleges of physicians and surgeons, as well as provincial law societies, "adopt strict codes of conduct, disciplinary measures and severe penalties, including loss of licence to practise, against members involved in brokering or performing assisted insemination ... to facilitate a preconception arrangement" (ibid., p. 691).

What lies behind this adamant position is the sacredness of procreation. Anything that secularizes it does injury to a moral fabric that has traditionally meant more to women than to men, and through which women have, in the past, found their primary identity. Over and over again, the commission referred to commodification as the debasement of the procreative process. Marx never used "commodity" or "commodification" in that way. Strictly speaking, there is also no supply and demand, no market, no invisible hand. Nevertheless, the term metaphorically suggests that the harsh realities of the competitive marketplace should not be imported into the private sphere, where one might hope for countervailing values. The report suggests that

> the fundamentally repugnant aspect of preconception arrangements is that they instrumentalize human beings through the deliberate act of creating a child for the express purpose of giving it up, usually in exchange for money. The premise of commercial preconception contracts is that a child is a product that can be bought and sold on the market. (ibid., p. 682)

Preconception arrangements, according to the commission, do profound harm to women by placing them "in the situation of alienating aspects of themselves that should be inherently inalienable" (ibid., p. 683). Similar references throughout the report suggest a special inviolate quality of pregnancy that would apply with even greater force to abortion, where the fetus is surrendered without sentiment, and, where, to the dismay of pro-lifers, women often feel a great sense of relief when it is over.

Apart from the inherent wrongness of surrogacy, the commission found there were serious harms done to the family, in particular, to the gestational mother, who bonds with the fetus and must abruptly sever the connection. There is, according to the commission, "a substantial body of medical, gynaecological and psychological literature to support the view that the bonding takes place during gestation." Moreover, it argued "that any forced separation between mother and child may result in lasting harm to the mother" (ibid., p. 675). Harm is also done to the society "by diminishing the dignity of reproduction and undermining society's commitment to the inherent value of children" (ibid., p. 686).

The only persons who benefit from preconception arrangements, according to the commission, are the brokers. Although the commission could find none in Canada, it chose a pre-emptive strike, or what it kept referring to as a "window of opportunity," to prevent this group of intermediaries from ever appearing. Nor was the commission willing to make an exception for private arrangements between family members or friends (ibid., p. 696). According to the commission's view, the affront to the dignity of the child is the same whether the child is a gift between close friends and no money is exchanged or is the subject of an impersonal commercial contract between strangers.

The supposed alienation experience that a woman who provides a procreative service undergoes is assumed, not demonstrated. Women who have served as gestational mothers deny **bonding** with the fetus they are carrying for others. The commission was not prepared to take their word for it, and implied that they were in denial. Women who relinquish a child with little distress, the commission said, "can later suffer from the experience" (ibid., p. 676). The children, according to the report, suffer as well:

> First, they have been created not as ends in themselves but to serve the needs of others.... Second, there is the issue of multiple parenthood when genetic gestations and social roles are separated as a result of a preconceptions arrangement ... a situation that we know, based on experience with adoption, can have a significant impact on a child's personal and emotional development and sense of identity. (ibid. p. 677)

The commission acknowledges that a child born of a preconception arrangement is truly wanted, but it is still not convinced that the child would not be psychologically handicapped as a result. According to the commission, the child will know that it "has nonetheless been 'bought at a price' which would make the child feel like a commodity that can be bought and sold, and create pressure for him or her to live up to his or her 'purchaser's price.'" Finally, the commission says, "we have to consider the potential for conflict within families. For example, non-participating family members might disapprove of the arrangement and this would affect the children who feel, rightly or wrongly, that their existence is the source of the conflict" (ibid., p. 677).

Cultural Biases   Whatever one may think or feel about preconception arrangements, these scenarios are culturally biased. Whether a woman feels alienated or not depends on the total experience. Whether she is viewed as an altruist helping a couple who are unable to have a baby or whether she is viewed as, many critics have described her, a "womb for rent" is a cultural matter. In many cultures, children are "gifts" to childless couples, and those who make the gift and those who receive it are drawn closer together (Fischer, 1963). The commission cites adoption practices in aboriginal communities where precisely this happens, but they did not see it as an alternative perspective.

Studies of women who plan to have or have had an abortion indicate that women do not automatically or naturally bond with a fetus (Zimmerman, 1977; Crum and McCormack, 1992). Instead, such bonding is encouraged by the use of ultrasound, imaging technology, and virtual-reality pictographs, as well as by groups who lobby to have the fetus declared a person. A pregnant woman who may have felt very little attachment to the fetus (other than heartburn, nausea, backaches, and insomnia) is persuaded by others, including maternally oriented doctors, nurses, and technicians, to see herself as a mother long before the fetus comes down the birth canal. It is at that moment when the play-acting stops and the serious role of parenting begins. If there is alienation, and it would be hard to tell it from post-partum depression, it is in a socially constructed pregnancy not the preconception contract. In any event, the concept of neonatal bonding and its importance for the emotional and cognitive, social, and physical development of children has been questioned (Chess and Thomas, 1982).

The commission also misunderstood the function of money in surrogacy by taking it literally. The payment is for a service, but it is also symbolic, closing a circle around the nuclear family. It insures against any future emotional claims on the child by the third party and protects the couple from any suggestion that they were engaged in a *ménage à trois*. Money depersonalizes, and this is exactly what the middle-class nuclear family wants to happen. It is part of a contract to exclude outsiders from the intrapsychic family economy. When the money is paid, it ends any future emotional claim on the child. The criminalization of surrogacy implies that the surrogate woman is a non-person, someone who would sink so low or would be so desperate that she would become a "breeder." It is not surrogacy that dehumanizes her, however; instead, it is language and the law.

We should remember that the way reproductive technologies are applied are effect, not cause. As we move toward a mixed system of home birth and hospital, doctor and midwife, the system may loosen up to allow women more active management of pregnancy, less passivity and less hospital dependency. Meanwhile, assisted preconception arrangements are arguably no more alienating to women than any other forms of pregnancy and childbirth.

The report's discussions of surrogacy spread a veil of sentiment over child bearing—"a child being wanted for its own sake"—concealing the institutionalized status of children in our society. Failure of the society to allocate resources to disadvantaged children, failure to universalize the cultural rights of children, failure to provide the disturbed or delinquent child with humane treatment and justice are some of the indicators of the low status of children in what is often misleadingly described as a child-centred society. If children are valued highly, we need not worry about how they are conceived or whether the motivation is "to please his parents," to drop out of school, "because we both come from large families," "because I just love babies," or something more edifying.

Further, the report revalorizes the biological mother and wipes out the years of efforts by social workers and others to recognize the social or adoptive mother as, in every sense, a mother. Not only is this a return to the mystique of biology, but it also disregards all that we have learned from the studies of "other mothering," of cultures where the biological parent is only one of several who take responsibility for a child, or where grandmothers rear their grandchildren, or where sisters exchange children (Stack, 1974; Ladner, 1971; Ruggles, 1994). Parenting is the crucial factor in the cognitive, emotional, and social development of children. Giving the woman who carries the fetus a higher status and a legal priority reinforces a simplistic and essentialist image of women as bodies. Once again, biology is destiny.

Prenatal Screening

Three chapters of the report and 51 of its recommendations concern prenatal diagnosis (PND): research, use, and regulation. Scientists may see this area as the cutting edge of research in genetics, but for the layperson it represents many different things. "At our public hearings," the commission writes,

> we heard perceptions that prenatal diagnosis is being used as a "search and destroy" mission to "weed out defective fetuses" ... that counselling is biased and predicated on the assumption that it is better to abort a fetus found to have an anomaly than to consider raising a child with a disability ... that some of the newer developments ... are being used for eugenic purposes and that women were coerced into termination of pregnancies. (Report, vol. 2, 1993, p. 845)

The commission regarded these and similar complaints as misinformation, and urged the scientific community to work harder to communicate better. "There is a great deal of misinformation and need for accurate, unbiased and accessible information about genetics." Indeed, the public is not well informed about PND but, among those persons who were aware of the opportunity, a large percentage indicated that they themselves would use the services. The commission recognized the moral dilemma of withholding services from couples who are at high risk and providing services whose results can be misleading and hurtful. It came down on the side of increasing opportunities for those who might wish to have PND. However, it also hopes to reduce both errors and the emotional consequences by providing **non-directive counselling** at all stages— prior to conception, and during and after screening. Further protection of the client is achieved through the licensing of genetics centres (vol. 2, 1993, p. 845). Providing prenatal diagnosis services without a licence issued by the commission "constitutes an offence subject to prosecution." Under no circumstances should women be required to undergo testing. Testing, however, may reveal information that could cause strain in a family, and many who do counselling see little value in full disclosure. In general, the Canadian geneticists favour disclosure. They do so—and this is perhaps more important—on the grounds that information given to women increases the autonomy of the woman, to give her a choice not, as feared by many, for **eugenics** reasons. The choice may be imperfect and the counselling biased, but there is a deep resentment over information being withheld.

In short, the commission stated emphatically that the provision of prenatal diagnosis does not devalue those with physical handicaps, and genetic counselling does not lead to eugenics. If all the cases of congenital anomalies and genetic disorders were eliminated, there would still be a sizable population of newborn infants who will need special care and legal protection. "We do not believe ... that there is a trade-off between providing PND and providing support for people with disabilities. On the contrary," the commission continues, "the two go hand in hand" (ibid., p. 799). Elsewhere, it says that using PND "is both beneficial to individual women and couples at risk and consistent with social values regarding equality for persons with disabilities and respect for life" (ibid., p. 810).

The Anti-Abortion Agenda There are some feminists who see in the counselling process a pressure to choose abortion on what may be false tests or problems of interpreting data. There is, I suggest, a latent anti-abortion policy running through this, that is, abortion when necessary but not necessarily abortion. The decisions are difficult because so many of the test results are borderline and ambiguous. But abortion does not preclude the social imperative to provide living, educational, occupational, recreational, and commercial environments adapted to persons with a disability. **Inclusivity** means that we welcome difference, and, to put it bluntly, put our money where our mouths are.

Ethically, there is no problem with the principle of inclusivity as difference, but the value system of the disabilities lobby should not be foisted on a couple who prefer to adopt or try again, as if the desire to have a healthy child was a form of narcissism or consumerism. Once again, we are laying a guilt trip on women who elect to have an abortion. Many of the arguments used to discourage PND and subsequent abortion return us to images of the fetus as person. A fetus with a chromosomal defect becomes a person who is being discriminated against. There are several places in the report where it recommends not counselling but specifically "grief counselling." Grief counselling comes from the literature on miscarriage where parents are urged to treat the miscarriage as the loss of a child and to go through burial and bereavement rituals.

I have discussed at some length the parts of the report that deal with prenatal diagnosis, in part, because it links the reproductive technologies to abortion services. It also has been widely discussed by groups who are usually pro-choice, but are concerned about the attitudes generated toward persons with disabilities. But there is another reason. I think we can begin to see the extent to which the practice of medicine is increasingly driven by research, how the research agenda of laboratory-based scientists who never see a patient influences what happens in the physician's office.

Doctors have, to some extent, become the scapegoats in this process. This attitude was reflected in some of the briefs to the commission, which advanced the view that doctors have an unusual degree of negative control or positive power over women and the obstetrical choices they have. Trashing doctors is one of our favourite forms of conversation, but the reality is that practising physicians are no longer at the pinnacle of the health-care and medical-research hierarchies. In assessing blame, we need to look more critically at the way in which medicine has been collectivized. Physicians are no longer an uncontested elite. Indeed, they are now less important than the research elite, and both are increasingly dependent on health-care administrators and the exigencies of hospitals and other administrative structures.

Fetal Tissue

At the present time, human fetal tissue is used primarily for research.[3] But the demand for it comes both from scientists doing basic research and from persons with Parkinson's disease and their families. In the future, as more disorders are treatable through fetal-tissue implantation, the demand will increase and may even exceed the supply. Can Canadians sell their own fetal tissue to those who need it? Can they donate it to parents or loved ones who need it, as is the case with blood transfusions? And can we purchase fetal tissue from outside Canada as a matter of free trade (see Cameron, this volume)?

Once again the public-opinion surveys conducted for the commission indicated strong positive support for donating fetal tissue and using it if the individual had a disorder that could benefit from it. Some fear was expressed that the donors might not know that they were donors, that hospitals conducting abortions would not seek consent from donors, or that women might be pressured into donating fetal tissue. But the overriding concern of the commission was commercialization. Accordingly, it recommended that fetal tissue not be sold or bought, that any advertising about the availability of tissue that might involve a payment be prohibited.

Recommendation 287 of the report seeks to protect women. No "fetuses or fetal tissue are used in Canada for which women have received payment, or where a profit has been made by an intermediary" (vol. 2, 1993, p. 1003). What it does not say is what happens when the demand for fetal tissue by Canadians exceeds the supply and Canadians know it is available elsewhere at a price. Taking the profit motive out of reproductive services is laudable, but doomed to failure because much of the technology has multiple purposes, and hence will continue to enrich the companies that manufacture or sell it. Also, if too many services are delisted, the emergence of a supplementary private system is inevitable (*Globe and Mail*, December 11, 1993, p. A2). Finally, the report does not separate the abortion issue from the questions about fetal tissue, although it does recommend two separate consent forms—one for the abortion and one for the uses of fetal tissue. In general, the commission was primarily concerned with regulations regarding the acquisition of the tissue.

We need to remind ourselves that science really does not have borders. We can prohibit certain forms of research being done in Canada, but the knowledge of research being done elsewhere does not stop at international airports. Canadian scientists, Canadian physicians, and Canadian women will eventually know about treatments for infertility, despite efforts by Canadian activists to keep it out of sight and out of mind.

A FLAWED REPORT: DETERMINISTIC FALLACIES

Although the report attempts to balance numerous competing interests and perspectives, it nonetheless remains a deeply flawed text. It is a bitter disappointment to infertile women who had hoped to hear a more positive message, an insult to women of colour, an embarrassment to anti-essentialist feminists, and a return to **modernization** theory *circa* 1950. Part of the problem is its single-minded focus on technology. The commissioners framed their inquiry by asking what the impact of these new technologies would be on law and social policy, on women and the family. For those who viewed the technology with hope, the promise of genetic screening meant liberation from the tragedy of genetic anomalies. For its critics, however, it was a straight line to eugenics. But whether the scenario was utopian or dystopian, it assumed technology was the prime mover, and that any social outcome could be deduced from the technology itself. According to some feminists, a patriarchal bias is inherent in technology; according to others, patriarchy is the multiplier of the negative effects. But the assumption is that technology makes history, not that history creates technology.

The same fallacy lies in the new biological determination that attempts to map our genes and locate the origin of certain medical defects with the expectation that we can find a factor that determines complex social behaviours such as delinquency, alcoholism, rape, altruism, depression, and other social disorders (Gould, 1992). At best, we can only know a predisposition, a susceptibility to these behaviours—the rest is social interaction (see Armstrong, this volume). But the policies based on this new knowledge may depend less on the reliability of the data than on the way it shapes our interpretations. Had the commission started with history, with the historical experience of men and women trying to overcome their inability to produce children, the scenario would have been different.

The new reproductive technology, then, is a continuation of an older reproduction technology and supplements traditional medicine and psychotherapy. Like the older science and technology, it is effect, not cause. Projecting forward, it is a necessary, though not a sufficient, condition for reproductive freedom. Whether these possibilities will be achieved, or when, depends on a political climate, on racism, levels of employment, standards of living, and the various factors that influence birth rates and the diffusion of medical innovations.

As they exist now, the technologies are far from perfect, and critics of them, including the commission, have a tendency to dwell on their shortcomings. These include low success rates, possible side effects, emotional strains, and the as yet unknown long-range consequences. But surveys of opinions conducted for the commission by Angus Reid and Decima polling companies indicate more public confidence and a tough-minded realism about any new medical development. In time, the technologies will be cheaper, safer, and more predictable, although for the present there are enough uncertainties to keep the dialogue open.

Everyone agrees that some infertility can be prevented through better health, environmental policies, the elimination of sexually transmitted diseases, and changing our lifestyle in terms of smoking, drinking, and overeating. Beyond that, demographers and epidemiologists are not optimistic that infertility can be significantly reduced if only because an increasing number of women are starting families later, often in their thirties, an age when all procreational risks increase. None of these reservations, then, should cloud our feminist vision of reproductive choice.

FEMINIST THEORY, CHOICE, AND INCLUSIVITY

Although most feminists have distanced themselves from modernization theory, they nonetheless share many of its premises. Principal among these is the assumption that a small family was better for a woman's health, education, and participation in the labour force than a large one. The second premise is that infertility was not God's punishment for promiscuity, not a species aberration, not a tragic fate but, instead, a medical problem that can be prevented and/or cured. Far less attention was given to women of colour or Third World women for whom **genocide** was a more immediate threat than unwanted pregnancy, and for whom involuntary sterilization, not abortion, shaped their consciousness. Indeed, for all groups who were powerless and live with genocidal population policies or the threat of them, there is a deep fear of extinction, a collective anxiety that takes the form of **pro-natalism** and stands in opposition to the benign anti-natalism or modernization theory, a theory shared by white Euro-centred feminists.

A feminist theory of choice that is inclusive of a broader range of women's experience would begin with the recognition that the desire to have children does not disempower women and, second, that large and alternative family systems further cultural diversity and inclusivity. Finally, it must recognize that the issue of infertility is not medical, psychiatric, or environmental, but political (anti-imperialism). Empowerment in this context assumes access to the technologies as symbolic of the right to have a family guaranteed by the International Convention of Human Rights, and to advocate their control by women through women-run clinics for birthing, abortions, and other forms of reproductive services (McCormack, 1991). In this woman-friendly, woman-centred environment, counselling and decision making would take place between the parties directly instead of being mediated by a large federal bureaucracy. In short, when we examine these two models—one based on modernization, the other on the politics of diversity—we can see the weaknesses of the report for Canadian women trying to build a new feminism.

Instead of limiting the reproductive choices of individual women in the name of *all* women, a new and inclusive feminist conception of choice would include different principles. Box 8.1 outlines some of them.

These are the foundations for choice. *How* we have our children—whether in-vitro fertilization, coital intercourse, or immaculate conception—is of no consequence. And that is the choice for which we have waited a very long time. The empowerment of women is contingent on access and whether they control it, but how women become pregnant has no implications for the state, for feminism as a social movement, or for the everyday life of women. Infertility becomes a function of age in the life cycle, and, as the life span extends, infertility may become the norm.

BOX 8.1

Feminist Principles for Choice

1. Pro-choice does not mean the status quo. The pro-choice movement is part of a larger feminist movement and an agenda for social change. The goals of the feminist movement remain the same: structural equality and autonomy, and these are one and the same; they cannot be split or played-off against each other

2. Pro-choice does not mean acceptance of our health-care system and our health-care economics as they now are

3. Pro-choice does not mean that we deliver women into the hands of a scientific research establishment. The politics of the science establishment, and, in particular, the human genetics group who are mapping our genetic systems, are politics, not science. (Lewontin, 1992)

CONCLUSION

The commission's recommendations fell just short of three hundred. This essay has touched on only a few. Neither does it discuss the structural administrative changes proposed—in particular, a new federal body of twelve persons, of whom at least six must be women (see Cameron, this volume). The National Commission would license, oversee the practices and research being carried out, and generally rationalize the system. At the same time, it would humanize the system by providing greater participation for various lay groups while undercutting the bias of experts, specialists, and professional medical and scientific communities.

When the report was issued, the federal Health minister, Diane Marleau, indicated that she would act quickly on health and safety issues. But the major recommendations of the report involve federal/provincial and territorial jurisdictions, and they are not likely to be easily worked out. (A PQ government in Quebec anticipating separation may want to increase the birth rate, especially among the well-educated, new young technocrats as well as the professional and managerial classes.) The Parliamentary Committee on Health is, at present, preoccupied with tobacco regulations.

But, if the recommendations discussed here were implemented, Canadian women would be the most overprotected from risk and the most underserviced women in the industrial world. We would have one of the best systems in terms of quality; one of the worst in terms of range; one of the least costly, if it works; one of the most costly, if it does not.

What are the chances of the report being acted on? All we can say is that the timing could not have been worse: regulation in an era of deregulation, protectionism in a time of free trade, administrative centralization in a period of decentralization. It could be dead-on-arrival. But whether the ideas and recommendations in *Proceed with Care* are ever enacted, they will still be part of our continuing dialogue on women and reproductive freedom.

NOTES

1. If the commission compared the self-selective briefs by women who were strongly opposed to the new reproductive technologies with surveys of opinion based on a sample of men and women, there would be an error that overestimates opposition. The differences of opinion between men and women were made clear in a poll conducted by Louis Harris and Associates in the United States which found that woman approved the new methods of reproduction more than men, although both were supportive (Francoeur,

1970). The true difference between women in the surveys and women who sent in briefs is probably much greater than is suggested by the report.

2. The exception is where there is complete bilateral blockage of the fallopian tubes. Even this group of women will have to look elsewhere if, after three cycles of treatment, they have not become pregnant.

3. One of President Clinton's first acts in office was to lift the ban on federally funded research using fetal tissue.

REFERENCES

Basen, G.; Eichler, M.; and Lippmann, A. (Eds.). (1994). *Misconceptions.* Toronto: Voyageur Publishing.

Camp, J. (1973). *Magic, myth and medicine.* New York: Taplinger Publishing Company.

Chess, S., MD, and Thomas, A., MD. (1982). Infant bonding: Mystique and reality. *American Journal of Orthopsychiatry, 52* (2), 213–222.

Congregation for the Doctrine of Faith. (1984). *Instruction on respect for human life in its origin and on the dignity of procreation: Replies to certain questions of the day.* Vatican City.

Crum, G., and McCormack, T. (1992). *Abortion pro-choice or pro-life?* Washington, D.C.: American University Press.

Deutsch, H. (1945). *The psychology of women: A psychoanalytic interpretation,* Vol. 2: *Motherhood.* New York: Grune and Stratton.

Dworkin, R. (1977). *Taking rights seriously.* Cambridge and New York: Harvard University Press/McGraw-Hill.

Eccles, A. (1982). *Obstetrics and gynaecology in Tudor and Stuart England.* Kent, OH: Kent State University Press.

Fischer, A. (1963). Reproduction in Truk. *Ethnology, 2,* 526–540.

Francoeur, R.T. (1970). *Utopian motherhood.* New York: Doubleday.

Gold, M. (1988). *And Hannah wept.* New York: Jewish Publication Society.

Gould, S.J. (1992). Genes, sex and altruism. *New York Review of Books,* November 19.

Guttmacher, A.F. (1953). Attitudes toward infertility. *Fertility and Sterility, 4* (4). 253–254.

Kennet, F. (1976). *Folk medicine fact and fiction.* London: Marshall Cavendish.

Ladner, J.A. (1971). *Tomorrow's tomorrow: The black woman.* Garden City, New York: Doubleday.

Lewontin, R. (1992). Doubts about the human genome project. *New York Review of Books,* May 28, 31–40.

Lippmann, A. (1994). Worrying—and worrying about—the geneticization of reproduction and health. In G. Basen, M. Eichler, and A. Lippmann (Eds.), *Misconceptions* (pp. 39–65). Toronto: Voyageur Publishing.

McCormack, T. (1991). Public policies and reproductive technology: A feminist critique. In D. Wertz (Ed.), *Research in the sociology of health care*, Vol. 9 (pp. 105–124). Greenwich, Conn.: JAI Press.

Morgan, D., and Lee, R.G. (1991). *Blackstone's guide to the Human Fertilisation & Embryology Act 1990*. London: Blackstone Press.

Ontario Law Reform Commission. (1985). *Report on human artificial reproduction and related matters*, 2 vols. Toronto: Queen's Printer.

Rebick, J. (1994). Is the issue choice? In G. Basen, M. Eichler, and A. Lippmann (Eds.), *Misconceptions* (Chap. 4). Toronto: Voyageur Publishing.

Royal Commission on New Reproductive Technologies. (1993). *Proceed with care*, 2 vols. Ottawa: Minister of Government Services.

Ruggles, S. (1994). The origins of African-American family structure. *American Sociological Review, 59* (1), 136–151.

Stack, C.B. (1974). *All our kin: Strategies for survival in a black community*. New York: Harper and Row.

Warnock, M., DBE. (1984). *Report of the Committee of Inquiry into Human Fertilisation and Embryology*, Cmnd. 9314. London: Her Majesty's Stationery Office.

Zimmerman, M.K. (1977). *Passage through abortion*. New York: Praeger.

SUGGESTED READING

Basen, G.; Eichler, M.; and Lippmann, A. (Eds.). (1994). *Misconceptions*. Toronto: Voyageur Publishing.

McCormack, T. (1991). Public policies and reproductive technology: A feminist critique. In D. Wertz (Ed.), *Research in the sociology of health care*, Vol. 9 (pp. 105–124). Greenwich Conn.: JAI Press.

QUESTIONS TO CONSIDER

1. One objection to surrogacy, or preconception contracts, is that the fetus has bonded with the gestational mother and that any disruption of this tie may have harmful effects on both child and mother. Discuss this issue and how it impacts on other policies, such as adoption.

2. The new reproductive technologies make it possible to have children without coital intercourse, thus enabling lesbian women to

have families. Discuss this in terms of recent debates on the legal status of same-sex families.

3. Critics of the new reproductive technologies suggest that allowing women to have children in this way is not pro-choice, that women are coerced into having children at great risk to their own health. Too little research is available on the long-term effects used to induce ovulation. Many infertile women say that their decisions are well thought-out and that they do not regard the risk as serious. Discuss the role of research in modern medicine, and the meaning of "informed consent" and reproductive choice.

4. On the basis of the Charter of Human Rights and Freedoms and the Human Rights Declaration, what can be said about the rights of infertile women, or couples, to have children? Consider, too, the problem of involuntary sterilization imposed on the mentally handicapped, women on welfare, and other disadvantaged groups.

CHAPTER 9

Same-Sex Couples and the Politics of Family Status

Brenda Cossman

"We're here, we're queer,
we're Family. Get Used to it!"
— Campaign for Equal Families, 1994.

In May 1994, the Ontario NDP government introduced the Equality Rights Statute Amendment Law. This long-awaited bill was intended to remove discrimination against gay men and lesbians by extending the definition of "spouse" to include partners in same-sex couples. The government had announced its promise to undertake a review of "all pertinent laws and policies pertaining to spousal benefits" in late 1990. It took another two and a half years, however, before the Attorney General of Ontario announced the government's intention to introduce a bill dealing with the rights of same-sex spouses. The Equality Rights Statute Amendment Law was intended to ensure that same-sex couples had rights identical to those of unmarried, cohabiting heterosexual couples— so-called common-law couples. In other words, gay and lesbian couples would have been entitled to the same rights and responsibilities as heterosexual couples who live together outside of marriage.

The bill was short-lived. In an act lacking in political courage, the government decided to proceed by way of an open vote, which was virtually guaranteed to result in the defeat of the legislation. Instead of using its majority in the legislature to ensure the bill's passage, the government allowed MPPs from all parties to vote on the issue according to their "conscience." The bill narrowly escaped a rare vote to have it defeated on First Reading in the legislature, before any debate was possible. After two weeks of intensive lobbying, both for and against the bill, Attorney General Marion Boyd attempted to save the legislation by promising to introduce amendments to its more controversial provisions before it was brought into the legislature for Third Reading. However, the promise to amend came too late in the day. The Liberals, whose support was required to get Bill 167 past Second Reading, refused to be moved by the promised amendments, notwithstanding the fact that these amendments were in direct response to their criticisms. The fierce opposition to gay and lesbian rights, from opposition parties as well as from within the NDP caucus itself, ultimately led to the defeat of Bill 167 on Second Reading. The NDP government has since made clear that it will not attempt to reintroduce same-sex equality legislation during its current term of office.

The same-sex equality rights legislation was the result of many years of political lobbying and litigation by gay men and lesbians, including many human-rights cases and constitutional-equality challenges in which gay men and lesbians claimed that their exclusion from family status violated their right to non-discrimination under the Human Rights Code, and under s. 15 of the Canadian Charter of Rights and Freedoms.[1] These previous cases were an important impetus for this legislative reform.

The legal and political strategy of claiming spousal status has been controversial within gay and lesbian communities themselves. Unlike the opposition to same-sex spousal status from most right-wing critics, the controversy among gays and lesbians is not based on homophobic and heterosexist discourses. Instead, it reflects a disagreement about the most appropriate political strategy for the gay and lesbian rights movement's struggle against pervasive homophobia and heterosexism. Some gay men and lesbians have opposed the political and legal strategy of seeking spousal and family status. Others have questioned whether gay men and lesbians should be arguing that same-sex relationships are "just like" heterosexual relationships. This political strategy, it is argued, may do more harm than good for gay and lesbian rights.

The first part of this essay examines the divisions within the gay and lesbian communities on this legal and political strategy. In it, I argue that the debate on family status has been polarized in a way that does not adequately capture the contradictory way in which gay men and lesbians live in families. Further, I suggest that we need to move beyond this polarized debate in a way that will allow lesbians and gay men to both claim family status and decentre the family. My argument is that our experiences of family do not fit neatly within either of these two positions. We are always both inside and outside of family at the same time. We therefore need to develop approaches and legal strategies that can embrace this contradiction.

The second part of this essay examines a specific example of law reform in relation to gay and lesbian couples and family status: the report of the Ontario Law Reform Commission (OLRC) on same-sex couples and the Family Law Act (FLA), and the background report for the OLRC, which I co-authored with Bruce Ryder.[2] This report fed into the policy process of developing the Equality Rights Statute Amendment Act, although, as will be illustrated, the proposed act differed significantly from the recommendations of the OLRC, and even further from those of the Cossman and Ryder report. In this section of the essay, I review the recommendations for reform of the Family Law Act and highlight the extent to which our background report included an effort to embrace a more complex understanding of the claim to family status that attempted to redefine the family and to include gay and lesbian couples within the family.

SAME-SEX COUPLES AND FAMILY STATUS

The Coalition for Lesbian and Gay Rights in Ontario (CLGRO) has argued for many years for the recognition of same-sex spousal relationships in Ontario legislation. In its brief *Happy families*, for example, the CLGRO makes the case that equality necessarily requires that gay and lesbian relationships have the same benefits, rights, and obligations as heterosexual couples. It continues: "All people, regardless of sexual orientation, have the right to determine for themselves their primary personal relationships and to have these relationships supported and recognized in law and by social institutions" (CLGRO, 1992, p. iv). Many gay and lesbian couples have sought to have their relationships legally recognized by arguing that the exclusion of same-sex partners from definitions of "spouse" constitutes discrimination on the basis of sexual orientation and/or family status prohibited by human-rights codes and/or s. 15 of the Charter. On this side of the debate, following on the political and legal strategy initiated by Karen Andrews in her constitutional challenge to the Ontario Health Insurance Program for excluding her same-sex partner, gay and lesbian couples have claimed that "We Are Family." This slogan has come to represent the political demand of lesbian and gay couples to be let inside the family. Some make the demand in a manner that is explicitly and unapologetically **assimilationist**; others argue that their claim to be let inside the family is inherently subversive, suggesting that the inclusion of gay and lesbian couples within the definition of "family" will radically transform the nature of the institution and subvert its traditional gender roles; still others just want the state and employment benefits that continue to be distributed on the basis of spousal and familial status to which they believe they, their partners, and their children are rightly entitled. In this view, gay men and lesbians emphasize that they, too, are taxpayers—that they pay for benefits but are unable to claim them.

DIFFERENT RELATIONS

Not all gay men and lesbians agree with the argument for same-sex spousal and familial status largely because they are sceptical of the claim to family. This position, often referred to as the **anti-assimilationist** position, raises questions about the political strategy of gay and lesbian couples claiming "We Are Family." Some lesbians and gay men resist the assimilation of their relationships by the traditional heterosexual model, and therefore disagree with the inclusion of same-sex couples in the definition of the "family." From this perspective, gay and lesbian relationships are simply different from heterosexual relationships, and any attempt to depict gay and lesbian relationships as "family" would therefore undermine the importance of this difference. There are, however, different themes within this critique. One theme is that gay and lesbian relationships do not fit the model of the heterosexual family. Gay and lesbian relationships are not functionally equivalent to heterosexual relationships: they do not necessarily purport to be based on sexual or emotional exclusivity, nor do they necessarily involve a high degree of interaction among the various dimensions of family life.

Within this view, there is a concern that the struggle for legal recognition requires lesbian and gay couples to downplay the ways in which their relationships differ from that of the traditional heterosexual family and have had to emphasize the ways in which their relationships parallel those of the heterosexual family. This strategy of inclusion within the family is thus seen to erase the important ways in which gay and lesbian relationships differ from heterosexual relationships (Report, 1993, p. 136). Further, it is argued that giving family benefits to lesbian and gay couples will result in a hierarchy of relationships modelled on the traditional family. The more gay and lesbian relationships challenge this dominant model, the less likely they are to be recognized and accorded legal status. Inclusion in the legal definition of "family," it is argued, will undermine the ways in which gay and lesbian relationships are different and marginalize those gays and lesbians who choose to live in relationships that deviate from the dominant model (ibid., p. 137).

THE FAMILY AND THE OPPRESSION OF WOMEN

A second theme within this critique of the claim to family status focusses more specifically on the role that the traditional family has played in the oppression of women. Feminist scholars have illustrated the critical role of the family, both historically and today, in the social and economic subordination of women (Barrett, 1980; Barrett and MacIntosh, 1991; Smart, 1984; Hamilton, 1988). The legal recognition of same-sex spousal relationships is thus seen to contribute to and reinforce the institution of the family, which has contributed to the oppression of women (Herman, 1990; Robson and Valentine, 1990; Gavigan, 1994). Some critics are particularly concerned with the political discourse that has been adopted by lesbians and gay men seeking legal recognition of their relationships. Shelley Gavigan (1994), for example, has criticized the language of "spousal benefits" as obscuring the oppressive nature of heterosexual familial relationships for women. Within the discourse of spousal benefits, unequal gender relations are erased, and heterosexuality becomes the site of privilege instead of oppression.

The two sides of this debate are far more complex than can be captured by a simple pro-family/anti-family opposition. When translated into legal and political arguments, however, this complexity tends to collapse into a simple debate about family/not family. The result has been a polarized debate which assumes that lesbians and gay men can be situated absolutely either inside or outside of family. One either supports or opposes inclusion within the family. This debate around family can be understood as an "inside/out" opposition. On one side, gay and lesbian couples are arguing that we are outside of the family and are demanding that we be allowed inside. On the other side, gay men and lesbians are arguing that we are outside of family and that we ought to remain there. Dianna Fuss suggests that this inside/out opposition characterizes much of contemporary lesbian and gay theory and practice. However, the problem with this opposition, and with the debate around family more generally, is that we are never unequivocally located inside or out. Thus, the opposition obscures "the fact that opts of us are both inside and outside at the same time." (Fuss, 1991, p. 5). In the context of the claim to family, we can say that we are never unequivocally located inside or outside the family. Since there is no singular or uniform discourse of experience of family, but rather a multiplicity of experiences.

WE ARE FAMILY

Consider the debate over whether gay and lesbian couples are family. The focus of the debate has been over whether gay and lesbian couples who live together ought to be entitled to consider themselves as "spouses." It is a question about the way in which people enter into spousal-like relationships, sharing both economic decisions and emotional intimacy. Yet, these are not the only ways in which we live as a family, and in which the claim that we are/not family acquires meaning. We live in a myriad of less than voluntary family subject positions. Lesbians, for example, are daughters, sisters, mothers, cousins, aunts. In this context, neither we (lesbian and gay couples) nor the state solely has the power to assert whether we are/are not family. Every day, our families, whoever they may be, give meaning to who is "family." If we are "out" as lesbians and gays, are we still inside "family"? Is one's partner "family"? The definitional boundaries of who's inside/out are drawn in and through the lived experiences and interaction of family

members. Moreover, the process of inclusion and exclusion is a complicated and potentially contradictory one. Some members of our family
may include us while others may not. We are, then, both inside and outside family at the same moment. The power of inclusion and exclusion
is diffuse, shifting, and often the site of conflict. Whether we are inside
or outside family in any particular context depends on particular config-
urations of power, and thus on who has the power to set the definitional boundary within that context. This power of inclusion and exclusion
is missed by the construction of We Are Family as spoken only by gay
and lesbian couples about themselves (Cossman, 1994, p. 24).

At the same time, the definitional boundaries of who's inside/out may
or may not correspond to our own position on the political claim that
"We Are Family." In fact, our own experience may be contradictory. We
may never claim that "We Are Family"—that is, never claim the privileges
that designation has in law or that it has meaning for us in spousal-like
terms—yet, our positions within our broader families may still have
meaning for us. In that case, it may be important that our broader families accept our partner as a member; in other words, it may be less
important that we claim that *we* are family than that each partner's family claims "we are family"—that is, the other partner is family. This latter
claim has a very different meaning. It is not based exclusively on spousal
relationships but on broader kinship relationships. Alternatively, we may
claim that we are family precisely because our families have refused to
take our partner into their fold. We may even lose our own family status
within this process. Our claim to be family is often in response to those
definitional boundaries that have excluded us from family. Naming ourselves as family when others refuse to do so is a challenge to those with
the power of inclusion and exclusion (Cossman, 1994, p. 25).

Our individual and collective experiences of family are multiple and
contradictory. Gay men and lesbians have some experience placing
them inside of family and other placing them outside of family. These
experiences must, in turn, be related to the broader discursive relations through which they have been constituted. Lesbians and gay men
have particular experiences of family as a result of historical and social
processes that have located them outside of family. Kath Weston's
work has traced some of this history. Until recently, gay and lesbian
identity has been constructed in opposition to family. To be a lesbian
or a gay man was to be without family—to be excluded from one's biological family and from the possibility of creating one's own family. In
the last decade, however, lesbian and gay couples have begun to challenge directly this social and cultural representation by claiming membership to a distinctive type of family characterized as "families we
choose" (Weston, 1991, pp. 28–29).

Lesbians and gay couples who have begun to claim family status are
challenging both the dominant representation of lesbian and gay identity
(as not family) and the dominant representation of family (as not lesbian

and gay couples). Those who resist this claim to family are not denying the historical exclusion of lesbians and gay men from family, nor even that this exclusion has discursive significance in lesbian and gay oppression. The point of disagreement is, more significantly, in the strategy of challenging dominant representations. Instead of focussing on their exclusion from family, these lesbians and gay men focus on challenging the opposition between family and not family, in which family is assumed to be naturally and normatively superior to its opposite, not family. In the same way that married is better than single, living in family is better than living outside family. In this view, it is not so much the exclusion of lesbians and gay men from family per se that has been oppressive. Instead, it is the family/not family opposition, and the tendency to characterize those excluded from family as deviant and other. Instead of claiming family status—of trying to get inside of the family—these lesbians and gay men are more concerned with displacing the opposition between family and not family, and the negative depictions of those living outside family (Cossman, 1994).

FALSE CHOICES

The political dilemma as it has been constructed for lesbians and gay men, then, is one of choosing between two equally oppressive discourses. Either they can challenge their oppression through the exclusion from family, or they can challenge the oppressive nature of family. The debate sets up, in turn, two opposing strategies to challenge gay and lesbian oppression—one of equality and one of family. Challenging the exclusion of lesbians and gay men from family relies on the discourse of equality. In other words, legal and political demands are framed in terms of a violation of the right to non-discrimination. According to this discourse, gays and lesbians have been and are oppressed by the continued discrimination against them. Challenging the oppressive nature of the family, on the other hand, relies on the feminist critique of the family. According to this latter perspective, gays and lesbians have been oppressed by the very institution of family. The inclusion within family, therefore, would only further inscribe this oppression.

The dilemma has forced a false set of choices on lesbians and gay men. Either they are oppressed by exclusion from family, or they are oppressed by the discourse of family itself. Either they should challenge their exclusion from family as a violation of their equality rights, or they should challenge the dominant discourse of family. The problem is that these political strategies, and the underlying oppressions that these strategies are intended to challenge, are not mutually exclusive but, rather, mutually constituting. The debate has been structured as if we must choose between oppressive discourses when, in fact, both dis-courses contribute to dominant depictions of gay and lesbian identity as well as gay and lesbian subordination. Lesbians and gay men have been oppressed by both these dimensions of family: because they have been excluded from family and because they have been oppressed through the very discourse of family. The dichotomy presents lesbians and gay men with an impossible choice: that of choosing which of two oppres-sive discourses is more oppressive (Cossman, 1994).

Further, the debate assumes that the family has an essential nature. It is represented as good, and the exclusion of gay and lesbian couples is bad (or, alternatively, the family is bad, and the exclusion of lesbian and gay couples is good). There has not been any political space within which to say that family is complicated—that it is both a site of oppres-sive social relations and a site of interdependence and support. We need to recognize that the family is a site of contradiction. In so doing, we create space for the recognition that the exclusion of lesbians and gay men from family is discriminatory while, at the same time, recog-nizing that the simple inclusion of gays and lesbians within family will not address the ways in which the dominant model of family is oppres-sive for individuals both inside it and outside it.

As long as the family remains an important social, economic, and ide-ological unit, around which social goods, rights, and responsibilities are organized and distributed, the exclusion of gay and lesbian couples will continue to be a source of discrimination and oppression. Moreover, as long as the dominant representation of gay and lesbian identity is one of otherness, of deviance, the discourse of equality remains a powerful and subversive strategy in the struggle against homophobia. The contin-ued escalation of the New Right's campaign against gay men and les-bians suggest that arguments based on sameness and equality have hit a social nerve, and that legal recognition and equality for same-sex cou-ples will not be easily won. Indeed, the rapid defeat of the Equality Rights Statute Amendment Act demonstrates all too well that equality for gay and lesbian couples has yet to become a politically viable concept.

Nevertheless, the mere inclusion of gays and lesbians within the family does not directly challenge the dominant representation of fami-ly, nor the continued unequal gender relations within it. The discourse of equality cannot challenge the assumption that family is an appropri-ate unit through which to distribute social goods. Nor can this dis-course of equality challenge the assumption that living in families is always preferable to not living in families. In other words, it does not challenge that family/not family hierarchy, in which family is always assumed to be the better way. There is a need to challenge, for exam-ple, the extent to which family is assumed to be an appropriate unit by which to distribute social benefits and rights. It continues to be impor-tant to engage in defamilializing strategies designed to disarticulate social rights and benefits from family status.

Our position in family is contradictory, and therefore it should come as no surprise that our political strategies must also be contradictory. Gay men and lesbians are both inside and outside of the family. Gay and lesbian couples need to be challenging their exclusion from family at the same time as they, and others, should be challenging the centrality of family. Gay men and lesbians need to be trying to get inside of the family at the same time as they need to be changing the very nature of the inside.

The question then becomes how we can pursue two seemingly contradictory strategies at the same time. The problem is heightened in the context of legal strategies, since law is particularly resistant to complexity. As Frug says, "law requires all legal claimants to assume a particular posture—a partial identity—in seeking judicial assistance; we must leave aside much of the multiplicity and complexity of our lives in order to engage in legal discourse" (1991, p. 487). Yet law's requirement that we speak in simple monotones does not extend to include the necessity that we abandon efforts to complicate our strategies. Neither does it demand that we forgo the hope of capturing the more complex nature of our identities. There are simpler ways that we can integrate the insight of being both family and not family into our political strategies. We can, for example, begin to recognize the falsity of the debate that has been foisted upon us. We can accept the validity of those on the "other side" of the debate by recognizing that there is, in fact, no "other side." Instead, there are a multiplicity of sides, all concerned with improving the lives of lesbians and gay men. We can also go a step farther by considering how we can take the arguments and analysis of the "other side" into account in formulating our own strategies. It might be possible to consider ways to make equality challenges in a way that does not rely on the dominant representation of family. For example, we could attempt to challenge provisions that exclude same-sex couples without simply relying on traditional definitions of "family."

Much of the attention paid to same-sex couples and spousal status has focussed on the courts and on the question of litigation strategies. This attention was sparked by legislatures hostile to the claims of gay men and lesbians whose political strategies then shifted to challenging discriminatory laws in the courts. More recently, however, there has been an opening within the legislative arena. The NDP government in Ontario indicated its commitment to legislative reform of the definitions of "spouse" that excluded same-sex couples, and NDP governments in other provinces are also considering the possibility of such reform. Furthermore, the federal Minister of Justice has indicated his interest in broadening the definition of "household" and the way in which government benefits are distributed to families. The issue of same-sex couples, in other words, is on the political agenda, and the difficult issues that have arisen in the context of litigation strategies must now be applied to the legislative arena. Below, I examine these

issues in the context of how the recognition of family as a site of contradiction can be brought to bear on the development of public and law
reform.

"ACCOMMODATING A DIVERSITY OF FAMILY FORMS": A REPORT FOR THE ONTARIO LAW REFORM COMMISSION

In May 1993, the provincial NDP government asked the Ontario Law
Reform Commission (OLRC) to study the reform of family law in
Ontario, including the question of whether gay men and lesbians
should be included within the Family Law Act (hereinafter "the act").
The OLRC, in turn, commissioned a background report, to be prepared
by Bruce Ryder, and me, to study the question of the applicability of
the act to unmarried cohabiting couples—both same-sex and heterosexual. In focussing on our recommendations regarding same-sex couples, my objective is to highlight the ways in which we sought to capture the complex nature of the gay and lesbian claim to spousal status,
and the extent to which it may be possible within the context of law
reform to pursue the contradictory strategy of trying to claim family status and, at the same time, decentre it.

The Family Law Act

The Family Law Act (FLA) is a provincial statute, governing the rights
and responsibilities of spouses. Parts I–III deal primarily with the equitable resolution of the economic consequences of the breakdown of
spousal relationships: Part I deals with **family property**; Part II, with
possession of the **matrimonial home**; and Part III, with spousal support. Further, Part IV allows spouses to enter into **domestic contracts**,
and Part V sets out the right to bring a tort action to recover economic
losses flowing from the negligently caused death or injury of a family
member. The scope of the act, as reviewed in Box 9.1, is determined
by the definition of "spouse." Married couples are considered as spouses throughout the act, and thus are included in all parts of the act. In
Part III, dealing with spousal support, "spouse" is more broadly defined
to include cohabiting heterosexual couples who have lived together for
three years, or are in a relationship of some permanence if they are the
natural or adoptive parents of a child. Part IV of the act, dealing with
domestic contracts, allows cohabiting couples to enter into cohabitation contracts. Cohabiting heterosexual couples are not, however,
included within the property provisions of Part I of the act, nor within
the matrimonial-home provisions in Part II. As Table 9.1 also indicates,
same-sex couples are excluded from the act as a whole.

TABLE 9.1
FAMILY LAW ACT: WHO'S IN/WHO'S OUT

Parts of Act	Included	Excluded
Part I - Family Property	- married couples	- all cohabiting heterosexual couples - all cohabiting same-sex couples
Part II - Matrimonial Home	- married couples	- all cohabiting heterosexual couples - all cohabiting same-sex couples
Part III - Support Obligations	- married couples - heterosexual couples cohabiting for at least three years and/or with a child in relationship of some permanence	- heterosexual couples cohabiting for less than three years, without a child - all same-sex couples
Part IV - Domestic Contracts	- married couples - all cohabiting heterosexual couples	- all same-sex couples
Part V - Dependant's Claim for Damages	- married couples - heterosexual couples cohabiting for at least three years or, with a child, in a relationship of some permanence	- all same-sex couples - heterosexual couples cohabiting for less than three years, without a child

We were asked to examine whether the current scope of the act was appropriate, or whether it should be extended to include cohabiting heterosexual couples and/or same-sex couples. In relation to same-sex couples, the questions that we addressed were: (1) whether the exclusion of same-sex couples from the act was justifiable; and (2), if not, how same-sex couples should be included within the act.

Is the Exclusion of Same-Sex Couples Justifiable?

In considering whether the exclusion of same-sex couples from the Family Law Act was justifiable, we began with a review of the constitutional status of this exclusion. We considered whether the act was consistent with the prohibitions on marital-status and sexual-orientation discrimination in s. 15 of the Charter of Rights and Freedoms and the Ontario Human Rights Code. Although the case law on this point is divided, we concluded that the exclusion did constitute discrimination (see Cossman and Ryder, 1993).

We then considered whether there was a policy consideration that could justify this discrimination. The rationale for the exclusion of gays and lesbians from the rights and responsibilities under the FLA lies in the traditional exclusion of gays and lesbians from marriage. The FLA and its precursor, the Family Law Reform Act, were intended to regulate spousal and spousal-like relationships. The relationships of gay men and lesbians, which have been legally excluded from the institution of marriage, have therefore never been recognized as spousal or spousal-like. The heterosexual assumption has been so deeply embedded in dominant understandings of marital and marital-like relationships that no consideration was given at the time of drafting the FLA to the inclusion of same-sex relationships. These policy considerations, based on an appeal to the sanctity of marriage, were not valid justifications for the continued exclusion of same-sex couples. Discrimination on the basis of marital status is expressly prohibited under the Ontario Human Rights Code. The courts have also concluded that marital-status discrimination (although not expressly mentioned) is included within s. 15 of the Charter. As a result, it is no longer legally justifiable to defend and promote marriage and marital relationships at the expense of other spousal and familial relationships (Cossman and Ryder, 1993, pp. 54–57).

However, a second policy consideration, which we considered to have much greater weight, was the anti-assimilationist position taken by lesbians and gay men. In addressing this policy question of whether to include same-sex couples, we directly confronted the conflict between the discourse of equality and the discourse of family. We tried to emphasize that, although we took this position very seriously, we did not believe that it could justify the continuation of the blanket exclusion of same-sex couples. However, our decision to prioritize the discourse of equality at this point of the analysis did not mean that we rejected the relevance of the anti-assimilationist position to the project as a whole. Rather, as the subsequent discussion will illustrate, our conclusion simply shifted the point at which this anti-assimilationist position might be relevant in the analysis.

How Should Same-Sex Couples Be Included?

After concluding that the exclusion of same-sex couples was not justified, we then turned to the question of how these couples should be included within the act (see Box 9.1). It is important to note that our report also included a review of the legal treatment of cohabiting heterosexual couples, and considered whether their exclusion from Parts I and II of the act justifiable. We concluded that cohabiting heterosexual couples should be

included within the property provisions and matrimonial-home provisions. Following from these recommendations, giving same-sex couples
identical treatment to that given to cohabiting heterosexual couples
would involve also including same-sex couples in Parts I and II of the act.

The first two options for including same-sex couples—as contract
and/or domestic partnerships—would be based on the choice of the
individual couples. In our view, there was no legitimate reason to prohibit same-sex couples who wanted to contract in, or to opt in through
registration, from doing so. The anti-assimilationist position seemed to
be least compromised by this option, insofar as only those couples
who choose to be included would be. Further, neither contract nor registered domestic-partnership agreements would require that same-sex
couples prove that their relationships were "just like" heterosexual relationships. Instead, they could structure their relationships according to
their own choices.

BOX 9.1

Degrees of Inclusion We considered these different approaches according
to the degree of inclusion, from the least to the most inclusive.

▶ *Contract*: Same-sex couples could be given the option to contract in
   to the statutory scheme. A specific provision could be included in Part
   IV of the act, which sets out the rights and obligations in relation to
   domestic contracts, expressly granting same-sex couples the right to
   negotiate enforceable contracts.

▶ *Domestic Partnership Regime*: Same-sex couples could be given the
   option to register their relationships as domestic partnerships, and thereby be included within the rights and obligations of the act as a whole.

▶ *Treat Same-Sex Couples in an Identical Manner to Unmarried
   Heterosexual Couples*: Same-sex couples could be treated the same as
   unmarried heterosexual couples by including them within the extended definition of "spouse." Under the existing legislation, cohabiting heterosexual couples are included within the support provisions in Part III
   if they have cohabited for three years, or have lived in a relationship of
   some permanence if they are the parents of a child. Treating same-sex
   couples and unmarried heterosexual couples the same could thus
   mean including these couples within this extended definition of
   "spouse." Further, cohabiting heterosexual couples are included within
   Part IV of the act, which allows for these couples to enter into valid
   and enforceable cohabitation contracts. Same-sex couples could thus
   also be included within the domestic-contract provisions in Part IV of
   the act, allowing them to enter valid and enforceable cohabitation contracts in the same manner as can unmarried heterosexual couples.

However, the issue of ascribing spousal status is more difficult. This option would require ascribing spousal status to couples who do not choose to enter contracts, or to designate their relationship as a domestic partnership. It requires addressing the question of whether spousal status should ever be ascribed to same-sex couples who do not opt in of their own volition. The question of ascribing spousal status raises the further question of whether this status should be partial (only for certain parts of the act) or comprehensive (for the act as a whole). Finally, it raises the question of how spousal status should be defined.

Fitting Same-Sex Couples In

In an effort to address these questions in relation to ascribing spousal status, our analysis was twofold: (1) we examined each part of the act and considered the objectives of the statutory provisions and whether these objectives applied to same-sex couples; (2) we considered how spousal status would be ascribed. How would "spousal" be defined in cases where couples have not chosen to designate their relationship as such. As I will describe, in our analysis, we returned to the question of the contradictory nature of same-sex couples' claim to spousal status.

Property Rights

The objective of the property provisions in Part I of the act is the recognition that the relationship is an economic partnership in which household work, child care, and financial provision are the joint responsibility of the spouses, and in which the contribution of each of the parties is deemed to be equal (s. 5(7)). The spousal relationship is seen to be based on the joint and equal responsibilities of the spouses. On the breakdown of the relationship, both spouses are seen to be equally entitled to share in the value of the property acquired during the partnership.

In our view, the rationale for the equalization of property in Part I is equally applicable to same-sex couples. The ideal of an equal partnership promotes a way of thinking about relationships that ought to be appropriate in any community (Cossman and Ryder, 1993, p. 141). If people live together in an economic partnership during which they pool their financial and non-financial resources, they should be equally entitled to share in the value of the property acquired during that partnership. The practical dimensions of Part I are equally applicable to same-sex couples. Most people acquire at least some property (however nominal) during the course of a relationship, and the requirement that couples share in the value of this property on the breakdown of the relationship would fit with the reasonable expectation of the parties. Further, we do not believe that lesbians and gay men are necessarily any more immune to disputes over the appropriate divisions upon the breakdown of the relationship. The law has an important practical role to play in promoting the efficient and equitable resolution of the ex-partners' affairs (ibid.).

Possessory Rights

Part II of the act is intended to recognize that the matrimonial home is an asset with special significance, in both financial and non-financial terms. The matrimonial home is often the major asset owned by either spouse. Further, the matrimonial home "is the place around which family life revolves" (Hovius and Youdan, 1991, p. 574). It often provides a family with a sense of financial security and accommodation, and children with a stable environment, as well as being the focus of emotional attachment. On the breakdown of a relationship, the equalization of property often requires that the home be sold. However, selling the home may create undue hardship for one of the spouses. Often, the spouse who has custody of the children may be unable to find affordable accommodation and/or may have to disrupt the educational routine of the children. Part II of the act is intended to address these special problems by giving the non-titled spouse the right to live in the matrimonial home and to make an application for the exclusive possession of it under certain circumstances (s. 24).

The rationale for possessory rights to the matrimonial home might apply equally to same-sex couples. As for unmarried heterosexual couples, the primary residence is likely to be the major asset of the same-sex relationship, as well as the focus of the family life. On the breakdown of the relationship, same-sex couples may similarly be in a difficult position in locating alternative, affordable housing. Further, the same factors relating to the best interests of the children may apply. One of the factors to be taken into account in an application for exclusive possession to the matrimonial home is the best interest of the child, which is defined in s. 24(3) as including "(a) possible disruptive effects on the child of a move to other accommodation, and (b) the child's views and preferences, if they can reasonably be ascertained." It ought not to matter whether the child's parents are heterosexual or same-sex. Another factor set out in that section (s. 24(3)(f)) is violence committed by one spouse against the other or the children. Protecting spouses and children from violence is thus one of the objectives of this part of the act, and, again, the sexual orientation of the couple should not be a relevant consideration in terms of this protection.

Support

The objective of the spousal-support provisions in Part III of the act are less clear. There are a number of different, and not entirely consistent, rationales underlying spousal support (Rogerson, 1989), some of which may fit lesbian and gay relationships better than others, and some of which are completely unsuited to lesbian and gay relationships. For example, in the traditional approach, spousal support was based on the assumption of women's economic dependency on men, and on the life-long promise of support. This model of support was based in the sexual division of labour, and the economic dependency of women that has resulted from it. Such a model would be inappropriate in the context of same-sex partners, who do not tend to adopt such traditional gender roles. Indeed, many gay men and lesbians explicitly reject such traditional gender roles, along with the social and economic inequality which these roles produce.

A second approach to spousal support is a needs-based model which is directed to addressing the economic need of spouses on marital breakdown. Although considered a significant improvement over the traditional approach to support, it has been criticized insofar as it encourages ex-spouses to look to each other for income security long after the relationship has broken down. This model seemed problematic in the context of same-sex partners, who have not traditionally looked to each other as sources of income security on the breakdown of their relationship. Moreover, it is an approach that is premised largely on the assumption on economic dependency that informed the traditional model of support—that is, on the family as the key source of individual financial security, especially for women.

A third, and opposing, model is one of self-sufficiency, or a clean break, in which spousal support is kept to a minimum and in which the primary objective is to promote the economic self-sufficiency of ex-spouses as soon as possible on marital breakdown. In the context of same-sex couples, arguments can be made both for and against this model. On the one hand, this approach can be seen to be based on assumptions of dependency. However, this approach would be limited to addressing those situations in which one of the partners was actually economically dependent on the other partner.

A fourth approach to spousal support is based on the idea of compensation—that spousal support should compensate a spouse for the contribution that he or she made to the relationship. This approach struck us as the most appropriate in the context of same-sex spouses. A partner would be entitled to spousal support based on the actual contribution made to the relationship. There is no assumption of economic dependency, but simply recognition of contribution. If an individual in a same-sex relationship has contributed to the relationship in a way that has resulted in personal economic disadvantage or economic advantage to his or her partner, then the individual should be entitled to support.

Dimensions of all four of these approaches to support can be found in the FLA. The problem with the law of spousal support was, then, that some of the approaches were appropriate in the context of same-sex couples, and others were not. As a result, we could not simply conclude that the rationale unequivocally applied, or did not apply, to same-sex couples. Although the compensatory approach to spousal support was unproblematic, it was not the only approach contained in the legislation. As a result of these problems and inconsistencies, we believed that there was a very serious question as to whether these obligations for spousal support should be ascribed to same-sex couples. Historically, gays and lesbians have not organized their lives according to this sexual division of labour, and, as a result, their lives have not been characterized by the same type of economic dependency. Nor have they looked to each other for support on the breakdown of relationships. Therefore, in relation to the issue of spousal support, the anti-assimilationist position seemed most compelling (see Cossman and Ryder, 1993, pp. 142–147).

Domestic Contracts

Part IV of the act allows individual couples to structure their relationship according to their own choices, and to define for themselves the rights and responsibilities inherent in their relationship. Part IV is intended to promote the values of autonomy of the parties, by allowing them to structure the terms of their relationship and providing a legal framework within which these terms will be enforced, subject to certain equitable considerations. The provisions allow married and cohabiting heterosexual couples to contract out of rights and obligations otherwise imposed by the act (married couples cannot contract out of the rights in Part II). Further, unmarried cohabiting couples who are not subject to Parts I and II can enter contracts in relation to issues of property and the matrimonial home.

The rationale of promoting autonomy and self-determination, while also providing for a minimum of fairness in the bargaining process, is equally applicable to same-sex couples. There is no legitimate reason that gay and lesbian couples should not be able to enter into valid and enforceable contracts that set out their rights and responsibilities during the relationship or on the breakdown of the relationship. We were of the view that the anti-assimilationist argument was not applicable to the issue of contracts, insofar as domestic contracts would simply allow gay and lesbian couples to define their relationship, and the legal consequences of their relationship, on their own terms.

Table 9.2 shows our recommendations for reform of the act. In sum, cohabiting heterosexual couples should be included in all sections of the act; same-sex couples should have the option of registering their relationships as domestic partnerships, and in so doing, becoming eligible for inclusion in all sections of the act; same-sex couples who do not register their relationships, however, should be included in only some parts of the act.

TABLE 9.2

Cossman and Ryder Recommendations for Reform of the FLA

Parts of the Act	Included	Excluded
Part I - Family Property	- all married couples - all heterosexual cohabiting couples living together for three years - all registered domestic partners - all same-sex cohabiting couples living together for three years	- heterosexual cohabiting couples who have lived together for less than three years (unmarried and unregistered) - same-sex couples who have lived together for less than three years (unmarried and unregistered)
Part II - Matrimonial Home	- all married couples - all heterosexual cohabiting couples living together for three years - all registered domestic partners - all same-sex cohabiting couples living together for three years	- heterosexual cohabiting couples who have lived together for less than three years (unmarried and unregistered) - same-sex couples who have lived together for less than three years (unmarried and unregistered)
Part III - Support Obligations	- all married couples - all heterosexual cohabiting couples living together for three years - all registered domestic partners	- heterosexual cohabiting couples who have lived together for less than three years (unmarried and unregistered) - all same-sex couples who have not registered their relationship
Part IV - Domestic Contracts	- all married couples - all heterosexual couples - all same-sex couples	- none

(continued)

(continued)

Parts of the Act	Included	Excluded
Part V - Dependent's Right to Sue	- all married couples - all heterosexual couples - all same-sex couples	- none

Defining "Spouse"

The next question we addressed was how spousal status should be ascribed. The act currently includes an extended definition of "spouse" for the purposes of spousal support in Part III:

> "spouse" means a spouse as defined in subsection (1), and in addition includes either of a man and woman who are not married to each other and have cohabited, (a) continuously for a period of not less than three years, or (b) in a relationship of some permanence, if they are the natural or adoptive parents of a child.

The term "cohabit" is defined in s. 1(1) of the act as meaning "to live together in a conjugal relationship, within or outside marriage." "Conjugal relationship" is not defined in the act, but it has been considered and defined by the courts. Two different approaches have emerged in the case law. In the first approach, the economic relationship between the parties is emphasized, and the court examines whether there is a relationship of economic dependency. In *Stoikiewicsz v. Filas* (1978), 7 R.F.L. (2d) 366 (Ont. Unif. Fam. Ct), the court stated: "unmarried persons cannot be found to be cohabiting ... unless it can be determined that their relationship is such that they have assumed an obligation to support and provide for the other in the same manner that married spouses are obliged to do" (pp. 369–70). In the court's view, since there was no relationship of economic dependency in the case, the parties could not be said to be cohabiting within the meaning of the act. This first approach has been criticized. In *Armstrong* v. *Thompson* (1979), 23 O.R. (2d) 421, the court considered and rejected this economic-dependency approach: "To say that because the dependent spouse worked outside the home, maintained her own bank account, and spent her own money, is reason to deny the rights (to spousal support) is not, in my view, what is contemplated in the Act."

The second, and more common, approach examines whether the relationship is functionally equivalent to marriage. In *Feehan and Attwells* (1979), 24 O.R. (2d) 248 (Co. Ct), the court considered the meaning of "conjugal" and "cohabitation." Citing the *Shorter Oxford English Dictionary*, which defines "conjugal" as "of or pertaining to marriage or to husband and wife in their relationship to each other," the court concluded that "cohabit" means "living together in a 'marriage like' relationship outside marriage" (p. 251). This second approach requires identifying the basic dimensions and functions of marital relationship. These functions of marriage have been defined as including a common residence; a sexual and emotional relationship; an economic relationship, including financial dependence or interdependence; a social relationship, wherein the individuals hold themselves out to family and community as a couple; a reproductive relationship; and a service relationship, that is, whether one of the individuals (the woman) provided domestic services for the other (see *Moldowich* v. *Pentinnen*, [1980] 17 R.F.L. (2d) 376 (Ont. Dist.Ct))

Both the economic-dependency approach and the functional approach have been based on very traditional conceptions of marriage and marital roles. These approaches have been informed by, and have served to reinforce, dominant familial ideology, which is problematic even in the context of heterosexual relationships. Measuring all relationships against this norm of an idealized marital relationship is extremely problematic. In attempting to reduce a spousal relationship to certain idealized marital functions, this approach assumes that there is a single and dominant model of marriage and family that can be clearly defined. The reality, in contrast, is that marital relationships are extremely diverse. The idealized functional approach sets up a monolithic and mythical image of the marital relationship against which all relationships are evaluated. In so doing, this approach undermines the diverse ways in which individuals may choose to live in relationships, and thereby undermines the goal of accommodating and respecting the diversity and equality of living arrangements (Cossmar and Ryder, 1993, p. 78).

In our view, neither the functional nor the dependency approach to cohabitation as currently defined in the case law promotes the values of equality, diversity, and self-determination in intimate relationships. The problems with the existing definition are only heightened in the context of same-sex relationships. Same-sex couples should not have to be just like "traditional" married couples in order to qualify for the rights and responsibilities in the act. The anti-assimilationist position seemed to be particularly compelling on this point. If same-sex couples have to "cohabit" within the meaning of s. 1(1)—that is, "live together in a conjugal relationship" as defined by the courts—the way in which same-sex relationships are different from traditional heterosexual relationships could lead to their exclusion. Same-sex couples would be recognized only to the extent that these relationships measured up against the traditional married, heterosexual requirements (ibid., p. 157).

The problem of measuring gay and lesbian relationships by reference to an idealized marital model is particularly problematic when seen in the light of several of the elements of "living together as husband and wife." Consider, for example, the requirement that the partners hold themselves out to society as a couple. While holding oneself out as married may bring community approval and support for heterosexual couples, the same result does not necessarily accrue to same-sex couples. The hetero-sexism and homophobia that gay men and lesbians face every day may operate as a strong incentive against holding themselves out as a couple. Being "out" as a couple also means being "out" as gay or lesbian, which may result in social condemnation, ostracization, and even violence.

We therefore concluded that the extended definition of "spouse" found in Part III, was in need of revision. We recommended that that definition be changed before same-sex couples could or should be included within its parameters. In other words, a redefinition of "spouse" was a prerequisite to ascribing spousal status to gay and les-bian couples. A new definition of "spouse" must address the problems in the existing definition, and attempt to embody more adequately the values of equality and diversity that must be promoted in the legal reg-ulation of intimate relationships.

We accepted that the definition had to be functional—that there was no other way to ascribe spousal status. Self-designating definitions of "spousal status" are more appropriate in that they avoid an **essentialist** definition of "family," but the very problem that this question of ascribed spousal status is intended to address is couples who do not self-designate. We concluded that the definition of "spousal" should have three stipulations:

▶ a residency requirement (the couple must live together)

▶ an economic-interdependency requirement (the couple must live in a form of economic partnership)

▶ an emotional requirement (the relationship must be of primary importance in both partners' lives)

These three dimensions seemed to us to approximate the nature of the relationship that the act was designed to include and protect.

The act is based on a conception of relationships as economic part-nerships, and attempts to deal with the economic consequences that flow from the end of those partnerships. It follows, then, that the exis-tence of economic interdependence or an economic partnership ought to be a defining characteristic of relationships that are covered by the act. Only where there is economic interdependence is there a valid pre-sumption that an equal division of property is the equitable solution on the breakdown of relationships. Similarly, only where there is economic partnership or interdependence is there a possibility that one party has diminished the market value of her or his human resources during the relationship (Cossmar and Ryder, 1993, p. 82). Interdependence does not mean that one party is necessarily more dependent on the other, although, in financial terms alone, that may frequently be the case. Rather, it means that the parties are mutually dependent during the course of the relationship (ibid.).

The economic relationship alone, however, did not seem to be sufficient for an extended definition of "spouse." It is, rather, the combination of emotional intimacy and economic partnership that creates the unique vulnerability of spouses to harsh consequences arising on the breakdown of a lasting relationship. Thus, the inclusion of some reference to emotional intimacy in the definition of "spouse" seemed appropriate.[3]

In summary, we recommended that same-sex couples be included within the act through contract, registered domestic partnership, and (in part) through ascription. Same-sex couples should be free to enter valid and enforceable contracts. They also should be allowed to opt into the FLA scheme by registering their relationships as domestic partnerships. Finally, spousal status should be ascribed to same-sex couples in relation to property equalization and the matrimonial home, but not in relation to spousal support. However, this spousal status should be ascribed only if the extended definition of "spouse" is reformed to capture better the nature of the relationships to be included.

The project of studying the inclusion of same-sex couples within the FLA scheme, and the particular conclusions that we reached, are on one level, an inherently assimilationist project and overly determined by the discourse of equality. Nevertheless, I believe that our study attempted to capture some of the more complex dimensions of gay and lesbian claims to family status. Our effort to embrace the contradictions inherent in these claims was apparent in two specific areas. The first was stopping short of complete assimilation. We endeavoured to include same-sex couples as spouses where the fit was appropriate. Same-sex couples could thus be included as spouses for some purposes, but not others. Second, we attempted to redefine the very thing in which same-sex couples were being included. We subtly attempted to deconstruct and decentre the dominant constructions of "family" at the same time as we tried to include same-sex couples inside it.

THE ONTARIO LAW REFORM COMMISSION REPORT

Our report was only background material for the Ontario Law Reform Commission, and the OLRC report falls short of fully embracing these contradictions. However, the contradictory nature of gay and lesbian claims to spousal status was not lost on the commission. While the commission agreed with our assessment of "conjugal" as problematic, it concluded that our proposed redefinition was too broad. According to the commission, there were two problems with our proposed definition:

> First, the meaning of the term "economic partnership" is unclear.
> Individuals may have difficulty demonstrating to a court that such a "part-
> nership" existed. Second, even when modified by the phrase "in a relation-
> ship ... of primary importance in each other's lives" the proposed definition
> potentially applies to many relationships that are not currently within the
> purview of the Family Law Act. It could conceivably apply, for example, to
> business partnerships, as well as to relationships between parents and
> their children, or between friends. (OLRC Report, 1993, p. 62)

In relation to where to draw the line between inclusion and exclusion,
the commission concluded that no spousal status should be ascribed
to gay and lesbian relationships without further consultation with the
affected community. Interestingly, this conclusion was based on the
commission's taking the anti-assimilationist position seriously. In the
commission's view, it was not possible to evaluate the anti-assimilationist position, nor the appropriateness of ascribing spousal status for
same-sex couples, without more evidence about the patterns of these
relationships than is currently available.

Table 9.3 sets out the final recommendations of the OLRC. They
directly parallel our recommendations, with the exception of ascribing
spousal status to same-sex couples who do not register their relationships as domestic partnerships. The OLRC recommended that these
relationships should not be ascribed as spousal without further consultation with the gay and lesbian community.

We did not ultimately disagree with these recommendations, although
further consultation had not been presented to us as a viable option. In
many ways, a recommendation to not ascribe spousal status to same-
sex couples might have been a better way to capture the complexity of
same-sex relationships. In this way, there would be no question of
developing an extended definition of "spouse" that would be applicable
to gay and lesbian couples. This would avoid the problems of assimilat-
ing gay and lesbian relationships into an essentialist (though redefined)
conception of family. By drawing the line at self-designation, only those
gay and lesbian couples who specifically choose to have their relationships included would fall within the scope of the act. Gay and lesbian
couples would thus be families only if they said that they were.

The problem that we perceived with this model was that it would be
creating a two-tier system—one for heterosexual and one for same-sex
couples—and might be seen to be in violation of equality rights.
Evaluated within the discourse of equality, it seemed to be ripe for
challenge. Indeed, on the release of the OLRC's report, representatives
from the gay and lesbian lobby for spousal status criticized the recommendations on precisely the ground that it did create such a two-tier
system, in which same-sex relationships were still being treated in a
discriminatory manner. The demand for formal equality—for treatment
identical to that accorded to heterosexual couples—was a powerful
one. And the appeal of formal equality proved to be irresistible at least
for the attorney general in her formulation of Bill 167.

TABLE 9.3
OLRC RECOMMENDATIONS FOR REFORM OF THE FLA

Parts of the Act	Included	Excluded
Part I - Family Property	- all married couples - all heterosexual cohabiting couples living together for three years - all registered domestic partners	- heterosexual couples cohabiting for less than three years - same-sex couples who have not designated their relationship
Part II - Matrimonial Home	- all married couples - all heterosexual cohabiting couples living together for three years - all registered domestic partners	- heterosexual cohabiting couples who have lived together for less than three years - same-sex couples who have not registered their relationship
Part III - Support Obligations	- all married couples - all heterosexual cohabiting couples living together for three years - all registered domestic partners	- heterosexual couples cohabiting for less than three years - same-sex couples who have not registered their relationship
Part IV - Domestic Contracts	- all married couples - all heterosexual couples - all same-sex couples	- none
Part V - Dependant's Right to Sue	- all married couples - all heterosexual couples - all registered domestic partners	- heterosexual couples cohabiting for less than three years, without a child - same-sex couples who have not registered their relationship

THE NDP'S BILL

The reforms introduced by the NDP government were a far cry from the recommendations of the Ontario Law Reform Commission. The Equality Rights Statute Amendment Act would have redefined "spouse" in such a way that same-sex couples would receive identical treatment to that given to cohabiting heterosexual couples. It was based on a model of formal equality in which same-sex couples and common-law couples would be treated exactly the same. Within the context of the Family Law Act, this would have meant amending the definition of "spouse" in s. 29 of the act, as well as amending the definitions of who can enter into cohabitation and separation agreements in Part IV of the act.

Table 9.4 lists these proposed reforms in relation to the Family Law Act. As indicated, same-sex couples are to be included for the purposes of Part III of the act if they have lived together in a conjugal relationship for not less than three years. Same-sex couples will also be allowed to enter into cohabitation and separation agreements within the purview of Part IV of the act. Both same-sex couples and cohabiting heterosexual couples would continue to be excluded from Part I of the act, dealing with property, and Part II of the act dealing with the matrimonial home.

The government did not accept the recommendations of the OLRC in relation to registered domestic partnerships, which would have allowed same-sex couples to self-designate their relationships as spousal. Nor did the government heed the warning of the OLRC in relation to not ascribing spousal status without further consultation with the gay and lesbian community, particularly in the context of spousal support. The model followed by the government was one of pure formal equality, that is, of treating same-sex couples and cohabiting heterosexual couples in an identical manner.

Throughout the legislative debates, this emphasis on formal equality featured prominently in the speeches of supporters of Bill 167. Over and over again, members of the House who supported the bill rose to emphasize that Bill 167 was a matter of equality—that it would simply extend the same rights and responsibilities to same-sex couples that are currently enjoyed by common-law couples. The comments of Frances Lankin, Minister of Economic Development and Trade, exemplified this theme:

> The reforms that have been put forward before us for second reading today, first of all, eliminate discrimination. They provide same sex couples with rights and obligations equal to those of opposite sex common-law couples. That is the equation we have to continue to keep in our mind as we go through this debate and look at these amendments. Specifically, the reforms will eliminate discrimination against same sex couples by amending the interpretation of all provincial laws which provide the benefits and the obligations or the rights that are based on that spousal status of being an opposite-sex common-law couples. (*Hansard*, June 1, 1994, p. 6586)

TABLE 9.4
EQUALITY RIGHTS STATUTE AMENDMENT ACT
REFORMS TO THE FAMILY LAW ACT

Parts of the Act	Included	Excluded
Part I - Family Property	- married couples	- all cohabiting heterosexual couples - all cohabiting same-sex couples
Part II - Matrimonial Home	- married couples	- all cohabiting heterosexual couples - all cohabiting same-sex couples
Part III - Support Obligations	- married couples - heterosexual couples cohabiting for at least three years, and/or with a child in relationship of some permanence - **same-sex couples cohabiting for at least three years**	- heterosexual couples cohabiting for less than three years, without a child - same-sex couples cohabiting for less than three years
Part IV - Domestic Contracts	- married couples - all cohabiting heterosexual couples - **all same-sex couples**	- none
Part V - Dependent's Claim for Damages	- married couples - heterosexual couples cohabiting for at least three years, and/or with a child in relationship of some permanence - **same-sex couples cohabiting for at least three years**	- same-sex couples cohabiting for less than three years - heterosexual couples cohabiting for less than three years, without a child

On the other side, opponents of the bill cast their arguments in the discourse of the family—more specifically, in terms of the "traditional family." Speaker after speaker rose to defend the so-called traditional family from the demise that would follow on the heels of the passage of this bill. Most opponents of the bill refused to frame the issue with the language of equality rights; though some did insist instead that the bill would give gay and lesbian couples "special rights."

It is also important to recognize that the extent to which visible and vocal dissent within the gay and lesbian community virtually disappeared during these debates on Bill 167. Regardless of individuals' views about the relative wisdom of obtaining same-sex benefits, the gay and lesbian community came together to speak with a strong and united voice. Debates about the wisdom of claiming family status were left for another day. There was little doubt within the community that Bill 167 was going to be won or lost on the simple question of equality rights—of whether the time had come for society to recognize the claims of gay and lesbian couples to those rights. It was a question of equality rights, pure and simple, and a defeat would be a victory for the forces of homophobia and heterosexism.

In the end, arguments in defence of the traditional family and against extending spousal status to gay men and lesbians won the day, defeating arguments based on formal equality. The model of formal equality, which the NDP government had chosen, presumably as the path of least resistance, proved to be all too easy for the majority of Ontario's politicians to resist. In wake of the defeat, it is difficult to sustain an argument that the government ought to have pursued a more complex vision of equality, which would require that groups be treated differently in order to be treated equally. If formal equality could not be realized, a model based on substantive equality would perhaps have been sheer fantasy.

On the other hand, it is possible that a different approach might have been less provocative. In the final hour of the debates, when the attorney general promised to introduce amendments to the bill before it was brought back to the House for its third and final reading, one of the proposed amendments was to replace the word "spouse" with the word "partner." This amendment was a direct response to the opponents of the bill, particularly the Liberals, who argued that, although they favoured equality rights for gay men and lesbians, they could not support this redefinition of "spouse." While the amendment came too late in the day to have any impact on the vote, it is intriguing as an alternative model. Ironically, the term "partner" is one that could gain greater favour from some anti-assimilationist gay men and lesbians. Using the term "partner" as the means to extend equal rights and responsibilities to gay and lesbian couples could minimize the slippage into a direct comparison between same-sex and heterosexual couples. It is possible at least to speculate that such a model might have had a better chance to succeed precisely because it did not make a direct parallel between gay and lesbian couples, and the so-called traditional family.

CONCLUSION

Our experience with this process of policy development and law reform indicates that it is possible to reflect complex positions in law reform and to develop proposals that could capture the complicated nature of gay and lesbian relationship to family. It was more difficult, however, to ensure that such proposals were accepted. Our experience with this process of policy development was also one in which these complexities were lost on the path through the stages of law reform. While the Ontario Law Reform Commission was able to see the need to examine legislative provisions piece by piece to evaluate whether the objectives could and should be applied to same-sex couples, the government was not. Rather, the government retreated to a position of formal equality. This perspective does not examine the specific objectives of legislative provisions, or recognize that substantive equality may sometimes require treating different groups differently. In the government's view, this model of formal equality would be more politically viable—it would be easier to explain, and easier to sell. And, at the end of the day, the government was probably right. Even the simple principle of formal equality proved to be too difficult to sell.

Law reform is not bursting with opportunities to embrace complexity and contradiction. It is, rather, a process in which complexity and contradiction are progressively weeded out, in which both the problem and the legislative response to the problem are simplified. Engaging in the process of law reform, whether as lobbyists, legal experts, or policy-makers, requires that strategic choices be made along the way. These choices, in turn, may simplify complex issues and compromise a more sophisticated understanding of the issues. However, recognizing the nature of the process need not mean that we abandon all efforts to address the complex and contradictory nature of the issues before us. Rather, our theoretical understanding of the problem will continuously provide the framework against which we can evaluate our choices. Politics, of necessity, means making compromises. But a theoretical framework can serve to remind us that we choose to compromise. I believe that it is possible to bring a more complex understanding of social issues, which can capture the contradictory nature of issues concerning the family, to the process of law reform.

Finally, although the bill was defeated, the issue has not gone away. Ironically, the defeat of the bill has had the effect of mobilizing the gay and lesbian community in Ontario. In the immediate aftermath of the defeat, gay and lesbian couples have come forward in unprecedented numbers to challenge discriminatory laws. And Gay and Lesbian Pride Day, in Toronto, at the end of June 1994, a few weeks after the defeat, saw an unprecedented 300 000 lesbians and gay men, and their friends and families come out to celebrate and protest, and to make the message of the Campaign for Equal Families loud and clear: "We're here, we're queer, we are family. Get used to it."

For the time being, the discourse of equality has won the day as the dominant political strategy in the struggle for gay and lesbian rights. In the shadow of the defeat of Bill 167, and the political mobilization behind the "We Are Family" campaign, it may be difficult and not politically expedient to make arguments complicating this claim. Indeed, the defeat of the bill was a powerful reminder of the extent to which the demand for basic equality rights for gay and lesbian couples continues to be a very radical claim.

Yet, it is essential that we not forget the contradictions inherent in this claim. We must not fall back into the either/or trap, the all-or-nothing proposition, of choosing whether or not we are family. Gay and lesbian claims to spousal status, and to family, more generally, are complicated. In a world in which lesbians and gay men have been denied their humanity through their exclusion from family, laying claim to family status remains an important strategy. Yet, in a world in which the boundaries between family and not family continue to demarcate access to social goods, and social identity, challenging the centrality of family will also remain an important political strategy. We live in a world in which we are oppressed by exclusion from family and in which we may be oppressed through our inclusion within family.

NOTES

1   The We Are Family campaign was launched by Karen Andrews in her constitutional challenge to the Ontario Health Insurance Plan for its failure to extend health benefits to her partner and her partner's children. Although the case was unsuccessful, the legacy of her case has been important in setting the stage within which other lesbians and gay men have sought to have their relationships recognized: *Andrews* v. *Ontario (Minister of Health)* (1988), 49 D.L.R. (4th) 584 (Ont. H.C.). More recently, Brian Mossop's case, in which he claimed that he had been discriminated on the basis of family status in the denial of employment benefits that were available to heterosexual couples, was the first gay-rights case to reach the Supreme Court of Canada. The Supreme Court rejected his claim on the basis that sexual orientation was not a prohibited ground of discrimination under the Canadian Human Rights Act, and the discrimination that Mossop and his partner had faced was really a question of sexual orientation, not family status. In the absence of a constitutional challenge to the exclusion of sexual orientation, the Court was of the view that the case could not succeed: *Canada (Attorney General)* v. *Mossop*, [1993] S.C.R. 544 (S.C.). The Supreme Court of

Canada will, however, shortly have another opportunity to consider the claims to spousal status and same-sex spousal benefits in the case of another gay couple, Egan and Nesbitt, which is expected to be heard in early 1995.

2. The report of the Ontario Law Reform Commission is titled *Report on the rights and responsibilities of cohabitants under the Family Law Act* (and hereinafter cited as Report, 1993). The background study prepared by Bruce Ryder and me is titled *Gay, lesbian and unmarried heterosexual couples: Accommodating a diversity of family forms* (hereinafter cited as Cossman and Ryder, 1993).

3. In regard to emotional intimacy, we adopted the language of the recent Consent to Treatment Act, which describes "spouse" as "a person of primary importance in each other's lives."

REFERENCES

Barrett, Michele. (1980). *Women's oppression today: Problems of Marxist feminist analysis.* London: Verso.

Barrett, Michele, and MacIntosh, Mary. (1991). *The anti-social family* (2d ed.) London and New York: Verso.

Coalition for Lesbian and Gay Rights in Ontario (CLGRO). (1992, April). *Happy families: The recognition of same-sex spousal relationships.* Toronto: CLGRO.

Cossman, Brenda, and Ryder, Bruce. (1993, June). *Gay, lesbian and unmarried heterosexual couples and the Family Law Act: Accommodating a diversity of family forms.* Unpublished report prepared for the Ontario Law Reform Commission. Copies available from the Ontario Law Reform Commission.

Cossman, Brenda. (1994). Family inside/out. *University of Toronto Law Journal 44* (1).

Frug, Mary Joe. (1991). Law and postmodernism: The politics of marriage. *University of Colorado Law Review, 62,* 483.

Fuss, Dianna. (Ed.). (1991). *Inside/out: Lesbian theories, gay theories.* New York: Routledge.

Gavigan, Shelley. (1993). Paradise lost, paradox revisited: The implications of familial ideology for feminist, lesbian and gay engagement with law. *Osgoode Hall Law Journal 31* (3).

Hamilton, Roberta. (1988). Women, wives and mothers. In Nancy Mandel and Ann Duffy (Eds.), *Reconstructing the Canadian family: Feminist perspectives.* Toronto: Butterworths.

Herman, Didi. (1990). Are we family? Lesbian rights and women's liberation. *Osgoode Hall Law Review, 28,* 789.

Herman, Didi. (1994). Rights of passage: Struggles for lesbian and gay legal equality. Toronto: University of Toronto Press.

Hovius, B., and Youdan, T.G. (1991). The law of family property. Toronto: Carswell.

Ontario Law Reform Commission. (1993). *Report on the rights and responsibilities of cohabitants under the Family Law Act.* Toronto: Queen's Printer.

Robson, Ruthann, and Valentine, S.E. (1990). Lov(h)ers: Lesbians as intimate partners and lesbian legal theory. *Temple Law Review, 63,* 511.

Rogerson, Carol. (1989). The causal connection test in spousal support law. Canadian Journal of Family Law, *8,* 95.

Smart, Carol. (1984). *The ties that bind: Law, marriage and the reproduction of patriarchal relations.* London: Routledge and Kegan Paul.

Weston, Kath. (1991). *Families we choose: Lesbians, gays, kinship.* New York: Columbia University Press.

SUGGESTED READING

Arnup, Kathy. (1991). "We Are Family": Lesbian mothers in Canada. *Resources for Feminist Research, 20* (314), 101.

Cossman, Brenda. (1994). Family inside/out. *University of Toronto Law Journal, 44* (1).

Gavigan, Shelley. (1993). Paradise lost, paradox revisited: The implications of familial ideology for feminist, lesbian and gay engagement with law. *Osgoode Hall Law Journal* (forthcoming).

Herman, Didi. (1990). Are we family? Lesbian rights and women's liberation. *Osgoode Hall Law Review, 28,* 789.

Herman, Didi. (1994). Rights of passage: Struggles for lesbian and gay legal equality. Toronto: University of Toronto Press.

Robson, Ruthann, and Valentine, S.E. (1990). Lov(h)ers: Lesbians as intimate partners and lesbian legal theory. *Temple Law Review, 63,* 511.

QUESTIONS TO CONSIDER

1. Compare and contrast the relative merits and weaknesses of assimilationist and anti-assimilationist approaches to gay and lesbian rights.

2. Compare the recommendations of Cossman and Ryder's report with the NDP's proposals in the Equality Rights Statute Amendment Act.

3. How should future strategies for gay and lesbian rights be formulated?

CHAPTER 10

Familial Ideology and the Limits of Difference

Shelley A.M. Gavigan

> Successful ideologies are often thought to render their beliefs natural and self-evident—to identify them with the "common sense" of a society so that nobody could imagine how they might ever be different. (Eagleton, 1991, p. 58)

> Attacking the family wage is a bit like an atheist attacking god the father. She wants to say that it does not exist, that the false idea that it does exist has evil consequences and that even if it did exist it would not be a good thing. (Barrett and McIntosh, 1990, p. 139)

Theoretical complexities confronting Canadian feminists are not new so much as newly acknowledged. The most recent and most powerful among them is the imperative to address racism and its implications in our work, and in our society more generally. Lesbians and gay men also challenge feminists to struggle against homophobia and to unravel the myriad ways heterosexual assumptions and prescriptions inform and deform social relations and social life. Additionally, feminists who problematize questions of class structure and class relations are illustrating that class is a concept and a relation that is inevitably mediated by gender and race relations. Those of us who work in law endeavour to explicate the roles played by legal actors as well as state and legal institutions, and the significance of legal principles and processes in all of this. This is not a modest task.

A serious challenge has been issued by critical scholars, political activists, and lawyers who are committed to the elimination of the social and legal marginalization of women of colour, and of lesbians and gay men. In particular, feminist criticism of "the family" has been challenged both by scholars and activists analyzing the effects of racism and by the current campaign to extend "spousal benefits," if not full family status, to lesbian and gay couples. This challenge can be stated succinctly: feminists who adopt a critical stance toward "the family" have been urged to acknowledge and rethink the White and heterosexual privilege apparently implicit in such an analysis.

The heightened visibility of these issues is timely, as is the necessity to respond to and engage in this important discussion. In this essay, I propose to do this, first, by analyzing the implications of the qualified pro-family stance in the critiques advanced or influenced by women of colour. I then engage with the argument that current legal definitions of spouse mean that the family is a site of "heterosexual privilege." In the final section, drawing upon a socialist feminist conceptualization of familial ideology, I illustrate with reference to Canadian welfare and immigration law (notably the legislative definitions of "family" and "spouse") that analysis and advocacy must encompass both the specificity and the interrelatedness of gender, race, and class relations.

It is not sufficient to declare as self-evident the significance of race, class, sexual orientation, and gender; rather, it is necessary to illustrate and analyze the inequalities that flow from those relations. Despite the insistence by many feminists, including many feminists who are women of colour, that, by nature, gender, race, and class inequalities are simultaneous and intersecting (e.g., Carby, 1982; Parmar, 1982; Cook and Watt, 1987; Williams, 1990; Collins, 1991; Bannerji, 1991), the image that often emerges is one of discrete compartments in a pyramid of oppressions. Gender becomes only a site of privilege, class drops out, or worse, becomes a bad attitude—"classism" (Harriss, 1989; Eastleton, 1992). In this essay, I hope to illustrate that this layering or compartment approach to analysis of social relations obscures more than it reveals. In particular, I hope to illustrate that "class" as an analytic concept and its expression in social relations cannot be neglected in feminist theorizing, political strategies or critical public policy.

FEMINISM, THE "FAMILY," AND THE LAW

A t the outset, it needs to be acknowledged that not all feminists adopt a deeply critical stance vis-à-vis the family. However, feminist scholars who have examined the operation of family law historically and in the current context (Boyd, 1987; 1989; Gavigan, 1987; Arnup,1989; see also Ryder, 1990) have illustrated that, while the precise form of the legal supports has shifted, a dominant model of family has been reproduced and reinforced through law (see, e.g., Chunn, 1988, 1992; Freeman, 1980; Backhouse, 1981; Smart, 1984). This family is heterosexual and nuclear in form, and patriarchal in content. Despite the celebration of its naturalness, timelessness, and ubiquity, feminist historians illustrated that the configuration of personal relations that our society has come to understand as the family emerged at a distinct historical and material conjuncture (Hall, 1979; Hall and Davidoff, 1987). The consolidation of its dominance occurred over the course of a century or so (Hall, 1979; Hall and Davidoff, 1987; Smith, 1981; Seccombe, 1986). As Dorothy E. Chunn says, this dominant family form, "which remains hegemonic today," is premised upon a "particular type of household arrangement—a nuclear unity of husband/father, wife/mother and their children—" and upon the ideological doctrines of "domesticity and privacy" (1988, p. 138).

Chunn's study of the formation and operation of early family courts in Ontario found that families who did not fit this model were to be made to fit, and their familial privacy was readily invaded to accomplish the task. "Recalcitrant families, located among the working and dependent poor, were subject to direct state regulation in the form of 'socialized' legal coercion" (Chunn, 1988, p. 138). Chunn describes how this posture was enforced through the courts. Ontario's early family courts "worked hard to repair and maintain nuclear family units in danger of disintegration; to buttress the ideology of 'the family' among that section of the population most resistant to it using mediation and conciliation if possible and overt coercion as a last resort" (ibid., p. 144).

Jane Lewis's research on the British case also points out that this coercion was class-based: "During the late nineteenth century, the courts frequently tried to force the working class husband to support his wife so that she would not become subject to the poor law." Moreover, "middle-class legislators readily blamed working class men for failing to maintain their wives" (1986, p. 21).

The Family Wage

The idea of the family (subsistence) wage, although arising in part from trade union demands, emerged at approximately the same time that the courts were forcing working men to support their wives. With it came the idea that a working man should earn enough to support his family, and "ideally, the wife's place was at home, or at least that any wage earning she did was of secondary importance" (Lewis, 1986, p. 106; see also Acker, 1988; Barrett and McIntosh, 1990; May, 1990). Certainly, the struggle for the family wage was one in which the rights of the woman worker were sacrificed. There have been other long-term and far-reaching problems associated with the family wage, not the least of which is that it remained, and still remains, for many, if not most, working-class people an unrealized and unrealizable ideal. It also forced women to assume the double burden of poorly paid employment, and devalued domestic labour and child care in the home (Lewis, 1986; Acker, 1988; Seccombe, 1988).

It is clear, however, as Jane Lewis also reminds us, that the idea of the family wage was not foisted upon an unwilling or duped working class, including women trade unionists who were mindful of the double burden imposed upon women who worked outside the home. The family wage promised one solution to inadequate wages, marginal subsistence, and grinding hardship (Lewis, 1986, p. 106; Lewis, 1983; Acker, 1988; May, 1990). The ideal of the family wage, and the respectability it conferred upon those working-class men whose wives "did not have to work" and those married women "who did not have to work" outside the home, held out a better, easier life for working-class people. Joan Acker captures the enormity and the complexity of the dilemma, which is no less apt today:

> Economic support through the family wage, to the extent that it was achieved for the working class, was the result of conflict, reform, resistance and accommodation occurring in political, trade union, legal, and familial arenas as people tried to cope with the destructive effects of capitalist development and secure for themselves and their families economic survival and a satisfying daily life. (1988, p. 485)

Familial Ideology

The significance of familial ideology was certainly not confined to trade union analyses and wage demands. In Canada, as Jane Ursel (1986) and Dorothy E. Chunn (1988; 1992) have illustrated, it came to inform a sweeping range of legislative initiatives as apparently disparate as child protection and minimum wages. Chunn, for example, argues that those unwilling or unable to conform to middle-class norms concerning child rearing and family life were readily subjected to state coercion. Before and after the turn of the century, Canada's federal and provincial governments "enacted a spate of criminal and quasi-criminal legislation that was ostensibly applicable to all children and all families but, in effect, targeted the non-middle classes" (1988, p. 44).

The model of the family wage also informed the earliest minimum-wage legislation in Canada. Minimum-wage standards anticipated that women who worked for a wage would be single, and certainly not supporters of dependants (McCallum, 1986; Hobbs, 1985; Russell, 1991; May, 1990). More profoundly, commitment to the idea of the patriarchal nuclear family as the exemplar model for the distribution of wages and social benefits came to inform all aspects of social, economic, and legal postures vis-à-vis the "family," notwithstanding significant historical, regional, and ethnic differences in wage forms in actual households (Russell, 1991, pp. 66–69). And, as Chunn has found, "when ideology failed," this model was coercively applied to the very section of the population least able to attain it: the labouring and dependent poor (Chunn, 1988).

The commitment to the form and content of familial relations expressed in the family wage is not a relic of less enlightened times. The primary responsibility for familial financial support continues to be regarded as personal, private, and intrafamilial. For example, the

Ontario Family Law Act explicitly states that "every spouse has an obligation to provide support for himself or herself, in accordance with need, to the extent that he or she is capable of doing do" (SO 1990, c.F.3, s.30) The capacity to do so is no less problematic for poor and working-class women now than it was in the nineteenth century.

Dissidence and Dissonance: Different Families?

Feminists, regardless of perspective, now acknowledge the significance of multiplicity and difference in women's experience. However, not all feminists agree about what "experience" really means or that it continues to be a relevant or unifying analytic concept. Most feminist scholars agree that there is no such thing as a singular "women's experience" or, for that matter, no singular experience of family. Indeed, the experience of family is quite different both between men and women and among women themselves. Few feminists, for example, would endorse Christopher Lasch's (1977) description of the patriarchal nuclear family as a "haven in a heartless world." At the same time, many Black feminists disagree with a feminist depiction of the family as a bastion of patriarchy. In their view, the Black family provides a haven in a racist society (Carby, 1982; Cook and Watt, 1987; hooks, 1990).

These differing perceptions of the importance of family have struck a chord with Canadian feminists who have incorporated the anti-racist critiques into their work and used them to interrogate Canadian feminist legal scholarship. There is, of course, no contrived uniformity to be found in the experience or writing of women of colour. For instance, the published work of aboriginal women is more resonant of community and nation (Monture, 1989; Ontario Native Women's Association, 1989; Turpel, 1991) than of "family" as we have come to understand it.

In a similar way, we can not assume that women of the same race share similar experiences. Patricia Hill Collins, for example, has suggested that, in the United States, class differences increasingly mediate the life experiences of African-American women. She argues that the "commonality" of race, gender, and class oppression "is experienced differently" by middle-class and working-class African-American women (1990, pp. 64–66). In the English–Canadian literature, Toni Williams (1990) and Nitya Duclos (1991) have offered trenchant critiques of the **essentialist** notion that all women share the same experience, while Himani Bannerji (1991) has extended her critique of the racism of conventional feminism to encompass as well a critique of a politics of difference.

In my view, what is exposed is how complex and contentious is the issue of "experience" within feminism, and how pervasive the notion of the "family" has become. On the one hand, there is a powerful injunction to remind us that there is no one unified "experience" that can be claimed to be woman's and, as such, challenges feminist work purporting to speak for all women. This is, however, not a completely new issue or struggle within feminism. For instance, class relations and class divisions between women, including feminist activists, have figured more prominently than is often acknowledged in the history of women's movement in Canada and elsewhere.

As historian Judith Walkowitz (1980) has illustrated, the nineteenth-century British middle-class feminist campaign to repeal the contagious-diseases legislation (and not incidentally to rescue and save prostitutes from the evils and perils of prostitution, and in particular from aristocratic male vice) was often resisted by working-class prostitutes. Although they also wanted the odious laws repealed, they did not want to be saved by middle-class women and/or transformed into rescued fallen angels. In other words, feminist reformers were often told that they did not speak for the very women to whom they were committed. Thus, while common cause was made between "respectable" feminists and their vilified working-class sisters, class tensions and antagonisms in this successful campaign were significant and important (Phillips, 1987).

The difficulty with the identification and juxtaposition of apparently differing and divergent experiences is that it can result in the assertion rather than the interrogation of the nature of these experiences. Himani Bannerji, while critical of race blindness in feminist theory and practice, has reservations about the implications of the "politics of difference." "In the name of 'difference'," she writes, "we tend not to go beyond a rich and direct description of personal experience to a social analysis which will reveal the sameness of social relations that constructs the experience of 'white' privilege and 'black' oppression" (1991, p. 83).

Barrett (1987) also suggests that the concept of difference has at least three distinct meanings within feminist writing, ranging from sexual difference to experiential diversity, to positional meaning. Clearly, feminists must be conscious of their usage of the term, and its meaning for feminist research. In other words, the significance of "experience" as a relevant analytic concept has to be rethought in its entirety. It surely cannot be the case that the lives and familial experiences of one group of women are devoid of contradiction and complexity, whereas others' lives are characterized only by contradiction and complexity. In my view, the acknowledgement of the partiality of experience, and the need to analyze all experience, is a more fruitful line of inquiry.

The Partiality of Experience

One way to analyze this tension is offered by a marxist conceptualization of ideology, which, as Michele Barrett recently suggested, offers "a reading, rather than a direct translation, of the political meaning of 'experience'" (1987, p. 32). For Barrett, the concept of ideology is particularly useful because "whatever its undoubted and manifest failings, (it) speaks both to and beyond the experience of the individual subject" (ibid., p. xix). The analysis of "experience" through the use of the concept of "ideology" may offer an illumination with respect to the significant dissonance between many (but not all) people's lived experience and the dominant ideology of the family. Despite this dissonance, paradoxically, the ideology of the patriarchal nuclear family provides the prism through which relationships are examined, and the measure against which they are judged, notwithstanding shifts which indicate that the idealized nuclear-family household may be becoming increasingly less typical. The distinction between actual households and the ideology of family households drawn out by Mary McIntosh and Michele Barrett (1983) in their early collaborative work continues to be imperative, even though they readily admit that they initially failed to identify and analyze adequately the range and diversity of British households (see, e.g., Carby, 1982; Barrett and McIntosh, 1985).

Douglas Hay has suggested that an ideology has both an elasticity and a generality, and thus "remains a *reservoir of belief* throughout society and flows into the gaps of individual protest" (1975, p. 55; emphasis added). The struggles of people who can never fit into the ideal of the nuclear family illuminate, rather than negate, what some feminists identify as the oppressive implications of the generality of the idealization and romanticization of the nuclear family, and the reservoir of belief that it offers sanctuary in a hard world. The strength, affirmation, and resistance (Herman, 1990, p. 799) that women of colour attribute to their often non-nuclear families similarly illustrates rather than negates that a great many people (Black people, aboriginal people, poor people of any race) have never experienced their households as cherished nuclear havens or the promise of a family or living wage. For example, apartheid in South Africa denied family life to Black men and women workers. In Canada, immigrants and foreign workers, especially female domestic workers, are often similarly denied a family life. Canadian immigration law has only limited provisions for family reunification, and even this is under constant attack. Meanwhile, the requirement that foreign domestic workers live in the homes of their employers effectively means that they must enter the home alone and under the constant scrutiny of their employer. Thus, a foreign domestic lives in a home but is never in her own home. As Arat Koç observes, the domestic worker today is like a stranger, "being in the family, but not of it. She is involved in the work of the house, but not the pleasures and intimacies of a home" (1990, p. 86). The policing of poor and aboriginal people via child-welfare and **social-assistance** legislation is another example of how the experience of family is mediated by race and class.

In fact, it would seem that the idealized nuclear family, premised, as it is, upon assumptions of privatized female dependence and domesticity, is especially problematic for Black women in the British and North

American contexts. Both Hazel Carby (1982) and Prathiba Parmar (1982) have illustrated in their work that Black and Asian women in the British context have long been integrated into the labour force, and that Black women in fact are often not dependent upon men. The oral histories of Black women in Ontario suggest that this may be the case in Canada as well (Brand, 1991). Juliet Cook and Shantu Watt (1987) in Britain, and Maxine Baca Zinn (1990) and Patricia Hill Collins (1990) in the United States, similarly have shown how deeply interrelated are class and racial inequalities in Black women's lives, and the lives of their children, affecting and affected not only by the work they do, but also by the work and wages of men in their lives.

However, the difficulty with the fact of Black women's independence is that it is both belied and denied by the state through the premises and definitions of, at the very least, welfare and immigration law. In other words, irrespective of their varied experiences of family, work, and culture, and notwithstanding their often de facto independence from men, poor women, including poor visible-minority and immigrant women, and yes, even poor lesbians, cannot "opt out" of the law (Brophy and Smart, 1985, p. 1) and the legal relations of enforced dependency. The state's legislatively expressed commitment to the primacy of "private" responsibility for spousal or child support is nothing less than a commitment to state-enforced patriarchal relations of private male responsibility and female dependence (Fudge, 1987; 1989).

This commitment is illustrated graphically in the context of Canadian immigration law for women seeking to immigrate to Canada. In effect, they are required to acquire the status of dependency in the process of being sponsored to Canada by a Canadian citizen or permanent resident, most often a spouse or fiancé (Seward and McDade, 1988; McIntosh, 1987). The significance of sponsorship is principally financial, as the sponsor undertakes to provide for the immigrant so as to ensure that the latter will not become a burden on the Canadian state. These sponsorship undertakings, to which the sponsored immigrant is not formally a party, are designed to ensure private financial support and to limit a sponsored immigrant's access to social assistance. The implications of the requisite sponsorship undertaking for the poor must not be missed. Poor Canadian citizens and permanent residents are less able than the more economically advantaged to sponsor their family members. A parent on social assistance, for example, might not be able to sponsor a spouse to come to the country, even though, together, they might make enough to get the family off of social assistance (Ontario, 1991, p. 85)

When a "sponsored" marriage ends, or, if at an early point in the process, the sponsor elects to withdraw the sponsorship, the precariousness of the position of the sponsored immigrant woman cannot be overstated. If the marriage has been the site of violence by her sponsoring spouse, the woman will nevertheless be required to pursue him for support unless she can convince welfare officials that her personal safety is at risk and that the relationship with the sponsor has really ended. Thus, for many immigrant women in Canada, most especially, the poor, the opportunity to be independent of their spouses, both in fact and in law, is almost impossible (Ng, 1988, pp. 187–189). The presumption of women's familial dependence once again finds legislative enforcement, irrespective of a woman's actual wishes, needs, or experience.

THE PROBLEM OF THE NUCLEAR-FAMILY FORM: HETEROSEXISM OR HETEROSEXUAL PRIVILEGE?

There are a number of different sources for my next area of concern: the call to legalize and thereby, it is implicitly argued, legitimize the lesbian and gay household. One great impetus for the current interest in formal recognition may derive from the devastation of AIDS, and breast cancer, and the heart-breaking struggles that some gay men and lesbians have had in the aftermath of the death of their loved ones. The expression "long-time companion" seems to understate the relationship. While I find the phrase evocative of a voluntary egalitarian intimacy, one understands the perceived, or indeed experienced, invisibility of surviving companions who are unable to find themselves named with the "real" family as survivors.

The pain, the grief, the compelling facts, the obvious discrimination (Ryder, 1990; Duclos, 1991) and judicial subscription to familial ideology are undeniable. Nonetheless, my questions remain: do lesbians and gay men really need a "spouse in the house"? Is the fact that the threshold definition of "spouse" in law as a person of the opposite sex best characterized as an instance or source (Ryder, 1990) of "heterosexual privilege"? Would this form of legalization of lesbian and gay relationships correct the injustices of a heterosexist society? Is the definition of "spouse" in other respects neutral? Can the social and legal concept of "spouse" be plucked from its heterosexual familial context and dropped into the lesbian and gay context? And, if so, should it be?

For the editors of the *Harvard Law Review*, in their review of American law *Sexual Orientation and the Law* (1990), these questions address non-issues. They conclude that marriage has always been regarded as a central institution in U.S. society. Alongside its strong symbolic meaning to the partners, marriage bestows concrete legal advantages on the couple: tax benefits, standing to recover damages for certain torts committed against spouses, and rights to succession and insurance benefits, to name a few (ibid., p. 95). And, marriage is also constitutionally protected because it promotes familial and social stability (ibid., p. 97).

264 PART III RESTRUCTURING PRIVATE LIFE

As I have suggested above, feminists and lesbians writing with a feminist perspective tend to be wary in their analyses. Didi Herman, for instance, worries that "by appropriating familial ideology, lesbians and gay men may be supporting the very institutional structures that create and perpetuate women's oppression" (1990, p. 797). Herman takes no comfort from this position:

> One could conclude that the response to the experience of oppression cannot lie in a retreat into family, whatever the form, and certainly not into the discourse of familial ideology. Our families may be different in that they are not premised upon on the subordination of women by men.... (However,) we must also reconcile ourselves with the reality that for some, families and oppositional familial ideologies are important sites of resistance and affirmation. (ibid., p. 804)

But, my own questions remain. Is there not more to "the family" than different familial experiences? And while, as Nitya Duclos (1991), also insists, there is no essential family, and surely no essential lesbian or gay family, there is something beyond the sum of contesting dissident experiences and beliefs, something against which we all are measured. The premises of "the family" neither begin nor end with the legislated definition of "spouse." This is clearly illustrated when one interrogates the notion of heterosexual privilege. It implies symmetry when asymmetry is surely a more accurate characterization of spouses in the familial context (Freeman, 1980, pp. 236–237), notwithstanding the contrived formal equality, gender-neutrality, and contractual language of family law legislation. In my view, an analysis of the concept "spouse" that concludes it confers privilege is too narrow despite its progressive and critical complexion. "Heterosexual privilege" posits a bifurcated gender-netural dyad of homosexual/heterosexual. It is resonant of anti-discrimination language (in/out, inclusion/exclusion). Ruth Colker, for instance, explicitly draws upon the imagery of segregation when she characterizes marriage as a restricted club (to which she reluctantly belongs) (1991, pp. 323–324).

The exclusive focus on the specific contexts of lesbian and gay relationships paradoxically has decontextualized heterosexual relationships. More precisely, it has decontextualized and declawed heterosexism. The analysis must be extended to explain core familial phenomena in our country, such as wife assault and child abuse, the presumed dependency upon a man of a woman in need of either social assistance or a job, the enforced dependency (read: poverty) of many sponsored immigrant women, the terrifying isolation of the battered woman whose first language is not one of our two official languages, and the dearth of quality and accessible child care and safe, affordable, housing and a modicum of economic and physical security of women who leave unhappy or violent relationships, and the different class positions reflected and reinforced in different legislation. The concept of "heterosexual privilege" does not even begin to do this. It simply cannot cope with the enormity of the family as an ideological construct, and as a result it is neither a helpful analytic concept nor an accurate descriptive tool. To speak in terms of heterosexual privilege declaws.

While there has been a too long unquestioned and consistent reference to a "person of the opposite sex" at the heart of the legal definition of "spouse," (see Box 10.1), married women, common-law wives, and single mothers historically have been dealt with differently in family and welfare law. Historically and presumptively today, family law legislation restricts legislative rights to family property to legally married spouses; resort to the concept of constructive trust must be had when a woman's real trust is betrayed by a common-law spouse. In the 1970s, when, as Mary Morton (1988) has observed, the ideological climate shifted, Canadian legislators felt compelled to correct the most obvious inequities. The definition of "spouse" in many provincial family-relations statutes was relaxed for the purpose of child and spousal support.[1]

Current conventional wisdom is that common-law spouses are just like real spouses "in law." In fact, even the most cursory examination of the legislation and case law in the area of pensions, insurance, and survivor's benefits reveals that there is no one definition of "common-law spouse" and no single legislative approach thereto. Indeed, woe betide a surviving common-law partner who, prior to 1993, came up against a legal (read: real) widow over the issue of survivors' benefits under the Canada Pension Plan. For many, access or relegation to the status "spouse" is a question of class. As an elderly homeless woman attempting to establish that her relationship with her deceased "special friend" measured up to the definition of "common-law spouse" in the Canada Pension Plan Act expressed it: "We just loved each other. We planned to marry, but we were always too sick or too poor. We had no fixed address. How do you get married on the street?"[2]

THE CASE OF WOMEN IN WELFARE LAW: HETEROSEXUAL PRIVILEGE?

For Canadian women, most especially sole-support mothers on social assistance, the definition of "spouse" has always been relatively relaxed and intrusively enforced. Feminist scholars have illustrated the myriad ways in which the fundamental premises of this area of law have both assumed and enforced women's dependency upon men (Abner, 1989; Brenner, 1990; Leighton, 1987; Lewis, 1985; Smith, 1981). Not only have poor women been expected to conform to this model of appropriate family life and responsibilities, historically, to ensure that they were deserving, but they have been subjected to legislatively mandated harassment by the virtue of the notorious "spouse in the house" rule. Prior to the most recent amendment of the Ontario

---

BOX 10.1

Different Legal Definitions of "Spouse"
Statute:
Family Law Act, RSO 1990 c. F.3, s. 1(1)
Meaning:
"spouse" means either of a man and woman who,

(a) are married to each other,

or

(b) have together entered into a marriage that is voidable or void, in good faith on the part of the person asserting a right under this Act. ("conjoint")

Statute:
Family Law Act, RSO 1990, c. F.3
Meaning:
"spouse" means a spouse as defined in subsection 1 (1), and in addition includes either of a man and woman who are not married to each other and have cohabited,

(a) continuously for a period of not less than three years,

or

(b) in relationship of some permanence, if they are the natural or adoptive parents of a child. ("conjoint")

Statute:
Canada Pension Plan Act, SC 1993 c. C–8
Meaning:
"Spouse", in relation to a contributor, means,

(i) if there is no person described in subparagraph (ii), a person who is married to the contributor at the relevant time,

or

(ii) a person of the opposite sex who is cohabiting with the contributor in a conjugal relationship at the relevant time, having so cohabited with the contributor for a continuous period of at least one year.

---

legislation, the courts were fairly routinely presented with appeals from the Social Assistance Review Board (SARB), which required a determination of whether a particular relationship was sufficiently conjugal to warrant the characterization "spousal."

Paradoxically, welfare advocates have actively resisted and campaigned to prevent the kind of inquisitorial analysis of recipients' personal and sexual lives that has occurred in the lesbian and gay cases in their efforts to litigate the acceptance of their intimate relationships (Herman, 1990, pp. 797–799). Recently, in Ontario, the Regulations to the Family Benefits legislation[3] were amended, reflecting, in part, this concern. In addition to the now conventional definitions of "spouse," a new definition was introduced.

The legislative changes to the definition of "spouse" were intended to bring Family Benefits law more into line with family law principles,[4] and to eliminate the automatic presumption that a man's presence in a woman's house was a fairly reliable marker of a spousal relationship. As long as the man in the house is not the father of the woman's children, the couple has a three-year grace period before he is deemed to be her spouse. Then she had to provide evidence to satisfy the Family Benefits officials that the relationship does not warrant the label "spousal." In determining whether or not a person is a spouse, the regulations stipulate that sexual factors *shall* not be investigated. The restriction of the consideration of sexual factors undoubtedly was intended to protect the privacy of Family Benefits recipients. As I will illustrate below, however, this reform has had a contradictory result.

Erika Abner's (1989) assessment of this reform is that the position of women receiving Family Benefits has been improved only in marginal terms. Beyond this, she argues, "welfare administrators appear to expect more from mey by way of support than is frequently ordered by judges for support applications under family law provisions" (1989, p. 22). Furthermore, by operation of the presumption of a spousal relationship following not less than three years' cohabitation with a person of the opposite sex, the onus is placed on a recipient to show that the social, economic, and familial aspects of the relationship are such that it does not amount to cohabitation.

Two "spouse in the house" cases[5] illustrate the paradox that has resulted. In the first, Ms C.B. separated from her husband and, with her children, moved into her mother's home. Almost immediately, the mother herself had to move, and C.B. and her children were faced with the task of finding yet another home. Her estranged husband located an apartment for her, in a house in which he, too, proposed to live. The Social Assistance Review Board that subsequently heard her appeal noted that she had agreed to the unusual arrangement because of the difficulties in securing affordable and safe housing. She would rent the upstairs unit, while her husband rented the downstairs, to which the landlord had said he would add a kitchen and bathroom. However, the landlord never fulfilled his promise, and consequently the husband had to use his wife's kitchen and bathroom. Although he had agreed to pay child support, the tribunal noted that he was seldom working, so nothing was paid. The evidence from the SARB was that she had been "emotionally, financially and practically a single parent," had made all the arrangements for day care and school, and was regarded in the community as a single parent. She did not have joint meals or enter-tainment with her spouse, but felt she had no choice but to accept the living arrangement because of the then low vacancy rate and high rents. She was declared by the Director of Income Maintenance to be ineligible as she living with her spouse within the meaning of the Family Benefits Regulations.

C.B. appealed unsuccessfully to the Social Assistance Review Board, which found that she had always been honest and straightforward with the Family Benefits officials. They nonetheless held that

> while the Board may accept the evidence given by the Appellant that there is no longer a relationship that most people would call spousal between her and this person, the fact that he is the father of both chil-dren and has the obligation to support them, makes him her spouse under this legislation.

In another, and more recent, case[6] a woman who had been receiving an allowance under the Family Benefits Act as a sole-support parent with two independent children (aged two years, and eight months) appealed against a determination by the Director of Income Maintenance that she had received an overpayment during a period in which the father of her two children had moved back into her home. After the separation, and while she was receiving Family Benefits, he had moved back in an attempt to reconcile. The SARB was informed that she had been near exhaustion and "at that point reconciliation sounded good if only that it might allow her to get a little extra sleep." Within a few weeks, she realized that the reconciliation was not going to work, and she spent the next several months trying to remove him from her home. The relationship during this period was marked by his vio-lence toward her. Approximately two months after K.S. had moved back into the house, she called the police; but, according to her statement, they declined to assist—in fact, she said that they told her they could do nothing if his belongings were in the house. Expressing the conflict and contradictions that many women in violent relationships may expe-rience, she did not call the police again because, as she explained, his family, "particularly his mother, had provided her with a lot of support" and "he was the father of her children," which made it difficult for her to call the police. While K.S. was back in the house, he had his own room, paid a modest amount in room and board, and insisted that she pay him $5 each time she used his car. During the entire period (unlike C.B.'s case), he had continued to pay $500 per month in child support, which had been assigned by the recipient to the Provincial Treasurer. The board, not surprisingly, found this odd. The recipient responded that, if "Mr. K.S. had really been living with her, she would have changed the arrangements so they would have had the money." The director declared an overpayment for the ten-month period during which K.S. had resisted her efforts to remove him from her home.

The issue before the SARB was whether she was a sole-support parent with dependent children, and hence eligible for an allowance under Family Benefits, or had been living with her spouse, and hence was ineligible. As with C.B., the board found that Mr. K.S. fell squarely within the definition of "spouse" in Regulation 1 (d)(iii), and applying, it seems, a common-sense interpretation of the phrase "living together," the board found that, during the ten months, they had been living together to satisfy the letter of the act and regulations. These women found themselves caught by the definition of "spouse" within the regulations; the board was inhibited by s. 1(1)(a) from considering the non-existent sexual relationship and by s. 1(1)(b) from considering the dearth of economic, social, or familial aspects. As father of the woman's children with an obligation to support them, he was her spouse, even though poverty forced them to live in the same building. As a result, each woman was ineligible to receive Family Benefits as a **single mother** with dependent children as she was not living separate and apart from her spouse.

For women on social assistance without men in their immediate vicinity, in and around the house, the problems that attend s. 8 of the Family Benefits Act Regulations loom as large. This regulation authorizes the director to reduce a monthly allowance where he or she is not satisfied that an applicant or recipient is making reasonable efforts to obtain support. Included within this category is a recipient or applicant who is a sponsored dependant within the meaning of the Immigration Act.[7]

Recently, the Ontario Divisional Court considered the appeal of a single mother who had been subjected to a Regulation 8 reduction of $40 per month because she had refused to make an application for child support.[8] Her position was that she neither knew nor wanted to know the whereabouts of the father of her little boy. She said he had a alcohol/drug habit, was in and out of jail, and just generally "messed up." And, finally, she said she did not want to "bring him to court because she didn't want him to have any rights to Joey." O'Driscoll J., writing for the court, agreed with the director's view. The appellant's view that an application for support would be both fruitless and potentially problematic for her did not absolve her of the obligation to make reasonable efforts to obtain compensation from the father. However, the court found that there had been no evidence that would justify a conclusion that, even had she undertaken the application, she would have received $40 per month in support. Thus, she lost a little and won a little.

In a study of the operation of Regulation 8, former Family Benefits case worker Kathleen Lawrence (1990) has alleged that a disproportionately high number of racial-minority Family Benefits recipients have "Regulation 8 charges" deducted from their allowance. She suggests that racial minority recipients are six times more likely than White recipients to experience these charges, which prompted her to file a complaint with the Ontario Human Rights Commission in 1990.

As preliminary as Ms. Lawrence's study may be, it illustrates again that feminists committed to understanding the operation and conditions of women's subordination must be attentive not only to gender, race, class, and heterosexism, but to the manner, sites, and sources of their inter-connectedness. Not only for poor women of colour who are single parents in need of social assistance, but for all of us, the interrelationships of gender, class, and race have to be understood. There are no discrete variables, no one crucible, only complex social relations in which the "family," with all of its ideological baggage, is most clearly expressed.

CONCLUSION

In the current global economic crisis, I am mindful that it surely seems mean-spirited to deny anyone access to whatever modicum of economic or family-based benefit that is available, especially as the Canadian welfare state shrinks, relegating ever more responsibility for the social well-being and welfare of its citizens to the private familial sphere. Nonetheless, I have attempted here to illustrate the difficulties with a strategy that appears to offer a self-evident short-term solution. Those of us with our doubts may encounter the suggestion that we want others to wait for "the revolution" (Herman, 1990, p. 802). Do we? It depends. A fundamental transformation of the social order seems as impossible as the rebuilding of the Berlin Wall. And yet, the women's movement and the trade union movement have sparked important "defamilializing" campaigns, significantly for universal child care, for women's access to safe birth control and legal abortion free from spousal hindrance, against family violence, for equal pay and employment equity. Beyond these have been the campaigns for full participation of the disabled in work and culture, and for protection and extension of universal health care. None of these struggles has been won yet, but in pressing each and every demand, we implicitly chip away at the ideological assumptions about the family. Women have a right to good jobs. Children flourish in excellent child-care centres. People with disabilities should neither be under de facto house arrest nor consigned to their families for care. Publicly funded, universal health care, not privatized and privately funded home care, is a fundamental (if perilously fragile) social right.

It is my view that one's access or entitlement to social benefits, to health care, dental care, long-term disability benefits, bereavement leave—in sum, one's dignity and personal and economic security—ought not, and need not, depend upon being situated in or relegated to a familial relationship. And when this seems impossible, we might remember Antonio Gramsci: while we have "pessimism of the intellect," we must have "optimism of the will."

NOTES

1. The Family Law Act, R.S.O. 1990, c. F.3, Part III (Support Obligations), s. 29, provides this expanded definition of spouse:

> "spouse" means a spouse as defined in subsection 1(1), and in addition includes either of a man and woman who are not married to each other and have cohabited

> (a) continuously for a period of not less than three years, or

> (b) in a relationship of some permanence, if they are the natural or adoptive parents of a child.

2. Evidence of Olive Cowan before the Review Committee under the Canada Pension Plan Act, *Olive Cowan* v. *Minister of National Health and Welfare*, unreported decision of Review Committee, October 1989, at 3. The committee's decision to allow Mrs. Cowan's claim was appealed by C.P.P. and ultimately set aside under the terms of a settlement reached between the parties. This unreported decision is on file with the author.

3. The Family Benefits Act Regulations, RRO 1980, Reg. 318, now R.R.O. 1990, Reg. 336. In the other subsections of the regulation, the now conventional definitions of "spouse" are also retained:

> (i) a person of the opposite sex to an applicant or recipient who together with the applicant or recipient have declared to the Director or a welfare administrator appointed under section 4 of the General Welfare Assistance Act that they are spouses,

> (ii) a person who is required under the provisions of a court order or domestic contract to support the applicant, recipient or any of his or her dependent children,

> (iii) a person who has an obligation to support the applicant, recipient or any of his or her dependent children under section 30 or 31 of the Family Law Act, 1986 notwithstanding a domestic contract or other agreement between the person and the applicant or recipient whereby they purport to waive or release such obligation to support ...

4. This was recommended *Transitions* (1988, p. 161). Recently, this recommendation has been taken up and extended by *Back on Track* (1990, p. 87): "We would argue that couples of the same sex should be treated the same way as those of the opposite sex for the purpose of determining the benefit unti for social assistance."

In Action 46, the authors of *Back on Track* recommended that the Minister of Community and Social Services press the Attorney General to implement changes in the Family Law Act to extend laws relating to support obligations for couples of the same sex.

5. The Family Benefits Act, RSO 1990, c. F.2, and Regulation 366, RRO 1990.

6. *XX* v. *The Director, Income Maintenance Branch* (Appeal No. J-06-06-03) (unreported decision of Social Assistance Appeal Board, November 29, 1990).

7. Family Benefits Act Regulations, RRO 1990, Reg. 366 s. 9. The section, in its entirety, provides:

> Where the Director is not satisfied that an applicant or recipient is making reasonable efforts to obtain compensation or realize any financial resource that the applicant, recipient, or a beneficiary included or to be included in the recipient's allowance, may be entitled to or eligible for including where the applicant, recipient or beneficiary is a sponsored dependent or nominated relative within the meaning of the regulations under the Immigration Act, 1976 (Canada), any compensation or contribution to the support and maintenance of the applicant, recipient or beneficiary that may result from any undertaking or engagement made on his behalf under the said regulations between the Government and the sponsor, the Director may determine that the applicant, recipient or beneficiary is not eligible for a benefit or he may reduce the amount of the compensation, contribution of financial resource, as the case may be, that in his opinion is available to the applicant, recipient or beneficiary.

8. *Campbell* v. *Director, Income Maintenance Branch, Ministry of Community and Social Services* (25 June 1990), No. 329/88 (Ont. Div. Ct) (unreported)

REFERENCES

Abner, Erika. (1989). *The merits of the use of constitutional litigation to unravel the fabric of the feminization of poverty in Canada.* LL.M. thesis, Osgoode Hall Law School, York University.

Acker, Joan. (1988). Class, gender, and the relations of distribution. *Signs, 13.*

Arat Koç, Sedef. (1990). Importing housewives: Non-citizen domestic workers and the crisis of the domestic sphere in Canada. In Meg Luxton, Harriet Rosenberg, and Sedef Arat Koç (Eds.), *Through the kitchen window: The politics of home and family* (2d ed.). Toronto: Garamond.

Arnup, Katherine. (1989). Mothers just like others: Lesbians, divorce and child custody in Canada. *Canadian journal of women and the law. 3.*

Backhouse, Constance. (1989). Shifting patterns in nineteenth century custody law. In David H. Flaherty, (Ed.), *Essays in the history of Canadian Law, 1.* Toronto: The Osgoode Society.

Bannerji, Himani. (1991). But who speaks for us? Experience and agency in conventional feminist paradigms. In Himani Bannerji, et al. (Eds.), *Unsettling relations: The university as a site of feminist struggles.* Toronto: Women's Press.

Barrett, Michele. (1987). The concept of difference. *Feminist Review, 26.*

Barrett, Michele, and McIntosh, Mary. (1983). *The anti-social family.* London: Verso.

Barrett, Michele, and McIntosh, Mary. (1985). Ethnocentrism and socialist feminist theory. *Feminist Review, 20.*

Barrett, Michele, and McIntosh, Mary. (1990). The "Family Wage": Some problems for socialists and feminists. Ian T. Lovell (Ed.), *British feminist thought: A reader.* Oxford: Basil Blackwell.

Boyd, Susan B. (1988). Child custody, ideologies, and employment. *Canadian Journal of Women and the Law, 3,* 111.

Boyd, Susan B. (1989). Child custody law and the invisibility of women's work. *Queen's Quarterly, 96,* 831.

Brand, Dionne. (1991). *No burden to carry: Narratives of black working women in Ontario 1920s–1950s.* Toronto: Women's Press.

Brenner, Joanna. (1990). Feminist political discourses: Radical versus liberal approaches to the feminization of poverty. In Karen V. Hansen and Ilene J. Philipson (Eds.), *Women, class and the feminist imagination: A socialist feminist reader.* Philadelphia: Temple University Press.

Brophy, Julia, and Smart, Carol. (1985). Locating law: A discussion of the place of law in feminist politics. In Julia Brophy and Carol Smart (Eds.), *Women-in-law: Explorations in law, family and sexuality.* London: Routledge and Kegan Paul.

Carby, Hazel V. (1982). White woman Listen! Black feminism and the boundaries of sisterhood. In Centre for Contemporary Cultural Studies (Ed.), *The empire strikes back: Race and racism in 70s Britian.* London: Hutchinson.

Chunn, Dorothy E. (1988). Rehabilitating deviant families through family courts: The birth of socialized justice in Ontario, 1920–1940. *International Journal of the Sociology of Law, 16.*

Chunn, Dorothy E. (1992). *From punishment to doing good: Family courts and socialized justice in Ontario, 1880–1940.* Toronto: University of Toronto Press.

Colker, Ruth. (1991). Marriage. *Yale Journal of Law and Feminism, 1.*

Collins, Patricia Hill. (1990). *Black feminist thought.* New York: Routledge.

Cook, Juliet, and Watt, Shantu. (1987). Racism, women and poverty. In Caroline Glendenning and Jane Millar (Eds.), *Women and poverty in Britain.* Brighton: Wheatsheaf Books.

Duclos, Nitya. (1991). Some complicating thoughts on "same-sex" marriage. *Law and Sexuality, 1.*

Eagleton, Terry. (1991). *Ideology: An introduction.* London: Verso.

Eagleton, Terry. (1992). Defending the free world. *The Socialist Register.*

Editors of Harvard Law Review. (1990). *Sexual orientation and the law.* Cambridge, Ma: Harvard University Press.

Freeman, M.D.A. (1980). "Violence against women": Does the legal system provide solutions or itself constitute the problem?" *British Journal of Law & Society, 7.*

Fudge, Judy A. (1989). The privatization of the costs of social reproduction: Some recent Charter cases. *Canadian Journal of Women and the Law, 3,* 246.

Fudge, Judy A. (1987). The public/private distinction: The possibilities of and limits of the use of Charter litigation to further feminist struggles. *Osgoode Hall Law Journal,* 485.

Gavigan, Shelley A.M. (1987). Law, gender and ideology. In Anne F. Bayefsky (Ed.), *Legal theory meets legal practice.* Edmonton: Academic Printing.

Hall, Catherine. (1979). The early formation of Victorian domestic ideology. In Sandra Burman, (Ed.), *Fit work for women.* London: Croom Helm.

Hall, Catherine, and Davidoff, Lenore. (1987). *Family fortunes: Men and women of the English middle classes, 1780–1850.* Chicago: University of Chicago Press.

Hay, Douglas. (1975). Property, authority and the criminal law. In Douglas Hay, (Ed.), *Albion's fatal tree: Crime and society in eighteenth century England.* London: Allen Lane.

Herman, Didi. (1990). Are we family?: Lesbian rights and women's liberation. *Osgoode Hall Law Journal, 28.*

Hobbs, Margaret. (1985). *"Dead horses" and "muffled voices": Protective legislation, education and the minimum wage for women in Ontario.* M.A. Thesis, University of Toronto.

hooks, bell. (1990). Homeplace: A site of resistance. In *Yearning: Race, gender and cultural politics.* Toronto: Between the Lines.

Kline, Marlee. (1988). Race, racism and feminist legal theory. *Harvard Women's Law Journal, 8.*

Lasch, Christopher. (1977). *Haven in a heartless world: The family besieged.* New York: Basic Books.

Lawrence, Kathleen. (1990). Assessing the discriminatory outcomes of the application of a family benefits policy. *Journal of Law and Social Policy, 6.*

Leighton, Margaret. (1987). Handmaids' tales: Family benefits and the single-mother-led family. *University of Toronto Faculty of Law Review, 45.*

Lewis, Jane. (1983). Dealing with dependency: State practices and social realities, 1870–1945. In Jane Lewis (Ed.), *Women's right's, women's welfare.* London: Croom Helm.

Lewis, Jane. (1986). The working-class wife and mother and state intervention, 1870–1918. In Jane Lewis (Ed.), *Labour and love: Women's experience of home and family, 1850–1940.* London: Basil Blackwell.

McCallum, Margaret E. (1986). Keeping women in their place: The minimum wage in Canada, 1910–1925. *Labour/Le Travail, 17.*

McIntosh, Deborah. (1987). Defining "family": A comment on the family reunification provisions in the Immigration Act. *Journal of Law and Social Policy, 3.*

May, Martha. (1990). The historical problem of the family wage: The Ford Motor Company and the five dollar day. In Ellen C. Dubois and Vicki L. Ruiz (Eds.), *Unequal sisters: A multi-cultural reader in U.S. women's history.* New York: Routledge.

Monture, Patricia. (1989). A vicious circle: Child welfare and the First Nations. *Canadian Journal of Women and the Law, 3.*

Morton, Mary E. (1988). Dividing the wealth, sharing the poverty: The (re)formation of "family" in law in Ontario. *Canadian Review of Sociology and Anthropology, 25.*

Mossman, Mary Jane, and MacLean, Morag. (1986). Family law and social welfare: Toward a new equality. *Canadian Journal of Family Law, 5.*

Ng, Roxanna. (1988). Immigrant Women and Institutionalized Racism. In Sandra Burt, Lorraine Code, and Linda Dorney (Eds.), *Changing patterns: Women in Canada.* Toronto: McClelland and Stewart.

Ontario. (1991). *Back on track: First report of the Advsory Group on New Social Assistance Legislation* (Chair: Alan Moscovitch). Toronto: Province of Ontario.

Ontario Native Women's Association. (1989). *Breaking free: A proposal for change to Aboriginal family policy.* Thunder Bay: Ontario Native Women's Association.

Ontario Social Assistance Review Committee. (1988). *Transitions: Report of the Social Assistance Review Committee.* Toronto: Queen's Printer.

Parmar, Prathiba. (1982). Gender, race and class: Asian women in resistance. In Centre for Contemporary Cultural Studies (Ed.), *The empire strikes back: Race and racism in 70s Britain.* London: Hutchinson.

Philipson, Ilene J. (1990). Heterosexual antagonisms and the politics of mothering. In Karen V. Hansen and Ilene J.Philipson (Eds.), *Women, class and the feminist imagination: A socialist feminist reader.* Philadelphia: Temple University Press.

Phillips, Anne. (1987). *Divided loyalties: Dilemmas of sex and class.* London: Virago.

Robson, Ruthann, and Valentine, S.E. (1990). Lov(h)ers: Lesbians as intimate partners and lesbian legal theory. *Temple Law Review, 63.*

Russell, Bob. (1991). A fair or a minimum wage? Women workers, the state and the origins of wage regulation in Western Canada. *Labour/Le Travail, 28.*

Ryder, Bruce. (1990). Equality rights and sexual orientation: Confronting heterosexual family privilege. *Canadian Journal of Family Law, 9.*

Scott, Joan W. (1992). Experience. In Judith Butler and Joan W. Scott (Eds.), *Feminists theorize the political.* New York: Routledge.

Seccombe, Wally. (1986). Patriarchy stabilized: The construction of the male breadwinner wage norm in nineteenth century Britain. *Social History, 11.*

Seward, S.B. and McDade, K. (1988). *Immigrant women in Canada: A policy perspective.* Ottawa: Canadian Advisory Council on the Status of Women in Canada.

Smart, Carol. (1984). *The ties that bind: Law, marriage and the reproduction of patriarchal relations.* London: Routledge and Kegan Paul.

Smart, Carol. (1989). *Feminism and the power of law.* London: Routledge.

Smith, Dorothy E. (1981). Women's inequality and the family." In Alan Moscovitch and Glenn Drover (Eds.), *Inequality: Essays on the political economy of social welfare.* Toronto: University of Toronto Press.

Turpel, Mary Ellen. (1991). Home/Land. *Canadian Journal of Family Law. 10.*

Ursel, Jane. (1986). The state and the maintenance of patriarchy: A case study of family, labour and welfare legislation in Canada. In J. Dickinson and Bob Russell (Eds.), *Family, economy and state: The social reproduction process under capitalism.* Toronto: Garamond.

Walkowitz, Judith. (1980). *Prostitution and Victorian society: Women, class and state.* London: Cambridge University Press.

Williams, Toni. (1990). Re-forming women's truth: A critique of of the Report of the Royal Commission on the Status of Women in Canada. *University of Ottawa Law Review, 22.*

Zinn, Maxine Baca. (1990). Minority families in crisis: The public discussion. In Karen V. Hansen and Ilene J. Philipson (Eds.), *Women, class and the feminist imagination: A socialist feminist reader.* Philadelphia: Temple University Press.

Cases

Andrews v. *Ontario (Minister of Health)* (1988), 49 DLR (4th) 584 (Ont. H.C.).

Anon. v. *General Manager, Department of Social Services, Metro Toronto* (Appeal No. G-02-27-01), (unreported decision of Social Assistance Review Board, September 12, 1988).

Burton and Minister of Community and Social Services, Re (1985). 52 OR 211 (Ont. Div. Ct).

C.B. v. *The Director, Income Maintenance Branch, North East Local Office* (Appeal No. G-06-15-05), (unreported decision of Social Assistance Review Board, February 20, 1989).

Campbell v. *Director, Income Maintenance Branch, Misinstry of Community and Social Services,* No. 329/88, (unreported decision of Ont. Div. Ct, June 25, 1990).

Ms. v. *The Administrator, Department of Social Services, United Counties of Prescott and Russell* (appeal No. F-11-08-020), (unreported decision of Social Assistance Review Board, November 4, 1988).

Pitts and Director of Family Benefits Branch of the Ministry of Community and Social Services, Re (1985), 51 OR (2d) 302 (Ont. Div. Ct).

S.A.B. v. *The Director, Income Maintenance Branch, Toronto North East Local Office* (Appeal No. H-02-16-18), (unreported decision of Social Assistance Review Board, October 20, 1989).

Warwick v. *Minister of Community and Social Services, Re* (1978), 21 OR (2d) 528 (Ont C.A.).

Willis v. *Minister of Community and Social Services, Re* (1983), 40 OR (2d) 287 (Ont. Div. Ct).

Statutes

Canada Pension Plan Act, RSC 1985, c. C-8.

Divorce Act, RSC 1985, (2nd Supp.), c. 3.

Family Benefits Act, RSO 1990, c. 151.

Family Benefits Regulations of Ontario, RRO 1990, Reg. 318, as amended to OR 548/88.

Family Law Act, RSO 1990, c. F.3.

General Welfare Assistance Act, RSO 1990, c. 188.

SUGGESTED READING

Arat Koç, Sedef. (1990). Importing housewives: Non-citizen domestic workers and the crisis of the domestic sphere in Canada. In Meg Luxton, Harriet Rosenberg, and Sedef Arat Koç (Eds.), *Through the kitchen window: The politics of home and family* (2d ed.). Toronto: Garamond.

Bannerji, Himani. (1991). But who speaks for us? Experience and agency in conventional feminist paradigms. In Himani Bannerji, et al. (Eds.), *Unsettling relations: The university as a site of feminist struggles*. Toronto: Women's Press.

Barrett, Michele, and McIntosh, Mary. (1990). The "family wage": Some problems for socialists and feminists. In Ian T. Lovell (Ed.), *British feminist thought: A reader*. Oxford: Basil Blackwell.

Chunn, Dorothy E. (1988). Rehabilitating deviant families through Family Courts: The birth of socialized justice in Ontario, 1920–1940. *International Journal of the Sociology of Law, 16.*

Duclos, Nitya. (1991). Some complicating thoughts on "same-sex" marriage. *Law and Sexuality, 1.*

Herman, Didi. (1990). Are we family? Lesbian rights and women's liberation. *Osgoode Hall Law Journal, 28.*

QUESTIONS TO CONSIDER

1. What is meant by "heterosexual privilege"?

2. Why might the definition of "spouse" vary in different pieces of legislation?

3. In what contexts could one say that the dominant model of family is "imposed coercively"?

CHAPTER 11

Policing Desire: Obscenity Law, Pornography Politics, and Feminism in Canada

Lise Gotell

Over the past two decades, the feminist campaign against pornography has enjoyed remarkable success in the courts, in the legislatures, and in the realm of public opinion. Prior to the 1970s, debates about sex and censorship were polarized between civil-libertarian advocates of free expression and moral conservatives. The voices of women and the question of pornography's relation to gender power were largely absent from these debates. Increasingly, however, a "new" and feminist-inspired discourse, defining pornography as the expression of male sexual violence, has become the constraining norm of the pornography debate. A concern with pornography's gendered "harms" influenced the obscenity-law reform initiatives of successive federal governments over the 1970s and 1980s. Recently, feminist anti-pornography discourse has found expression in law in the landmark Charter case *R. v. Butler* (1992), 8 C.R.R. (2d) 1 (S.C.C.)—a Supreme Court decision that upheld Canadian obscenity prohibitions on the basis that pornography degrades and dehumanizes women.

From one perspective, feminist struggles against pornography, culminating in the Supreme Court decision in *Butler*, may be viewed as paradigm examples of feminist influence on a policy field (Busby, 1994). This essay, however, advances another interpretation. The very definition of "pornography," the nature of pornography's relation to sexual domination, as well as the wisdom of state censorship, remain deeply contested issues within Canadian feminism. Despite the claims of anti-pornography activists, there exists no universal feminist position on pornography. As Arcand has astutely observed, pornography is not a thing but an argument (1991, p. 58). The question "What is pornography? is one that has consistently defied authoritative response. Shifts in debates around pornography and new political and legal responses to this issue do indeed signal the growing influence of a particular feminist position. But the official embrace of feminist anti-pornography discourse can only at a most superficial level be read as a feminist success story.

It is the purpose of this essay to trace the development of Canadian obscenity law and pornography policy. As I illustrate, this story is primarily one about the changing character of **moral regulation**, marked by periodic fears about moral decline and social disorder. Initial sections explore the conservative origins of Canada's obscenity policy, the more recent emergence of pornography as a social problem, and the widespread partisan support for a new law on pornography that has arisen over the past twenty years. Through this discussion, I suggest that political receptiveness to feminist anti-pornography mobilization may have less to do with the persuasiveness and strength of this campaign than with the state's own agenda. In keeping with the other contributions to this volume, I attempt to locate evolving policy responses—in this case, to pornography—within the profound changes in state form that are currently occurring. The place of feminist anti-pornography politics within the new politics of anti-pornography, however, remains tenuous. By drawing parallels between old obscenity politics and the new politics of anti-pornography, I emphasize their similarities; both are founded upon the attempt to create moral order in an unstable world.

While the 1970s and 1980s witnessed a new political openness to anti-pornography feminism, government law-reform initiatives did not ultimately lead to definitive policy changes. Failed efforts to establish a new legislative consensus on obscenity reform served to push pornography conflicts into the courts and the realm of constitutional litigation. The character of feminist anti-pornography litigation is, therefore, the focus of remaining sections of this essay. Through a careful examination of *Butler*, and of feminist intervention in this case, the impact of anti-pornography feminist discourse on law will be disentangled. My intent is to interrogate critically the underlying assumptions of anti-pornography feminism; to question the appropriateness of its preferred policy recommendation, state censorship; and to challenge the interpretation of *Butler* as an unequivocal victory for feminism.

THE CANADIAN STATE AND OBSCENITY LAW: HISTORICAL DEVELOPMENT

Moral Regulation

State censorship of sexual imagery has always functioned to establish and reinforce what is to be seen as "normal," "healthy" sexuality and to repress that which falls outside this boundary—that is, allegedly "abnormal" and "deviant" sexualities. Along with a whole set of other rules, including those defining marriage; those regulating abortion, contraception, and prostitution; and those criminalizing certain forms of sexual behaviour like homosexuality, obscenity law has played a central role in moral regulation (Valverde and Weir, 1988). By erecting legal prohibitions to some sexual materials, states have sought to condition sexual behaviour, to maintain moral order, and, in this manner, to shore up the "foundations" of society.

The underlying assumption informing the legal, and especially criminal, regulation of obscenity is the belief that law should be used to enforce a particular standard of morality. The original concern of obscenity law was to reinforce a conservative sexual morality and to guard against "depravity." While the twentieth century witnessed some liberalization of legal prohibitions on obscenity, the moral foundations of obscenity law remained intact. More recent, and specifically feminist, critiques of pornography have served to incorporate an emphasis on sexual representation, sexual equality, and sexual harm into the moral rationale of obscenity law. Overall, the evolution of legal regulation and debates about sexual imagery reveals a constant concern for ensuring some form of moral order and stability.

The British Origins: Re-creating Moral Order

As with much of our criminal law, Canada's original obscenity regime was an inheritance from Britain. Prior to the nineteenth century, sexual publications themselves were not legally punishable in British law; only when sexual content was combined with sedition or blasphemy was it considered a criminal offence. The first laws placing prohibitions on sexual publications or "obscenity" coincided with the Industrial Revolution—a period of great disruption during which the social foundations of the old pre-industrial order were eroded, with nothing yet to replace them.

Historically, campaigns for the regulation of obscenity have tended to intensify during periods of social disorder and perceived moral decline (Arcand, 1991, p. 143; Lacombe, 1994, p. 19; Rubin, 1993). The first great anti-obscenity movement, the moral purity movement of the nineteenth century, occurred amid rapid urbanization and the emergence of an urban working class. Simultaneously, advances in printing technology heralded the beginnings of "popular" sexual texts, now much more widely available to the "urban masses." It was the coincidence of these factors—social disruption, enhanced availability of sexual publications, and the emergence of movements determined re-create moral order—that set the context for the codification of legal restrictions on obscenity.

Criminalization

The prohibition of obscenity through the British Obscene Publications Act of 1857 was part of a broad parcel of policies designed to establish a conservative sexual morality, to affirm heterosexual marriage as the only legitimate site of sexuality, and to protect those deemed vulnerable to being led astray through vice and obscenity (Mort, 1987; Valverde and Weir, 1988, p. 31; Rubin, 1993, p. 4). Canadian legislation against obscenity soon followed. The first Criminal Code of Canada (1892) proscribed obscenity under the heading "Offenses Against Morality," which forbid the public sale or exposure of any obscene book or printed matter. While criminalization was clearly the intent of both of these early laws, neither statute attempted to specify a precise definition of "obscenity." Instead, it was left for the courts to determine the boundaries between the "obscene" and the "not obscene" (see Box 11.1).

CANADIAN OBSCENITY LAW EVOLVES

Prior to 1944, the *Hicklin* precedent constituted the sole test for obscenity within Canadian law. The central legal criterion demarcating the "obscene" was the degree of explicitness. By the 1940s and 1950s, however, a series of important legal decisions signalled some marginal liberalization of obscenity law. The courts introduced certain qualifications into *Hicklin*, including:

▶ a requirement of "intent" to deprave;

▶ a requirement that there be an element of contemporariness in the definition of "obscenity";

▶ a requirement that the "offending" passage must be viewed in the context of the entire work (Campbell and Pal, 1989, pp. 114–115; Lacombe, 1988, pp. 35–36).

Through the adoption of these criteria, the courts were effectively narrowing the grounds for the criminal prosecution of obscenity. Implicit in the requirement that an entire work must be considered, for example, was the notion that depictions of sex could be redeemed if associated with some higher purpose. Nevertheless, the context requirement affirmed the view that "sex for sex's sake," or sex that was not associated with literary or artistic purpose, would unequivocally be viewed as "obscene" and a danger to society. Furthermore, while judicial decisions altered standards of obscenity, the moral and conservative foundations of the *Hicklin* test clearly remained intact. Works would continue to be judged primarily on their perceived effects on public morality.

BOX 11.1

The *Hicklin* Test: Moral Conservatism and Gender Subtexts In the famous 1868 *Hicklin* case, the British courts established a test for obscenity that would set precedent for legal interpretation in both Canada and Britain lasting for almost the next century. The **Hicklin test** explicitly articulated the moral-conservative underpinnings of obscenity law. As it elaborated, the legal definition of obscenity was its potential to corrupt:

> the test of obscenity is this,... the tendency ... to deprave and corrupt those whose minds are open to such immoral influences, and into whose hands a publication of this sort may fall ... it would suggest into the minds ... thoughts of an impure and libidinous character. (*R. v. Hicklin* [1868] 3 L.R.Q.B., 360)

Through this test, the court clearly identified "adverse moral impact" as the definition of "obscene." The legal regime which *Hicklin* founded was based on the assumption that sex itself constitutes a powerful danger to society, and sexual publications possess a particular ability to deprave.

Although largely unarticulated, it was assumed that only adult and educated men were able resist to the power of the "obscene." As Arcand observes,

> (only adult men were deemed) capable of remaining calm, dignified and moderate, whereas a more delicate or impressionable creature, such as a woman or a child or a member of the unsophisticated poor, would be unable to resist the destabilizing power of pornography ... pornography thus becomes a "social problem" when it is no longer the preserve of gentlemen whose reactions to it are predictable. (1992, pp. 117–118)

Lurking at the foundations of early obscenity law, then, was a gendered moral subtext. While the discourse of conservative moralism casts the impact of "obscenity" in largely gender-neutral terms, it nevertheless has profoundly gendered implications. Women, along with children and working-class men, were constituted as incapable of rational judgment and, therefore, particularly vulnerable to being swayed through sexual texts. Women's sexuality was, in this way, viewed as something passive, dependent and to be protected. It is not simply coincidental that the criminal regulation of obscenity coincided with the extension and strengthening of laws against prostitution in Canada and in Britain (Shaver, 1994, p. 128; Burstyn, 1985, p. 12; Rubin, 1993, p. 4). Again, the desire to rescue women from "victimization" and "male sexual excess" underpinned the efforts of both moral-purity activists and legislators. In effect, conservative moral discourse strives to contain, circumscribe, and hide female sexuality within the boundaries of heterosexual marriage. Women's sexual expression outside this context was denied any meaning, and female chastity was affirmed as a normative standard, against which deviations would be judged (Burstyn, 1985, p. 13).

284 PART III RESTRUCTURING PRIVATE LIFE

Criticisms of Hicklin

The liberalizing thrust of judicial decisions coincided with the emergence of criticisms of the *Hicklin* test. Legal experts extensively criticized it for its vagueness and subjectivity and because it did not require actual proof of harm (Campbell and Pal, 1989, p. 114). Nevertheless, when Parliament moved to address the obscenity-law reform in the 1950s, it was not to move away from the *Hicklin* test but to toughen it up. Much like the set of conditions that inspired original legal prohibitions on obscenity, the issue of "decency" in writing was thrust onto the public agenda just as changes in printing technology allowed for production of cheap, widely accessible books and magazines (ibid., p. 115). Once again, concerns about moral corruption framed the identification of obscenity as a political problem. And although the law-reform initiatives of the 1950s rested upon an implicit gendered subtext, questions of sexual representation, gender relations, and sexism would remain unstated during this round of reform.

The 1959 Reform: Moral Anxiety Revisited

Canada's existing obscenity legislation, passed in 1959, emerged from a set of conservative and moral anxieties about the increased availability of sexual materials. Beginning in the 1950s, many Members of Parliament, both Liberal and Conservative, began to argue that the 1892 criminal provisions on obscenity were inadequate to deal with a perceived explosion of "filthy" literature. The *Hicklin* test was castigated because it was subjective and, it was argued, thereby permitted certain "trashy" publications to escape criminal punishment. For this reason, there were calls within the House of Commons and the Senate for legislative clarification of the definition of "obscenity" (Campbell and Pal, 1989, pp. 116–117). Significantly, concern over the issue of obscenity remained very much confined to the legislative and legal arenas. The emergence of pornography as a "social" problem, as an object of conflict and debate, would not occur until the 1970s, with the rise of the civil libertarian, gay rights, and feminist movements.

The Amendment: Catching "Muck" and "Trash"

It was perhaps this absence of social debate and scrutiny that allowed the Conservative government to amend the Criminal Code provisions on "obscenity" and, for the first and only time, to codify some definition of "obscenity"—"any publication a dominant characteristic of which is the undue exploitation of sex, or of sex and any one more of the following subjects, namely crime, horror, cruelty and violence."[1] As explained by then Justice minister David Fulton, this definition was adopted in order to catch within obscenity law "muck" and "trash" that had no artistic or literary merit (Campbell and Pal, 1989, p. 116; Lacombe, 1988, p. 37).

"Objectivity" and "Reasonable Men"

The new law was explicitly intended create an "objective" test for the determination of criminal obscenity, to supplement the *Hicklin* test. As Fulton explained, "The word undue is one which the courts are familiar as meaning generally something going beyond what men of good will and common sense will tolerate" (quoted in Campbell and Pal, 1989, p. 116). Implicit here is the legal notion of the "reasonable man" standard; according to this standard, the perspective of the hypothetical "reasonable man" provides a standpoint for objective legal judgement and, in this case, for policing the boundaries of the obscene. This equation—the viewpoint of the "reasonable man" equals a standpoint of objectivity—embeds an unarticulated **phallocentricism** and serves to cast women as "irrational others." Obscenity law, both as it was created in the nineteenth century and as it was altered in the 1950s, was quite clearly about morality and constructed from a specifically masculine point of view (MacKinnon, 1989, p. 196).

The Community Standards Test

While the criminal law on obscenity was amended to clarify in statute the definition of "obscenity," the boundaries established by the new legislation nevertheless remained vague—"undue exploitation of sex." For this reason, state regulation of sexual imagery continued to rely considerably on judicial discretion and elaboration. In a series of 1950s and 1960s decisions, Canadian courts established a test, known as the **community standards test**, by which obscenity was defined as sexual material which offended the "community," as reflected in the views of the "average" person (*R. v. Brodie*, [1962] SCR, p. 705).

The problem with the community standards test, as with the *Hicklin* test which had preceded it, was its thinly veiled subjectivity. The Canadian community is neither monolithic nor static; consequently, efforts to define an average Canadian standard of acceptance remained illusory. But, as if to sidestep this problem, the courts determined that evaluations of community standards required neither empirical proof nor expert evaluation. As it was elaborated, the judiciary's "general instinctive sense" of the sexual norms of the Canadian community came to represent "community standards" in obscenity case law (Busby, 1994, p. 167). Of course, these judicial determinations often relied on the view that all sexual imagery is immoral. And because of its subjective character, the community standards test was applied very inconsistently, resulting in a series of uneven obscenity judgements (Campbell and Pal, 1985, pp. 118–119). In effect, the reformed obscenity law, though intended to ensure moral order and shrouded under the guise of "objectivity," was premised upon highly unpredictable judicial interpretation. This law would increasingly be viewed as unworkable as pornography was politicized as a social problem.

PORNOGRAPHY EMERGES AS A SOCIAL PROBLEM: THE DEBATES

During the 1970s, there were increasing calls for the amendment of Canada's obscenity legislation coming from diverse perspectives (See Table 11.1). The emergence of pornography as a "social problem," as a object of intense conflict that engaged a wide variety of social actors, served to transform the obscenity debate and, for the first time, to problematize questions of gender and pornography. While conservative moralism had long constituted the foundation of the Canadian state's regulation of sexual imagery, social change and the voices of new social actors opened to contestation the very rationale of Canadian obscenity law.

Liberalization and Civil-Libertarian Critics

The 1960s witnessed some alteration in the state's role as guardian of the moral order, and this set the context for the emergence of a broader and more politicized obscenity debate. In Canada, as in many other Western liberal democracies, laws concerning previously defined "moral" issues (divorce, contraception, abortion, and homosexuality) were reformed and liberalized. This liberalization was not wholesale; it involved a retraction, but not a complete withdrawal of legal regulation. Nevertheless, informing these policy changes was the notion that immorality was no longer sufficient grounds for legal restriction; instead, legal prohibition must be justified on the basis of preventing social harm.

Initially, however, changing ideas about morality and law did not prompt the Canadian state to reconsider its obscenity legislation. In the United States, by contrast, the Commission on Obscenity and Pornography was created to investigate the effects of pornography. Reporting in 1970, the commission articulated a liberal rationale for the decriminalization of obscenity. It contended that obscenity laws infringed on freedom of expression and concluded that pornography is not harmful, but instead promotes liberal and tolerant attitudes (Berger, Searles, and Cottle, 1991, pp. 22–23). Echoing the findings and orientation of the U.S. commission, Canadian civil-libertarian and law-reform groups began to pressure the federal government to liberalize or decriminalize obscenity. The Law Reform Commission of Canada, for example, argued that, while it may be reasonable for the Criminal Code to proscribe "public" obscenity, soft-core pornography that was privately consumed should not bring criminal penalty (Law Reform Commission of Canada, 1975). Some civil libertarians went farther in their critiques, asserting that pornography is liberating and that its restriction was, therefore, entirely unjustified (Lacombe, 1994, p.25).

TABLE 11.1
CONTENDING POSITIONS ON PORNOGRAPHY

	Sexuality	Law/Morality	Pornography/Obscenity	Censorship
Civil Libertarian	A terrain of freedom and privacy devoid of power	It is not legitimate for law to enforce a particular standard of morality; law should not infringe on privacy unless harm can be proven	Pornography is primarily a means of sexual expression and education; obscenity is subjective and not open to clear definition	State censorship is unjustified, in most cases, because it represses sexual freedom and infringes on expression rights
Gay Rights	Heterosexual norm must be challenged; a sphere of repression and potential liberation	Law has played a role in repressing gay sexuality; law must not reinforce sexual morality	Pornography is primarily a means of liberation; gay pornography challenges dominant sexual norms; obscenity is subjective and reinforces heterosexuality	State censorship is unjustified; obscenity law has been used to silence gay sexual expression
Anti-Pornography Feminist	A sphere of masculine power through which women are oppressed; women's consent and sexual agency are illusory; a central underpinning of patriarchy	Law has been used to reinforce male power; it is not legitimate of law to uphold conservative sexual morality; a concern for sexual equality and sexual harm must be built into moral rationale of law	Pornography is a core practice that institutionalizes sexual inequality and violence; pornography which degrades and dehumanizes women can be demarcated from erotica which depicts	State censorship of pornography is justified because pornography infringes on sexual equality; a harms-based test must be the rationale of obscenity law

(continued)

(continued)

	Sexuality	Law/Morality	Pornography/Obscenity	Censorship
Anti-Pornography Feminist			equality in sexual relations; pornography is obscenity	
Anti-censorship Feminist	A sphere of domination and struggle; women have sexual agency and should struggle against heterosexual, patriarchal norm	Law has reinforced a conservative sexual morality; it is not easy to disrupt the conservative morality of law and, therefore, law is an unreliable ally for feminists in their struggles	Pornography resists clear definition; it both reinforces sexual inequality and offers spaces for challenging sexual norms; alternative sexual imagery, including gay and lesbian pornography, is likely to be considered obscene	State censorship has been used to repress marginal and alternative sexual representations; state censorship is unjustified because it restricts women's efforts to challenge dominant sexual norms
New Right	Sexuality is a sphere of nature which must be bounded by morality; sexuality must be confined to procreative activities within heterosexual marriage; unleashed from this boundary, sexuality has the power to disrupt society	Law's primary role is to uphold a common morality	Pornography can be clearly defined through sexual explicitness; pornography undermines the family, traditional authority, and the moral fabric of society; pornography degrades "women"; pornography is obscenity	State censorship is necessary to prevent moral decline

Sexuality, Freedom, and Expression

The arguments of civil libertarians are premised upon a particular conception of sexuality and sexual expression. For civil libertarians, central to the pornography debate is the issue of freedom, that is, freedom from state censorship and state invasion of privacy. Sexuality is constructed as a terrain of individual freedom and privacy, devoid of power relations. State intervention in this sphere, without empirically proven evidence of harm, is thus seen as illegitimate (Berger, Searles, and Cottle, 1991, pp. 20–22). Civil-libertarian claims challenged the legitimacy of law as guardian of the moral order and, for much of the 1960s and early 1970s, the pornography debate was polarized between civil-libertarian and moral-conservative positions.

Gay Liberation and Pornography

The 1970s, however, saw a further politicization of the pornography issue, as new voices and concerns were inserted into this debate. Coincident with, though not entirely consistent with, the civil-libertarian position, gay rights activists and sex radicals argued for the repeal of obscenity law. Emerging out of the so-called sexual revolution of the 1960s, the gay-liberation movement identified obscenity law as a central concern because of the way it has repressed and targeted gay pornography. For many gay men and some lesbians, gay pornography is seen as an affirmation of their sexuality, particularly important for those in the process of coming out (Berger, Searles, and Cottle, 1991, pp. 82–84; Bearchell, 1993, p. 37; Lacombe, 1994, p. 20). In a context where gay sexual representations were (and are) forced to exist underground and at the extreme margins of society, pornographic texts and images provided one of the few available sources of information about gay sexuality.

Challenging the Heterosexual Norm

In some ways, then, the claims of gay activists echoed civil-libertarian views on freedom of sexual expression and the importance of pornography for sexual education. Nevertheless, what grounds this position is a critique of heterosexual dominance. In contrast to the central assumptions of civil libertarians, the gay-rights movement understands sexuality as a site of struggle and power. The creation of gay sexual imagery is one mechanism, and part of a broad strategy, aimed at challenging the dominant heterosexual norm (Rubin, 1993).

Feminist Debates

Perhaps the most critical "new" interventions in the pornography debate came with the emergence of the second-wave women's movement. Prior to the 1970s, as we have seen, the gendered dimensions of obscenity law and of pornography remained obscured. The central question framing the pornography debate was whether sex should be depicted, and not how sex is depicted within pornography. Beginning in the late 1970s, some Canadian feminist activists began to mobilize around violent and degrading images of women in pornography and formed organizations devoted to fighting pornography, including Women Against Violence Against Women, the Committee Against Pornography, and the Canadian Coalition Against Media Pornography (Lacombe, 1994, p. 29). From the outset, however, feminist interventions in the pornography debate were multivocal. Coinciding with the development of an anti-pornography feminist campaign, there also emerged feminist-oriented anti-censorship groups, such as the Ontario Film and Video Appreciation Society and Censorstop (Lacombe, 1994, p. 57; see Box 11.2).

Moral Order: Anti-Pornography Feminism and the New Right

While all feminist intervenors in the pornography debate articulated a critique of the moral conservative foundations of Canadian obscenity law, anti-pornography feminists did not reject the notion that law should be used to ensure some form of moral order. The feminist campaign against pornography seeks to reform and recast the moral foundations of law to incorporate a normative concern for sexual harm. In accepting the moral regulatory function of law and in other significant respects, anti-pornography feminism thus enters into an uneasy rhetorical and political alliance with the moral right.[2]

THE NEW RIGHT AND PORNOGRAPHY

The Social Articulation of Conservative Obscenity Discourse

As the final voice present in the emerging pornography wars of the 1970s and 1980s, the New Right's position did not necessarily represent a discursive shift from previous eras. The emergence of a grass-roots and conservative movement against pornography (based in the churches and in conservative and anti-feminist groups, such as the Coalition for Family Values, Canadians for Decency, and R.E.A.L. Women) can be viewed as a reaction to anxieties about the "explosion" of pornography and the perceived liberalization of obscenity case law (Lacombe, 1994, pp. 45–53; Vance, 1993b). The concerns of this movement were, in fact, similar in thrust to concerns that had prompted state legislators to enact and tighten obscenity laws during earlier periods. The significance of the New Right's intervention in the contemporary pornography debate was that now moral-conservative discourse on obscenity was being articulated through a social movement.

BOX 11.2

Comparing Feminist Positions Both feminist anti-pornography and anti-censorship activists seek to problematize the relation between sexual representation and sexual inequality. By framing their discussions of pornography within the structural context of gender oppression, feminist contributors to pornography debate, of whatever stripe, challenged the decontextualized and power-blind positions of civil libertarians (Currie, 1992, p. 193). In some respects, feminist interventions were similar those of gay activists in their common critiques of dominant heterosexuality. While sharing certain concerns, however, the differences between anti-pornography and anti-censorship feminist positions remain stark (Wilson, 1993, pp. 15–18, 22–28; Lacombe, 1994, pp. 26–44, 56–63; Vance, 1993b):

‣ whereas anti-pornography feminists condemn sexuality as a sphere of male power, anti-censorship feminists highlight the potential of women's sexual agency and pleasure;

‣ whereas anti-pornography feminists contend that pornography eroticizes male domination, anti-censorship feminists emphasize the impossibility of literalist readings of pornography (i.e., the meaning of any sexual representation depends on its context and the subjectivity of the consumer);

‣ whereas anti-pornography feminists argue that pornography causes sexual violence, anti-censorship feminists assert the complex roots of sexual violence;

‣ whereas anti-pornography feminists support state censorship of pornography that degrades and dehumanizes women, anti-censorship feminists contend that state censorship is most likely to be deployed against lesbian, feminist, and other marginalized groups.

Despite these significant and ever-present divisions among Canadian feminists on pornography and censorship, anti-pornography feminism has come to be seen as the public face of the women's movement and the hegemonic feminist position. The embrace of anti-pornography politics by major feminist organizations, the simplicity and clarity of this discourse, and the coincidence of this position with dominant political and legal agendas would all work, as we will see, to ensure the growing influence and legitimacy of anti-pornography feminism.

The social articulation of moral-conservative discourse can be linked to two factors. First, given the politicized and plural character of the pornography debate, there existed, for the first time, a perceived imperative to defend the moral regulatory basis of obscenity law against a wide range of challenges. Second, as analysts of the New Right have contended, the origins of this social movement must be understood in the context of social change, including the decline of the nuclear-family form, and the successes of feminist and other progressive movements in challenging traditional structures and attitudes (Petchesky, 1984, p. 247; Erwin, 1988, pp. 147–148).

The Right, Moral Anxiety, and Pornography

The New Right's anxiety about change and the decline of traditional authority structures, such as patriarchy, grounds its critique of pornography. Conservative groups contend that pornography offends public decency and promotes moral decline. While incorporating some elements of anti-pornography feminist rhetoric, such as the arguments about sexual violence, the axis of New Right pornography discourse is the claim that pornography poses a threat to the family (Vance, 1993b, p. 35; Lacombe, 1994, p. 48; Currie, 1992, p. 195). By endorsing "extra-marital" sex, pornography is seen to unleash sex from the bounds of heterosexual marriage and to undermine traditional gender roles within the family (Berger, Searles, and Cottle, 1991, p. 18). And because the family is constituted as the foundation of society, pornography thereby threatens social stability. For this reason, the Right, like anti-pornography feminism, seeks tougher laws on pornography. From this position, however, "indecency" and "sexual explicitness" would constitute primary criteria for criminalization.

ONTO THE POLITICAL AGENDA: THE NEW POLITICS OF ANTI-PORNOGRAPHY

The emergence of pornography as a social problem called into question both the rationale and the effectiveness of Canadian obscenity law. On the whole, the articulation of diverse challenges threatened the legitimacy of the existing legal regime but posed conflicting, if not irreconcilable, proposals for law reform. Social pressures and critiques pushed the issue of obscenity law reform onto the Liberal government's political agenda in the late 1970s. In the 1980s, the election of the Progressive Conservatives and the ascendance of neoconservatism made state actors increasingly open to law-and-order policy, among which efforts to restrict pornography assumed some place of importance. Overall, these law reform efforts mark the ascendance of a "new" politics of anti-pornography.

Liberal Government Initiatives

It was within the context of the heightened politicization of pornography debates that Liberal governments sought to amend the 1959 law, introducing three anti-pornography bills and establishing two commissions concerned with obscenity reform (See Table 11.2). These efforts spanned the period between 1977 and the Liberals' resounding electoral defeat in 1984, and coincided with the social escalation of pornography conflicts. Each attempt to pass new legislation, however, met with criticism from all sides. In particular, these exercises illustrated the difficulties of establishing a legislative definition for pornography (Campbell and Pal, 1989, pp. 119–127). Paradoxically, the emergence of pornography as a social problem acted to push obscenity law reform onto the political agenda, but it simultaneously made authoritative policy response increasingly difficult.

While Liberal governments were unable to construct a new policy consensus on pornography, it is possible to identify certain underlying themes of their reform initiatives and proposals (See Table 11.2):

▶ first, Liberal efforts emphasized the "urgency of the problem of sexually explicit material" (Canada, House of Commons, Standing Committee on Justice and Legal Affairs, 1978, 18:3);

▶ second, the Liberals accepted that problem of pornography should continue to be addressed primarily through criminalization;

▶ third, these efforts recognized the principle of sexual equality and proposed to introduce the concept of "undue degradation of the human person" into the Criminal Code provision on obscenity (Campbell and Pal, 1989, p. 122);

▶ fourth, child pornography was identified as a central concern and specific and harsh prohibitions were proposed (ibid.).

The Incorporation of Anti-Pornography Feminist Discourse

In sum, the Liberal approach to pornography accepted the existing criminal obscenity framework but sought to insert into it new concerns about sexual inequality and child abuse. Despite their failure to become law, these efforts do indicate, as Lacombe contends, "the extent to which the anti-pornography movement had made itself gradually heard in Ottawa" (1994, p. 79). In particular, significant shifts in legislative discourse, from an emphasis on "decency" to one focussed on "harm"—in particular, harm to women and children—signalled the growing influence of anti-pornography feminism on this policy area. Yet, despite this shift, and indeed existing alongside it, the moral-conservative foundation of obscenity law remained present. While dressed up in feminist rhetoric, Liberal initiatives proposed to broaden the definition of obscenity, raising, for some critics, concerns about overzealous prosecutions of sexually explicit material (Campbell and Pal, 1989, p. 122). It is therefore possible that the traditional state preoccupation with sexual explicitness was in the process of being modernized—modernized by couching it in more contemporary and feminist arguments (Vance, 1993b, p. 33).

TABLE 11.2

LEGISLATIVE INITIATIVES ON OBSCENITY AND PORNOGRAPHY, 1892–1993

Year	Party	Initiative	Outcome of Bills	Description
1892	Conservative	Criminal Code s.179(2)	Enacted	Criminalized "obscenity" under the heading "Offenses Against Morality"; "obscenity" not defined
1959	Conservative	Amendment to Criminal Code–s.150(8)	Enacted	Codified a definition of obscenity—"any publication a dominant characteristic of which is the undue exploitation of sex"
1977	Private Members Bill (Conservative)	Bill C-207	Was defeated	Would have criminalized any "explicit representation" of a "sexual act" (i.e., almost all printed and pictorial matter which dealt with sex)
1978	Liberal	Referred pornography to Standing Committee on Justice and Legal Affairs		Placed pornography on the political agenda
1978	All party (chaired by Liberal Mark MacGuigan	Standing Committee on Justice and Legal		Report emphasized the urgency of the "problem" and

(continued)

(continued)

Year	Party	Initiative	Outcome of Bills	Description
1978		Affairs issued report on pornography		embraced anti-pornography feminist view that pornography degrades women and abuses the principle of sexual equality. Recommended adding "undue degradation of the human person" to obscenity law and separate criminal sanctions for child pornography
1978	Liberal	Bill C-21	Never debated and died on the parliamentary order paper	Would have introduced strict penalties on child pornography; redefined obscenity to include "undue degradation of the human person"; and separated sex from violence in the definition of obscenity
1981	Liberal	Bill C-53	Government withdrew bill	Omnibus bill dealing with a wide range of Criminal Code amendments. Would have introduced harsh penalties

(continued)

(continued)

Year	Party	Initiative	Outcome of Bills	Description
1981				against child pornography
1983	Liberal	Established Special Committee on Pornography and Prostitution (Fraser Committee)		Establishment of committee signalled Liberal government's commitment to introducing new pornography legislation
1984	Liberal	Bill C-19	Died on the parliamentary order paper	Omnibus bill dealing with Criminal Code amendments. Would have amended definition of obscenity to include "degrading representations of a male or female person"; disentangled sex from violence in definition of obscenity.
1985	Reported under Conservative government	Special Committee on Pornography and Prostitution (Fraser Committee), Report		Proposed a pornography law founded upon a harms-based approach; located pornography within an equality framework; recommended tough criminal sanctions for violent, degrading, and child

(continued)

(continued)

Year	Party	Initiative	Outcome of Bills	Description
1985				pornography; "soft core" pornography would be decriminalized
1986	Conservative	Bill C-114	Died on the parliamentary order paper	Proposed to criminalize pornography. Pornography was defined very broadly as any material showing vaginal or oral intercourse, ejaculation, sexually violent behaviour, bestiality, incest, necrophilia, masturbation, or other sexual activity
1987	Conservative	Bill C-54	Died on the parliamentary order paper	Allowed for limited display of and access to "erotica," but prohibited the depiction of vaginal, anal, and oral intercourse, lactation, menstruation, and ejaculation.
1993	Conservative	Bill C-128	Enacted	Creates separate and harsh penalties for child pornography; makes possession of child pornography a

(continued)

(continued)

Year	Party	Initiative	Outcome of Bills	Description
1993				crime; child pornography is defined as the representation of anyone depicted as being under the age of 18 engaged in sexual activity

Disunified State: Contradictory Trends in Obscenity Regulation

The legislative stalemate on the issue of pornography did not, however, mean that there existed a regulatory vacuum. In the absence of a coherent, definitive response by the federal government, obscenity law continued to be applied and elaborated upon by a disparate collection of state actors, including the courts, customs officials, provincial attorneys general, and police.

Intensified Regulation?

This decentralized legal environment provided a political space for the mobilization of those concerned with the "explosion" of sexual materials. Consequently, during the 1960s and 1970s, anti-pornography squads were established within some police forces (Campbell and Pal, 1989, p. 120; Lacombe, 1988, pp. 59–64), and customs regulations on obscene materials were refined (Gilmour, 1993, pp. 31–34, 66–67; Bearchell, 1993, pp. 37–40). By 1980, Canada Customs's index of prohibited material included some 35 000 titles (Campbell and Pal, 1989, p. 136). Predictably, police and Customs scrutiny for obscenity was guided by a zealous respect for moral standards, resulting particularly in the targeting of non-dominant sexual representations. Many key obscenity cases during this period involved lesbian and gay materials (Bearchell, 1993; Toobin, 1994, pp. 72–74; MacKinnon and Dworkin, 1994, p. 2). In 1985, for example, in a cases decided against Glad Day Bookshop, it was determined that images of gay and lesbian sex were more offensive to community standards than were similar heterosexual materials (Kinsman and Brock, 1985, p. 35). And, throughout this period, gay and lesbian novels, sex manuals, and magazines were exponentially added to Customs's list of banned materials.

Liberalization?

In some respects, then, legal regulation seemed to intensify; but the dis-unified character state regulatory mechanisms allowed for the develop-ment of certain contradictory trends. Over the 1970s and 1980s, some obscenity decisions signalled the development of an increasingly tolerant judicial attitude. Courts narrowed the definition of "obscenity" to exclude portrayals of sex that had a "serious" purpose and treated sex with "sin-cerity" (Cossman, 1994, pp. 8–10; Lacombe, 1994, p. 88). In addition, the community standards test appeared to be evolving to encompass anti-pornography feminist concerns about degradation and dehumaniza-tion (*R. v. Doug Rankine Co.* (1983), 9 CCC (3d) 53 (Ont. Co. Ct); *R. v. Towne Cinema Theatres* (1985), 18 CCC (3d) 193; Cossman, (1994), pp. 5–8). Nevertheless, inconsistencies in judicial interpretation remained, and an emphasis on sexual explicitness and "deviance" con-tinued to inform many obscenity decisions (Lacombe, 1994, p. 78).

The Tories and Family Values: Moral Discourse Recast

With the election of the Mulroney Conservatives, the creation of a new and coherent pornography policy took on new urgency. The Fraser Commission on Pornography and Prostitution, commissioned by the Liberals, reported in 1985, soon after the Conservative's remarkable elec-toral victory. The Fraser Commission served to legitimize the identification of pornography as a policy priority, but its report reflected an orientation that would differ quite markedly from Tory anti-pornography discourse.

The Fraser Commission

On the whole, the Fraser Commission appeared to capture the mood of pornography policy during the previous Liberal regime. While the commission had heard witnesses representing diverse perspectives, anti-pornography discourse—in particular, anti-pornography feminist discourse—clearly informed the commission's report (Lacombe, 1994, p. 97). The Commission's report proposed a new pornography law founded upon a **harms-based** rationale; it located the problem of pornography with-in a discourse of equality and human rights; and it recommended tougher penalties on child pornography and on "degrading" and violent pornogra-phy, while endorsing the decriminalization of non-violent and "soft-core" pornography (Canada, Special Committee on Pornography and Prostitution, 1985). In effect, the commission supported a criminal-law framework for addressing the "problem" of pornography, but sought to construct a new balance between freedom and equality within this framework.

The Tory Initiatives

In marked contrast to Fraser, the Mulroney government's anti-pornogra-phy agenda was lodged squarely within a conservative moral discourse.

Immediately after their election in 1984, the Conservatives embraced a so-called family values platform, promising measures to control pornography. While adopting certain elements of anti-pornography feminist rhetoric, especially regarding the connection between pornography and sexual violence, the government justified tougher criminal restrictions on pornography as necessary for the preservation of the "family." As expressed by the prime minister:

> Our Canadian family is the cornerstone of all decent social initiatives. The Canadian family will be defended in this Parliament by this government, at all times and in all circumstances.... With more threats to the fabric of our family life, it is the government's duty to act in response. That is why we will be moving in this session against pornography, child abuse and drug abuse. (quoted in Campbell and Pal, 1989, p. 128)

The government's express commitment to pornography reform resulted in the introduction of two extremely tough anti-pornography bills (see Table 11.2). Both Conservative bills sought to move away from an approach based upon broadly worded provisions to be interpreted by the courts, and instead provided a set of quite specific statutory definitions of "pornography."[3] These initiatives embraced the view that pornography was amenable to categorization and clear definition.

The Mulroney government's second pornography bill (Bill C-54), for example, proposed to allow for limited access to "erotica," but prohibited the following sweeping categories of pornography: sexually violent conduct; a degrading act in a sexual context; lactation or menstruation in a sexual context; masturbation or ejaculation; and vaginal, anal, or oral intercourse. Reflecting a repressive intent, the legislation also proposed to criminalize "any matter that incites" or "advocates" any of these acts (Scheier, 1988, pp. 61–62). In effect, this bill represented an attempt to instill an almost Victorian sexual Puritanism. It ambitiously sought to cordon off pornography into a discrete and broad realm of representations. Pornography was defined through a literalist interpretive framework (the "I know it when I see it" approach to pornography)[4] and the breadth of the legislation's categories encompassed, if not nudity, then virtually all depictions of sexual activity.

Moral Discourse/Feminist Rhetoric

Within the Conservative government's pornography initiatives, we can observe a rearticulation of moral-conservative discourse on sexual representation. Reflecting most closely the claims of New Right rhetoric, this recasting of official obscenity discourse also relied on feminist arguments about degradation and sexual violence. As Vance notes, it is now no longer acceptable to cast the dangers of sexual imagery as a threat to morality alone. In this context, the incorporation of anti-pornography feminist rhetoric provides an opportunity to modernize what is at heart an older conservative agenda (1993b,

p. 39). The assimilation of feminist rhetoric, which began with the Liberals, was raised to an artform under the Tories. Through this exercise in discursive blending, the Conservative government, especially with Bill C-54, sought to construct a "compromise" on pornography which would appeal both to its conservative constituency and to feminist anti-pornography activists.

However, this compromise proved difficult to craft. While many major Canadian feminist groups, including the Canadian Advisory Council on the Status of Women and NAC, originally supported the intent of the bill, most feminists disagreed with the breadth of its definition of "pornography" (Lacombe, 1994, pp. 120–123; Canadian Advisory Council on the Status of Women, 1988). Conservative groups also wavered in their support; while Bill C-54 was initially applauded, criticisms of the bill's allegedly "liberal" "erotica" provisions soon intensified. Not surprisingly, civil libertarians, artists, writers, librarians, and some gay and lesbian activists united to mount a visible and highly charged campaign against the government's proposed anti-pornography legislation (Lacombe, 1994, pp. 123–132).

Explaining the New Politics of Anti-Pornography

Ultimately, the Mulroney government allowed both of its very controversial pornography bills to die on the order paper. There are many possible and complex interpretations for this decision to set aside obscenity law reform. These include the sorts of familiar problems experienced by the Conservative government's predecessor:

▶ the difficulties of creating social consensus on such a divisive issue;

▶ the problem of codifying a clear legislative definition of pornography;

▶ and, consequently, an alteration of legislative priorities.[5]

One could engage in an extensive analysis of Conservative and Liberal failures to establish a new legislative consensus on pornography. A more interesting question, however, is "why has pornography emerged as a significant issue for political parties over the past 15 to 20 years?" Even though successive attempts create a new law have not been resulted in policy change, these efforts have illustrated a high level of political support for the idea of tougher restrictions on pornography. The objective of legislating against pornography was shared by all three of our old national parties—Liberal, New Democratic (NDP), and Conservative. This partisan support for some form of anti-pornography law, albeit rooted in different objectives and ideologies, has been expressed in successive parliamentary debates; in electoral promises; in the proceedings of parliamentary committees; and in the unanimous multiparty support for the Tories' one successful pornography bill, Bill C-128—the 1993 child pornography legislation (see Table 11.2).

Political Calculations

Why, then, has there been this coalescing of political interests behind an anti-pornography agenda? On one level, we might attribute the new politics of anti-pornography to political opportunism. The movement against pornography does serve to unite many interests across the political spectrum, from feminists to the New Right. And in this drawing together of competing interests, pornography law reform appears to offer the promise of electoral gains.

There is some value in this explanation. The Conservatives, for example, appear to have been convinced by their pollsters that there was a moral majority on this issue (Campbell and Pal, 1989, p. 139). For parties, such as the NDP, who wish to appeal to a different con-stituency, anti-pornography politics can also offer distinct political advantages. Wilson suggests that attacking pornography provides Left parties with an opportunity to appear supportive of feminist demands while avoiding political debts that are difficult to repay. In her analysis of the British Labour Party and pornography politics, she observes:

> The anti-pornography position is consistent with (Labour's) new respectable image, and, they hope will draw women's votes. At the same time, it costs nothing to implement and the constituency that apparently has the most to lose from any such legislation, the producers and retail-ers of pornography, is not a pressure group that can wield significant muscle or moral force. (1993, p. 21)

Another Explanation: Post–Keynesian Instability and Anxiety

Beyond these political calculations, however, there may be a more fun-damental explanation for the increased sway of an anti-pornography agenda. It is critical to situate anti-pornography politics within the broader context of this post-Keynesian era. In fact, recent promises to contain pornography coming from across the partisan spectrum may tell us a great deal about the kind of state that is emerging from the ashes of the old Keynesian state. The post-Keynesian state is both lean-er and meaner is exemplified by the anti-pornography agenda. Just as anxieties about moral disorder and social disruption prompted original prohibitions on obscenity as well as their reform in the 1950s, so too may current instabilities explain the new popularity of anti-pornography politics.

That we live in uncertain times may seem to be somewhat clichéd. We do, however, inhabit a political space characterized by great insta-bility, equal in magnitude to the Industrial Revolution. All of the familiar foundations that served to ground the citizens of the postwar order are in decline (Brodie, 1994, pp. 2–10). The cold war is over; the nuclear-family form is in decline; national economies are being globalized; and cradle-to-grave employment is being replaced by "flexible" and precari-ous work. In sum, Brown describes this era as one of "fragmentation

without corresponding wholes, heterogeny without unity ..., deterritori-
alization of production and peoples, social surfaces without depths"
(1991, p. 64).

Critically, the era of the Keynesian state is also ending. The idea that
the state can manage to economy to create growth, maintain employment, as well as a social safety net, has been attacked from many sides.
The Keynesian state has been discredited by the Right as the cause of
burgeoning deficits and declining competitiveness. Its defenders on the
Left seem to give in to the new logic of neoconservatism as soon as they
manage to gain electoral power. In this new era of post-Keynesian, neoconservatism, state actors have thus surrendered certain policy instruments. They have also lost their ability to justify their actions through the
now outdated Keynesian rhetoric of state interventionism. Policy-makers
face an extremely anxious electorate; but, at the same time, the old
Keynesian notion that governments must spend to create stability has
now been discredited. This context of instability, anxiety, and the decline
of the Keynesian state frames the new politics of anti-pornography.

Law and Order, Sexual Violence, and Pornography

As some analysts have observed, the neoconservative state has moved
to strengthen its coercive powers. The reduction in state size and
spending that has characterized neoconservative governments of the
1980s has coincided with growth in state power and authority (Gamble,
1988, p. 30, 36; McBride and Shields, 1993, p. 37, 88; Whitaker,
1987, p. 2). As the threads of the postwar order are dismantled, including the **Keynesian welfare state**, the need for strong government to
maintain social authority correspondingly increases. In this conjuncture, then, a law-and-order agenda becomes enormously popular with
neoconservative politicians and policy-makers.

The ascendance of neoconservatism in both Britain and the United
States has been accompanied by an erosion of civil liberties and an
increase in state coercion. In Canada, under Progressive Conservative
governments, law-and-order policy has also taken on new urgency
(Whitaker, 1988; McBride and Shields, 1993, p. 37). As other essays in
this volume indicate, for example, Tory efforts to appear responsive to
"women's" issues were framed almost entirely within a law-and-order
agenda. While the former federal government came to loggerheads
with the organized feminist movement because of its steady assault on
social policy, it simultaneously began a series of initiatives designed to
combat the problem of "violence against women." These included new
sexual assault legislation; new gun control legislation; a new anti-stalk-
ing law; a parliamentary inquiry on violence entitled "The War Against
Women"; the commission of a Panel on Violence Against Women; new
research funding on family violence; and, importantly, two failed
attempts to pass tough pornography laws (Levan, this volume).

These moves do recognize sexual violence as a social problem and one worthy of government intervention. Nevertheless, and much like the moral-purity discourse of the last century, the violence initiatives also promote an image of women as silent and passive "victims" and idealize the state as "protector." On the whole, recent violence initiatives participate in the creation of a climate of sexual fear, partake in a radical simplification of gender relations, and operate to contain women within the narrow band of "safety" afforded through the "protectionist" activities of the state (Pidduck, 1994, pp. 7–8, 10–12). At the same time, however, feminist organizations have been deemed special-interest groups, incapable of representing women's true interests. As a result, a whole series of feminist-run projects on sexual violence have suffered in the wake of federal funding cuts (NAC, 1990; Gotell, 1993, p. 450).

In sum, in the context of the decline of the Keynesian state, anti-pornography politics, like the broader law-and-order agenda in which they are inscribed, become hugely seductive to neoconservative and to other political actors. Law-and-order policy presents itself as a means of appearing concerned with popular anxieties; at the same time, however, it avoids the discredited policy instrument of social spending. It is here that we must situate recent attempts to pass tough anti-pornography laws, as well as the broad partisan support for new anti-pornography policy.

SHIFT TO THE COURTS: LEAF, *BUTLER*, AND PORNOGRAPHY

Legislative decisions to set aside obscenity law reform did not mean a deescalation of pornography struggles nor an end to the what I have termed the new politics of anti-pornography. Conflicts over pornography continued unabated in the wake of defeated bills and altered political agendas. As both cause and effect of this ongoing struggle, Canada's criminal obscenity law was widely perceived as lacking legitimacy. And despite legislative stalements on this issue, political commitments to anti-pornography policy did not subside. In the absence of a definitive political response, however, pornography struggles moved into to the courts.

The Charter: A New Role for the Courts in Obscenity Law

As we have seen, the legal arena has always been a key site for the elaboration and development of obscenity policy. In many ways, then, this shift to the courts represented a continuation of long-established patterns. Yet the entrenchment of the Charter of Rights in the Canadian constitution signalled a new and more authoritative role for the judiciary in the realm of obscenity policy. Given the Charter's protection of expression rights (s. 2(b)), it was inevitable that obscenity legislation would be the object of a constitutional challenge (see Box 11.3). Nevertheless, because the Charter also recognizes that rights may be reasonably limited (s. 1) and because of its guarantees of sexual equality (ss. 15 and 28), the results of such a challenge were not easy to predict. In effect, constitutional support for most sides of the pornography debate could be found in the text of Charter.

The New Feminist Politics of Anti-Pornography

During the 1980s, there occurred an escalation of feminist anti-pornography struggles in the United States, Britain, and Canada (Lacombe, 1994, p. 29; Vance, 1993a and 1993b; Frug, 1992, pp. 145–153; Wilson, 1993, p. 18). As feminist anti-pornography campaigns have intensified, they have also become more focussed and more fundamentalist in their claims about pornography and women's oppression. There has been a shift from an effort to understand women's sexuality and how we internalize oppressive notions of femininity, toward a simpler view which squarely blames pornography for creating a climate of sexual violence (Wilson, 1993, p. 18). As Lacombe notes, the feminist campaign against pornography "increasingly neglected to address the complexity of social relations organizing sexism, thus betraying its original premise that pornography is a product of sexism" (1994, p. 29). Instead, pornography has been deemed the ultimate foundation of women's oppression.

Explaining the New Fundamentalism: Feminist Anxieties

In attempting to account for this shift to a more fundamentalist discourse, Merck and Wilson both suggest that the recent trends within anti-pornography feminism may represent a response to current uncertainties

---

BOX 11.3

R v. *Butler* The first constitutional challenge to obscenity law to reach the Supreme Court was *R.* v. *Butler*, a case involving criminal charges laid against a Manitoba video store. What was perhaps most significant about this case was the nature and apparent influence of anti-pornography feminist discourse on the Court's decision and reasoning. In *Butler*, the feminist litigation organization **LEAF** intervened to advance an unequivocally anti-pornography and pro-censorship position. If the 1980s witnessed the dawn of a new politics of anti-pornography, so too did LEAF's position in *Butler* express a new feminist politics of anti-pornography. This politics was, at once, more intractable and highly sweeping in its assertions.

(Merck, 1993, p. 60; Wilson, 1993, p. 28). As we have seen, at the level of the state, moves to regulate obscenity and to restrict pornography have been motivated by fears of social instability and moral disorder. The New Right, for its part, has also embraced anti-pornography politics in reaction to anxieties about decline—in particular, about the decline of the nuclear family. The more fundamentalist orientation of feminist anti-pornography politics can also be understood as a reaction to instability—specifically, to the political splits and reversals that have beset the feminist movement over the last fifteen years.

As this volume illustrates, feminism occupies a highly tenuous position within the current political context. The rise of neoconservatism as a new governing consensus has meant the erosion of many of the women's movement's early political gains. In addition, conflicts within feminism have escalated. Both feminist theory and feminist strategy have been exposed as representing a narrow set of concerns, reflecting the experiences of White, middle-class, Western, and able-bodied women (Gabriel, this volume). In short, struggles around differences among women and the exclusive character of much feminist politics have made it increasingly difficult to speak of feminism in singular or universal terms (Flax, 1990, p. 50). One reaction to these current conflicts is to embrace diversity and to try to craft a feminist politics which is more attentive to differences, and necessarily more complex. Another reaction is to retreat to the safety of universal claims and fundamentalist approaches in the attempt to re-create some principle of feminist unity (Brown, 1991, p. 64).

The new feminist politics of anti-pornography may be understood as exemplifying the latter strategy. It reflects a politics of simplified certainty in which the complexities of sexuality are reduced to an assertion of male domination and pornography is constructed as both the ideological support and the expression of male sexual power. Pornography is a particularly clean site for demonstrating the practice of feminist theoretical insight (Frug, 1992, p. 151). It remains exceedingly difficult to illustrate, for example, the complex nature of women's positions in the economy and in the labour force. By contrast, anti-pornography feminism's claim that sexuality is the linchpin of male domination can be graphically illustrated through the ritualistic showing of pornographic slides with women being tortured and beaten (Kaminer, 1992, p. 116). This is asserted as the "Truth" of pornography and any feminist position which challenges this "Truth" is presented as being not really feminist at all (see MacKinnon, 1987). In short, Wilson describes the new feminist politics of anti-pornography as a form of secular fundamentalism, "a way of life, or a world-view ... which insists that the individual lives by narrowly prescribed rules ... a faith that offers certainty." As she explains, although "the search for a new life can be exhilarating,... it can also lead to anxiety." But fundamentalism, even in its feminist guises, also has its price; the price paid for certainty is rigidity and intolerance for those who question foundational "truths" (1993, pp. 28–29).

Law's Truth and Categorical Claims

On one level, then, we might explain LEAF's embrace of the new feminist politics of anti-pornography in *Butler* as a search for a feminist grounding in an unstable world. On another level, the character of LEAF's intervention must be seen in relation to the nature of legal discourse itself. As pornography struggles shift into the courts, social groups who wish to influence judicial responses must couch their arguments in a language and structure compatible with law. As some feminist theorists have emphasized, law's power rests on its promise to determine the "truth" of social events. Law claims to be "objective," to be able to determine true from false. For this reason, legal arguments which can assert "truth," and which can present simple, certain, and clear assertions of social reality, are likely to be privileged within legal discourse. In effect, law seems to hear feminists best when they can speak in authoritative tones (Smart, 1989, p. 71).

Anti-Pornography Feminism in the Courts: LEAF'S Intervention

In *Butler*, LEAF intervened on the side of the federal government to defend the existing obscenity law against a Charter freedom-of-expression challenge. Despite the continued and contentious debates within Canadian feminism on pornography and censorship, LEAF made the decision to intervene in this case without the benefit of outside consultations and the tone of its factum is unequivocal. The absence of consultations with other women's groups may seem surprising, because LEAF, as a litigation organization devoted to advancing women's Charter equality claims, is widely perceived as a constitutional voice of Canadian feminism. Nevertheless, for much of LEAF's history, links of accountability with other feminist organizations have not been well established. In the absence of formalized consultation procedures, LEAF's authority has often rested on an assertion of legal expertise (Gotell, 1993, Chap. 4).

Familiar Arguments as Charter Claims

In its intervention in *Butler*, LEAF articulated many of the familiar arguments of anti-pornography feminism, but reframed these claims in the language of Charter rights. The first thread of LEAF's argument in *Butler* was to contend that women are subordinate group and to insist that it is from this context that pornography and obscenity law must be assessed (LEAF, 1991, p. 7, p. 17). When viewed from the standpoint of women, the impact of pornography is clear, according to LEAF; it is degrading and dehumanizing. In fact, it is in these terms that pornography is defined—"a systemic practice of exploitation and subordination based on sex that differentially harms women" (1991, p. 7). The harms of pornography emphasized in the LEAF factum include: direct physical violence used to make some pornography; connections between pornography and violence against women; and the way in which pornography creates a social climate of disrespect for women. On this basis, pornography is presented as a violent form of expression, a form of hate propaganda and thus not protected under the Charter. Given its claim that pornography contributes to the social context of women's disadvantage, LEAF contended that state censorship of pornography through obscenity legislation is constitutionally mandated (1991, p. 7).

In effect, through this intervention LEAF deployed Charter guarantees of sexual equality to argue for the maintenance of state regulation of obscenity. But consistent with the overall thrust of anti-pornography feminism, LEAF sought to reframe the moral rationale of obscenity law. Specifically, LEAF encouraged the Supreme Court to adopt a harms-based test for determining obscenity. Obscenity under this test would be defined as material which is "dehumanizing, degrading, subordinating and dangerous for women" (LEAF, 1991, p. 6). When interpreted through this approach, LEAF contended, the Criminal Code's obscenity provision is "neither vague nor over broad" (1991, p. 19).

LEAF and the New Feminist Politics of Anti-Pornography

If LEAF's intervention rearticulated many long-established themes of anti-pornography feminism, so too did it reflect the newer and more fundamentalist orientation of this position. An appeal to "truth" grounds this intervention in several important ways:

▶ First of all, LEAF's position is presented in categorical terms, as if it were revealing a singular feminist "truth" to the judiciary—"prohibiting pornography promotes equality" (LEAF, 1991, p. 17). The *Butler* factum embodies the characteristic narrative style of legal argument—it is closed and unequivocal; it refuses contingency and complexity.

▶ Second, and much like the Conservatives' pornography bills, LEAF's factum relies on a literalist interpretation of pornography. In this view, the pornographic possesses a singular and universal meaning, readily apparent to anyone. The importance of context and personal experience in the interpretation of sexual imagery is thus effectively denied. The task of defining what is "degrading and dehumanizing" is seen to be open to objective legal determination.

▶ Third, the factum uses social science research to make the claim that pornography promotes sexual violence and contends that "it is uncontroversial that exposure to such materials causes aggression towards women in laboratory settings" (LEAF, 1991, p. 11). This research is, however, extremely controversial (McCormack, 1993, p. 311). It has been plagued by methodological problems and inconclusive results (King, 1993, pp. 57–72). According to the report of the Fraser Committee, there is no pursuasive evidence that pornography is causally related to sexual violence (Canada, Special Committee on Pornography and Prostiution, 1985, p. 99). A 1990 British inquiry reached a similar conclusion (*Toronto Star*, October 29, 1994, p. L7). In contrast to LEAF's assertions, then, this resrach is inconclusive or, at the very least, open to conflicting interpretations.

In these ways, LEAF's intervention shrouded what is a particular feminist position and approach under the guise of "objectivity" and "truth." Its factum denied the complexity of feminist debates around pornography and censorship.

As if to add moral force to its already categorical assertions, LEAF also made the claim that women are "victimized" by pornography. Underlying its position is a view of sexuality as domination and of pornography as being about the domination of women by men. Within this repressive view of power, women are constructed as "victims," passive "objects" of male sexual domination. The "passive victim" is deployed here in strikingly similar terms as within Tory violence rhetoric. Echoing nineteenth-century moral-purity discourse, women's powerlessness becomes moral rationale for their protection through law. In this process, however, both women's sexual desire and their political agency are erased (Wilson, 1993, p. 27).

The *Butler* Decision: Old Morality/ New Feminist Justification

The Supreme Court's 1992 decision in *Butler* appeared to lay to rest moves for pornography law reform and, some have argued, succeeded in transforming the old conservative foundations of obscenity policy (Busby, 1994). In affirming the constitutionality of existing criminal obscenity provisions, the Court condemned further legislative efforts to criminalize obscenity, emphasizing the illusive character of "pornography" and, consequently, the impossibility of greater legislative precision (*R. v. Butler* [1992], 8 CRR [2d] 1 [SCC] p. 506). While this case had provided a forum for the articulation of conflicting perspectives on pornography and censorship, including interventions by civil-libertarian and conservative groups, the Court appeared most influenced by LEAF's anti-pornography position. Despite its embrace of feminist rhetoric, however, the Supreme Court did not completely uproot the older conservative moral basis of obscenity legislation. Instead, it seems as if the *Butler* decision may have achieved what previous legislative efforts had failed to do—that is, the reinscribing of obscenity policy within a new and modernized feminist rhetoric.

310 PART III RESTRUCTURING PRIVATE LIFE

A Feminist Victory? A Harms-Based Approach

LEAF's claim that degradation is the "truth" of pornography did carry some force in the Supreme Court. In the *Butler* decision, the Court upheld the obscenity legislation, arguing that it constituted a reasonable limit on the Charter's guarantee of freedom of expression. In so doing, however, the Court effectively altered the objective of s. 163 of the Criminal Code. Purporting to reject "moral" standards for determining criminal obscenity, the decision embraced an approach which defines obscenity as material that exploits sex in a "degrading and dehumanizing manner" (*R. v. Butler*, p. 596). Here, the Supreme Court's thinking appeared clearly influenced by LEAF's factum; as the decision stated, "Among other things, degrading or dehumanizing materials place women (and sometimes men) in positions of subordination, servile submission or humiliation. They run against the principles of equality and dignity of all human beings" (ibid.). This is the basis for the claim that *Butler* represents a feminist victory—a legal recognition of the goal of gender equality in the context of the pornography debate.

Moral Foundations Affirmed

The Court's shift of emphasis from "decency" to "harm" and "equality," however, coexists with an affirmation of a more traditional conservative sexual morality. As Cossman (1994) has illustrated, underlying this decision is a profoundly "moralistic" sexual subtext. The majority decision is riddled with references to sex as "base" and "dirty." Sexual materials which are not produced for some "meritorious" purpose (artistic, literary, or educational) thus represent, in the Court's view, lesser forms of expression.

In addition, while the decision undeniably imported feminist anti-pornography discourse into the meaning of obscenity, the test established to define what is "degrading and dehumanizing" remains profoundly conservative. In *Butler*, the Court restated the validity of the community standards test, suggesting that the standard to be applied is a national one (p. 595). Further, in explaining how judges should determine what is "degrading," the decision contended that that which is harmful is degrading. And harm, according to the Court, means materials that predispose "persons to act in an anti-social manner"—that is, conduct which "society formally recognizes as incompatible with its proper functioning" (pp. 600–601).

The notion of "anti-social conduct," together with *Butler's* embrace of a national community standard, invites those who apply obscenity law to restrict sexual representations that challenge dominant sexual norms. In this manner, the decision appears to condone the long-established foundations of Canada's criminal obscenity regime. Obscenity is viewed as something that offends a "common morality" and incites people to act in ways which threaten this moral order. In effect, while

Butler may have opened a new chapter in Canadian obscenity law, it may not constitute a complete break from the past.

Aftermath: Obscenity Chill

The aftermath of *Butler* appears to confirm this interpretation—that is, that the decision does not entirely uproot the older, moral basis of Canada's obscenity law. It is in the context of gay and lesbian sexual representations that we can most clearly observe the extent to which obscenity law is still based on the legal regulation of morality. In the first cases following *Butler*, the *Glad Day Bookshop* case and the *Scythes* case, the words "degrading" and "dehumanizing" were applied in a very decontextualized and arbitrary manner to deem several gay and lesbian pornographic works criminally obscene (*Glad Day Bookshop Inc.* v. *Canada* (14 July 1992), Toronto 619/90 [OJC]; *R.* v. *Scythes* (16 January 1993), Toronto [OCJ] [unreported]; Cossman, 1994, pp. 28–37; Toobin, 1994). The sexual morality underlying the Supreme Court's *Butler* decision frames and sets the context for these lower-court decisions (Cossman, 1994, pp. 27–28). Given the heterosexist bias which underpins the sexual norms of the Canadian community, it was not surprising that gay and lesbian sexual representations would continue to be viewed as more offensive to community standards, as "anti-social" and, therefore, "degrading."

While it may still be early to predict the impact of *Butler* for legal interpretation, defence lawyers describe the re-emergence of an "obscenity chill," existing underneath and prior to the judicial arena. Most important, police and Customs's particular scrutiny of gay and lesbian sexual materials has continued in the wake of the Supreme Court decision (Barclay, 1992–93; MacKinnon and Dworkin, 1994, p. 2; Toobin, 1994, pp. 72–74).[6] Less visible, but equally important, *Butler* has also promoted a climate of "censorship" fear, in which those who produce sexual images are increasingly reluctant to exhibit their work and galleries are reticent to display this work (Barclay, 1992–93, p. 19).

As this chapter has demonstrated, the repression of marginal sexual voices preceded *Butler*; but it is possible that this decision condones and may intensify this silencing. In affirming the validity of obscenity legislation, the Supreme Court bestowed new legitimacy on a law that lacked legitimacy; it gave a new, contemporary and feminist rationale to a law rooted in sexual morality.

CONCLUSION

The criminal regulation of obscenity in Canada has long been framed within a discourse of conservative moralism. While feminist interventions in the pornography have challenged this discourse, the story of obscenity law suggests that these moral foundations may be difficult to disrupt.

As this essay has demonstrated, the old politics of obscenity and the new politics of anti-pornography share certain common characteristics. Both emerged within contexts of social and "moral" disruption; both seek to re-create stability in an unstable world; both imagine women as passive "victims"; and both participate in moral regulation by seeking to criminalize sexual representations that offend the, albeit, evolving moral order. What marks the new politics of anti-pornography as distinct from the old politics of obscenity, as we have seen, is an emphasis on anti-pornography feminist assertions of sexual harm. Nevertheless, from the Tories' "sexual violence" initiatives, to the Supreme Court's decision in *Butler*, older discourses of sexual moralism continue to resonate alongside new gestures to anti-pornography feminism.

Overall, these shifts in pornography politics and obscenity regulation suggest complexity, ongoing contradiction and, therefore, the insufficiency of interpretations which assert a feminist-inspired transformation of this policy area. To be certain, the "official" recognition of sexual equality within the context of the pornography debate does represent a partial feminist victory. But the inscription of feminist rhetoric within conservative and morally based political and legal discourses also illustrates the dangers of co-optation.

The impact of the *Butler* decision, as a turning point in struggles around pornography, is not yet certain and will depend upon ongoing social conflicts and mobilization. The Canadian state's efforts to regulate obscenity will also continue to be marked by disunity. While the post-*Butler* legal terrain is still taking shape, it is clear that this decision has had the effect of granting official legitimacy both to anti-pornography feminist claims and to the criminal regulation of obscenity.

Because of this, *Butler* has inspired new mobilization by anti-censorship feminists. Since *Butler*, LEAF's anti-pornography intervention has repeatedly been challenged by a diverse group of feminists who resist the construct "women as victims" and all that it entails. These women, among them artists, writers, lesbians, bookstore and media workers, and sex-trade workers, have reacted with outrage to LEAF's whole-hearted support for state censorship through criminal obscenity legislation.[7] Anti-censorship feminists contend that, far from constituting a feminist legal victory, *Butler* merely provides a new feminist language to legitimize and modernize what is really an old conservative, moral agenda.

As anti-censorship feminist critics remind us, the meaning of sexual images, like their effects, is not always clear. For this reason, sexual representations remain the focus for a struggle over meaning, and the impact of state censorship for such struggles could be repressive. State censorship can close off spaces for feminist conversations about sexuality, just as it has tended to forestall efforts to create alternative sexual images. In conclusion, sexuality is a critical field of feminist struggle; pornography, as one way in which sexuality gets represented, will continue to occupy an important, if always contradictory, space in attempts to disrupt sexual norms. Consequently, support for criminal obscenity regulation, even though cloaked under a new rhetoric of sexual harm, should be approached with some caution.

NOTES

1. I do not mean to suggest that an absence of democratic debate and social scrutiny is a precondition of effective policy-making. Nevertheless, particularly in policy areas which have been identified with morality, legislatures have often found it very difficult to act when there is widespread politicization and social division on an issue. A similar pattern has been observed with abortion policy.

2. As Lacombe documents, anti-pornography feminist organizations entered into formal alliances with Right organizations during the 1980s, working closely with churches and other groups in the anti-pornography campaign. In 1984, for example, a symposium on media violence held in Toronto brought together several feminist and conservative organizations (Lacombe, 1994, pp. 47, 52–53).

3. For a discussion and analysis of Bills C-114 and C-54, see Campbell and Pal, 1989, pp. 135–150, and Lacombe, 1994, pp. 99–136).

4. This approach is based on the notion that pornography has a clear and unambiguous meaning that depends neither on context nor on the perspective of the consumer. For a discussion and critique of this approach, see Vance, 1993b, pp. 39–45, and Arcand, 1991, pp. 24–25.

5. This is the explanation put forward by Campbell and Pal (1989).

6. In a 1994 interview, the manager of Glad Day Bookshop, one of Canada's few gay bookstores, indicated that at least one in four of their shipments continues to be seized by Canada Customs (Toobin 1994, p. 72). Canada Customs has admitted in the press that it has not altered any of its policies or practices to conform to *Butler*'s harms-based approach to obscenity (MacKinnon and Dworkin, 1994, p. 2).

7. According to artist Elaine Carol, anti-censorship feminist activists in groups such as Ontario Coalition Against Film and Video Censorship (OCAFVC) and Censorstop reacted with shock to the *Butler* decision and to the position which LEAF had taken in it. These women formed a task force charged with contacting LEAF to

voice criticism and setting up a meeting with LEAF to "call it to task." Ultimately, these anti-censorship feminists formed an Ad Hoc Coalition of Anti-Censorship Women which drew together representatives from OCFVAC, Censorstop, Maggies (a group of sex-trade workers), the Lesbian and Gay Film Festival, *Fireweed* (a feminist periodical), Toronto Women's Bookstore, Playwrights Union of Canada, York University Centre for Feminist Research, Glad Day Bookshop, and lawyers and academics (Interview, Elaine Carol, June 6, 1993; Minutes of meeting, Ad Hoc Coalition of Anti-Censorship Women, June 17, 1993).

REFERENCES

Arcand, Bernard. (1991). *The jaguar and the anteater: Pornography and the modern world.* Toronto: McClelland and Stewart.

Barclay, Claire. (1992–93). Obscenity chill—Artists in a post-*Butler* era. *Fuse, 16* (2).

Bearchell, Chris. (1993). Gender bender: Cut that out. *This Magazine, 26.*

Berger, Ronald; Searles, Patricia; and Cottle, Charles. (1991). *Feminism and pornography.* New York: Praeger.

Brodie, Janine. (1994, March). Politics on the boundaries: Restructuring and the Canadian women's movement. Eighth Annual Robarts Lecture, York University.

Brown, Wendy. (1991). Feminist hesitations, postmodern exposures. *Differences, 5.*

Burstyn, Varda. (1985). *Women against censorship.* Vancouver: Douglas and McIntyre.

Busby, Karen. (1994). LEAF and pornography: Litigating on equality and sexual representations. *Canadian Journal of Law and Society, 9* (1).

Campbell, Robert, and Pal, Leslie. (1989). *The real worlds of Canadian politics.* Peterborough: Broadview.

Canada, House of Commons, Standing Committee on Justice and Legal Affairs. (1978). *Report on pornography.* Ottawa: Queen's Printer.

Canada, Special Committee on Pornography and Prostitution. (1985). *Report* (Vols. 1 and 2). Ottawa: Queen's Printer.

Canadian Advisory Council on the Status of Women.(1988). Pornography: An analysis of proposed legislation (Bill C-54). Ottawa: Queen's Printer.

Cole, Susan. (1989). *Pornography and the sex crisis.* Toronto: Amanita.

Cossman, Brenda. (1994). Feminist fashion or morality in drag? The sexual subtext of the Butler decision. Unpublished paper, Osgoode Hall Law School.

Currie, Dawn. (1992). Representation and resistance: Feminist struggles against pornography. In D. Currie and V. Raoul (Eds.), *The anatomy of gender.* Ottawa: Carleton University Press.

Erwin, Lorna. (1988). Challenging feminism: The organized antifeminist back-lash. *Resources for Feminist Research, 17* (3).

Flax, Jane. (1990). Postmodernism and gender relations in feminist theory. In L. Nicholson (Ed.), *Feminism/postmodernism.* New York: Routledge.

Frug, Mary Joe. (1992). *Postmodern legal feminism.* New York: Routledge.

Gamble, Andrew. (1988). *The free economy and the strong state.* London: Macmillan.

Gilmour, Don. (1993, March). Strange customs. *Saturday Night.*

Glad Day Bookshop Inc. v. *Canada* (14 July 1992), Toronto 619/90 (OJC).

Gotell, Lise. *Feminism, equality rights and the Charter of Rights and Freedoms in English Canada.* Ph.D. dissertation, Department of Political Science, York University, Toronto.

Kaminer, Wendy. (1992, November). Feminists against the First Amendment. *The Atlantic Monthly.*

King, Allison. (1993). Mystery and imagination: The case of pornography effects studies. In A. Assiter and Avedon Carol (Eds.), *Bad girls and dirty pictures: The challenge to reclaim feminism.* London: Pluto.

Kinsman, Gary, and Brock, Deborah. (1985). Porn/censor wars and the battle-fields of sex. In *Issues of censorship.* Toronto: A Space.

Lacombe, Dany. (1988). *Ideology and public policy.* Toronto: Garamond.

Lacombe, Dany. (1994). *Blue politics: Pornography and the law.* Toronto: University of Toronto.

Law Reform Commission of Canada. (1975). *Limits of the criminal law: Obscenity.* Working paper no. 10. Ottawa: Law Reform Commission of Canada.

LEAF. (1991). Factum of the intervenor, the Women's Legal Education and Action Fund. *Butler* v. *Her Majesty the Queen.* 1991 (SCC), court file number 22191.

MacKinnon, Catherine, and Dworkin, Andrea. (1994, August 26). *Statement by Catherine A. MacKinnon and Andrea Dworkin regarding Canada Customs and legal approaches to pornography.*

MacKinnon, Catherine. (1987). *"On Collaboration": Feminism unmodified.* Cambridge, MA: Harvard University Press.

MacKinnon, Catherine. (1989). *Towards a feminist theory of the state.* Cambridge, MA: Harvard University Press.

MacKinnon, Catherine. (1993). *Only words.* Cambridge, MA: Harvard University Press.

McBride, Stephen, and Shields, John. (1993). *Dismantling a nation.* Halifax: Fernwood.

McCormack, Thelma. (1993). If pornography is the theory, is inequality the prac-tice? *Philosophy of the Social Sciences, 23* (3).

Merck, Mandy. (1993). From Minneapolis to Westminster. In L. Segal and M. McIntosh (Eds.), *Sex exposed: Sexuality and the pornography debate.* New Brunswick, NJ: Rutgers University Press.

Mort, Frank. (1987). *Dangerous sexualities*. London: Routledge and Kegan Paul.

NAC. (1990). *We're worth more*. Toronto: National Action Committee on the Status of Women.

Petchesky, Rosalind. (1984). *Abortion and women's choice*. Boston: Northeastern University Press.

Pidduck, Julianne. (1984). *Feminist rhetoric on violence against women and the production of everyday fear*. Paper prepared for the York University Feminist Political Science Conference, Toronto.

R. v. *Brodie* (1962), SCR 681.

R. v. *Butler* (1992), 8 CRR (2d) 1 (SCC).

R. v. *Doug Rankine Co.* (1983), 9 CCC (3d) 53.

R. v. *Hicklin* (1868), 3 L.R. Q.B. 360.

R. v. *Scythes* (16 January 1993), Toronto (OJC) (unreported).

R. v. *Towne Cinema Theatres* (1985), 18 CCC (3d) 193.

Rubin, Gayle. (1993). Thinking sex: Notes for a radical theory of the politics of sexuality. In H. Abelove et al. (Eds.), *The lesbian and gay studies reader*. New York: Routledge.

Scheier, Libby. (1988, June). Bill C-54: Tying tongues. *Saturday Night*.

Shaver, Frances. (1994). The regulation of prostitution. *Canadian Journal of Law and Society, 9* (1).

Smart, Carol. (1989). *Feminism and the power of law*. London: Routledge.

Toobin, Jeffrey. (1994, October 3). X-rated. *The New Yorker*.

Valverde, Marianne, and Weir, Lorna. (1988). The struggles of the immoral: preliminary remarks on moral regulation. *Resources for Feminist Research, 17* (3).

Vance, Carol. (1993a). Feminist fundamentalism—women against images. *Art in America, 29*.

Vance, Carol. (1993b). Negotiating sex and gender in the Attorney General's Commission on Pornography. In L. Segal and M. McIntosh (Eds.), *Sex exposed: Sexuality and the pornography debate*. New Brunswick, NJ: Rutgers University Press.

Whitaker, Reg. (1987). Neo-conservatism and the state. In R. Miliband and J. Saville (Eds.), *The socialist register, 1987*. London: Merlin.

Wilson, Elizabeth. (1993). Feminist Fundamentalism: The shifting politics of sex and censorship. In L. Segal And M. Mcintosh (Eds.), *Sex Exposed: Sexuality and the pornography debate*. New Brunswick, NJ: Rutgers University Press.

SUGGESTED READING

Arcand, Bernard. (1991). *The jaguar and the anteater: Pornography and the modern world*. Toronto: McClelland and Stewart.

Assiter, Alison, and Avedon, Carol. (Eds.). (1993). *Bad girls and dirty pictures: The challenge to reclaim feminism*. London: Pluto.

Berger, Ronald; Searles, Patricia; and Cottle, Charles. (1991). *Feminism and pornography*. New York: Praeger.

Burstyn, Varda. (1985). *Women against censorship*. Vancouver: Douglas and McIntyre.

Busby, Karen. (1994). LEAF and pornography: Litigating on equality and sexual representations. *Canadian Journal of Law and Society, 9* (1).

Cole, Susan. (1989). *Pornography and the sex crisis*. Toronto: Amanita.

Lacombe, Dany. (1994). *Blue politics: Pornography and the law*. Toronto: University of Toronto Press.

MacKinnon, Catherine. (1993). *Only words*. Cambridge, MA: Harvard University Press.

McCormack, Thelma. (1993). If pornography is the theory, is inequality the practice? *Philosophy of the Social Sciences, 23* (3).

Segal, Lynne, and McIntosh, Mary. (Eds.). (1993). *Sex exposed: Sexuality and the pornography debate*. New Brunswick, NJ: Rutgers University Press.

QUESTIONS TO CONSIDER

1. Discuss the implications for women of conservative moral discourse on obscenity.

2. What are the similarities and differences between the old obscenity politics and the new politics of anti-pornography?

3. Explain the relationship between law-and-order policy and moves to toughen obscenity laws.

4. What are the implications of state disunity for obscenity policy?

5. Discuss the contradictory nature and implications of the Supreme Court's *Butler* decision. Can *Butler* be seen as an unequivocal feminist victory? What are some positive and some negative aspects of this decision?

6. Compare and contrast contending feminist positions on pornography.

CHAPTER 12

Violence Against Women

Andrea Levan

The establishment of the Canadian Panel on Violence Against Women in 1991 marked more than two decades of struggle between feminists and the state to recognize, define, and develop policy to address violence against women. Since the report of the Royal Commission on the Status of Women (RCSW) (1970) twenty years before, which had been virtually silent on the subject, feminists had come to understand violence against women as a pervasive problem with important implications for women's equality. However, policy tended to evolve piecemeal, focussing on particular forms of violence (such as wife battering) and conceptualizing them as problems faced by individual victims. Further, it was assumed that these problems could be ameliorated by reforming the law. As feminists developed a theoretical understanding of the systemic causes of violence against women and the common links between its various forms, they became increasingly critical of what they perceived to be the state's "tinkering" approach.

These tensions crystallized in the aftermath of the Montreal Massacre. For the first time, feminist analysis of the problem gained wide currency. Theoretical disagreements about both the meaning, extent, and causes of violence against women, and the strategies that should be put in place to eliminate it, quickly came to dominate the public discourse. The decision to set up a panel that would consider these questions and investigate the issue as a whole represented a significant change from earlier policy and was something of a victory for feminists. Some groups reacted with cautious optimism. Others, however, saw the process as just another in a long series of consultations and reports the state had used to contain protest while appearing to be responsive. Given the theoretical problems and unresolved debates that had been developing over twenty years of policy-making, it is not surprising that the panel's activity was characterized by divisions and a lack of credibility. Five major national women's organizations withdrew their support from the process a few months before the final report was published, and the report itself was bitterly criticized for its unwieldy plan of action, including nearly 500 unprioritized recommendations. The process resulted in further polarization, and it remains to be seen what the long-term consequences will be.

THE 1970S: BUREAUCRATIZATION OF WOMEN'S ISSUES

Although its profound silence about women's experience of violence is shocking from a modern perspective, the RCSW (1967–70) is still the formative event in the development of Canadian government policy on women and had an important influence on how policy on violence against women would develop. The report covers many areas of Canadian life such as the family, the economy, taxation, immigration, education, child care, and the participation of women in public life. The terms of reference of the commission clearly limited the inquiry to economic matters and questions of equal opportunity, and these priorities determined the pattern of state policy in reference to women through the 1970s. In addition, especially in the first half of the decade, energies were directed toward the creation of new women's organizations and bureaucratic structures within the federal government to deal with issues made visible by the report (see Table 12.1). Women's groups who had participated in the call for a royal commission also tended to support its agenda for action. It took some years before the women's movement moved beyond the agenda of the RCSW to issues considered historically to be private matters (including violence issues such as rape, wife-battering, and pornography). For example, the National Action Committee on the Status of Women (NAC), a coalition of women's groups founded in 1972 to monitor and pressure the government to ensure that the recommendations would be carried out, did not begin to function as a policy-making entity until the end of the 1970s (Vickers, Rankin, and Appelle, 1993, Chap. 2). NAC's policy on violence also developed piecemeal in response to various government legislation. Indeed, it was not until the 1994 annual general meeting that the first comprehensive policy document was put before the floor.

According to Sue Findlay, one of the most important outcomes of the RCSW was that a majority of women came to believe that the government would respond to their concerns if faced with appropriate pressure, and liberal feminism became the "public face" of the women's movement (1988, p. 31). Organizations such as NAC and the National Association of Women and the Law (NAWL), founded in 1975, adopted a strategy of lobbying and submitting briefs that was welcomed by the

TABLE 12.1
THE 1970s—KEY EVENTS

1970	Royal Commission on the Status of Women report
	Coordinator on the Status of Women is placed in the Privy Council Office
1971	Minister Responsible for the Status of Women is appointed
	First women's centres in Canada
1972	First rape crisis centre in Canada
	First transition house in Canada
	NAC is founded at "Strategy for Change" conference
1973	CACSW is established
1975	United Nations International Women's Year
	NAWL is founded
1976	Bill C-71 (sexual assault) is in force
1978	Standing Committee on Justice and Legal Affairs report on pornography
	Bill C-52 (sexual assault) is introduced, never passed
	Constitutional Amendment Bill containing Charter is introduced into the House
	Law Reform Commission of Canada report on Sexual Offences
	Bill C-51 (pornography) is introduced, never passed
	Supreme Court decision *R. v. Hutt* (narrow interpretation of soliciting makes it difficult to prosecute street prostitutes)
1979	*Towards equality for women.* As part of a response to the U.N. World Plan of Action, the government publishes its first policy statement on violence against women.

government, but which in the long run served to marginalize grass-roots groups, including most of those active on violence issues, who used more confrontational tactics and were more vocal in their insistence on systemic reform. Findlay argues that an analysis of the period after the RCSW shows not only the success of the women's movement in pressuring the state to respond to their demands for equality, but also "the success of the state in constructing this representation in a way that controlled women's demands and limited reforms" (1987, p. 33). One method of containing reform was to segregate and disperse women's issues throughout the federal bureaucracy.

As a direct result of the RCSW, government structures were created to deal with women's issues. In 1970, a Co-ordinator on the Status of Women was placed in the Privy Council Office, and a Minister Responsible for the Status of Women was appointed in 1971. The Women's Program in the Office of the Secretary of State was established as the main funding body for women's groups. In addition, women's advisors were placed in the ministries of Justice, Employment and Immigration, and Health and Welfare. However, these offices had little formal communication with one another and had little formal connection to the women's movement, except for the Women's Program. Similarly, the Canadian Advisory Council on the Status of Women (CACSW), established in 1973 as a direct result of a recommendation in the royal commission report, has had little credibility with the women's movement, although it has produced some useful research. It has suffered from its lack of real influence and has been perceived as feminist from within the bureaucracy and subject to state interference from without.

The Women's Program gained credibility with feminist organizations in the mid-1970s because it was originally staffed by feminists who had strong connections to the movement. The program was given a particular impetus in International Women's Year (1975), when it was responsible for distributing $2.5 million to women's projects. Women's Program funding was widely used to help establish or stabilize feminist organizations such as women's centres (first established in Canada in 1971), rape crisis centres (1972 and after), and transition houses (also 1972), which were front-line service providers to women victims of violence. The Women's Program also played a role in the formation of the Canadian Association of Sexual Assault Centres (CASAC). The first national convention in 1975 was funded by a grant in International Women's Year. A "national assister" was put in place with special funds from the Department of Health and Welfare in order to co-ordinate the activities of fledgling rape crisis centres (Kasinsky, 1978).

By the late 1970s, however, the influence of the Women's Program began to wane. In 1976, the Office of Co-ordinator of Status of Women was moved from the Privy Council Office and given independent responsibility, reporting directly to the Minister Responsible for the Status of Women (Findlay, 1988, p. 43). It assumed a major role in developing the first federal plan of action on women's issues, *Towards Equality for Women* (Status of Women Canada, 1979). This was the first federal document to identify violence against women as a priority issue. In contrast to government practice in the earlier years, neither the CACSW nor representatives from the women's movement were consulted in writing this plan. Sue Findlay states that "the final plan is correctly seen as a political decision to limit reform policies," making no reference to day care, abortion, or mandatory affirmative action, issues that were the major focus of the organized women's movement (1987, p. 46). With respect to violence against women, some key recommendations include a promise to undertake a major study on the problem, to establish a national clearinghouse of information, and to review amendments to the Criminal Code related to the offence of rape. Status of Women Canada emerged from the exercise with a stronger, better-defined mandate, including a Cabinet directive to co-ordinate federal policies on sexual violence.

THE 1980S: THE EMERGENCE OF FIVE POLICY ISSUES

Sexual Assault

Although *Towards equality for women* had referred to violence against women in general, during the 1980s federal policy focussed on several distinct issues that were subject to different bureaucratic jurisdictions (see Table 12.2). The first issue to emerge was rape. Partly because some brief references had been made to it in the RCSW report, the Minister of Justice proposed changes to the rape law as early as September 1974. Passed in 1976, these changes were designed to limit questioning about the past sexual conduct of the victim. The reforms had little real effect, however, and pressure continued to build for more extensive legislation. By 1978, more than 30 rape crisis centres were operating in Canada, which helped to build awareness of the difficulties faced by raped women in the justice system.

Beginning in 1978, a series of bills were proposed that addressed these concerns. The final version came into effect in 1983:

▶ It replaced rape with a three-tiered offence of "sexual assault" in order to ensure that all forms of assault would be dealt with under the law.

▶ Rape was redefined as a crime against the person rather than an offence against public morals.

▶ The crime was degendered, so that men and women could be equally victims or offenders.

▶ The marital exemption was eliminated, making it possible for a woman to charge her husband with rape for the first time.

▶ In addition, the 1976 reforms were clarified by setting parameters on what judges could allow in the questioning of the sexual background of victims. This became known as the "rape shield."

Women's groups, however, had a number of serious concerns with these reforms. In the first place, they were concerned that their analysis of the social causes of rape had been sidestepped to place the emphasis on the victim, who was seen to be in need of professional assistance (Ellis, 1988). Some critics observed that rape continued to be overwhelmingly a crime committed by men against women, and that the degendering of rape had simply obscured its political meaning. The procedures of legislative change also undermined confidence. Apparently the bill kept changing and being amended throughout the parliamentary process, so that at times even MPs were unsure about which version they were debating (Los, 1994, p. 28). Some eleventh hour amendments became known to women's groups only weeks after the Bill was passed (Ellis, 1983).

TABLE 12.2
The 1980s—Key Events

1980	Canadian Congress of Black Women is formed at the seventh annual conference for Black women
1981	Bill C-53 (sexual assault, child sexual abuse, and pornography) is introduced, never passed
	Badgley Committee is constituted
1981–82	Hearings and final report of the Standing Committee on Health, Welfare, and Social Affairs (wife-battering)
1982	National Clearinghouse on Family Violence (Health and Welfare) is established
	The Canadian constitution is repatriated, and the Charter of Rights entrenched
	Report of the Standing Committee on Health, Welfare, and Social Affairs (wife-battering) is introduced to the House; greeted by laughter
1983	Bill C-127 (sexual assault, prostitution) in force
	Standing Committee on Justice and Legal Affairs report on prostitution
	Fraser Committee is established
1984	Bill C-19 (prostitution and pornography) is introduced, never passed
	Meeting of Federal/Provincial/Territorial Ministers Responsible for the Status of Women focusses on wife-battering
	Badgley Committee produces its report
1985	LEAF is founded
	Fraser Committee produces its report
	Bill C-49 (prostitution) is in force
1986	NOIVM is formed
	Federal/Provincial/Territorial Ministers produce implementation report (wife-battering)
	Family Violence Prevention Division (Health and Welfare) is established
	Child Sexual Abuse Initiative is launched
	Bill C-114 (pornography) is introduced, never passed
	Bill C-15 (child sexual abuse) is introduced
1987	Bill C-54 (pornography) is introduced, never passed
	Special Advisor on child sexual abuse is appointed
1988	Bill C-15 (child sexual abuse) is in force
	Family Violence Initiative is launched by the federal government
1989	Supreme Court decision *R. v. Seaboyer* strikes down rape shield
	Bill C-61 (prostitution) is in force
	Montreal Massacre

The machinery of reform also served to privilege certain profession-al, educated women and to exclude others. The CASAC, for example, had little input into the new bill. The government's withdrawal of funding for the national assister after three years had once again decentralized the work of rape crisis centres and made the rapid communication that was necessary to respond to legislative developments difficult. Time and money concerns inhibited the participation of many groups. In an article written after the bill was passed, Barnsley, Ellis, and Ranson (1982) claimed that the government had preferred to consult NAC and NAWL women because their positions were compatible with its own preferences. In contrast, government representatives attending the CASAC annual meeting in 1978 had not even bothered to mention the first proposal for reform, which was introduced into the House the next day.

Finally, serious doubts about the long-term value of pursuing solutions within the legal framework emerged. After the 1983 reforms, judges continued to have a great deal of discretion in the way the law would be interpreted. There also seemed to be no more likelihood that rapes would be considered founded or charged by police than they were under the old law, even though there had been an increase in reporting. The entrenchment of the Charter of Rights in the Canadian constitution, which had been used to justify rape law reform, had allowed men to make and win ten times as many equality claims as women (Fudge, 1989, p. 450). In 1989, a Charter challenge caused the Supreme Court to strike down the rape-shield provisions, one of the few real gains of the 1983 law, and forced the next round of rape law reform.

Child Sexual Abuse

Although the issue of child abuse was already well established by the 1970s, the report of the Committee on Sexual Offences Against Children and Youths (1981–1984; Badgley Committee) shifted attention to child sexual abuse. Although the Badgley Committee's research confirmed very high rates of abuse and provided the first comprehensive overview of the problem, most feminists were unhappy with the report. For one thing, by using degendered language such as "victim" and "assailant," the report obscured the fact that child sexual abuse, like rape, is a crime overwhelmingly committed by men. As had been the case with sexual assault, it situated child sexual abuse almost entirely as a legal problem, needing legal solutions, and didn't explore how societal structures such as the institution of the family might contribute to the problem. Many of the report's recommendations were incorporated in a bill passed in 1988 that revised the categories of sexual offences against children in the Criminal Code and the rules of evidence and testimony in child abuse cases.

Critics pointed out that the Badgley report's moralistic stance transformed all child and youth sexuality into a question of abuse requiring the specialized knowledge of professionals such as lawyers, doctors, and social workers. In fact, these people have come to dominate the consultation processes around the issue, and the voices of young people themselves are notably absent (Sullivan, 1992). Debi Brock (1991) argues that this emphasis on sexual abuse has made it the overriding definer of women's experience, minimizing and obscuring all the other ways—physical, emotional, and economic—in which children are abused in our society. By framing the issue this way, the state was able to avoid examining how other factors, such as its own economic policies, might reduce the vulnerability of children. In its social-policy initiatives in the late 1980s, the government did place an extraordinary emphasis on child sexual abuse. In 1986, it launched a Child Sexual Abuse Initiative with a budget of $20 million to promote education, demonstration projects, research, and consultative seminars and conferences. In the same year, a Child Abuse Secretariat was established within Health and Welfare and later incorporated into the Family Violence Prevention Division. In sharp contrast to the development of policy on sexual assault, Status of Women Canada had little role in these initiatives. According to Victorya Monkman (1988), who was hired as the coordinator of Child Sexual Abuse in the Health Services Promotion Branch of the department of Health and Welfare, the issue was rigorously degendered. References to women's groups or feminists were discouraged, staffing at the senior management level was almost entirely male, and women's perspectives were excluded from research.

The appointment in 1987 of a special advisor on child sexual abuse resulted in more than 1000 consultations, workshops, an initial discussion paper, and a final report, *Reaching for solutions* (Special Advisor to the Minister of National Health and Welfare on Child Sexual Abuse in Canada, 1990). Despite the appearance of openness and broad consultation, feminist groups tended to be poorly represented in this process. By and large, the issue of child sexual abuse had become the domain of professionals, and reflected more regulative processes centred on children and families (Sullivan, 1992, p. 106). For example, when the new law was reviewed four years after it came into effect, the only women's group appearing on the list of witnesses or those making submissions was the NAWL. In addition, the issue remained degendered. *Reaching for solutions* contains a short section on the gender dimensions of child sexual abuse in its preliminary discussion, but none of the 74 recommendations deals specifically with gender issues. Public policy reflected concern about the sexual abuse of children, but did not identify it as an issue of violence against women or place it in the broader context of women's inequality.

Pornography and Prostitution

The government attempted to employ a similar strategy of public consultation in order to generate support for policy change with the Special

Committee on Pornography and Prostitution (1983–1985; Fraser Committee). Even among feminists, there have been deep divisions over pornography, especially over the issue of censorship and the extent to which the state should intervene to limit pornography. Nevertheless, feminist response to the Fraser Committee report was generally much more positive than it had been to the Badgley report. In general, the Fraser report avoided recommendations that relied solely upon the criminal justice system and looked for solutions in economic and social policy. It acknowledged feminist concern about the sexist content of images, and the need for educational initiatives and an increased network of social services. In addition, it attempted to lay out different philosophical approaches and strategies for solutions to the two problems. However, the new Conservative government, which had inherited both the Fraser and Badgley reports from the Liberals who had commissioned them, rejected this approach.

With respect to prostitution, a Supreme Court decision in 1978 had made it difficult to enforce the law on soliciting, and street prostitution had increased in most Canadian cities in the 1980s. The Fraser Committee had recommended that laws on prostitution should be removed from the Criminal Code, and that existing laws which focussed directly on disorderly conduct and disturbing the peace should be used to address the public nuisance. However, the government passed a bill in 1985 which was designed to tighten up the old law so that street prostitutes could be charged more easily. In 1989, another law was adopted which made it possible to convict dependants of prostitutes for living on the avails of prostitution. These changes not only ignored, but also totally reversed the intention of the Fraser Committee recommendations. Their main effect was to increase the harassment of street prostitutes. These reforms were bitterly opposed by the Canadian Organization for the Rights of Prostitutes (CORP) and women's organizations such as NAC.

The government also attempted to enact a bill dealing with pornography. It had been recognized for some time that the definition of obscenity in the Criminal Code needed to be redefined. It put a primary emphasis on sex, rather than violence or sex with violence, and did not explicitly cover video and electronic forms of pornography. A series of attempts from 1978 to 1984, however, had failed to make the needed changes. The Fraser Committee recommended that three tiers of pornography, subject to different penalties, should be defined in the Criminal Code. However, in 1986 and 1988, the government's proposals for new pornography laws that superficially appeared to conform to this approach were almost immediately condemned by most organizations, even anti-pornography feminist groups. Both bills included "any sexual activity" in the list of pornographic activities, made no attempt to consider how or why acts were depicted, and didn't distinguish between acts that simply depicted violence and those that endorsed it.

Opposition to the bills was so universal that differences among feminists were put aside. Both died on the Order Paper, and after more than fifteen years of activity, no legislative change has been made with respect to pornography.[1]

Perhaps more than any other issue discussed in this essay, public-policy developments on pornography and prostitution generated cynicism and fatigue, and caused feminists to question the usefulness of investigative panels or committees. It became obvious that, even when a report was positive, the government was in no way bound to follow its recommendations. Some feminists concluded that the whole process contained protest by maintaining an appearance of responsiveness, and diverted energy and money that could be put to better use.

Wife-Battering

Like rape, wife-battering as a public-policy issue emerged from the grass roots and in many ways has been one of the more successful feminist initiatives. The RCSW report made no reference to wife-battering, but it is now well recognized as a social problem. Since the first transition house was established in 1972, the number of shelters in Canada has grown steadily to more than 400, and most have relatively secure funding. Much of the feminist analysis of the shelter movement, however, focusses on the mixed blessing of this success. Writers such as Currie (1990) and Hilton (1989) even refer to the "failure" of the Battered Women's Movement.

The publication of the CACSW study *Wife battering: The vicious circle* (MacLeod, 1980) played an important part in beginning to raise public awareness of the issue. In many ways, it set the tone for the development of policy, putting a strong emphasis on criminal justice solutions, including reform of criminal proceedings and the law. Hilton comments that, in its use of the phrase "one in ten women" it directed attention to official facts and figures and away from the underlying system that supports abuse (1989, p. 327). In 1981, acting upon the promise from the plan of action in *Towards equality for women* that a major study would be conducted, a parliamentary standing committee held hearings. Many women's groups and transition houses, some with ten years of feminist activism and practical work in place by this time, presented to the committee, and parts of the resulting report (Standing Committee on Health, Welfare, and Social Affairs, 1982) do reflect their analysis that the problem was grounded in attitudes prevalent in society at large. However, like the CACSW study, this report put a strong emphasis on the criminal justice system, insisting that wife-battering must be treated as a criminal activity.

The show of laughter and disrespect with which MPs greeted this report when it was introduced in the House helped to generate a high level of public concern about the issue. In July 1982, Parliament unanimously passed a motion to encourage police to lay charges in cases of wife-beating (Hilton, 1989, p. 329). The National Clearinghouse on Family Violence in the Department of Health and Welfare was established in the same year. In 1984, a meeting of federal, provincial, and territorial Ministers Responsible for the Status of Women focussed on wife-battering, and another meeting in 1986 reviewed implementation strategies of the various governments. A large number of ministries prepared reports for these meetings, and at this stage, as was the case with sexual assault, Status of Women Canada had the lead co-ordinating role. In 1986, however, the Family Violence Prevention Division was established in the Department of Health and Welfare.

By the mid-1980s, then, the process of institutionalization was firmly established, at provincial as well as the federal level of government. Provincial government activities often provided the most dramatic examples of how the issue was "taken away" from the grassroots women's movement. In Ontario, for example, the government began a project in 1983 to create new shelters in Northern Ontario. However, churches were named as the first choice for providing the services, and existing women's groups were not even consulted (Walker, 1990, p. 201). This meant that feminist analysis was eroded in the provision of help to battered women. In some communities outright animosity and suspicion were created between women's groups and the shelters.

By the time of Linda MacLeod's second study for the CACSW, *Battered but not beaten* (1987), feminists were beginning to re-examine the use of government intervention as a strategy to eliminate wife-battering. Although MacLeod emphasized positive gains, such as the growth in the number of crisis shelters, greater stability in funding, and the growing professionalism of staff, she also documented some of the compromises these changes entailed. Shelter staff no longer saw political activity as an important part of their work. Most shelters had moved away from the collective model to a hierarchical staff structure. Boards of directors were chosen for their influence rather than for their commitment to the issue. In addition, the pressure to cut costs and the reluctance to spread the social-welfare net were recognized as major new obstacles. Some feminist activists became highly critical of the way in which the process of institutionalization compromised the ideals of the movement.

As a result, the success of feminists in having the issue of wife-battering taken up by the state has generated debates over state intervention. As Barnsley describes the problem, feminists found themselves struggling against an analysis of wife-battering as a phenomenon caused by "individual pathology" or "faulty family interaction," a view which overlooked the role of misogyny, of women's economic dependency, of institutions such as the family (seen as private and sacrosanct), and of the widespread acceptance of violence as a way to maintain control (1988, p. 18). They experienced continual pressure to redefine the problem, and move toward individual and family treatment models rather than radical social change. "Wife assault" became "spousal assault"; terms such as "family violence" and "domestic violence" located the problem in the family rather than in a societal system of gender relations, and furthermore, obscured who was doing what to whom (Barnsley, 1988, p. 19; Walker, 1990, p. 98). Barnsley also identifies a danger in internalizing the state's limits, and defining demands in terms of what the state will accept. As Currie (1990) puts it, "the demand for *re-distribution of social power*, which can only result from radical social change and which underscored the early women's movement, has been translated into demands for *expansion of current institutions*" (p. 89).

As was the case with child sexual assault, many of the government's activities in this area seemed designed to undermine feminist analysis. For example, little of the money went directly to aid victims in the first "Family Violence Initiative," launched with a budget of $40 million in 1988. The primary focus of the initiative was on information dissemination. A consultation process was undertaken that included a half-day meeting in Ottawa with 50 non-governmental organizations, the production of a consultation document, and a big national forum held in November 1989. The forum was constructed as an assembly of family violence "experts" representing "special needs" groups, and many of these were not informed in any way by a feminist perspective. The significance of gender was not mentioned in the working documents. Feminists at the conference eventually withdrew from the main agenda and set up their own caucuses (Walker, 1990, p. 216). This was yet another example of how apparent consultation systematically erased feminist voices. Not surprisingly, a second Family Violence Initiative, announced in 1991, at the same time as the Panel on Violence Against Women, was not greeted with much enthusiasm in feminist circles.

Not all feminists, however, agree that state intervention has been a bad thing. Ursel (1991), for example, argues that the definition of the state as the enemy results in the failure to grasp opportunities and to recognize allies within the state. She finds it disturbing that ownership of the issue appears to be the primary consideration of some feminist groups, and that those who take an anti-state position do not look more closely at the many improvements for battered women themselves that have resulted from state intervention. While granting that agencies involved with battered wives are more heterogeneous since the intervention of the state, she points out that they meet the needs of many more women by including immigrant women's programs and Native services, and shelters in small rural conservative communities. In her view, contradictions within the state create the possibility of convergence of state and women's interests on certain issues. The policy implications are to approach the state strategically rather than adversarily.

ENTERING THE 1990S

The theoretical issues underlying the debate about state intervention informed some of the major confrontations that arose around the Canadian Panel on Violence Against Women. In particular, the question of whether to participate in state processes, or pursue a strategy of disengagement, had been given new weight by a decade of feminist disillusionment with the state. Feminists were upset by the ways in which their organizations were modified by state demands and their issues were redefined and located within limited areas of reform. The amount of energy that had been expended in processes of policy consultation orchestrated by the state, and the pressures this had created for feminist organizations, were a matter of serious concern as they entered the 1990s. An overriding question was how broad structural change could be effected in a system that discouraged analysis and put forward "tinkering" strategies. The knowledge that their work might very well be a waste of time was balanced by a fear of not participating and not being heard. The consequences of each strategy had to be considered carefully. These questions were closely related to issues of professionalization and expertise, and representation within the women's movement itself; in particular, the extent to which certain voices were privileged by the state and others were marginalized. These issues were made more complex by differences in race, sexual orientation, and abilities among women. The organization of many of these constituency groups during the 1980s (see Table 12.2) had forced older women's organizations to acknowledge issues of privilege and representation, and most were painfully struggling to address them.

By the end of the decade, relations between the federal government and feminists had deteriorated almost beyond repair. Feminist organizations regarded Tory policies such as free trade, taxation, cutbacks in transfer payments to the provinces affecting health and education, and privatization as detrimental to social programs and women's interests. This hostility had been exacerbated by the Tory record on such women's issues as abortion and day care. In the past several years, it had been increasingly difficult for feminist organizations even to meet with the government. Symbolizing the government's disregard for the concerns of women's groups was their refusal to attend the annual NAC lobby, in which the caucuses of the three major parties had traditionally been grilled about key policy concerns.

The emergence of R.E.A.L. (Realistic, Equal, Active for Life) Women in the 1980s had provided a focus for anti-feminism and an attack on the funding provided to women's groups by the Women's Program. Despite the fact that the government's own review in 1987 had recommended that funding to equality-seeking groups should continue, by the end of the decade groups such as NAC were beginning to suffer massive cuts to their operating budgets. At the same time, R.E.A.L. Women was granted conference funding. In this political climate, groups began to reject traditional lobbying techniques and experiment with more confrontational tactics. For example, in 1989, in a coalition with the Canadian Labour Congress and the Association of First Nations, NAC organized a series of protests on the VIA rail line, culminating in Ottawa, to protest the cuts to various social programs in the new budget. This initiative was not particularly successful. But when a group of women in St. John's, Newfoundland, staged a sit-in in the Secretary of State's office in 1990 to protest the elimination of funding to women's centres, similar actions quickly spread across the country and resulted in a reinstatement of the funding for that year.

The government's approach to the violence issue appeared to contradict its actions on other fronts. For example, at one point the Minister Responsible for the Status of Women announced that the issue of wife assault was one of the issues Prime Minister Mulroney cared about the most (Currie, 1990, p. 89). It was possible to maintain this contradiction as long as the links between various kinds of violence or between violence against women and other social and economic problems faced by women were unacknowledged. By the end of the decade, public-policy initiatives had still made few such links, even though a number of influential feminist texts had described male violence against women as a global and historical phenomenon of vast proportions. After the Montreal Massacre, the image of a "war against women," an overwhelming problem affecting the well-being of every woman (and not just a few victims) entered the public discourse in Canada and forced a change in policy direction.

The Montreal Massacre: Two Solitudes

On December 6, 1989, Marc Lépine entered L'École Polytechnique in Montreal with an automatic rifle; killed fourteen young women, mostly engineering students; and then committed suicide. He left behind him a note expressing his rage against feminists and stating clearly that he had committed this act for political reasons. In the days that followed, Canadians struggled to make sense of the events that had occurred. In the first early, confused reports, the significance of gender was not even noted, but as it became evident that women had been deliberately targeted, media coverage shifted from the event itself to how it was to be interpreted. Almost immediately, the debate became polarized, with "two solitudes" of opinion emerging (*Calgary Herald*, December 14, 1989, p. A1).

Most feminists saw the massacre as an extreme example of the violence against women that was woven into the fabric of Canadian life. They pointed to the number of women killed by their husbands each year, the violent and misogynist attitudes promoted in pornography, and the harassment and hostility still faced by many women entering the professions. Lépine's own actions were significant. He chose as the site of the massacre an institution where women were entering a traditionally male domain. He separated the women from the men, he murdered only women, and he left a letter explaining his hatred of feminists. He also named numbers of prominent women he would like to kill. Nothing could provide a more brutal example of the meaning of misogyny or the importance of the work feminists had been doing for years.

Others, however, rejected this explanation and argued that the shooting was the "isolated act of a madman." They focussed on the psychopathology of Marc Lépine, providing evidence of his aberrant social behaviour, his anger, and his inability to succeed. Lépine came from a poor background and was found to have a history of childhood abuse. This last fact supported those who saw the Montreal Massacre as a reflection of the general breakdown of society. As they saw it, men and children suffered violence as much as women, and to dwell exclusively on male violence against women was inappropriate. Many public figures and journalists attempted to minimize the gender dimension of the tragedy.

In the public debates that emerged after the killings, the two explanations were thought to have no common ground. However, most feminists do not discount the importance of economic factors, nor the horrific impact of child abuse, in perpetuating cycles of abuse and despair. To focus on violence against women does not deny that other forms of domination and abuse exist. Quite the contrary, it can make us more sensitive to them. But feminists did object to the focus on Lépine's individual problems, without considering the social context that had helped him to see women as acceptable targets of violence. The same reluctance to acknowledge the social factors that reinforced these problems and created the conditions under which they could grow seemed to have characterized government strategies during the previous ten years. Feminists were pained by the refusal to acknowledge the prejudice and hatred that many women face every day. They experienced this as a further violence, a further denial of their right to speak or organize themselves.

This feeling was confirmed and strengthened by the wave of antifeminist sentiment that emerged. By naming male violence as the problem, feminists were seen to be extreme, manipulative, and capitalizing on personal tragedy for their own ends. Gwen Landoldt of R.E.A.L. Women, for example, said that feminists were using the tragedy to "push for more government funding for their cause" (ibid., 1989). In the right-wing rhetoric, informed by the belief that feminism was largely responsible for the breakdown of society and that women abandoning the home were the root cause of society's ills, feminism was ultimately responsible even for the massacre itself. One Thunder Bay newspaper went so far as to say that the killings were the result of "the divisions created in Canadian society by the mere presence of the women's movement" (Baril, 1990, p. 19).

After the massacre, feminists needed to validate their own perceptions for themselves. Many wanted a safe place to express their grief and anger, with other women who would believe them and understand. In mixed-sex groups, some felt intimidated or that their ideas were trivialized or not treated with the same weight as those of men. However, while some men respected the needs of these women, others felt threatened or angry because of their exclusion. When the women's centre in Thunder Bay organized a vigil for women only, the story was picked up by the national media. Attention then shifted from a focus on violence against women to feminist hostility toward men.

In the highly charged atmosphere after the killings, some feminists did polarize the debates even further. In some feminist discourse, "male" was an undifferentiated category in which all men were like Marc Lépine, and all men were guilty. For example, Benson suggested a year after the massacre that "it is not consoling to realize that awareness in the government has moved from laughter to boredom and disinterest in what must be the biggest private hobby of men in Canada, that is, the hurting of women" (1990, p. 7). It is not surprising that some men rejected this view of themselves and insisted on defining the meaning of violence against women in other terms. Still, one must be careful not merely to substitute the stereotype of men as beasts for another where they are all maligned victims. Women *are* vulnerable to violence from men. The fact that men as a group *are* in a position of privilege relative to women not only creates the context in which violence against women occurs, but is likely to make men more defensive when the status quo is challenged. Thus, the isolation of both "solitudes" of opinion was reinforced. Each side attacked the other; but, perhaps even more significantly, each side experienced themselves as *under* attack. The fear felt on both sides made communication less and less possible and hardened both positions. There is no doubt that the Montreal Massacre stimulated an intense anti-feminist backlash and a public debate on the meaning, extent, and causes of violence against women, which had emerged as a social problem.[2]

Close to the time of the massacre, several other incidents in the universities contributed to the public concern over the issue and kept feelings high. These included the Queen's University "No Means No" campaign, where posters were defaced with violent graffiti; the Wilfrid Laurier University panty raid in which women's panties were smeared with ketchup and peanut butter, captioned, and hung in the cafeteria; and the University of British Columbia Caribou House incident, in which women in residence were sent violent and misogynist "invitations" to a tug of war by a neighbouring fraternity. In such incidents, the same pattern of feminist reaction, alternative explanation, and anti-feminist backlash unfolded. In addition, anniversaries of the massacre continued to provoke commentary. Some men attempted to organize groups to combat male violence, and the white-ribbon campaigns, though criticized by some women's groups as mere show, became highly publicized. Meanwhile, the federal government exhibited a certain schizophrenia with respect to the problem. For example, it refused the petition from NAC to have December 6 named a national day of mourning in 1990, but passed a private member's bill to the same effect in 1991. While expressing concern about the high levels of violence experienced by women, it continued to enact severe funding cuts to women's agencies, some of them direct providers of service to victims of violence. It was in this climate, then, that women's groups began to search for strategies to address the problem and to force the government to respond.

THE CALL FOR A ROYAL COMMISSION

The decision to call for a royal commission came about as a result of discussions which began before but were given immediacy by the Montreal Massacre. The year 1990 marked the twentieth anniversary of the report of the RCSW, which many Canadian feminists recalled as a highly significant event in gaining recognition for women's issues and spurring legislative change to improve women's status. Some groups saw a new royal commission as an important way to publicize the relative lack of progress on some issues, and the emergence of new concerns, since the original report was published. At their annual general meeting in May 1989, for example, NAC passed a resolution to implement a new "women's commission." Significantly, however, much of the debate turned around the old question of state involvement. NAC, for example, proposed that this commission should not be state run, but instead run by women themselves. Unfortunately, such a mammoth undertaking proved impossible without resources, and the resolution was never implemented.

After the Montreal Massacre, and especially as the first anniversary approached, the focus shifted toward the idea that this royal commission should focus on violence against women—an issue hardly touched on in the RCSW report. On December 6, 1990, a coalition of 30 women's groups,[3] with the support of many provincial and municipal governments, submitted a formal petition for the establishment of a royal commission on violence against women. According to the final report of the Canadian Panel on Violence Against Women, more than 26 000 letters were received by the government in support of the idea (1993, p. B1).

The groups most instrumental in this initiative, for the most part liberal feminists with faith in the state as a mechanism for reform, believed that the RCSW had been directly responsible for many of the gains made by Canadian women. For example, in response to the argument that royal commission reports are often shelved, Kay Sigurjonsson, Associate Executive Director of the Federation of Women Teachers' Associations of Ontario (FWTAO), argued that this had not been the case with the 1970 report. She credited it with the establishment of institutional structures such as the CACSW and the Ministers Responsible for the Status of Women, as well as with legislative gains in "equal opportunity legislation." Sigurjonsson suggested a new commission would generate publicity and public support for government-funded initiatives and serve a co-ordinating function in bringing together "all the disparate elements (various) studies represent" (1991, p. 115). To this point, remember, there had been no public examination of the problem as a whole. Glenda Sims, President of the Canadian Advisory Council on the Status of Women, made a similar point, commenting on the need for a co-ordinated overview. Dawn Black, NDP Status of Women critic in the House of Commons, was another key player in the initiative. She stressed the importance of bringing the issue of violence against women into public view and argued that a royal commission could work as a national educational tool (Irving, 1991). The letter sent to the prime minister on behalf of the 30 women's groups argued that a high-profile public investigation with recommendations might have an impact similar to that of the report twenty years ago.

Other women's groups had reservations about the effectiveness of a royal commission. A recurrent theme in newspaper commentary for the next two years was that the issue had already been "studied to death," and the government had consistently failed to act on reports and recommendations. In a cautionary article published in *Canadian Woman Studies*, for example, Marie-Claire Lévesque pointed out that many of the recommendations of the RCSW report had still not been implemented (1991, p. 117). After a decade of state-run initiatives, considerable cynicism was expressed about the process as an excuse for inaction, and about the probable outcome—another report would simply be shelved. Moreover, grass-roots feminist groups were worried about further cuts to their operating budgets if money were funnelled to a new commission (Irving, 1991). This was not an unfounded fear, given that the government was currently cutting funding to all women's groups, including some shelters. Nevertheless, as the push for a royal commission took on a momentum of its own and began to have greater likelihood of success, groups added their name to the coalition.

The War Against Women

In the meantime, a process had been going on that helped to focus energies on the royal commission strategy. In the House of Commons, the Standing Committee on Health and Welfare already had in place a subcommittee on the status of women. Members included NDP and Liberal women's critics Dawn Black and Mary Clancy, and three women Tory MPs, including chair Barbara Greene. As a response to the massacre in Montreal and to the other incidents of university violence that year, this subcommittee set up hearings on the problem of violence against women, and asked groups to comment on the need for a royal commission and what issues such a commission should include. Most women's groups presented hard-hitting briefs.

Their submissions are interesting for what they reveal of the social and political climate—in particular, the strained relationship between some women's groups and the government. In retrospect, it is easy to see that this did not bode well for the effectiveness of a government-run commission on violence against women. NAC, for example, severely criticized the policies of the Conservative government, citing its funding cuts and its position on child care and abortion, and claiming that the government itself was perceived to be a major obstacle to any real change. Not surprisingly, this antagonized the Tories on the subcommittee, who accused NAC of taking the responsibility away from everyone by always blaming everything on the government.

The reception of the final report issued by the subcommittee in June 1991 illustrates even more dramatically the context of confrontation and anger in which the subject of violence against women was by now firmly situated. As one newspaper headline put it, the report was "sunk by its title": *The war against women* (*Vancouver Sun*, June 19, 1991, p. A13). The Standing Committee on Health and Welfare refused to endorse the report of its subcommittee. Astonishingly, MP Edna Anderson, who voted for the report while a member of the subcommittee, voted against it when it came to the standing committee. The right-wing periodical *Alberta Report* decried the "phoney war," labelled the report "virulently feminist," and commented that its rejection was "welcome news for anyone fed up with the extremes of feminism" (July 8, 1991, pp. 24–25).

The opposition to the report was spearheaded by MP Stan Wilbee. Wilbee's commentary, as summarized in newspaper reports, echoed familiar themes. He felt that the word "war" was "a bit extreme" and that it created divisions at a time when people needed to work together. Wilbee wanted to emphasize that men were supportive of women. This conciliatory stance was somewhat undermined, however, by the divisiveness he himself had caused in rejecting the report. His remarks about sexual assault—that a woman might say she hadn't consented to intercourse because she had "become angry or sobered up"—also made it clear how much support he was really ready to offer (*Vancouver Sun*, June 19, 1991, p. A13).

These events are yet another example of the public struggle to interpret the meaning of violence against women. *The War Against Women* report did get the approval of most women's groups. It put forward a broad definition of "violence" and reinforced the interpretation of the Montreal Massacre as "a dramatic expression of male rage against women ... an extreme form of the violence women regularly confront in their lives" (Standing Committee on Health and Welfare ..., 1991, p. 1). Not surprisingly, these were two of the points to which the *Alberta Report* article particularly objected (Koch, 1991). It called for:

- a national public-relations campaign, including mandatory education in the schools;
- mandatory gender-sensitivity training for the RCMP, judges, and MPs;
- mandatory counselling programs for offenders;
- increased stable funding for women's groups;
- elimination of systemic barriers to women's equality;
- development of a national housing policy;
- a task force to study violence in Native communities; and
- a royal commission.

It did, however, reject some of the specific suggestions that had been made by women's groups, in particular, that members of the commission should be selected by, and appointed to represent, women's groups (Lakeman, 1991). This would become a significant sticking point once the Panel on Violence Against Women was established. The embarrassment caused by the rejection of the report, sped up the prime minister's announcement of the panel of inquiry, which had already been promised in the Throne Speech in May.

THE CANADIAN PANEL ON VIOLENCE AGAINST WOMEN

On August 15, 1991, the membership and mandate of the Canadian Panel on Violence Against Women was made public (see Table 12.3). Pat Marshall, executive director of the Metro Action Committee on Public Violence Against Women and Children (METRAC), and Marthe Asselin Vaillancourt, a Quebec community activist, were appointed as co-chairs. The rest of the members represented a variety of backgrounds and experience, but all had substantial knowledge of violence against women. Many also had served in front-line service organizations. They included one Native woman, one immigrant woman, and one man. In addition, an aboriginal circle of four members was named, which was to focus on components of the process that concerned aboriginal women.

TABLE 12.3
The 1990s—A Panel Chronology

1990	Report of the Special Advisor on child sexual abuse; consultation hearings on the report
	Coalition of Women's Groups calls for a Royal Commission on Violence Against Women
1990–91	Subcommittee on the Status of Women of the Standing Committee on Health and Welfare, Social Affairs, Seniors, and the Status of Women, hearings and report (*The war against women*)
1991	Throne Speech announces a "Blue Ribbon panel" on Violence Against Women
	Second Family Violence Initiative is announced
	August: Canadian Panel on Violence Against Women is established
	October: December 6 is named a national day of remembrance
1991–92	October to January: Consultation hearings on Bill C-49 (sexual assault)
1992	January: The panel hearings begin across the country
	Bill C-49 (sexual assault) is in force
	Supreme Court decision *R. v. Butler*, upholds constitutionality of Criminal Code obscenity provisions
	June: NAC annual general meeting. Resolution is passed demanding increased representation for immigrant women, disabled women, and women's groups on the panel
	July: NAC, the Congress of Black Women, DAWN, and CASAC withdraw support from the panel and pull out of the advisory committee
	August: NOIVM withdraws support
	September: The interim report of the panel is released
1993	Standing Committee on Justice and the Solicitor General, four-year review of the C-15 (child sexual abuse) amendments, hearings and report
	July: The panel's final report, *Changing the landscape*, is released

Structure and Process

The announcement of the panel's formation was greeted with some cynicism in the press. Many commentators questioned the need for more public awareness of a problem that was already well known. Others saw it as an exercise in political opportunism. Some groups felt that the whole exercise would be a waste of time. For example, the Edmonton City Council passed a resolution asking the panel to leave Edmonton off its itinerary. The mayor commented that the government would be better to start spending money on programs, thereby solving the difficulties that women faced rather than simply studying them again.

In the feminist community, however, the announcement was met, for the most part, with cautious approval. Echoing the arguments that had been put forward around the call for a royal commission, Judy Rebick, president of NAC, felt that the panel could mobilize public opinion to make the issue of violence against women a top political and social priority. Lee Lakeman, a representative of the Canadian Association of Sexual Assault Centres (CASAC) and later to be one of the members to withdraw from the panel's advisory committee, wrote an analysis titled "How should radicals respond?" in which she laid out strategies to make the most of government processes while at the same time maintaining a policy of disengagement. Lakeman clearly did not see the establishment of the panel as a feminist initiative. She urged her readers not to feed the panel information about themselves and their organizations. In her view, the panel's job was to study the federal state and its institutionalized sexism in order to force reforms by the next election. Lakeman's article also focussed on some key structural problems. She pointed out that those appointed to the panel were tokens, rather than representatives of certain groups, in distinct contrast to the recommendations of women at the subcommittee hearings. To Lakeman, this meant that the government had succeeded in avoiding the political strength of a united women's movement on the panel. She warned that women's groups must insist on the panel's accountability. To whom were the members accountable? How might they be held accountable? Prophetically, Lakeman's answer was "we can raise a lot of hell" (1991, p. 5).

In its own retrospective analysis of the process, the Canadian Panel on Violence Against Women also identified "structure, always structure" as one of the key problems that it faced. Panel members had conflicting obligations to women's groups, Canadian women in general, and the federal government. Maintaining accountability for all these interests was an impossible task. They admitted that their failure to resolve it had resulted in "disarray and a sense of powerlessness within both the panel and the feminist community" (1993, p. B5). Much of the blame was attributed to the process by which such projects were constituted in the first place. In the future, they concluded, matters needed to be negotiated and discussed openly with all essential partners before the project took final form.

The report also commented on other awkward problems of structure. For example, the aboriginal circle had originally been set up as an independent body, but when it became evident that this was unworkable, the circle members were made full-fledged members of the panel. However, since they, unlike the other panelists, were representatives of aboriginal and Inuit women's associations, they were seen by other women's groups as a model for representation that had been denied them. Informed by the experience of past policy initiatives, the issue of appropriate representation from all groups, particularly of women of racial minorities and those with disabilities, was of major concern to the women's movement. Since such women were not adequately represented on the panel, the decision was made to include their perspectives by constituting an advisory committee that more accurately reflected the diversity of Canadian women. But the structural relationship of the panel to the advisory committee (including, again, the issue of accountability) was never resolved (Canadian Panel on Violence Against Women, 1993, p. B3). Some members came to feel they had no real ability to influence decisions.

A further problem facing the panel was time. Although the original coalition request for a royal commission had suggested a period of three years, the panel's mandate allowed only fifteen months to carry out a broad-based consultation in dozens of communities and to draft a progress report and a final report. According to the report, the difficulty of the limited time period was made apparent almost immediately to the members. When it became evident that its objectives were being compromised by the time limitations, the panel did secure an extension of its deadline. However, it never seriously challenged the limited timetable in which it was asked to work because it thought criticism might jeopardize the project. The political motivations behind the deadline also were never scrutinized, though it was clear that the government wanted the report to appear before the next election.

Five of the recommendations in the final report addressed these procedural and structural problems. It recommended that, in future inquiries of this sort, the mandate and rules of operating and procedure should be outlined as clearly as possible ahead of time. Members should be able to contact one another and exchange views on the task before they were appointed, and time and opportunity for negotiation should be given to allow them to refine the mandate before taking up their duties. In addition, the report recommended that ways be developed to guarantee better representation of all population groups in Canada and that new mechanisms be established for consultation between women's groups and the government.

Withdrawal

Bill C-49 Consultations

The importance of all these concerns was dramatized in July and August 1992 when five national women's groups—NAC, the Congress of Black Women, the Disabled Women's Network (DAWN), CASAC, and the National Organization of Immigrant and Visible Minority Women (NOIVM)—withdrew their support from the panel. The reasons for this decision can be partly understood in the context of their experience during the series of consultations around the reform of the sexual assault law, which took place from October 1991 to January 1992. The Supreme Court had recently struck down the sections of the rape law that protected a victim from having her past sexual history introduced as testimony in a rape trial, and representatives of various groups were called together by Justice minister Kim Campbell to solicit ideas for revising the sexual assault law.

Many feminists found the decision of whether or not to participate in this process extremely difficult. Issues from past experience were considered carefully. Was there value in working within the criminal framework yet again? Would certain groups of women be co-opted and/or marginalized? For example, many grass-roots and minority women were troubled by the question of whether to work with White women lawyers (McIntyre, 1994, p. 295). The government began the hearings with a limited proposal for redefining the conditions by which evidence of past sexual history would be admissible. The women's groups, driven by the Women's Legal and Education Action Fund (LEAF), however, argued that that this time a preamble contextualizing the equality implications of sexual assault should be included and that the issue of consent be addressed. Drawing upon the lessons of the last two decades, the feminist lobby attempted to challenge the framework of sexual assault law reform and situate the new law within a philosophical understanding both of women's experience of sexual assault and its role in maintaining women's oppression. Furthermore, Lee Lakeman insisted that consultations with representatives from the grass-roots women's movement and from the aboriginal, poor, disabled, and visible-minority communities, as well as sex-trade workers, were required.

The resulting consultations appear to have been a model of feminist practice. McIntyre describes the experience as one of power sharing through genuine diversity (1994, p. 309). Efforts were made to ensure that the legal reforms were made understandable and accessible to all the women participants. To a large extent, they succeeded in their objectives. Bill C-49

- set out a test for judges to determine whether a complainant's sexual history could be admitted as evidence;
- provided a definition of "consent" and outlined specific situations that did not constitute consent; and
- restricted the defence of mistaken belief so that an accused would have to show he had taken reasonable steps to ascertain that it had been given.

However, the bill did have a disappointing preamble. It did not, as the coalition requested, list the particular susceptibility of minority women, disabled women, and sex-trade workers to discriminatory treatment under the law. Nevertheless, the substance of the bill that was finally tabled in the House of Commons was essentially formulated by the coalition.

This experience was a central one. For the first time in their interaction with the state, feminists were able to shape not only the content, but the philosophical framework of reform and the process of consultation.

Also, they were able to present a united front based on inclusion and a consensus reached among many diverse groups. They were fully prepared to use a boycott as a weapon, and they emerged from the process with a strong sense of unity and efficacy. These lessons were important in shaping the expectations of women's groups for the Panel on Violence Against Women, which began its hearings in the same month as the Bill C-49 consultations ended. One of the first things they demanded was that the panel endorse the recommendations arising from the consultations. It refused, and in so doing appeared to align itself against the united front of the women's movement.

The Hearings

Although women's groups had been guardedly optimistic as the process began, discontent gathered momentum as hearings were held and, more important, as the time approached to prepare the interim report. Some objected to the use of the phrase "zero tolerance"—a term made popular by George Bush in his war on drugs—in the panel's press releases to the media. Duthie quotes Trisha Joel of Vancouver Status of Women, who observed: "soon we may be reading ads in the papers about how the government endorses zero tolerance on violence. Well, big deal. After all, the Tories are also promising to end child poverty by the year 2000. These are all great slogans with little behind them" (Duthie, 1992). In the same column, Lee Lakeman, revealing her expectations of the panel's role, said that it had not yet had the opportunity to make "bureaucratic waves." Clearly, these women were hoping that the government's own role in helping or hindering efforts to end violence was going to be examined.

The actual methods by which hearings were arranged and conducted also began to come under attack. In a column in which she explained the basis of the withdrawal of support, Sunera Thobani, co-chair of the NAC Violence Committee, condemned "the contempt with which the panel, notwithstanding its rhetoric, viewed the women of Canada." Complaints included the fact that hearings were conducted in buildings that were inaccessible to women with disabilities. The time allocated to women invited to the hearings of this panel was insufficient, and child care and translation for racial-minority women were not provided. Even more significantly, Thobani focussed on the exclusion of grass-roots women's organizations. Many organizations did not know the panel had come to town until after it had departed. Others were given such short notice that serious consultation was impossible. Thobani decried the panel's lack of accountability to the women's movement and commented that "if the panel had been serious about a partnership with the women's movement, its starting point would have been a meaningful consultation with and inclusion of national women's organizations in the planning of its work" (*Vancouver Sun*, July 21, 1992, p. A11).

A further concern of women's groups was the approach that had been taken in the hearings. At least in part, the structure of the hearings as private, invitation-only gatherings reflected an important feminist objective: to give a voice to women who were either silenced or never heard before. As outlined in the progress report published in September 1992, the panel "took great effort to go beyond the service workers and helping professions to reach individual women who are not, and may never be, a part of any organization or assistance network" (Canadian Panel on Violence Against Women, 1992, p. 10). While this was a laudable goal, the privacy surrounding the hearings meant, as Thobani pointed out, that even some feminist organizations were excluded. Ironically, in attempting to make the process more woman-centred and informed by a feminist perspective, the panel succeeded in antagonizing women's organizations even further. Other groups, such as the academic community, who presumably might have had something to contribute to the understanding of the problem, also were not encouraged to participate.

Instead, the hearings were structured in such as way as to facilitate the recounting of personal experiences of violence and abuse. Certainly, this is the aspect upon which newspapers and other media focussed in their reports. Even in the panel's own reports, however, the element of personal suffering was stressed. In both the interim and final reports, discussion was interspersed with frequent verbatim excerpts from women's testimonies. An entire publication produced by the panel, *Collecting the voices: A scrapbook*, consists of letters and stories received during the consultations. The major headings of the final report include the words "experiencing violence" and thus put the focus on individuals rather than social structures.

The panel seemed to adopt the strategy that publicizing individual experiences would arouse public indignation and determination to do something about the problem. However, it could as easily be argued that this strategy detracted from a sense of collective responsibility for action, since the stories could be explained away as someone else's problem. A number of feminists on the advisory committee, who were shown the progress report before it was published in September, were upset that it seemed to address violence as "an isolated thing of men beating women at home" without addressing its systemic causes. In addition, they thought that federal government's responsibility for funding transition houses, sexual assault crisis centres, women's centres, and national women's organizations needed to be stated (Huang, 1992).

The Ultimatum

At the NAC Annual General Meeting on June 8, 1992, the growing frustration with the process of the panel was outlined to the membership.

NAC voted to withdraw its support unless an ultimatum of three major demands was met. The panel should

▶ represent minority women on the panel by appointing three members to be named by the NOIVM and the Congress of Black Women;

▶ undertake a series of consultations with national women's groups and work with a body of delegates from these groups who would be consulted before releasing any reports;

▶ state its support for the recommendations arising from the Bill C-49 consultations (*Vancouver Sun*, July 21, 1992, p. A11).

Of the three demands, the second one is central and is a key to understanding the other two. Perhaps the most important factor influencing the political context in which the panel process occurred was the sense of extreme alienation and hostility most major feminist organizations felt toward the federal Tory government. The concern of national women's organizations that channels of communication be established so that their viewpoints on women's issues could be heard was central. Moreover, feeling that their expertise on violence against women had been developed through years of grassroots work, they wanted their analysis to be given primacy of place in any policy-making decisions. Quite to the contrary, in this process they felt their views had been marginalized or ignored altogether. With respect to the issue of violence, in particular, it can be seen how this sense of marginalization, of being rendered invisible, tied into the emotional debates that have already been examined. In most ways, a desire to force acknowledgment of their expertise had become the most important issue for feminists in their interaction with the state. This concern is an identifiable theme from the beginning of the panel inquiry process. The demand by many groups that panel members should be appointed by women's groups to represent them; the concern about consultation with women's groups, which is evident even in *The war against women* report; the commentary produced by feminists at the announcement of the panel— all reflected issues of representation.

It is possible that had more effective structures been developed to facilitate this consultation, as had happened during the Bill C-49 consultations, the issue of representation would not have caused the break that it did. After all, most major women's groups—including those representing particularly disadvantaged groups of women— began by supporting the process, even when the membership of the panel was known. The advisory committee to the panel included Flora Fernandez Ortega, a Chilean immigrant with experience working with Latin American women in shelters and co-chair of the NAC Violence Committee; Eunadie Johnson, president of NOIVM; Joan Meister, past national chairperson and supervisor of Violence Projects with DAWN;

and Esmeralda Thornhill, a founding member and president of the Congress of Black Women. However, the women working on the advisory committee were limited to discussing issues laid out by the panel and felt marginalized from the real decision-making processes. For this reason, the groups rejected the panel's offer of special advisors as a way to end the ultimatum controversy. Commented Justine Blake-Hill from the Congress of Black Women: "What the panel was saying to us is, 'you're going to stay in the kitchen, while we dine in the dining room'" (Huang, 1992).

Immigrant and visible-minority women compared their situation to the presence aboriginal women, representing particular organizations, had achieved on the panel. However, the circle members of the panel pointed out that they had lobbied successfully to have a strong voice in the panel's work, while others had shown little interest. Aboriginal women had already identified the issue of violence against women as a priority concern, had carried out their own studies, and had made representations to the subcommittee that had produced *The war against women*. Perhaps because interaction with the state is an unavoidable fact for aboriginal peoples in Canada, these groups were much quicker to identify and seize the opportunity to use the panel for their own purposes. Even though the ultimatum insisted that unequivocal support should continue to be given to aboriginal women, circle members were not sympathetic to the demands of visible-minority women and saw them as damaging the work done by and for aboriginal women on the panel (*Winnipeg Free Press*, August 1, 1992, p. A11).

For its part, the panel was working under tremendous time constraints to produce a report within the terms of the mandate. It had already completed the consultation hearings and did not feel it was appropriate to add new members at such a late date. Pat Marshall saw the representation issue as "an easy way for NAC to deal with issues it's been under fire for, to target something outside and build solidarity within" (*Globe and Mail*, August 1, 1992, p. A8). It is true that the NAC organizational review of 1988, which created tremendous divisions within the organization, had identified racism, and the exclusion of lesbians and women with disabilities, as serious issues within NAC (Vickers, Rankin, and Appelle, 1993, pp. 165–168). The issue of racism had surfaced at several contentious annual meetings since that time as well. Adequate consultation with regional and grass-roots groups continued to be a difficult problem, made even worse by funding cuts. Yet, Marshall's comment belittles the serious commitment that NAC had made toward recruiting and encouraging the participation of previously underrepresented groups. For example, the co-chairs of NAC's Violence Committee, Flora Ortega and Sunera Thobani, were both immigrant women with strong ties to their communities.

Public Response

Marshall's viewpoint was echoed in the press. When Jeffrey Simpson, in the August 20, 1992, edition of the *Globe and Mail* (p. A20), compared the withdrawal of women's groups to a "mosquito bite," Glenda Sims of CACSW responded (*Globe and Mail*, Decemer 4, 1992, p. A12) that he had minimized the very serious concerns about inclusiveness, which were now recognized as a fundamental principle of Canadian society. A general sense of public bewilderment about the reasons for the decision is evident. Some wondered why women were engaging in the very kinds of power struggles they condemned in male-dominated institutions. Showing a profound misunderstanding of the representation issue, they pointed to the quality of the people involved on the panel and wondered how it could produce a report that would reflect only the interests of White, middle-class women.

The withdrawal of support from the panel became an excuse to ridicule or vilify feminists, the women's movement, and NAC in particular. Simpson accused NAC of "an exaggerated sense of its own importance" and commented that its actions demonstrated it stood on "the margin of the political spectrum, further left in many cases than even mainstream NDP thinking" (*Globe and Mail*, August 20, 1992, p. A20). *Alberta Report* gleefully reported that "Canada's fringiest feminists won't be wooed" (September 7, 1992, pp. 8–9). Antifeminist organizations, who were also bitter that they had been excluded from the process, took pleasure in the apparent divisions among feminists. Presumably, the panel's objectives in excluding groups such as R.E.A.L. Women arose from the wish to avoid another round of protracted and painful debate. However, if one purpose of the process was to educate and convince those who were not already aware of the urgency of the problem, little could be gained by closed hearings.

Other members of the press focussed less on the reasons for the withdrawal strategy than on its long-term outcome. What purpose would be served by the boycott? Was it the case, as many commented, that such strategies were invariably destructive? Certainly, the panel's work was seriously undercut. In addition, the credibility of the issue of violence against women, already under attack in the popular debates, was further eroded. It is clear that NAC and the other women's groups were hoping to use the ultimatum to force a more inclusive consultation model, and felt that the issue of representation was of enough importance to justify such a stand. It remains to be seen whether the disengagement strategy in this case was the best choice. Presumably, by remaining true to its ideological commitment to full participation of all women, the women's movement will be strengthened. On the other hand, its effectiveness may have been weakened by the popular perception of marginalization.

The Final Report

Certainly, the popular response to the final report, released at the end of July 1993, suggests that little was gained by the exercise. The report contained 494 recommendations, touching on a broad range of themes. However, these recommendations were not prioritized in any way. Critics commented that the report was poorly written and often very naive—simply a rehash of similar studies. NDP and Liberal women's critics Dawn Black and Mary Clancy, along with many feminist groups, condemned it. Sunera Thobani, for example, pointed out that there was neither a time frame nor any indication of where the money for the implementation of the weak and unprioritized recommendations would come from, and concluded that the report was a step backwards for women's groups in Canada (Pilot and Brown, 1993). Some saw it as a cheap public-relations ploy, released on the eve of an election. Others were angry that the report was unlikely to generate the political will to change. Seeming to bear this out, Minister Mary Collins said the government would adopt "zero tolerance" of violence against women as a philosophy, but would not promise any new money to address the problem.

The plan of action, calling for zero tolerance within seven years, appeared to most critics to be unworkable. Most agreed that there were far too many recommendations, targeting a range of players (such as the churches, the media, other levels of government, and individuals) over which the federal government had no control. On the other hand, the government's own role in the problem, such as the funding cuts that affected women, or the abolition of the Court Challenges program to help fund Charter cases, was given very little comment.

Predictably, editorial responses were contradictory. For example, while the *Toronto Star* thought that mandatory gender-sensitivity training for judges should be quickly rejected, the *Montreal Gazette* focussed upon this as one of the more suitable recommendations. Nevertheless, familiar themes emerged. The *Globe and Mail* found the report "bloated" with feminist jargon, "more of an obeisance to orthodox feminism than an honest inquiry." In particular, it lamented the absence of men's voices: "Men, the report tells us, must be part of the solution. But how, if their voices are censored?" Pointing out that abusive men may in fact feel powerless and desperate, the writer wondered why that fact was never found worthy of exploration. "Do the authors think that suppressing the experience of boys and men will help us find answers?" (*Globe and Mail*, July 21, 1993, p. D6).

Many critics also felt that the panel had used misleadingly wide definitions of violence. As the *Montreal Gazette* put it: "one sometimes suspects this panel thinks that all misfortune anywhere, including the eruption of Mount Pinabuto, constitutes violence against women" (August 1, 1993, p. B2). A number of commentators took particular issue with the

Women's Safety Project study, which was included in the report and which found that 98 percent of a sample of Toronto women had suffered some form of sexual violation (Canadian Panel on Violence Against Women, 1993, p. 10). These statistics were found to be alarmist and implausible. The careful explanation of their work and methods which researchers Lori Haskell and Melanie Randall published in the *Globe and Mail* did not really take away from the public perception that the statistics did not reflect reality (September 9, 1993, p. A23).

The *Toronto Star* also reported rumours of dissatisfaction among panel members, some of whom apparently did not see a final version of the report until the day before it was released. Some had not been consulted since May. The only visible-minority member of the panel, Mobina Jaffer, is quoted as saying that the groups who boycotted the panel were right: "The women of colour have got five pages in the report. I believe being the lone member was a mistake" (July 30, 1993, p. A23).

Thoughtful feminist analysis of the report that seeks to determine how it might be used to good purpose is only starting to emerge. At this point, however, it is difficult to dispute the *Globe and Mail* editorial that observed that the report "will polarize rather than unite, reduce to the fringe what might have been at the centre, and set back society's efforts to root out violence committed by men against women" (July 31, 1993, p. D6). As a project originally undertaken by feminists to act as a public education tool and generate a broad base of support, it was a dismal failure.

CONCLUSION

In retrospect, it is easy to see how some of the reasoning behind the decision to request a royal commission was flawed. It was a mistake, for example, to equate the social climate in 1967, when the RCSW was established, with the situation in 1990. In 1967, almost no information about women's status in Canada was on record, but by 1990 there had been a virtual explosion of information centred in the government, the universities, and a variety of institutional and grass-roots women's groups. For this reason, the co-ordinating function of the panel might be regarded as an almost impossible task. It is really quite difficult to understand why those in favour of a royal commission thought that the issue needed more publicity than had already been generated by the Montreal Massacre. It is highly debatable whether the public either wanted or needed more information about violence against women, or whether existing biases, polarized as they were, could be overcome by an inquiry.

Furthermore, the economic and political climate had changed drastically since 1967, when government funding was perceived as the ready

solution for social problems. Now, the whole discourse was characterized by a general atmosphere of mistrust and a well-organized backlash
against feminism. Expensive projects were resented. The $10-million
cost of the panel became a source of frequent commentary and ire. In
a climate where even essential social programs such as health and education were under increasing pressure to be financially accountable,
new ones were hardly likely to be launched. Furthermore, in contrast to
the spirit of optimism exhibited during the RCSW, many contemporary
women's groups were weary and cynical about the time and effort
required to undertake such a mammoth project. Relations between the
Conservative party and organized women's groups had deteriorated to
the point where they interfered with any attempt to work co-operatively.

The final report did make it clear that any plan to attack violence at
its roots would require major policy initiatives affecting nearly every
aspect of society. Combatting violence against women challenges traditional sex-role ideology and has a cataclysmic potential to overturn present structures and norms, as the "war" imagery used in the public
debates suggests. For these reasons, it is likely that future governments
will revert to addressing single issues and working within limited and
familiar arenas such as the criminal justice system. But, at the same
time, the issue has become too visible to be hidden away again. At the
1994 annual meeting of the Ministers Responsible for the Status of
Women, for example, a declaration of rights of women subjected to violence was issued, and the community kit produced by the panel has
begun to be distributed.

Most women's groups were disillusioned after the panel exercise,
but they may have realized from this experience the need to become
less reactive and to develop their own policy on violence. NAC, for
example, put forward its first comprehensive policy on violence and
adopted it as a working paper at its annual meeting in 1994. This document has already become the basis of consultations with the government. The panel experience, nevertheless, did emphasize the importance of adequate time for negotiation and the need for groups to have
some say in how their voices would be represented. Perhaps these
lessons will be remembered in the future. In the meantime, violence
against women is a continuing problem in Canada, and adequate solutions have not yet been devised to eliminate it.

NOTES

1. A shift to the Charter litigation milieu, however, has helped to define
   the meaning of "obscenity." In 1992, the Supreme Court in *R.* v
   Butler upheld the constitutionality of the Criminal Code obscenity
   provisions. However, as gays, lesbians, and anti-censorship feminists

had predicted, the impact of the decision may not be felt where it was most wanted. Ironically, the first obscenity charges after the *Butler* decision were laid against the Glad Day Bookshop in Toronto for selling a lesbian magazine about women's sexuality.

2. The *Canadian news index*, which lists by subject stories in major Canadian newspapers, gives a startling indication of how dramatically the problem came to public consciousness after the Montreal Massacre. The volume for 1989 did not even have a subject category "violence against women," but by 1992 there were five columns of entries (about 200) under this category.

3. These groups included CACSW, NAC, LEAF, NAWL, MATCH International, the Canadian Nurses Association, the Federated Women's Institutes of Canada, Women in Science and Engineering, the FWTAO, the Girl Guides of Canada, and the Ontario Association of Interval and Transition Houses.

REFERENCES

Baril, J. (1990). Excerpts from "The centre of the backlash." *Waterlily 1* (4), 19–20.

Barnsley, J. (1988). Feminist action, institutional reaction. *Resources for Feminist Research 17* (3), 18–21.

Barnsley, J.; Ellis, M.; and Ranson, J. (1982, October). Bill C-127: How did we get there? Where do we go from here? *Kinesis*, pp. 10–11.

Benson, C. (1990, December). The war on women. *Policy Options 11* (10), 7–12.

Brock, D. (1991). Talkin' bout a revelation: Feminist popular discourse on sexual abuse. *Canadian Woman Studies 12* (1), 12–15.

Canadian Panel on Violence Against Women. (1992). *A progress report.* Ottawa.

Canadian Panel on Violence Against Women. (1993). *Changing the landscape: Ending violence—achieving equality.* (Final report). Ottawa: Minister of Supply and Services.

Committee on Sexual Offences Against Children and Youths. (1984). *Sexual offences against children.* (The Badgley Report) (2 vols. and summary report, vol. 3). Ottawa: Minister of Supply and Services Canada.

Currie, D. (1990). Battered women and the state: From the failure of theory to a theory of failure. *Journal of Human Justice 1* (2), 77–96.

Duthie, K. (1992, February). Panel on violence: The public process begins. *Kinesis*, p. 4.

Ellis, M. (1983, February). New rape bill weakens statutory rape provisions. *Kinesis*, p. 13.

Ellis, M. (1988). Re-defining rape: Re-victimizing women. *Resources for Feminist Research 17* (3), 96–99.

Findlay, S. (1987). Facing the state: The politics of the women's movement reconsidered. In M. Luxton and H.J. Maroney (Eds.), *Women's work, women's struggles* (pp. 31–50). Toronto: Methuen.

Findlay, S. (1988). Feminist struggles with the Canadian state: 1966–1988. *Resources for Feminist Research 17* (3), 5–9.

Fudge, J. (1989). The effect of entrenching a bill of rights upon political discourse: Feminist demands and sexual violence in Canada. *International Journal of the Sociology of Law, 17,* 445–463.

Hilton, Z. (1989). One in ten: The struggle and disempowerment of the battered women's movement. *Canadian Journal of Family Law 7,* 313–335.

Huang, A. (1992, September). Canadian Panel on Violence Against Women: Some things never change. *Kinesis,* p. 3.

Irving, K. (1991, April). Violence against women: Do we need a royal commission? *Kinesis,* p. 5.

Kasinsky, R. (1978). The rise and institutionalization of the anti-rape movement in Canada. In M. Gammon (Ed.), *Violence in Canada* (pp. 151–167). Toronto: Methuen.

Lakeman, L. (1991, September). How should radicals respond? New panel to study old violence. *Kinesis,* p. 5.

Lévesque, M. (1991, Fall). The Panel on Violence Against Women: Strategy or smoke screen? *Canadian Woman Studies, 12* (1), 117–119.

Los, M. (1994). The struggle to redefine rape in the early 1980s. In J.V. Roberts and R.M. Mohr (Eds.), *Confronting sexual assault: A decade of legal and social change* (pp. 20–56). Toronto: University of Toronto Press.

MacLeod, L. (1980). *Wife battering: The vicious circle.* Ottawa: Canadian Advisory Council on the Status of Women.

MacLeod, L. (1987). *Battered but not beaten: Preventing wife battering in Canada.* Ottawa: Health and Welfare Canada.

McIntyre, S. (1994). Redefining reformism: The consultations that shaped Bill C-49. In J.V. Roberts and R.M. Mohr (Eds.), *Confronting sexual assault: A decade of legal and social change* (pp. 293–317). Toronto: University of Toronto Press.

Monkman, V. (1988). Silences: Child sexual abuse and the Canadian government. *Resources for Feminist Research, 17* (3), 56–58.

Pilot, J., and Brown, J. (1993, September). Canadian Panel on Violence Against Women: What else is new? *Kinesis,* p. 5.

Royal Commission on the Status of Women in Canada. (1970). *Report.* Ottawa: Information Canada.

Sigurjonsson, K. (1991, Fall). Not another royal commission! *Canadian Woman Studies 12* (1), 114–116.

Special Advisor to the Minister of National Health and Welfare on Child Sexual Abuse in Canada. (1990). *Reaching for solutions: The report.* Ottawa: National Clearinghouse on Family Violence, Health and Welfare Canada.

Special Committee on Pornography and Prostitution. (1985). *Pornography and prostitution in Canada* (The Fraser Report) (2 vols.). Ottawa: Minister of Supply and Services Canada.

Standing Committee on Health, Welfare, and Social Affairs, House of Commons. (1982). *Report on violence in the family: Wife battering.* Ottawa: Queen's Printer.

Standing Committee on Health and Welfare, Social Affairs, Seniors, and the Status of Women, House of Commons, Canada. (1991). *The war against women.* Ottawa.

Status of Women Canada. (1979). *Towards equality for women.* Ottawa: Minister of Supply and Services Canada.

Sullivan, T. (1992). *Sexual abuse and the rights of children: Reforming Canadian law.* Toronto: University of Toronto Press.

Ursel, J. (1991). Considering the impact of the battered women's movement on the state: The example of Manitoba. In E. Comack and S. Brickey (Eds.), *The social basis of law: Critical readings in the sociology of law* (2d ed.) (pp. 261–288). Halifax: Garamond.

Vickers, J.; Rankin, P.; and Appelle, C. (1993). *Politics as if women mattered: A political analysis of the National Action Committee on the Status of Women.* Toronto: University of Toronto Press.

Walker, G. (1990). *Family violence and the women's movement.* Toronto: University of Toronto Press.

SUGGESTED READING

Canadian Panel on Violence Against Women. (1993). *Changing the landscape: Ending violence—achieving equality* (Final Report). Ottawa: Minister of Supply and Services.

Resources for Feminist Research. (1988). Vol. 17, No. 3.

Roberts, J.V., and Mohr, R.M. (Eds.). (1994). *Confronting sexual assault: A decade of legal and social change.* Toronto: University of Toronto Press.

Walker, G. (1990). *Family violence and the women's movement.* Toronto: University of Toronto Press.

QUESTIONS TO CONSIDER

1. What are some of the major ways in which feminist explanations of the meaning and causes of violence differ from the explanations implied in most policy initiatives? How might you account for these different points of view? Which set of explanations do you favour, and why?

2. Give some examples of strategies of engagement and disengagement with the government that the women's movement adopted in the struggle to have the issue of violence against women addressed. Why had this question of strategy become so important by the end of the 1980s? Do you think the decision of major women's groups to withdraw support from the panel was a good one? Why or why not?

3. What issues and debates were brought out by the Montreal Massacre? How these are relevant to: (a) public-policy initiatives in the preceding decades; (b) the Canadian Panel on Violence Against Women?

4. Why is the issue of representation such an important one for the women's movement? How have government processes in the past inhibited proper representation of some women's concerns? In your view, what changes in process could address this problem?

GLOSSARY

Affirmative action policies are those that seek to redress historic patterns of discrimination for a particular group.

Androcentric refers to a male-centred or male-as-norm approach that assumes a male standard of being and knowing as the standard for all people, both women and men.

Anti-assimilationist refers to an approach in which marginalized groups resist inclusion within existing legal structures and institutions, and seek instead to transform those institutions. Within the context of same-sex couples, an anti-assimilationist approach resists inclusion with existing definitions of family, and emphasizes that same-sex relationships are different from heterosexual relationships.

Anti-natalism is a population policy initiated by the state to discourage high birth rates and large families. It was advocated by Thomas Malthus, an eighteenth-century English economist, who formulated the proposition that the population increases geometrically while the food supply increased arithmetically, thus leading, according to Malthus, to large-scale famines. There is still much concern today about "overpopulation" and world food supply.

Assimilationist refers to an approach to equality in which marginalized groups seek to be included within existing legal structures and institutions. Within the context of same-sex couples, an assimilationship approach seeks inclusion within existing definitions of family, and emphasizes that same-sex relationships are essentially the same as heterosexual relationships.

Bonding refers to a close connection established between mother and newborn after birth and in early years of childhood. It is believed by many psychologists to determine the social and emotional development of the child. Recent discussions emphasize the bonding when the fetus is *in utero*, that is, prior to birth. Empirical studies however, offer only weak evidence for the theory, and many have become critical of the concept, in particular, the emphasis placed on the mother ("guilting the mother") to the exclusion of fathers, other siblings, and the total social environment of the infant.

Charlottetown Accord was the Mulroney government's second failed attempt at constitutional renewal in Canada. It was a complicated document that proposed to reform federal institutions such as the Senate, devolve more powers to the provinces, and grant aboriginal people the right to self-government. It was rejected in a national referendum held in the fall of 1992.

Community standards test is a test for the determination of obscenity established by Canadian courts in the 1950s and 1960s and reaffirmed by the Supreme Court in 1992. Through this test, "obscenity" was defined as material that offended the standards of the community as reflected in the views of the average person. This test is both vague and subjective, and has been applied by the courts very inconsistently. Under this test, neither expert opinion nor evidence of Canadian public opinion is required to define community standards; subjective judicial evaluation of Canadian sexual norms is enough to establish the community standard in any individual case. In 1992, this test was reaffirmed by the Supreme Court; the Court argued that a national community standard was the most appropriate standpoint for determining "degrading and dehumanizing" sexual material, the boundary of criminal obscenity.

Contingent work force refers to contract or short-term employment with no job security or benefits such as pensions or unemployment insurance, often termed "flexible labour." More jobs in Canada are taking on the characteristics of contingent labour.

Deinstitutionalization refers to the process to taking people out of institutions and sending them to be cared for in communities or in households. It was introduced to describe the movement of people out of mental-health institutions.

Domestic contracts include contracts entered into before, during, and after the marital relationship. A couple can enter into a cohabitation agreement (if they plan to live together outside of marriage), a marriage agreement (if they are or plan to be married), or a separation agreement (on the breakdown of the relationship). The Family Law Act provides that, subject to certain very limited exceptions, the decisions that individuals make will be respected, and these contracts will be upheld.

Employment equity refers to a set of activities designed to ensure that an organization has equality for all its employees in all aspects of employment such as recruiting, hiring, compensation, and training. The goal of these activities is to have organizations' work forces mirror or reflect the composition of the labour market from which it recruits.

Essentialism   refers to the tendency in feminist theory to assert that there is an inherent "women's nature" that is shared by all women, regardless of race, class, sexuality, or some other indicator of difference.

Eugenics   rests on the belief that human species can be changed through control of hereditary factors in procreation. Positive eugenics intended to improve species by procreation by persons with desirable characteristics. Negative eugenics discourages procreation by persons with undesirable characteristics. Eugenics was a popular belief following Darwin. It was later refuted but was revived by the Nazis to protect the purity of the Aryan race; thus, it is a constituent of racism.

Fallopian tubes   carry the egg from the ovary to the uterus. A major form of infertility is scar tissue in the fallopian tubes.

Family property   is property that is acquired by either spouse during the course of the marital relationship. According to the Family Law Act, the value of all property acquired during the relationship is to be shared equally between the spouses on the breakdown of the relationship.

Feminization of labour   refers to the two-fold change in the labour market that includes the increased participation of women workers in paid employment and the increase in the number of non-standard jobs.

Fordism   refers to a stage of capitalism based on mass production of industrial goods through regimented control of workers and a high degree of division of labour. It is seen as a basis for conditions of mass consumption, stable employment, high wages, and social benefits. This stage is generally dated from 1945 to the mid-1970s.

Genocide   refers to the total annihilation of entire groups of people with certain religious or ethnic or national identifications.

Harms-based approach to pornography   is advanced by anti-pornography feminists who have argued in favour of this approach. In 1992, LEAF (q.v.) urged the Supreme Court to adopt this approach to determining criminal obscenity. According to this approach, materials should be judged on the basis of whether or not they harm women—whether or not they contribute to women's subordination—and not on the basis of sexual explicitness.

***Hicklin* test**   is a test for the determination of criminal obscenity established by the British courts in 1868 and used in Canadian law until the 1940s. According to this test, the tendency to "deprave" or "corrupt" is the defining characteristic of criminal obscenity. This legal test is rooted in a conservative sexual morality. Under the *Hicklin* precedent, obscenity was judged on the basis of sexual explicitness.

Inclusivity   is the principle of correcting bias of existing knowledge or social action. In feminist theory, this refers to neglect in the second-wave feminist movement, which is based primarily on the agendas of European-American, White, and heterosexual women. Inclusivity shifts the emphasis to non-European, non-White groups (African, Asian, Native) women, and to lesbians.

Infertility   in women refers to the inability of a woman to conceive or carry fetus to term (repeated spontaneous miscarriages). Normally, a year of unprotected intercourse and no conception is regarded as evidence of infertility. Infertility in men is often the result of a low sperm count or defective sperm motility.

Keynesian welfare state   refers to a general set of post-Second World War welfare-state arrangements in OECD countries marked by redistributive measures such as social security, and income supplements such as unemployment insurance. The steady level of income in the hands of consumers (either through a job or welfare supplements) was thought to ensure a constant level of economic output and to avoid the long-term depression of the economy, as occurred in the 1930s. It often existed simultaneously with a Fordist (q.v.) mode of regulation.

LEAF,   or the Women's Legal Education and Action Fund, is a Canadian feminist litigation organization formed in 1985 to advance and defend women's Charter equality rights. LEAF is committed to using the courts and the Charter as instruments of feminist struggle. LEAF has been involved in more than 100 cases, including the 1992 Supreme Court decision on pornography.

Lifestyle in health care   refers to practices related to eating, drinking, smoking, exercise, and sex.

Macro-economics   is the study of economics concerned with the relationship between broad economic aggregates such as national income, employment, and inflation. The role of government expenditure, taxation, and monetary policy in determining the general level of economic activity is a major preoccupation.

Matrimonial home   is the property (home, cottage, apartment) that was ordinarily occupied by a person and his or her spouse as the family residence during their relationship. The matrimonial home is given special status in the Family Law Act, recognizing that it may be the major asset owned by the spouses, that it is the focus around which family life revolves, and that it provides shelter to the family.

Micro-economics   is the study of the economic behaviour of individual decision-making units such as people, families, businesses, labour unions, and government agencies.

Modernization   is a description of a social structure characterized by urbanization, industrialization of the economy, social individuation, and secularization of values.

Moral regulation   is a term used to describe relationships between state and non-state actors involved in developing and reproducing codes of morality. Moral regulation is the privileging of certain forms of expression that results in the subordination of other forms of expressive behaviours and controls forms of self-identification and social recognition. Sexual regulation forms a crucial part of the larger project of the production of moral subjects. The legal regulation of sexual representation through obscenity law and pornography policy are key examples of moral regulation.

Non-directive counselling   is an interpersonal therapy in which emphasis is placed on patient or client decision making about treatment or course of action.

Non-standard employment   refers to work forms other than the traditional model of a full-time, full-year job. It includes short-term work, own-account self-employment (work by the self-employed who do not themselves have employees), part-time work, and temporary-help agency work.

Pay equity   is a set of activities designed to evaluate men's and women's jobs with the goal that women's jobs of equal or comparable value to men's are paid the same wage rate as the latter.

Phallocentricism   describes a form of analytic sexism. Phallocentric approaches treat the male as universal. They assume that the masculine experience can stand in for and represent human experience. An example of phallocentricism is the "reasonable man" standard in law. By this standard, the standpoint of the "reasonable man" is treated the benchmark for legal decision making. Phallocentric approaches ignore women's experiences because the masculine experience is viewed as universal.

Prenatal diagnosis   is testing before birth to determine whether a fetus has specific abnormality.

Pro-natalism   encourages large families and a high birth rate and is often associated with labour-intensive agricultural economies. The Roman Catholic Church has strongly supported high birth rates by forbidding the use of contraceptives, any form of family planning, and abortion. In many societies, a low birth rate is maintained by raising the age of marriage.

Second-wave feminism refers to the period beginning in the 1960s and continuing after the report of the Royal Commission on the Status of Women (1970), when feminists focussed on achieving equality for women in the workplace and in the home. The goals of second-wave feminists, then, are substantially different from those of first-wave feminists (active in the period between 1880 and 1920), who fought to gain such political rights for women as the franchise.

Single mother, in this book, refers to any woman who is rearing children without another parent figure in the household. This includes women who have never been married, as well as those who are widowed, separated, or divorced, and can be used interchangeably with "lone" or "sole" mother. However, the gender-neutral term single "parents" should be avoided as an inappropriately gender neutral term. Almost all 'single parents' are women.

Social assistance is that part of the income-security system based on an assessment of need, and directed toward those with low incomes. It is also often termed "welfare."

Stabilization policies are a set of macro-economic (q.v.) policies directed at preventing or shortening recessions and counteracting inflation. Neoliberal stabilization policies typically consist of reductions in government spending and budget deficits, and holding down or cutting real wages. The social dimensions of neoliberal stabilization measures are thought to be a disproportionate burden of adjustment placed on the poorer segments of society, including women.

Total quality management, also called "continuous quality improvement," is a new way of organizing work designed to eliminate waste, ensure products have no faults, and speed up production by flattening the hierarchical organization of management and by involving teams of workers in the production process.

NOTES ON CONTRIBUTORS

PAT ARMSTRONG is a former Chair of the Department of Sociology at York University and the current Director of the School for Canadian Studies at Carleton University. She is an internationally recognized feminist scholar in the fields of women and work, and Canadian health-care policy. Among her numerous publications are *The double ghetto*, *A working majority*, *Theorizing women's work*, *Labour pains: Women's work in crisis*, and *Vital signs: Nursing in transition*.

ISABELLA BAKKER is a political economist and an associate professor of Political Science at York University. Her most recent publications are *The strategic silence: gender and economic policy* and *Changing spaces: Gender and state responses to restructuring in Canada*. Before coming to York, she was a consultant for the Royal Commission on Employment Equity, Status of Women Canada, and the Organization for Economic Cooperation and Development.

JANINE BRODIE is a professor of political science at York University, a former holder of the Robarts Chair in Canadian Studies, and a past director of the York Centre for Feminist Research. Her publications include *Crisis, challenge and change: Class and party in Canada*, *Women and politics in Canada*, *The political economy of Canadian regionalism*, *The politics of abortion*, and *Politics at the margins: Restructuring and the Canadian women's movement*.

BARBARA CAMERON teaches public policy in the Department of Political Science, Atkinson College, York University. Her research interests centre on women and public policy, particularly trade, employment, training, and labour-market policy. Prior to her appointment at York University, she held research and policy positions with the Ontario provincial government and with the trade union movement.

BRENDA COSSMAN is an associate professor at Osgoode Hall Law School, where she teaches family law, feminist legal theory, and law and international development. She is the Director of the Institute for Feminist Legal Studies at Osgoode Hall. Her research interests include feminist approaches to the legal regulation of the family, with a particular focus on gay and lesbian families. She co-authored a background report for the Ontario Law Reform Commission entitled *Gays, lesbians and unmarried heterosexual couples: Accommodating a diversity of family forms*, which provides a backdrop for her chapter in this volume.

PATRICIA EVANS is an associate professor in the School of Social Work at Atkinson College, York University. She has published extensively in the areas of women, work, and welfare in both the Canadian and comparative contexts. She is currently co-editing a book on women and the welfare state, and is researching patterns of social assistance for single mothers in Ontario.

JUDY FUDGE teaches at Osgoode Hall Law School and writes about the gender implications of labour law. She has recently published *Labour law's little sister: The feminization of labour and the Employment Equity Act* and is the co-editor of *Just wages: A feminist assessment of pay equity.*

CHRISTINA GABRIEL is completing her Ph.D. in Political Science at York University. Her dissertation focusses on how the struggles of Third World women in Canada are mediated by the politics of cultural pluralism. Her research interests include feminist theory and the intersections of gender, race, and class, and the implications of globalization for women in the south and the north. She was previously a journalist and an economic-policy analyst for the Ontario Women's Directorate.

SHELLEY A.M. GAVIGAN teaches at Osgoode Hall Law School and is the current Academic Director of Parkdale Community Legal Services in Toronto. She is an unrepentant socialist feminist and has written extensively in the areas of the legal regulation and abortion and is co-author of *The politics of abortion.*

LISE GOTELL teaches in political science and women's studies at Atkinson College, York University. She has written articles and monographs about the women's movement and the Charter of Rights and Freedoms, the Legal Education and Action Committee (LEAF), and women and neoconservatism. She is the co-author of *Bad attitude: Butler, pornography and censorship.*

ANDREA LEVAN is a professor of Women's Studies at Thornloe College, Laurentian University, where she teaches courses in feminist theory, woman and violence, and reproduction and mothering issues. She has been involved in various women's groups in her community of Sudbury, Ontario, and has served on the executive of the National Action Committee on the Status of Women. She is currently a Ph.D. candidate in the Women's Studies Graduate Program at York University and is working on her dissertation on the Canadian Panel on Violence Against Women.

THELMA MCCORMACK is a professor emeritus at York University and a fellow of the York Institute of Social Research. She is the former president of the Canadian Sociology and Anthropology Association, president-elect of the Canadian Women's Studies Association, former director of the Graduate Programme in Women's Studies at York University, former director of the York Centre for Feminist Research, and first incumbent to the Women's Studies' Chair at Mt. St. Vincent University. She has written extensively in the areas of communications, health policy, feminist theory, and human rights.

PATRICIA MCDERMOTT is an associate professor in the Division of Social Science at York University. She is a sociologist and labour lawyer and has written extensively on pay and employment equity. She is the co-editor of *Just wages: A feminist assessment of pay equity* and *Women challenging unions: Feminism, democracy and militancy*. She is currently working on a book on gender and the law in Canada and is the President of the York University Faculty Association.

INDEX

READER REPLY CARD

We are interested in your reaction to *Women and Canadian Public Policy*, by Janine Brodie. You can help us to improve this book in future editions by completing this questionnaire.

1. What was your reason for using this book?

   ☐ university course ☐ college course ☐ continuing education course
   ☐ professional ☐ personal ☐ other (please specify)
   development interest _____

2. If you are a student, please identify your school and the course in which you used this book.

3. Which chapters or parts of this book did you use? Which did you omit?

4. What did you like best about this book? What did you like least?

5. Please identify any topics you think should be added to future editions.

6. Please add any comments or suggestions.

7. May we contact you for further information?

   Name: _____

   _____

   Address: _____

   _____

   _____

   Phone: _____

   _____

(fold here and tape shut)

MAIL ➤ POSTE

Canada Post Corporation / Société canadienne des postes

Postage paid
If mailed in Canada

Port payé
si posté au Canada

**Business
Reply**

**Réponse
d'affaires**

0116870399   01

0116870399-M8Z4X6-BR01

Heather McWhinney
Publisher, College Division
HARCOURT BRACE & COMPANY, CANADA
55 HORNER AVENUE
TORONTO, ONTARIO
M8Z 9Z9